The Complete Idiot's

Internet Sites for Sma...

Federal Government

www.thomas.loc.gov
Congress site for a legislative up-date.

www.gpo.gov
U. S. Government Printing Office (GPO) links to federal laws

www.supremecourtus.gov
U. S. Supreme Court site includes cases

www.doj.gov
U. S. Department of Justice site includes antitrust laws

www.doc.gov
U. S. Department of Commerce site includes e-commerce

uspto.gov
U. S. Patent Office site for patent information

www.uspto.gov
U. S. Trademark Office site for trademark information

www.loc.gov
U. S. Copyright Office site for copyright information

www.eeoc.gov
EEOC site for employment anti-discrimination laws

www.nlrb.gov
NLRB site for union-related laws

www.osha.gov
OSHA site for laws on workplace safety

www.dol.gov
U. S. Department of Labor site includes employee benefit law

www.fmcs.gov
FMCS site for employee arbitration and mediation

www.sec.gov
SEC site for securities law regulation

www.ftc.gov
FTC site includes information on deceptive advertising

www.cpsc.gov
CPSC site provides information on defective products

www.irs.ustreas.gov
IRS site for tax forms and information

tear here

alpha
books

Internet Sites for Small Businesses (continued)

www.ssa.gov
Social Security site for retirement benefits

www.sba.gov
SBA site provides excellent information for small businesses

www.epa.gov
EPA site for environment laws and cleanup locations

www.hud.gov
HUD site for real estate information

www.census.gov
U. S. Census provides information about us

www.gsa.gov
GSA site for a multitude of federal links

Other Sites

www. [fill in your own state's two-letter postal code].us.gov
Find links to important legal information from your state

www.law.cornell.edu
Cornell University law articles, cases, links

www.law.indiana.edu
Indiana University links to law articles

www.findlaw.com
Findlaw links to many law articles

www.virtualchase.com
Virtual Chase legal research site

www.lectlaw.com
LectLaw site with legal information and forms

www.ilrg.com
Internet Research site for legal information and forms

www.lawguru.com
Law Guru site for links

www.aahbb.org
American Association of Home-Based Businesses site

www.nafep.com
National Association of Financial and Estate Planning site

www.seniorlaw.com
Senior Law site

www.aarp.org
AARP site for retirement information

www.naic.org
National Association of Insurance Commissioners site

www.atla.org
American Trial Lawyers Association site for plaintiffs

THE COMPLETE IDIOT'S GUIDE® TO

Law for Small Business Owners

by **Stephen M. Maple**

alpha books

Macmillan USA, Inc.
201 West 103rd Street
Indianapolis, IN 46290

A Pearson Education Company

International Standard Book Number: 0-02-863962-6
Library of Congress Catalog Card Number: Available upon request.

02 01 00   8 7 6 5 4 3 2 1

Interpretation of the printing code: The rightmost number of the first series of numbers is the year of the book's printing; the rightmost number of the second series of numbers is the number of the book's printing. For example, a printing code of 00-1 shows that the first printing occurred in 2000.

Printed in the United States of America

Note: This publication contains the opinions and ideas of its author. It is intended to provide helpful and informative material on the subject matter covered. It is sold with the understanding that the author and publisher are not engaged in rendering professional services in the book. If the reader requires personal assistance or advice, a competent professional should be consulted.

The author and publisher specifically disclaim any responsibility for any liability, loss, or risk, personal or otherwise, which is incurred as a consequence, directly or indirectly, of the use and application of any of the contents of this book.

Publisher
Marie Butler-Knight

Product Manager
Phil Kitchel

Managing Editor
Cari Luna

Acquisitions Editor
Renee Wilmeth

Development Editor
Suzanne LeVert

Production Editor
JoAnna Kremer

Copy Editor
Susan Aufheimer

Illustrator
Brian Moyer

Cover Designers
Mike Freeland
Kevin Spear

Book Designers
Scott Cook and Amy Adams of DesignLab

Indexer
Tonya Heard

Layout/Proofreading
Svetlana Dominguez
Mary Hunt
Ayanna Lacey
Heather Hiatt Miller
Stacey Richwine-DeRome
Gloria Schurick

Contents at a Glance

Part 1: Choosing Among the Business Entities   **1**

1 The Business for You   3
Begin your reading here for a preview of coming attractions. This chapter provides an overview of the kind of legal issues and challenges small business owners face.

2 Partnership in Harmony   15
Partnerships may seem commonplace whenever two or more gather to conduct business, but this chapter will point out potential pitfalls, including the fact that all partners are liable for the business debts.

3 The Inc. for You   29
Incorporation can protect your personal assets from business creditors, and you can choose to be taxed on the corporate income you receive or have the corporation itself taxed.

4 The Limited Liability Company Limits Your Liability   39
The LLC is the new kid on the entity block and has the advantage of partnership taxation without the members being liable for the business debts.

5 Going Solo as a Sole Proprietor   49
It might seem like all you need to do is hang out your business sign and begin, but keep in mind that the debts and taxes are yours. This chapter will help you consider all of the challenges and benefits awaiting you as a sole proprietor.

6 Taxing Matters   59
Your business entity choice determines the income tax effect. We'll show you the how it all should work.

7 Hiring a Lawyer, Accountant, and Other Advisors   71
You can't do it alone, so we'll show you why it makes sense to pay a fair price for the advice you need, and also take advantage of free resources.

Part 2: Beginning Your Successful Business   **81**

8 Buying an Existing Business: Traps for the Unwary   83
Spend time and seek advice on the best business that fits you personally and financially, then negotiate the best deal with the help of your advisors.

9 Franchising for Success   95
Franchising is big business for small businesses, but read the fine print before you sign.

10 Raising Money When You Need More Than You Have   107
*Borrowing to finance your operation requires good finan-
cial planning. Selling shares in your corporation may get
new money but at the price of diluting your control.*

11 Finding the Right Location: Realty Bites in
Leasing or Buying   119
*Read all the fine print on your proposed lease, then negoti-
ate the best terms. If you buy, check the zoning and liens
before you close.*

Part 3: Your Employees Matter   **131**

12 Selecting Employees Without Violating the Law   133
*Recruiting and hiring employees requires you to be aware
of and avoid violations of employment anti-discrimination
laws.*

13 Money and Other Matters in Employee Compensation   147
*Salary counts most, but fringe benefits save your employ-
ees substantial taxes; medical insurance and a 401(k)
may be the best fringes, but beware of medical insurance
cost.*

14 Keeping or Letting Go   161
*Some employees just don't seem to work out, but before
you fire, try to rehabilitate. If you must terminate, we'll
show you how to avoid violating the employment laws.*

Part 4: Running the Business   **175**

15 Insuring Your Business (and You) Against
Life's Disasters   177
*You need adequate insurance to protect against fire, theft,
and other natural disasters, as well as employees who run
red lights while on delivery.*

16 Contracts That Are Binding   189
*Your business contracts are your assets, so write them with
care.*

17 Employee Negligence and Other Harmful Behavior   205
*Your employees may be negligent or your product may in-
jure a customer. You'll find out here what you may be liable for.*

18 Suing and Being Sued: Basics of Litigation   221
*We live in a lawsuit-happy society, so you need to know
how to defend your company. You can also think of small
claims court as your collection agency.*

Part 5: Protecting Your Business Assets   **233**

19 Consumer Rights and Your Responsibilities   235
Customers expect honest dealings, and though you're fair, you'll need to know about the numerous consumer laws you may inadvertently violate.

20 Extending Credit and Collecting from a Reluctant Debtor   245
Protect yourself when you sell on credit by securing the debt with the debtor's collateral.

21 TMs, SMs, Copyright, Patents, and Trade Secrets   259
A name may say it all to your customers, so trademark it. Copyrights and patents could be your most tangible assets.

22 ABCs of Administrative Law   269
The alphabet soup of federal and state administrative agencies may regulate your business, so you need to know how to operate in their environment.

23 Wave of the Now: The Net or Home   279
E-commerce applies old laws to new situations; most home-based businesses operate under the same rules as any other business but there are exceptions worth noting.

Part 6: Looking Ahead and Closing Down   **293**

24 Insolvent: Coping with Bankruptcy Protection   295
Filing bankruptcy may not be the end, because Chapter 11 bankruptcy permits you to continue and work out an arrangement with creditors.

25 Your Estate Plan Includes the Business   307
Writing your last will and testament is just the beginning of estate planning for your retirement and for your heirs.

Appendixes

A Glossary of Legal Terms   325

B Basic Business Forms   332

Index   357

Contents

Part 1: Choosing Among the Business Entities   **1**

1 The Business for You   **3**

Choosing Your Entity 4
Personal Liability...5
Taxing Matters...5
Selecting Sage Advisors 7
Raising Cash to Grow 8
Employing the Best Staff..9
Contracts That Bind 11
Protecting Your Intellectual Property 12
Leaving the Business in Good Hands 13

2 Partnership in Harmony   **15**

Choosing Among the Choices 15
Regular Partnership Is General 16
Drafting the Best Agreement for All 16
Registering to Limit Liability 24
Limited Partnership Limits 25
Taxes Matter 26
Helpful Sources 26

3 The Inc. for You, or Sharing with Others   **29**

Incorporating Your Business for Protection 29
Shareholder Agreements to Agree............................31
Shareholders Share Almost Everything.....................32
Board of Directors and Officers Control...................33
Acquisitions and Dissolution Mean Change 35
Taxes Matter 36
Helpful Sources 38

**4 The Limited Liability Company Limits
Your Liability**   **39**

LLCs: The Basics 39
Your Organizing Articles Is the Beginning 40
Operating Instructions for the Business 41
Moving Forward 45
Taxes Matter 46
Helpful Sources 46

5 Going Solo as a Sole Proprietor   **49**

You and Your Choices...49
Financing for Now and the Future 51
Closing Out for New Beginnings 52
Taxes Matter 53
Helpful Sources 57

6 Taxing Matters   **59**

Taxing Choices for You to Make 59
IRS and You in Business 61
Operation: Making Tax Laws Work for You 62
Sale of Ownership Interest 65
All in the Family 65
IRS Looks at Your Business: Preparing for Your Appearance 65
States and Cities Want Their Share, Too...................................67
Helpful Sources 69

7 Hiring a Lawyer, Accountant, and
Other Advisors   **71**

Your Lawyer's Assistance 72
Accounting for Your Money 73
Insuring Against the Risks..75
Banking on You to Succeed..76
Brokering the Realty 76
Computer Sourcing 78
Investing the Cash 78
Retired Pros Playing for You 79
Helpful Sources 80

Part 2: Beginning Your Successful Business   **81**

8 Buying an Existing Business: Traps for
the Unwary   **83**

Selecting the Right Business for You...83
Using a Business Acquisition Team...85
Examining the Financials Closely...86
Looking for Any Legal Problems That May Arise.........................87
Making the Offer and Negotiating the Deal.................................90
Financing the Purchase 93
Taxing Matters..93
Closing Means Beginning 94
Helpful Sources 94

9 Franchising for Success   **95**

An Overview of Franchising Laws 95
Choosing the Right Franchise...97
The Franchise Disclosures Duly Noted 100
Your Franchise Agreement 103
Solutions to Franchisor Problems That Can Arise 106
Helpful Sources 106

10 Raising Money When You Need More
Than You Have   **107**

Figuring Out How Much You Need 107
Determining Your Assets...109
The Risks of Borrowing from Family and Friends 110
The Cost of Bank Borrowing 110

Small Business Administration Loan Guarantees....................................112
Investors and Securities Laws 113

11 Finding the Right Location: Realty Bites in Leasing or Buying — 119

Using a Broker to Find the Right Place.....................................119
The Way to Rent 120
Landlord Problems to Avoid 126
Buying Real Estate from Acquiring to Zoning 126
Purchase Agreement Terms That Benefit You.........................128
Helpful Sources 130

Part 3: Your Employees Matter — 131

12 Selecting Employees Without Violating the Law — 133

All the Major Employment Laws 133
Recruiting New Employees 137
Before You Hire 140
Testing and Passing 142
Hiring the Best That You Can Get 143
Independent Contractors Instead of Employees 143
Helpful Sources 145

13 Money and Other Matters in Employee Compensation — 147

Compensation Overview..147
Minimum Wage and Overtime Requires Punching the Clock.............149
Pay Practices to Avoid Lawsuits 151
Your Pay Package: Salary and Fringes 152
Pensions and Deferred Compensation to Delay Taxes.........................157
Helpful Sources 159

14 Keeping or Letting Go — 161

Put It in Writing 161
Review Performance Periodically 164
Employee Files..166
When Employees Go Bad 167
Sexual Harassment Is Serious Business 169
Safety on the Job...171
Workers with Disabilities 172
Labor Unions..173

Part 4: Running the Business — 175

15 Insuring Your Business (and You) Against Life's Disasters — 177

Insurance Basics from A to Z 177
Property Coverage That Is Adequate 180

Liability Protection That Can Save Your Business 181
Business Interruption and Other Worries................................182
Life and Health Insurance to Protect Your Employees...............184
Taxing Matters...186
Saving Premium Costs 187
Helpful Sources 187

16 Contracts That Are Binding   189

In Search of a Solid Contract 189
Forming a Solid Contract 190
Interpreting the Vague and Ambiguous 196
On Time and It Works 198
Drafting Checklist 201
Remedies for Breach of Contract 202
Your Agent May Bind You to a Contract 204

17 Employee Negligence and Other Harmful Behavior   205

Employee Torts and Your Liability 205
Negligence Can Hurt..208
Defenses to Negligence 210
Products Liability: Defects That Cause Harm 211
Intentional Torts from Battery to Libel 212
Remedies for the Injured...218
Helpful Sources 219

18 Suing or Being Sued: Basics of Litigation   221

Where to File Your Lawsuit 221
Civil Procedure: Complaint to Trial 223
Small Claims Court 230
Alternatives to Litigation 231
Helpful Sources 232

Part 5: Protecting Your Business Assets   233

19 Consumer Rights and Your Responsibilities   235

Advertising Without Misleading..235
Deceptive Sales Practices to Avoid 238
Consumer Safety Laws 240
Credit Where Credit Is Due 241
Helpful Sources 243

20 Extending Credit and Collecting from a Reluctant Debtor 245

Getting Paid: The Options 245
Securing the Loan with Collateral 248
Collection Process: Letter to Collecting the Judgment 252
Debtor Bankruptcy 253
Helpful Sources 257

21 TMs, SMs, Copyrights, Patents, and Trade Secrets — 259

Making Your Mark 259
Copyrighting Printed or Recorded Work 262
Patents for Useful Things 264
Trade Secrets Kept 266
Helpful Sources 268

22 ABCs of Administrative Law — 269

Agency Authority from Statutes 269
Agency Rules Are the Law 271
Adjudicating Rights and Wrongs 273
Agency in Action: The Zoning Board 275
Small Business Rights 277

23 Wave of the Now: The Net or Home — 279

Your Domain Is Your Kingdom 279
E-Commerce: Your Dot.Com 283
Cyberlaw: New Wine in Old Skins 284
Your Home Is Your Office 289
Helpful Sources 291

Part 6: Looking Ahead and Closing Down — 293

24 Insolvent: Coping and Bankruptcy Protection — 295

Protecting Your Personal Assets 295
Arrangements with Creditors 298
Making the Tough Decisions 301
Bankruptcy: 7 or 11 302
Taxes and Bankruptcy 304
Helpful Sources 305

25 Your Estate Plan Includes the Business — 307

Business and Other Assets 307
Avoiding Probate 310
Estate and Gift Taxes for Life Planning 313
Wills and Trusts: Documents You Need 316
Marriage and Divorce Has Its Effect 320
Business Successor Planning 323
Helpful Sources 324

Appendixes

A Glossary of Legal Terms — 325

B The Forms You'll Need — 333

Index — 357

Foreword

Owning your own business is an exciting, confusing, and often terrifying experience. It's something you don't want to do alone. Enlisting the help of professionals, such as accountants, lawyers, and other small business owners, is essential to the success of any business startup. And having *The Complete Idiot's Guide to Law for Small Business Owners* is like adding another professional to your business support circle.

From starting your entrepreneurial endeavor to creating a business successor plan, this is the handbook to make you feel at ease as you manage your own small business. When choosing the type of business you want to start—a partnership, corporation, limited liability company, sole proprietorship, or limited partnership—and the professionals who will help you every step of the way, discovering your insurance needs, answering your tax questions and liability fears, and addressing your needs for obtaining startup cash, *The Complete Idiot's Guide to Law for Small Business Owners* is an invaluable tool.

The in-depth discussions on employment law, ins and outs of contract negotiation, protecting intellectual property—from copyrights to patents to trademarks and trade secrets—and the distribution of your income are essential topics you won't want to miss. The clear and concise explanations of tax implications, allocating income among owners, timing of taxes, and dealing with the IRS will all help allay your fears and arm you with the knowledge you need to be a prepared and forewarned business owner.

I find choosing financial and other professional advisors stressful, so the sections on hiring professional advisors were particularly helpful to me. The tips on interacting with lawyers; the detailed list of services you should expect your accountants, lawyers, insurance brokers, and others to provide; and the advice on computer sourcing were also extremely useful. The book is also full of common sense pointers, such as avoiding those who speak a language only other consultants would understand and sticking with a financial planner who concentrates on planning and not selling.

This book is easy to understand and chock full of funny and thought-inspiring quotes and tips. Some of the quotes made me laugh out loud, and I tacked one up on the wall next to my computer for inspiration. I even found myself reading the chapters that did not apply to me, such as the sections on franchising. (One can dream big, right?)

Owning your own business is a dream come true. Don't let it turn into a nightmare by being unprepared and making unwise business decisions. Read *The Complete Idiot's Guide to Law for Small Business Owners* and fortify your dream with the facts, resources, and priceless information it provides.

—Jacky Sach, Cofounder of BookEnds, LLC

Jacky Sach is the cofounder of BookEnds, LLC, an editorial services and book packaging company. She and her partner, Jessica Faust, left their corporate publishing jobs to make a new start in book packaging. Together with the BookEnds staff, they offer an array of professional editorial services, including book producing, book doctoring, copyediting, developmental editing, rewriting, and proofreading. They can be reached through their Web site at www.book-ends-inc.com.

Introduction

If you're just starting out to create a new business, you'll need a guide through the laws that can cause more than a little consternation. I wrote this book to help you, the small business owner, who can't afford to call an attorney every time trouble appears. This book is not intended as a substitute for legal advice, but it does help you know *when* to ask for advice and *what* to ask.

Consider this book to be a preventive maintenance law manual. Scan the chapters. All of them may not pertain to your business right now, but most will be relevant at some point in the future. Read what applies, then shelve the book next to your personnel manual. Pick it up the next time you have a question of law.

Keep in mind that laws change and state laws vary so I can provide you with only a general understanding of the law. Often this is enough to protect you from being ensnared in legal traps. Fortunately, the Internet often will provide you with updates for free.

I admire small business owners for their hard work and enterprise. I hope that this book will help you avoid legal problems that could inhibit your success. Thank you for reading it.

What You'll Find in This Book

Part 1, "Choosing Among the Business Entities," permits you to review your business choices. You can choose to become a sole proprietor, limited liability company, or corporation, even though there is just one of you, or if two or more of you are in business, then a partnership, LLC, or corporation may be appropriate. Your personal liability for business debts and taxes depend on your choice.

Part 2, "Beginning Your Successful Business," discusses buying a going business or becoming a franchisee. Since you may need to rent or buy a building, my chapters take you through these transactions step-by-step. Then you must come up with the capital, so this part shows you how to do so.

Part 3, "Your Employees Matter," helps you traverse your way through the maze of hiring, managing, compensating, and firing employees.

Part 4, "Running the Business," covers insurance, contracts, torts, and lawsuits—the basic challenges you'll face when you operate your own business.

Part 5, "Protecting Your Business Assets," leads you through the numerous consumer protection laws. This part discusses selling on credit, getting collateral, and collecting from reluctant debtors. You may want to begin an e-commerce business or a home-based business, both of which are included in this section.

Part 6, "Looking Ahead and Closing Down," is frankly a potpourri of legal subjects, including business bankruptcy, business taxation, and estate planning.

Extras

As you go through this book you will note several boxes that provide you with various types of helpful information. Let's take a look at them.

Legal Eagle

This box provides legal advice for free (except for the price of this book).

Shark Attack!

This box alerts you to potential pitfalls so that you can avoid troubled waters.

Notes & Quotes

Statistics can inform us, and quotes entertain us. That's what you'll find here.

Legalese

Legal terms demand definition. This box provides you with what you need to understand them.

Acknowledgments

To Renee Wilmeth, the acquisitions editor, I offer my thanks for her support and encouragement. To Suzanne LeVert, my development editor, Susan Aufheimer, copy editor, and JoAnna Kremer, production editor, I express my appreciation. For the rest of the book team, I deeply appreciate your dedication to the world of the printed word. Finally, I want to thank my wife Sarah for her advice and support, and our school of business secretary, Debby McGary, for helping me transmit all my manuscript through the mysterious channel of e-mail attachments.

Special Thanks to the Technical Reviewer

The Complete Idiot's Guide to Law for Small Business Owners was reviewed by an expert who double-checked the accuracy of what you'll learn here, to help us ensure that this book gives you everything you need to know about the points of law encountered by many small business owners. Special thanks are extended to Deborah Henry.

Trademarks

Part 1

Choosing Among the Business Entities

To be or not to be was Hamlet's dramatic dilemma. Yours is more prosaic—to be a partnership, a corporation, a limited liability company, or a sole proprietor.

The choice of entities is yours to make, with the minor exception being that one person alone can't form a partnership. Your choice determines certain legal and tax consequences. If, for example, you and your co-owners create a partnership, then each one of you may be personally liable for the business debts, and each of you must report on your 1040 your share of the partnership's income or loss.

In this part, you will learn about the various entity choices, how you create the entity, and the consequences of each choice. You will be able to gain a thorough understanding of partnership, corporation, limited liability company, and sole proprietorship law. Taxes matter, so I discuss the tax results of your choice, which may help you to keep Uncle Sam from digging too deeply into your pocket.

You always can use some help, so I suggest ways of obtaining that help, some of which comes at little cost. Attorneys aren't cheap, but you can read this book and reduce your costs by doing some of the work yourself.

Chapter 1

The Business for You

In This Chapter

➤ What business entity is right for you

➤ How to get the money you need

➤ Contracts from A to Z

➤ Thinking of the end at the beginning

Since you're reading this book, chances are, you're an entrepreneur or want to become one. Owning and/or running your own business can be exciting and rewarding, but it is also a demanding master. For one thing, relatively complicated but essential legal matters are an integral part of any business, and without some knowledge of the law, you risk making potentially devastating decisions that can undermine your financial livelihood. This book won't get you past the bar exams, but it can help you make good business decisions based upon the law.

This chapter provides a brief overview of the book. It is somewhat like a movie teaser. You get a feel for business law without having to absorb too many details. Once you've seen what the book has to offer, you should feel free to skip ahead to read the chapters that are most relevant to your business, or read straight through. I've tried to make this book as comprehensive as possible, a working manual for business owners. Enjoy!

Choosing Your Entity

The first decision you'll need to make when you create a new business is just what type of new business you want to create. Here are your choices:

➤ **Sole proprietor.** This is a one-owner model; the owner receives all the income and is liable for the debts. It's easy to form and dissolve. The owner is taxed on the income.

➤ **Corporation.** One or more shareholders own the business, which is liable for its debts. It's formed and dissolved by filing documents with the state Secretary of State. Small business corporations may be taxed or elect to have the shareholders personally taxed.

➤ **Partnership.** Two or more persons establish this business and they are personally liable for its debts. Usually the partners enter into a partnership agreement that governs their rights and duties. Each partner is taxed on his or her share of the business income.

➤ **Registered limited liability partnership.** The basic features are the same as the partnership, but the partnership, not the partners, is liable for the business debts. The partnership has to register itself with the state Secretary of State.

➤ **Limited partnership.** One or more general partners and one or more limited partners form this business by filing an agreement with the state Secretary of State. Only the general partner is personally liable for the business debts. Each partner is taxed on his or her share of the business income.

➤ **Limited liability company.** One or more members may establish this business by filing its articles of organization with the state Secretary of State. The business, not its members, is liable for its debts. Each member is taxed on his or her share of the business income.

Going into business for yourself, with no partner, limits your choices to sole proprietorship or corporation (although some states recognize a one-member limited liability company). Co-owners have every choice except the sole proprietor.

When you select the entity that best fits your needs, you should ask at least three basic questions:

➤ Are you personally liable for the business debts?

➤ Who pays the taxes on the business income?

➤ How easy and expensive is the business to form?

The answers to these questions will determine the best entity choice for your business.

Notes & Quotes

"Being good in business is the most fascinating kind of art."

—Andy Warhol, artist

Personal Liability

Because bad things happen to good businesses, you'll want to limit your personal liability for business debts as much as possible. Corporate shareholders, partners in a registered limited liability partnership, and members of the limited liability company do not have any personal liability for business debts.

If you are a sole proprietor, I would suggest switching to a corporation, particularly if you have employees. Negligent employees cause damage. If they are on the clock when negligent, you as their employer will be liable. Insurance can cover only so much risk; after that, the business assets are subject to creditors' claims, and then you personally as the sole proprietor are liable (but not if you were a corporate shareholder).

If you are a co-owner, and concerned about liability, choose the registered limited liability partnership, limited liability company, or corporation. Personal liability is limited to your own negligence in these entities.

Taxing Matters

Needless to say, you should not pay any more taxes than absolutely necessary. The Sixteenth Amendment to the Constitution allows the federal income tax, but it doesn't require you to be generous to Uncle Sam. Choosing the right business entity can save cash that you can put to better use than Congress can.

Sole proprietors report business income and deductions on their personal returns (1040 Schedule C). Partners and limited liability company members report their share of the business income on their personal returns (1040 Schedule E). Corporations with 75 or fewer shareholders may elect to be treated the same as partnerships under Subchapter S of the tax code and report their share of the business income on their personal returns (1040 Schedule E). Or a corporation can be taxed on its income, and then the shareholders are taxed on dividends received (1040 Schedule B).

Shark Attack!

Your guaranty of a business debt—for example, cosigning a promissory note—could result in personal liability if the business defaults on the loan. Try not to mix personal and business finances; however, many business lenders insist on a personal guaranty from a partner or officer of a corporation.

Notes & Quotes

"What is the difference between a taxidermist and a tax collector? The taxidermist takes only your skin."

—Mark Twain, author

Since taxes matter, you need to sit down with your accountant and figure which entity gives you the best tax break. This choice may not be compatible with your entity choice to avoid liability. However, incorporating or becoming a registered limited liability partnership could be acceptable to protect personal assets, and provide taxes advantages.

Legal Eagle

If you are currently in business, consult your accountant about the need to switch entities to save taxes. You could, for example, switch from a sole proprietor to a corporation. You can usually change entitles by filing a new document with the appropriate state authorities. You must then be sure to transfer all real property, assets, and debts to the new entity, which can be costly.

Legalese

In most states, the office of the **Secretary of State** is where you file your business documents, including your Articles of Incorporation. However, your state may be the exception. Surf the Web to your state's site and check out which agency is the appropriate office to file your documents.

Ease of Formation

Your money and time are precious commodities. Initial costs of forming the business, the continuing costs of record keeping and filing, and the demands of the latter are important factors in choosing what type of business to form and run.

Sole proprietors just put up their signs and begin. No special filing with any agency is required. All forms of partnership require an agreement, which means legal expenses. Registered limited partnerships must register with the state *Secretary of State,* and limited partnership must file a certificate (or agreement) with that office.

The Limited Liability Company files its Articles of Organization with the Secretary of State and has an Operating Agreement, which details the way the LLC determines voting rights, profit distribution, etc. Again, these entail lawyer fees. The corporation files its Articles of Incorporation with the Secretary of State, has bylaws, and keeps detailed minutes, all of which require attorneys. But you can initially draft some of the documents and save some of the fees.

The corporation demands the most in ongoing record keeping and filings. These tasks are fairly uncomplicated and you can save money by doing them yourself.

Please read the rest of Part 1 for a thorough discussion of entities and tax law.

Selecting Sage Advisors

We all need advice. Your problem is to find good advice that you can use. This book can help you solve that problem. The best suggestion I can provide is to put together a team to help you run a better business. Your team should include as many of these persons as possible:

➤ Accountant

➤ Attorney

➤ Insurance agent

➤ Small business owner

Let's look at these professionals and what they can do for you one by one.

➤ **Getting Your Books in Order.** First, you need an accountant to help you set up the books. You can ask him or her for advice about what computerized bookkeeping system is best for your business. An accountant can also analyze the information and suggest ways to improve collection and save on paying bills. When tax time arrives, the accountant has all the information necessary to prepare your returns. Don't begin your business without a qualified accountant on your team!

➤ **The Real Legal Eagle.** Next, although lawyer jokes often do carry a measure of truth, you still need to be able to rely on a lawyer's advice to help you solve problems or avoid them in the first place. Documents must be drafted because, as an old Chinese proverb reminds us, the palest ink is better than the best memory. You can save on attorney fees by making preliminary drafts the lawyer can review for you, instead of the lawyer having to draft the entire document from scratch.

Notes & Quotes

"When the 30-year-old lawyer died he said to Saint Peter, 'How can you do this to me? A heart attack at my age? I'm only 30.' Replied St. Peter: 'When we looked at your total hours billed we figured you were 95.'"

—Anonymous. Quoted from *The Harper Book of Quotations* (Harper Perennial, 1993).

➤ **Getting It Insured.** Now, for insurance. If you're starting a new business, chances are you don't mind at least a little bit of risk because risk is a part of any business. No insurance can protect you against a change in customers' tastes and the sales flop that results. But if a fire breaks out or a tornado hits your building, insurance sure comes in handy, especially if your insurance advisor convinced you to purchase business continuation insurance, which allows you to continue to pay bills until you're up and running again.

➤ **Fellow Travelers.** Finally, it's invaluable to have a fellow small business owner on hand to give you advice about your own venture. Prime the pump, use the handle, and out flows some excellent advice. He or she probably has faced many of your same challenges, and you can certainly learn from his or her experiences. Please read Chapter 7, "Hiring a Lawyer, Accountant, and Other Advisors," for a more complete discussion of selecting and using advisors.

Raising Cash to Grow

Money is a necessary ingredient of any business, both to create it and to help it prosper. You'll probably never have enough money to do everything you want, but with advice from your accountant and business buddy, you can prepare a sound business plan with a realistic estimate of your need for capital.

Investment in your business comes from …

➤ You.
➤ Your family and friends.
➤ Business loans.
➤ Outside investors.

Let's start with you. Even if you don't have deep pockets now, you'd better have at least a little cash at the start. No one will invest in you if you don't have the assets—or the confidence—to invest in yourself. Your family and friends will certainly want to support you emotionally and maybe even help you out by working in the business. But be careful if you decide together that they should invest actual cash. If they do invest, make sure that everyone's very clear on the terms: Execute a promissory note with a market rate of interest and realistic repayment schedule. Be careful to keep all business and personal matters quite separate from each other at all times. The IRS is always watching, so document the loans.

When it comes to business loans from financial institutions, you'll need some collateral, which means that you may have to consider taking out a second mortgage on the home if you have no other assets to offer. Keep in mind, however, that you'll be taking a risk of losing your home if your business fails. On the other hand, there's a chance that the bank may be willing to forego collateral if someone cosigns or guarantees the promissory note, which would make that person liable if the company defaults on the loan. A family member, friend, or even a business investor may be willing to cosign your loan, but again, you must make sure to treat such a transaction as a business dealing, signed, sealed, and delivered. If you want to attract outside investors, you'll need to convince them that by investing cash now, they'll make more money later. And to do that you'll need a comprehensive, accurate business plan.

Do keep in mind, however, that individual or corporate investors will most likely want to become part owners of the business in return for their investment, which is called equity, so you may not have the final say in all business decisions.

When it comes to attracting investors by offering stock in your company, you may have to wait until your business is up and running—and making a profit. If you're ready for outside investors, then you'll want to consult an accountant and a financial planner about going public.

Please read Chapter 10, "Raising Money When You Need More Than You Have," for a thorough discussion of raising capital for your business.

Employing the Best Staff

As efficient and enthusiastic as you may be, you may need some help running your business. Unfortunately, hiring, compensating, promoting, and sometimes firing employees are demanding and thankless tasks. But your business success depends on how productive and enthusiastic your employees are.

Federal and state employment laws are a maze inside a labyrinth. The laws were enacted with the best of intentions and have a laudable goal, but you must carefully move through them to avoid their violation.

Just a few employment laws worth noting include …

➤ **Civil Rights Act of 1964.** The Civil Rights Act prohibits discrimination by employers against employees or potential employees on the basis of race, color,

Shark Attack!

Consult an attorney and accountant before soliciting investments. Federal and state securities laws are complex and exact severe penalties for their violation.

Notes & Quotes

"In the end, all business operations can be reduced to three words: people, product, and profits. People come first."

—Lee Iacocca, tycoon

religion, sex, and national origin. Employers may not discriminate in hiring, firing, promoting, and compensating, or in any other way, against any person within the protected classifications—which pretty much includes all of us.

➤ **Age Discrimination Act.** The Age Discrimination Act is my personal favorite, at least that's what I tell my young college students. It protects me and any other workers aged 40 and older from employment discrimination based on age.

➤ **Americans with Disabilities Act.** The Americans with Disabilities Act prohibits discrimination against qualified employees with mental or physical disabilities. The law broadly defines disability to include any impairment that substantially limits a major life activity, or is regarded as a disability, or a person who has a record of a disability. Employers must provide reasonable accommodation to help an employee perform the job.

➤ **Occupational Safety and Health Act.** The Occupational Safety and Health Act (OSHA) was designed by Congress to reduce workplace hazards and improve employee health and safety. Employers are required to provide a workplace free of physical dangers and to meet specific health and safety standards. OSHA inspects business sites, but usually only larger companies' premises unless there is a record of serious injuries or the business activity is inherently dangerous, such as the manufacture of toxic chemicals.

➤ **Fair Labor Standards Act.** The Fair Labor Standards Act requires the payment of minimum wage and overtime to many employees. Congress sets the minimum wage, but a state may establish a higher minimum wage. The overtime provisions (more than 40 hours in a week) do not cover executives and professionals. Businesses with annual sales of less than $500,000 may not be subject to overtime provisions; however, it's best to assume all hourly employees are covered, but check with the Wage-Hour Division of the Labor Department in your state for clarification.

➤ State workers' compensation acts. States establish their own workers' compensation statutes to pay employees for injuries on the job. The compensation varies considerably from state to state. The employer is generally held strictly liable for the injury, even if the employee or a fellow employee was at fault. There are minor exceptions to the rule, such as if an employee's own drunkenness causes his injury.

Please read Part 3, "Your Employees Matter," for a comprehensive discussion of employment law.

Legal Eagle

Do not over-react when faced with a difficult personnel decision. If an employee is not performing, then take the appropriate action, and just document the employee's conduct and your action in response.

Contracts That Bind

Your business will contract with suppliers, customers, employers, and landlords. The contract may be oral, written, or both. You may be content with a simple handshake, but put any important contract in writing. You may not need a lawyer, because there are relatively simple forms available for uncomplicated agreements, but for the big deals, seek legal advice. An attorney can draft a blank contract template for you to use over and over again for similar transactions.

Without being too pedantic, I should explain that your state's contract law has two primary sources: the Uniform Commercial Code (UCC) for the sale of goods, and common (court-made) law for every other type of contract.

There are some differences in writing requirements, warranties, and enforcement between the UCC sale of goods and other contract under common law. These differences will be discussed thoroughly in Chapter 16, "Contracts That Are Binding," and in other sections of the book, since contract law will have an impact on many areas of your business.

However, despite their differences, every valid contract consists of the following elements:

➤ Offer

➤ Acceptance

➤ Mutual voluntary assent to all terms

➤ Consideration

Here's an example of a successful contract properly performed: You offer to buy a #222 forklift from Lift Company for $10,000. Lift Company accepts your offer. The material terms of the purchase are specified in the order to which Lift Company agrees. You get the forklift and Lift Company receives your $10,000 check. The forklift works and your check does not bounce. Keep in mind—and we'll stress this again later—your contract offer must contain specific terms, such as price, delivery, and means of acceptance. Vague wording will haunt you. A contract doesn't need to be 10 pages of fine print, but the devil is always in the details.

Notes & Quotes

"The big print giveth and the small print taketh away."

—Anonymous

In order to form a contract, an acceptance must agree with the terms of the offer. Common law requires the offeree to accept each and every term—from the date of delivery to the price—while the UCC allows a little more latitude as long as the parties agree to certain significant terms. Don't leave anything to later interpretation. If in doubt, confirm the terms agreed upon one by one.

In addition, a valid contract is one into which both parties entered voluntarily. No force or fraud is permitted. The parties must be of legal age (18) and of sufficient mental capacity. Even if the price you pay is far more than the worth of the good or service, you'll be bound to the price if you agree to pay it in the contract.

Consideration is usually defined as a bargained-for exchange—you give something (money, product, or service) in return for something (money, product, or service). You may receive less of this for your that, but the law requires only an adequate exchange not an equal one. For example, you may pay more for a building than it's worth just to get a good location.

Some contracts, as a matter of law, must be in writing to be enforceable under the *Statute of Frauds*. For instance, the UCC requires all contracts for the sale of goods of $500 or more to be in writing. Under the common law, a written contract is required for real estate sales, leases for more than one year, a promise to pay someone else's debt, and transactions that will take more than one year to perform. Common law is based on court precedents (decisions), some going back decades or centuries.

Legalese

The **Statute of Frauds** is a statute used nationwide (harking back to early England) that makes certain unwritten contracts unenforceable.

Please read Chapter 16, "Contracts That Are Binding," for a complete discussion of contract law.

Protecting Your Intellectual Property

Not all of your assets are tangible. Some are very intangible, yet extremely valuable, and can be protected under federal and state law. These include …

➤ **Writings, artistic works, motion picture and sound recordings, which may be copyrighted.** Copyright protection begins when the creative work ends. When I finish writing this book, my copyright exists whether or not I register the book (my publisher will) with the Copyright Office, or even though I might forget to put the © symbol on the book. If you develop and market written materials, then copyright them to prevent others from using your work without your permission (or if with your permission, by agreeing to pay you). Protection extends for the creator's life plus 70 years.

➤ **Inventions of machines or computer hardware, which may be patented.** Invent a better mousetrap and the world will beat a path to your door, so the saying goes. I read an article in *The Wall Street Journal* several years ago that described a new mousetrap design that would entice the victim into the box-like trap with a food and sexual lure, incinerate it, and provide a readout of the number of mice executed. I trust the inventor patented this useful device through the Patent Office. Protection for most patents is for 20 years.

➤ **Business name, which may receive a trademark or service mark.** Your name marks your business. If you conduct business statewide and want to protect your name from others using it, then file with the trademark office in your state. If you have, or are planning, nationwide or international business, then register the name with the federal Trademark Office. Then use the name, protect it, or lose it. Aspirin was once a trademarked name.

➤ **Business trade secrets.** You may have a business plan, database, product, process, or confidential customer list that you can't protect with a copyright or patent. If you take reasonable efforts to keep these intangible assets secret, state law may protect them against misappropriation by competitors or disgruntled ex-employees. To be enforceable, these items must have independent economic value. Clearly, if your business plan is in the hands of a competitor, it may cost you dearly. Trade secrets cannot be registered. Just make sure that all employees are aware of the importance of secrecy, and have the employees sign an agreement not to disclose the secrets. Employee e-mail contains many loose missives that could sink your ship.

Please read Chapter 20, "Extending Credit and Collecting from a Reluctant Debtor," for a thorough discussion of intellectual property law.

Notes & Quotes

"Three may keep a secret if two of them are dead."

—Ben Franklin, printer

Leaving the Business in Good Hands

If you're just beginning your business, you probably haven't even considered its end. But you, yes, even you, should keep in mind the vagaries and uncertainties of life. Estate planning isn't just for senior citizens.

Any business owner should have ...

➤ **A Last Will and Testament.** When you and I pass to our reward, we hope to leave something for our heirs. We want to do this as effectively and as inexpensively as possible. You need an up-to-date will that specifies who gets what. If you don't have a will, state law determines which heirs get your assets. For example, if your spouse does not co-own your business, and you die without a will, then your children may inherit a portion.

➤ **Life insurance.** Life insurance is a must, just as health insurance is, although perhaps not as obvious or urgent. If you have dependents

Shark Attack!

Don't put off planning for the future. Federal estate tax and state death taxes can significantly reduce your estate if you fail to plan.

who will continue to need your support after your death, then term life insurance (no cash savings) is essential and relatively inexpensive. Life insurance can be used by your business to fund a buyout of a deceased co-owner's interest.

➤ **A business successor plan.** Plan now for a business successor. If you have one or more co-owners, execute a buy-sell contract. The contract should specify the method by which the value is determined (such as appraisal, for example) and the means of payment (option or mandatory purchase).

You may want to consider other estate planning documents, such as a revocable trust, durable power of attorney, and living will. Please read Chapter 23, "Wave of the Now: The Net of Home," for a comprehensive discussion.

The Least You Need to Know

➤ Sole proprietors and partners are personally liable for business debts.

➤ You can always use good advisors.

➤ Capital comes from you, family, friends, and sometimes investors, but not the last at first.

➤ Employment laws can be traps for the unwary or the discriminatory.

➤ Put your contracts in writing.

➤ Writing a will and a business successor plan should be priority items in your business planning.

Chapter 2

Partnership in Harmony

In This Chapter

➤ Find your partner—and dance!

➤ Writing a binding contract

➤ The limits to limited partnerships

➤ Understanding the tax liability

You and a friend want to go into business together. You need to select a business entity, and a partnership comes readily to mind. Two or more persons can establish a partnership. Usually, they sign a partnership agreement that specifies certain rights, such as profits, voting, and management. Each partner is personally liable for the business debts, and each partner is taxed on the partnership income. Is it the right choice? Please read on.

Choosing Among the Choices

You have a choice of partnership entities:

➤ Regular partnership

➤ Registered limited liability partnership (LLP)

➤ Limited partnership

Notes & Quotes

"A friendship founded on business is better than a business founded on friendship."

—John D. Rockefeller Jr., businessperson

Legalese

A **partnership** is an association of two or more persons who will act as co-owners of a business for profit. Individuals or business entities may form partnerships.

The partnership and now its alternative choice, the registered limited liability partnership, is the choice of many professional firms, including doctors, lawyers, and accountants to name just a few. Limited partnerships have been frequently used as tax shelters for oil, gas, and coal operations, as well as real estate investments. Each of the three business entities has its advantages and disadvantages. Let's look at them one by one to see which type might work best for you.

Regular Partnership Is General

You can create an informal partnership with a simple handshake, but executing a *partnership* agreement is a much better way to begin business.

Your partnership begins with an agreement. Included in the terms of agreement should be an explanation of voting rights, profit and loss sharing, and admission of new partners. Each partner is personally liable for the debts of the partnership. The death or withdrawal of a partner may terminate the partnership, but this can be changed by the agreement. Each partner reports his or her share of the profit or loss on his or her individual tax return, whether distributed or not.

Most states don't require the partners to file anything with the Secretary of State, unlike a corporation, which must file its Articles of Incorporation. If the partnership, like any entity, is doing business in another name, then state law generally requires filing a "Doing Business As" certificate locally.

Drafting the Best Agreement for All

Partnerships are of this world, and as such depend on trust and a good partnership agreement. If you shake hands and proceed without an agreement, then the Uniform Partnership Act will provide the terms of your agreement as the default choice. For example, if there is no partnership agreement, then the partners automatically share equally in the profits, losses, and votes.

If you decide to hammer out the terms and create an agreement (which I strongly suggest you do), then you'll be trying to foresee typical challenges that you may face. Just this process of hammering out the terms is perhaps the best test of whether or not you and your partner or partners are compatible.

For example, two of my clients were going through the proposed agreement, but became stuck at the point of check authorization. One client insisted that all checks over five dollars be cosigned. I suggested as gently as possible that perhaps they should reconsider being partners. The trust level wasn't particularly high.

The following is a discussion of some of the terms that you and your partners should consider as you create your agreement.

➤ **Choosing Your Name.** The partners can choose to include their own names, such as Able, Baker, and Charlie, or any name not previously trademarked. Since a name may say it all, choose one that fits nicely into your business advertising.

➤ **Laying Claim to a Purpose.** Indicating your business purpose—what you intend to sell, provide, or trade in—in the agreement, is not necessary, but doing so will help you avoid future confusion if, say, one or more partners wanted to go off in a direction different from what you anticipated when you signed up. Here's what can happen: My client originally established a partnership to sell wedding dresses and later discovered the other partner had decided to branch off into selling used cars. A more definite purpose statement would have required an amendment to the partnership agreement before one of the partners could start hawking cars instead of dresses.

➤ **Fixing the Term.** Most partnerships continue until the partners retire or die, or until the business is no longer profitable. Few of the agreements specify a time limit. Since a partnership dissolves upon the death or retirement of a partner, the agreement should include a clause permitting the remaining partners to continue the partnership (and pay off the retiring partner or deceased partner's estate). For instance, one law firm had existed for several years. The partners never got around to executing a partnership agreement. Suddenly one of the younger partners died of a heart attack. The partnership dissolved and had to reform, at some cost and tax expense.

In addition to these terms, you'll also want to pay careful attention to financial terms. Each partner's initial capital contribution must be specified in the agreement. A prospective partner who has second thoughts about coming up with the money may have third thoughts when that partner is reminded of his or her legally binding promise. Capital contributions may be in the form of cash, property, or services to the partnership.

If contributions are property or services, the agreement should indicate how and by whom these contributions are to be valued. You should clearly indicate what property the partnership will own. As an example, a partnership was about to break up, and

the major dispute involved who owned what. The agreement specified that each partner's contribution of property was listed on attachment A. Unfortunately, no one had put together the attachment A, and memories of what was contributed considerably differed.

If a partner is to lend money to the partnership, you should clearly state the terms of the loan, including the rate of interest and payment due date. The partnership should execute a promissory note as evidence of the debt. The partnership may need additional capital contributions in the future and you should provide for that contingency. Retaining some percentage of earnings or requiring additional capital contributions by the partners upon call of the partnership should be included in the agreement.

Understanding Profits and Losses

The partners can share profits and losses equally, in proportion to the capital contributions, according to the work performed, or any other way specified in the agreement. If there is no agreement then profits and losses are shared equally.

Determining profit and loss shares is never easy, and this can be further complicated if the partnership wants to distribute bonuses among the partners.

The partners may want to pay bonuses to one or more partners for superior performance. Beware that performance bonuses often engender resentment among those whose remuneration is not as generous. For example, a law partnership tried to allocate bonuses based on client revenue generated. This infuriated the partners with less lucrative but important practices. Losses can be allocated differently than profits, but usually are the same, and income tax reporting usually follows the allocated share of profit and loss. Some partners are more effective workers than others are. A partner's income is limited to his or her share of the profits, unless the agreement specifies a salary.

In one company, for instance, one set of partners had other jobs, which meant that they provided limited partnership services while others were able or willing to work more for the firm. Nevertheless, all partners—underachievers and overachievers alike—received the same share of the profits. The partnership dissolved because of the resentment that built up between the two groups. A salary scheme would have solved this problem.

Creating Management

Each partner has an equal vote in partnership business decisions, and a majority vote is usually required for approval. However, the partnership agreement may alter this equal vote and majority rule. For instance, partners could base voting rights upon the percentage of the profits or capital contribution. Other management concerns that you should specify in the agreement are quorum and notice requirements. For instance, your agreement should require periodic meetings, and minutes for each meeting should be kept. In fact, large partnerships often have a management committee elected by the partners to run the daily affairs. The agreement may want to designate a senior partner as the tie-breaker vote if there is a voting impasse.

Delineating Partner Duties

Partners owe a duty to properly attend to partnership business. But partners may have other jobs, particularly if they're just starting up a new company together. To avoid conflicts over work schedules, the partners may want to agree to a minimal amount of time that each partner must spend working for the partnership. Businesses vary, so no model provision specifying each partner's duties is appropriate. However, one partner may have expertise in marketing, another in accounting, and a third in management. An informal arrangement regarding these duties may be helpful.

If one or more partners end up working many more hours than the others work, the partners may want to pay the more dedicated partners more in salary or in profits. The thing to remember is that each partner owes his or her undivided loyalty to the partnership, called a *fiduciary* duty. This fiduciary duty requires every partner to eliminate any conflict of interest he or she may have and to keep his or her private business separate from the new partnership. For instance, you're not allowed to buy supplies for your new partnership concern from your personal business entity. Of course, a partner does not violate this duty if he or she discloses the potential conflict and receives partnership permission to proceed.

Legal Eagle

If you began the business and the other partners joined later, you might want to consider retaining a majority of the votes to maintain your position as senior partner. Someone has to make the final decision.

Legalese

A **fiduciary** is a person who is bound to act with the utmost good faith in the management of property or affairs for the benefit of another. A partner is a fiduciary to the partnership.

Making Clear a Partner's Right to Accounting

Each partner is entitled to review the financial records, but it is helpful to remind everyone of the law. The partner in charge of the accounting should readily respond to any partner's request for financial information. The agreement should specify at least quarterly profit-and-loss and balance-sheet financial information. Every partner should be aware of the partnership's financial situation. The books should be set up by an account-ant, who then provides the quarterly and annual re-ports. Here's what happens when such a process is not established: In one company, the partners relied on one of the spouses to do the bookkeeping. Unfortun-ately, she had other demands on her time. Accounts receivable went uncollected and accounts payable went unpaid. No one knew whether they were making or losing money. They lost money and went out of business.

Notes & Quotes

"Where large sums of money are concerned, it is advisable to trust nobody."

—Agatha Christie, author

Adding Partners

The law requires unanimous acceptance of a new partner by all current partners un-less the agreement states otherwise. Rejecting a potential partner may not be good business, so consider a majority or greater vote rather than a unanimous one. The partners should consider upon what terms a new partner is to be accepted, such as capital contribution, profit-and-loss share, voting rights, and so on.

Withdrawing Partners

At the same time, keep in mind that the partnership will have to provide for any partner who retires. Usually, the remaining partners agree to purchase the retiring partner's interest based upon an appraisal and make a periodic payout over several years. The buyout is typically paid over several years to ease the impact on the part-nership. The retiring partner usually has other sources of income, such as a new job or pension, so annual payments, rather than a lump sum, do not cause him or her a financial hardship.

Death can come to any partner, so your agreement should make provisions for that eventuality. One way to handle the payout to the deceased partner's estate might be through a term life insurance paid by the partnership. Since the partnership interest may be the most significant asset in the decedent's estate, the initial payment should be substantial. None of the deceased's family wants to wait around several years be-fore the payments are finished.

Appraisal of an Ownership Interest

Appraisal of a going business is difficult at best. Your accountant should suggest several alternatives, one of which may be included in the agreement. Sometimes the best solution is to have an appraisal made at the appropriate time, with criteria established in the agreement. A departing partner may want to compete in business with your partnership. Your agreement can restrict the departing partner by prohibiting him or her from working in the same business for a reasonable time after departure. Courts will uphold this restrictive covenant as long as it is no more expansive than necessary to protect the partnership. For example, if the partner is a sales rep, the agreement may exclude him or her from working in his or her sales area for two years.

Shark Attack!

Payment to a retiring partner or partner's estate usually involves significant tax implications. Consult a tax accountant or lawyer to properly structure the payment for tax advantage to the departed and remaining partners.

Expelling a Partner

Clearly, there are some things a partner may do that require his or her removal. A law partner who is disbarred, for instance, is of little use to the partnership. A partner who lies, cheats, and steals cannot be tolerated. The partnership agreement should provide just cause grounds for a partner's expulsion and a procedure by which the partner can be removed and repaid his or her capital contribution. The partnership may want to provide for a deduction of the partner's capital for the economic harm to the partnership. In one company, a partner was entrusted with client funds. Unfortunately, she stole the money to sustain her lifestyle and then the auditor caught her. The partners voted for her expulsion and denied her repayment of her capital, because the amount she had stolen was paid back by the partnership.

Dissolution and Winding Up

It's difficult to consider shutting down when you're just beginning, but almost all goods things must come to an end. This section of the agreement should specify what dissolution requires, such as a majority vote of the partners, and the procedure involved. The agreement should specify who will be in charge of winding up the business. An individual partner or committee of partners are both viable choices.

Winding up involves completing work in progress, collecting accounts receivable, and paying creditors. The law requires that creditors be paid first. If the creditors do not receive payment, then they may hold the partners personally liable for the unpaid debts. Since any partner may be liable for the entire partnership debt, it is important for all partners to make sure the business pays its creditors. If there are any contingent claims, the partnership may establish an account to handle the payments. After the business pays the creditors, then the partners are entitled to any undistributed share of the retained earnings and capital contributions. The agreement specifies the method by which this is determined.

Arbitration

Inevitably, disputes arise within a new business partnership. Rather than storming off to court and paying enormous legal fees to resolve the problem, you should consider an alternative called arbitration. A knowledgeable expert, usually a lawyer experienced in partnership law, will provide an interpretation of the agreement in a timely and less expensive manner.

Legal Eagle

Preparation is the key. If you go into arbitration, you need to prepare as much for that process as you would for a trial. A well-drawn agreement and detailed minutes of partnership decisions may settle a disputed point before it gets to arbitration.

The arbitrator's decision may be binding, which means it limits review by the courts, or it may be subject to court review. Your agreement should specify which type of arbitration you prefer. All of the partners may split the costs or the agreement may state that the losing party must pay. In one company, the retiring partner was unhappy about the appraisal of his interest. Instead of a lawsuit, the retiring partner and the partnership presented written and oral evidence to the arbitrator, who then determined that the appraisal procedure was followed and ruled for the partnership.

In summary, the agreement requires you to make some difficult decisions. If you can't work them out, then it is better to realize defeat now with a minimal investment, rather than wait for the anguish and anger that almost certainly occur when the unresolved issues arise.

Contract Liability

Each partner is considered an *agent* for the partnership. If a partner makes a contract with another party—a vendor or a client—then the entire partnership is bound to abide by the terms of that agreement. There are some exceptions, but remembering this general rule is helpful. Likewise, if the partner is negligent while working and injures someone or damages property, then the partnership is liable. You can see why choosing your partners wisely is important. But even then, negligence often just happens.

Partners should clearly understand the limits of their ability to bind the partnership to a contract. This understanding should be acknowledged in the partnership minutes or a memorandum. Then, a partner who violates this policy is on notice that he or she will be liable for any excess over the amount the partner is entitled to spend. Likewise, a partner's misconduct, such as negligence, can result in partnership liability for the negligence.

However, this policy would not affect creditors who are not aware of the partnership's policy, which means that if creditors lend money to one partner—unaware that two partnerships are required—you would nevertheless be required to repay the debt. In fact, you might want to notify major creditors of the policy or state on any order form that a certain partner or partners must authorize every transaction involving a certain amount of money or term.

In one company, one of the law partners liked to spend money on research books. He contracted with a law book sales rep to purchase a set for $4,000. The others found out and were furious, but the partnership had to pay. The book rep had dealt with the partner concerning book purchases, and reasonably believed that the partner had the authority to bind the partnership.

Tort Liability

People do get careless, and while a negligent partner is liable for any actions performed during business hours, it's usually the partnership or the partnership's insurance company that pays. Here's an example: One partner did not timely file a client's tax return. The unforgiving IRS imposed penalty and interest on the client, who in turn insisted that the errant partner pay the tab. In the end, the partnership paid the penalty and interest because the amount was substantially more than the one partner, alone, could afford.

If the partner's misconduct is intentional—punching an irritating customer or stealing from customer accounts—the partnership will almost certainly be held liable. Just be aware of the risk and do what you can to protect yourself, such as purchasing a performance bond for the partner who handles the customer funds if you have even an inkling of impropriety.

Legalese

An **agent** acts on behalf of his or her principal and the principal is liable for his or her acts. A partner acts as an agent for the partnership when purchasing for the partnership.

Legal Eagle

Consider requiring two partners to cosign any contract over a certain amount(maybe one thousand dollars), which can reduce your concern over an errant partner binding the partnership to a contract the majority does not want.

Shark Attack!

Tempers can be expensive. If a partner cannot keep his or hers, get that partner away from people or expel the partner from the partnership. A dog may be entitled to one bite before the owner is liable, but courts are less sympathetic to humans.

Whose Property Is It?

It's often difficult to discern the difference between partnership property and an individual partner's personal property. As previously indicated, make sure you designate any capital contribution of property as partnership property on your records. Any property a partner lends to the partnership should likewise be clearly designated as being that partner's property.

Property purchased with partnership funds is presumed to be partnership property, but make sure that title and records so indicate. For instance, a partner purchased a delivery truck with a partnership check, but put the title in his own name. Now the partner must prove that the truck is properly titled to retain his claimed ownership, since he bought the truck with partnership money. If the check represented a capital distribution to the partner, then he would be able to keep the truck, but he has the burden of proof.

All of this information is important when it comes to taxes (who receives the depreciation), creditor's rights (an individual partner's creditor cannot attach partnership property), and distribution of partnership assets on dissolution of the partnership.

Registering to Limit Liability

Partners are personally liable to partnership creditors. Each partner is liable for all of the debt, at least to the extent that other partners don't pay their fair share. Underpaying partners can be sued, but a judgment is only as good as its collection. In one company, the partnership went under, and the debts exceeded the assets. Two of the partners had substantial assets; the other two were mortgaged to the hilt. The partners with the money paid. The partners with no money filed bankruptcy and discharged their obligation to the partners who paid.

But wait! State legislatures have changed the rules of the game by creating a registered limited liability partnership (LLP). The change from a partnership to LLP is simple enough in most states. You must file a form with the Secretary of State declaring the partnership to be LLP, and thereafter a partner is personally liable only for his or her own misdeeds, such as personal negligence, but not for the other partners' wrongdoing.

For example, under agency law, if one partner ran a red light and wiped out most of the pedestrians, the partnership would be liable under agency law. In LLP, any excess liability beyond the LLP's assets would not be the liability of any partner other than the offending member.

Other than the change in liability, the LLP operates the same as a regular partnership.

Limited Partnership Limits

The *limited partnership* may be nearly extinct. Congress changed the tax code in 1986 to permit only certain tax losses to be taken by the partners, which denied considerable tax shelter advantages to the partners. Then came the limited liability company, and now the limited liability partnership, which provides the owner with limited personal liability for business debts but allows partnership tax treatment. But the old guy deserves some mention.

You can create a limited partnership by filing a certificate with the Secretary of State. The certificate is usually an abbreviated limited partnership agreement. Here are terms that the partners need to include in the certificate:

➤ **Name.** The limited partnership name must include its designation as a limited partnership or LP.

➤ **Partners.** The certificate should identify each partner as either a general partner or as a limited partner. The general partner has sole management responsibility; limited partners have no management rights. The general partner is personally liable for the business debts; the limited partners risk only their capital investment. In essence, the limited partners are passive investors.

➤ **Purpose.** In the past, limited partnerships usually involved investments that could generate a tax loss, such as real estate development and mineral extraction such as oil and gas. Since the limited partners have no management rights, a clear purpose statement is vital to their expectations.

➤ **Term.** A time limit for its existence may be set. A general partner is required, so the death of the sole individual general partner would cause its dissolution. However, most limited partnerships permit the limited partners to elect a successor general partner.

➤ **Capital contribution.** Each partner's capital contribution is recorded. The contribution may be in cash, property, or services. The value of the latter two should be clearly stated.

Legalese

A **limited partnership** is a partnership formed with two or more persons as co-owners, which means that it has one or more general partners and one or more limited partners.

Legal Eagle

A limited partnership may have a corporation as its general partner, thus avoiding co-owner personal liability for its debts.

25

While the limited partner may request a return of his or her capital within six months of written notice, the law does not permit this distribution if it would impair creditor rights. Usually a limited partnership has borrowed heavily (to maximize the tax loss pass through to his or her own 1040), so the return of capital is highly unlikely.

➤ **Profits and losses.** The agreement specifies the shares allocated to each general and limited partner. Usually this is a specific percentage, although some partnership tax shelters have a reallocation formula.

➤ **Admission of new partners.** The agreement usually provides the method of admitting new general and limited partners. If nothing is specified then all the partners must consent. The interests of the limited partners are usually transferable without limitation, and the heirs of a deceased limited partner may inherit his or her interest.

➤ **Dissolution and liquidation.** The agreement may specify an event causing dissolution, such as the death of the general partner before the election of a replacement or a specific time for termination. The liquidation of the limited partnership requires supervision by the general partner. Creditors are paid first, then partners according to the agreement.

Taxes Matter

Each partner, whether in a partnership, registered limited liability partnership, or limited partnership, reports his or her share of the distributable business income. The partnership reports the income and expenses on federal form 1065, and provides each partner with a form 1065 K-1. The K-1 specifies the amount and type of income the partner reports.

Shark Attack!

Beware of the limited partnership: It shouldn't be the entity of choice for most businesses. The limited liability is available for all owners in the limited liability partnership or the limited liability company.

For example, if you are one of two equal partners and the partnership net income consists of $60,000 ordinary income and $40,000 capital gains, then your K-1 will show $30,000 of ordinary income and $20,000 of capital gains. You'll report those amounts on Schedules E and D of your individual 1040, and so will your partner—even if you didn't actually receive it as income. For a more detailed discussion about taxes for the small business, please read Chapter 6, "Taxing Matters."

Helpful Sources

Almost all states have their laws available on their Web page. You can download your state's Uniform Partnership Act and Uniform Limited Partnership Act.

You may want to surf the Web. Several law firms have Web sites that may provide specific information about partnership law in your state. In addition, several software companies, such as Quicken, sell business forms, which are available at many computer stores; I would use those forms with some caution and suggest a review of your draft by an attorney. Finally, your local library usually has books related to business formation, as well as the state code.

The Least You Need to Know

➤ Partnerships should have a detailed written agreement.

➤ Partners are personally liable for business debts, unless the partnership is a registered limited liability partnership.

➤ Partnerships are liable for the contracts and misconduct of the partners acting on its behalf.

➤ Each partner reports his or her share of the distributable partnership income.

Chapter 3

The Inc. for You, or Sharing with Others

In This Chapter

➤ Using incorporation to protect yourself

➤ Agreeing to agree

➤ Setting up a board of directors

➤ Finding the right dissolution solution

You, too, can be a corporation. Corporate status provides you with the protection of limited liability. You can choose between being taxed personally or having the corporation taxed on its business income. The corporation can exist in perpetuity, which may mean beyond the initial shareholders' lives. The corporation can have as many shareholders as it wishes. I will assume for this discussion that it's either just you or a few other shareholders, and in this chapter show you all you need to know to get started.

Incorporating Your Business for Protection

Corporate organization is rather structured and, to become established, requires a number of documents, including ...

➤ Articles of Incorporation

➤ Bylaws

➤ Initial shareholder and board of directors minutes

When it comes to choosing what state in which to incorporate, you'll probably want to incorporate in the state where you'll conduct your business. By doing so, you'll avoid being treated as a foreign corporation in your own state. If you grow into a

giant dot.com, then you may want to consider the state of Delaware, which is the happy home for many large corporations, because of its favorable corporation tax laws.

If you are going solo, then you don't need what's known as a pre-incorporation agreement. With two or more shareholders, consider the pre-incorporation agreement to be a must-have document. Its primary purpose is to contractually bind all the potential investors/shareholders to their capital contributions. Many businesses fail because of insufficient initial capital, which is one good reason this contract is so important. The agreement can be as simple as including …

➤ Corporation name

➤ Amount of capital contribution

➤ Shares to be issued to each shareholder

Just a reminder: Please read Chapter 10, "Raising Money When You Need More Than You Have," before soliciting investments in your corporation. You must closely follow federal and state securities laws in order to avoid possible civil (and potentially criminal) lawsuits against you.

Choose a name and reserve it with the Secretary of State by filing a registration-of-name form. Avoid a name that's already trademarked ("Coke" is one). Many states require the use of Corporation, Incorporated, or an abbreviation thereof in the name. If your chosen corporate name is too similar to an existing entity, then the Secretary of State will reject your choice.

If you are the sole shareholder, then a bare-bones Articles of Incorporation is all that you need, and you can find the form on your Secretary of State's Web page. The Articles usually contain the following information:

➤ **Name.** Widget Company, Inc.

➤ **Authorized Shares.** One thousand shares of common stock.

➤ **Name and Address of the Registered Agent.** Sam Service, 1 North Street, None, IN 46222.

➤ **Name and Address of the Incorporator.** Sam Service, 1 North Street, None, IN 46222.

You file the form with the Secretary of State and pay a small fee. Congratulations, you have a new corporation!

Stock issued to the initial investors in a small corporation will be common stock. If you realize your fantasies and your corporation sells its stock to the general public, then you may want to create different classes of common or preferred stock. But by then you will have expensive lawyers, accountants, and brokers to shepherd you through the process.

Please read Chapter 10, "Raising Money When You Need More Than You Have," for a complete discussion of stock offerings.

The registered agent is the person designated to receive service of a summons should the corporation be sued. The incorporator (you or the person who filed with the state) signs the Articles. Once the Articles of Incorporation are filed, the shareholders, incorporator, and board of directors meet. The shareholders elect the board, and the board, in turn, elects the corporate officers. The board approves the bylaws, and receives the shareholders' payment for the stock. The board issues the corporate stock. If the corporation has numerous shareholders, things are more complex, so a more detailed Articles of Incorporation should be drafted. An attorney should be retained to prepare those Articles.

The *bylaws* establish the procedure for the shareholder and board meetings, such as notice and quorum requirements. The bylaws provide a brief description of the duties of the officers.

Shark Attack!

Beware of hidden costs. Some states charge a significant fee or special franchise tax for incorporation in addition to an annual fee. Check with your state Secretary of State for your state's fee schedule.

Legalese

Bylaws contain all provisions for managing the business and regulating the affairs of the corporation.

Shareholder Agreements to Agree

If your corporation has more than one shareholder, the shareholders should prepare a Shareholders' Stock Purchase Agreement. The agreement provides a method by which a retiring or deceased shareholder's stock may be purchased. Without this restriction, stock is freely transferable, meaning the stock can be sold to anyone. In a small corporation, shareholders are more like partners, so a new shareholder who is not approved by the other shareholders can cause problems if you don't have an agreement.

The shareholder agreement typically provides an option to purchase the stock of the retiring shareholder. The corporation and the shareholders have a right to purchase the stock by matching a price offered by an outsider. As an alternative, the agreement could determine the option price of the stock by an appraisal at its fair market value or at a fixed price previously established. A fixed price method is the least desirable because shareholders never seem to get around to adjusting the price as the business progresses.

For the shareholder who has died, the corporation and the shareholders agree to pay the estate for the stock. Usually the deceased's stock is appraised at its fair market value on the date of death.

The option payment for the retiring shareholder typically is a structured payout that occurs over four or five years, while the estate payout may involve a significant down payment and periodic payments. Term life insurance on each shareholder's life can substantially fund the estate payment. Since the option payment comes directly from corporate funds or shareholder pockets, these payments will usually take longer (and the departing shareholder usually is earning other income during this time).

In addition, the shareholders may want to maintain the same percentage of share ownership among each other; they may agree to allow each shareholder an option to purchase his or her pro rata share of any new stock offering by the corporation.

Legal Eagle

Make sure your Stock Purchase Agreement restricts transfer of the stock to only those approved by the other shareholders. This can avoid including the incompatible shareholder, but it can make selling the stock more difficult.

Legal Eagle

Establish the appraisal procedure in the stock purchase agreement. The corporation and the shareholder/estate may each appoint an appraiser. The appraisers will then select a third appraiser. This procedure should provide a fair means to determine value.

Shareholders Share Almost Everything

Your percentage of stock ownership determines your share of the corporate profit, the distribution of which is a dividend, usually in the form of cash. Large corporations pay dividends quarterly. Most small corporations do so less frequently.

If the shareholders are also employees of the corporation, which is typical, then most of their compensation comes from salary and fringe benefits. The choice of tax entity (*S corporation or C corporation*, discussed later in this chapter) may decide if it is advantageous to declare dividends. The board of directors declares the dividends, usually from corporate profits.

Shareholders are not personally liable for corporate debts unless they personally guarantee a debt. Banks typically require shareholders to guarantee loans, but most individual creditors do not.

Shareholders officially act in corporate meetings, and each shareholder is entitled to one vote for each share. Most states permit the meetings to be conducted telephonically. As an alternative, shareholders may approve a corporate resolution without meeting with unanimous written consent.

The bylaws usually require a quorum (majority of the stock shares) and majority vote for the approval of a corporate resolution. Annual shareholder meetings are required. The president of the corporation or a majority of shareholders can call a special meeting for important business such as electing a new director.

Legalese

An **S corporation or C corporation** is a tax designation only. In an S corporation, the shareholders are taxed on the business income, while in a C corporation, the corporation, itself, is taxed.

Board of Directors and Officers Control

Directors are elected by the shareholders, usually for a one-year term, but may serve up to three years. They may be compensated for their services, and if they are, may set their own compensation and record it in the minutes. In a small corporation, the shareholders often are the directors. While the Board sets corporate policy, its officers execute the Board decisions.

Legal Eagle

Guarantee as little as possible. Usually banks will insist that all shareholders personally guarantee the loan. Some landlords may require a guaranty.

The directors serve at the pleasure of the shareholders and may be removed with or without cause by the shareholders in a meeting specifically called for that purpose.

For instance, in one corporation, shareholder/director Bob had a personality that allowed him to dominate the other shareholders. Finally the other two shareholders had enough. They sent proper notice and held a shareholder meeting. The other partners removed Bob as a director; because the bylaws so stated, they didn't need to state or prove a cause for Bob's dismissal.

The Role of the Board of Directors

The bylaws specify notice, quorum, and voting requirements of the corporation. Like the shareholders, the board of directors may meet by telephone or video conference or may unanimously approve a written corporate resolution without any meeting

Shark Attack!

Don't neglect removal powers when you write your bylaws. Removal of a partner is always an acrimonious process and fraught with threats of litigation unless you carefully spell out the form of removal and the amount of notice required. Removing a partner is a powerful weapon and you may want to limit it in the bylaws by requiring a super-majority ($^2/_3$ or $^3/_4$) vote to enact it.

Legal Eagle

Talk to your accountant to make sure you don't establish an illegal dividend. In addition, since dividends may be taxable to the shareholder, consulting a tax advisor is important, particularly to the high tax bracket shareholder.

at all. The board of directors must meet annually, but the bylaws may specify more frequent meeting and the president may call special meetings. Board functions include …

➤ Approving/amending bylaws

➤ Electing/removing officers

➤ Establishing policy

➤ Declaring dividends

The board may remove an officer with or without cause in a meeting specifically called for that purpose. If an officer is also an employee, removal doesn't necessarily result in terminating employment.

The board acts to set policy and make major decisions, such as purchasing land or erecting an office building. The directors may also establish a personnel manual for employees, develop a business plan, and determine which offer has the authority to contract.

State law may restrict the board's authority to declare and pay a dividend. If a dividend is paid when corporate debts exceed assets, then that may be an illegal dividend that the shareholders are required to return.

Breach of Trust

Each board member has a duty of loyalty (fiduciary duty) to the corporation, so it's important that all board members avoid conflicts of interest. The board member who has a financial interest in the vote of a corporate resolution, for example, approving a contract between him or herself and the corporation, must declare that interest and abstain from voting.

Board members are not usually liable if they make poor decisions; however, if they breach their fiduciary duty by self-dealing, or if their conduct lacks good faith and prudent care, then they may be liable to the shareholders. Most statutes hold a director personally liable if the director's misconduct was reckless or willful. Some large corporations agree to purchase director and officer liability insurance to protect them from frivolous suits by disgruntled shareholders.

Here's a flagrant example of a fiduciary breach: A corporate director, who was secretly serving on a competitor's board, forwarded all the corporate plans to the other board. When the board discovered this double-dealing, it removed the director and sued him for the monetary damages suffered by corporation.

The Role of the Officers

The board members also elect corporate officers. Corporations need a president and secretary who, in a sole shareholder corporation, may be the same person. In addition, the corporation usually has a vice president and treasurer. In a small corporation the officers often are the shareholders (and directors).

The bylaws describe officer duties, but the board may augment them. Officers execute policy and make decisions within the parameters set by the board. For example, the board may authorize the president to lease an office building or negotiate a loan. The officers run the daily operations and may delegate authority to others, such as supervisors, to contract for the corporation or to hire and fire employees.

Since officers are agents for the corporation, they have the same fiduciary loyalty to the corporation as do the directors. Officers are agents for the corporation, and they can bind the corporation to contracts made on its behalf. Also, an officer's negligent conduct that harms another can result in a judgment against the corporation.

Legal Eagle

If you are buying corporate assets, hire a good accountant to allocate the asset purchase prices to maximize tax depreciation. If you are selling the business, insist on a premium to adjust for loss of the capital gain advantage.

Legal Eagle

If your corporation decides to employ an officer, consider drafting the officer's employment contract to allow termination as an employee if you terminate him or her as an officer. Disgruntled ex-officers don't make good employees.

Acquisitions and Dissolution Mean Change

In these heady days of mergers and acquisitions, anything is possible when it comes to the future of your corporation, so be prepared. The board and shareholders may one day be in a position to make decisions about a merger and dissolution of the corporation.

Merger and Acquisition

Merger is the purchase of Corporation A's stock by Corporation B, followed by A merging into B, and A going out of existence. Corporation B receives A's assets and is liable for A's debts.

The board and shareholders approve the merger, then the Articles of Merger are filed with the Secretary of State. If you are a shareholder in Corporation A, there may be an alternative to having your stock converted to Corporation B stock. If you voted against the merger, you can notify your Corporation A that you want cash for your stock. State law establishes the procedure, as dissenter's rights. However, some states permit this right only if Corporation A's stock is not listed on a public exchange, such as NASDAQ or New York Stock Exchange.

Corporations seem acquisitive of other corporations of late. Corporation A's stock may be acquired by Corporation B, but the two are not merged. This is referred to as a parent-subsidiary relationship. The two corporations are separate entities but the parent corporation (B) controls the subsidiary (A).

Sale of All Corporate Assets

When the shareholders decide to sell the business, most small corporations end up selling their assets to the purchaser instead of the shareholders selling their stock. That's because the buyer wants the assets but not the corporation's liabilities (which it would be obligated to pay if there were a stock acquisition). Also, there are tax advantages for the buyer to acquire the assets. Selling shareholders would prefer to sell their stock, because the capital gain from the sale of stock is taxed at a lower rate than the ordinary income resulting from the distribution of assets when the corporation is liquidated.

Dissolution

Corporations can exist in perpetuity, but small corporations seldom last that long. When the time comes to sell the business assets or when the business goes under, the board and the shareholders must approve dissolution of the corporation. The Articles of Dissolution are then filed with the Secretary of State. Upon dissolution, the debts (including the taxes) are paid first, then the shareholders receive any remaining assets based on their percentage share of the stock.

Taxes Matter

Corporate taxation may follow one of two paths: C or S. If you do not take an S corporation election by filing form 2553 with the IRS to tax shareholders directly on corporate income, then the corporate tax status is as a C corporation. Simply put, the net income is taxed to the corporation. The rates progress from 15 to 38 percent of the taxable income (gross income less deductible expenses). The federal tax is reported on form 1120 and the tax is paid by the corporation.

As a share holder in a C corporation, you must report on your own 1040 any dividends the corporation distributes to you. In essence, if you're not careful, you'll end up paying double taxes (corporate and individual). To avoid this, some small corporations pay higher salaries and fringe benefits (tax deductible to the corporation) and little or no dividends. However, the IRS may audit your corporation and determine that this compensation is excessive and therefore not a legitimate deductible expense for the corporation. You should consult your tax accountant or lawyer about this strategy.

Another tax alternative is to elect to be taxed as an S corporation. To qualify as an S corporation, your corporation must …

➤ Be incorporated and organized in the United States.

➤ Have only one class of stock (common).

➤ Be limited to a maximum of 75 shareholders.

➤ Have only individuals, estates, and certain trusts as shareholders.

➤ Have no nonresident aliens as shareholders.

To be effective for the first year, you must file the election (form 2553) with the IRS before the fifteenth day of the third month from incorporation. If the election is later, then it will be effective for all subsequent years after the year in which the election was made. All shareholders must consent to the election.

Here's an example: Corporation Alpha is a C corporation in 2000. The shareholders must file form 2553 no later than March 15, 2001 to convert to S status in 2001.

You'll report corporate income and expenses on the federal schedule 1120S, then each shareholder will receive notice of his or her taxable income, which is allocated according to his or her percentage of stock ownership and reported on the 1120 K-1.

Notes & Quotes

"Reflecting on a corporate merger, one executive noted, 'We got the mushroom treatment. Right after the acquisition, we were left in the dark. Then they covered us with manure. Then they cultivated us. After that they let us stew awhile. Finally, they canned us.'"

—Isadore Barmash, businessperson

Shark Attack!

Avoiding dividend payment to avoid higher taxation is risky strategy. The IRS may impose additional taxes on the corporation if there is an unreasonable accumulation of retained earnings (insufficient dividend payments).

The shareholder then reports this information on his or her 1040. The S corporation shareholder must report his or her share of the corporate income whether or not it is actually distributed to the shareholder.

Legal Eagle

As a shareholder of an S corporation, make sure your records are in proper order. The IRS will want to tax any dividends that shareholders receive unless the shareholders can clearly show that they have been previously taxed.

For example, assume that you are one of two equal shareholders and the corporation has $100,000 of taxable income. The 1120S K-1 will report $50,000 income for each of you, which you must on Schedule E of your 1040. If the corporation later pays a dividend from the previously taxed income, then such dividend is tax-free income to you (since you already paid the tax upon receiving the K-1).

Please note that some states do not recognize S corporation tax status for that state's income tax law, so that the corporation itself pays the tax on its income. This will not affect federal taxes, but you'll have to consider that fact when deciding whether or not to elect S status.

For a more complete discussion of tax law, please read Chapter 6, "Taxing Matters."

Helpful Sources

Most state Secretary of State Web sites contain all the corporate forms that you'll need to file with that agency. State Web sites contain the Corporation Code and you may download it for your reading pleasure. Also, some law firms in your state may have Web sites that discuss corporate formation and operation, as well as the tax elections. Local libraries, likewise, have books on incorporating.

The Least You Need to Know

➤ Corporate shareholders are not liable for business debts unless the debts are personally guaranteed.

➤ You can incorporate your business by filing Articles of Incorporation with the state Secretary of State.

➤ The board of directors elects the officers, establishes and amends the bylaws, and declares dividends.

➤ A corporation may be taxed on its profits (C corporation), or the shareholders may be taxed on the corporation's profits (S corporation).

Chapter 4

The Limited Liability Company Limits Your Liability

In This Chapter

➤ Limiting liability: the basics

➤ Creating your organizing articles is the beginning

➤ Understanding how an LLC operates

➤ The lowdown on taxes for LLCs

The limited liability company (LLC) can be an alternative to a partnership or corporation. An LLC is an unincorporated association organized under state law, and the members of the association are the owners of the company. A member may be an individual or business entity. The members of the LLC are not liable for the business debts, which is a distinct advantage over the regular partnership because the partners are personally liable for its debt; however, in the registered limited liability partnership (LLP) its partners are not liable for its debts. Each member reports his or her share of the business income (or loss). In this chapter, we'll discuss the pros and cons and ins and outs of this particular business entity.

LLCs: The Basics

What are the advantages of an LLC as compared to partnerships and corporations? Well, partnerships tend to be quite flexible because the partnership agreement permits the partners to work out an arrangement that best suits their needs. However, the partnership's downside is personal liability for business debts and each partner must report his or her share of the partnership taxable income on the partner's 1040.

LLCs also have advantages over corporations, which tend to be more structured and require filings with the state Secretary of State than do LLCs. In addition, LLC shareholders are not personally liable for the corporate debts. Any corporation with 75 or fewer shareholders can elect to have each shareholder report his or her share of the corporate taxable income on the shareholder's 1040. As an alternative, the corporation itself can be taxed on its profits. You may choose to convert your partnership into a limited liability company. The organization documents and steps are discussed in this chapter. The conversion to the LLC should be tax free, but always use an accountant to prepare for the details making that possible. Your corporation may also convert to LLC, although this is less likely, since there is no personal liability for the owners of either entity, and the corporation can elect to have its shareholders taxed on its income.

Your Organizing Articles Is the Beginning

The limited liability company (LLC) has the following features:

➤ Articles of Organization filed with the Secretary of State

➤ Operating Agreement with flexible terms

➤ Member management or appointed managers

➤ Profit and loss determined by members as stated in the Operating Agreement

➤ Members are not liable for business debts

➤ Members may restrict transfer of ownership

➤ Existence as an LLC for 30 years or more

➤ Taxation as a partnership unless members elect corporate taxation

Shark Attack!

Members of the limited liability company are personally liable only for the business debts that they personally guarantee, such as a bank loan.

The Articles of Organization must be filed with the state Secretary of State before the LLC may begin business. The Articles may be fairly abbreviated, but must contain the following:

➤ **Name.** Able Limited Liability Co., LLC.

➤ **Registered Agent and Address.** Al Able, 1 South St., Somewhere, IN. The registered agent accepts service of legal papers on the LLC.

➤ **Term of Existence.** Perpetual. (The term may be less than perpetual, such as 30 years, but most LLCs use "perpetual".)

➤ **Management.** By members.

The Articles of Organization may be more detailed if the organizing members want it to be. If there is just one member (allowed in some states) or only a few, a bare-bones document is likely all that is needed. At least one of the organizing members must sign them; however, all members must sign the Operating Agreement. (The Operating Agreement is more significant and must be carefully drafted.) Many states have preprinted Articles of Organization, some of which can be downloaded from the Secretary of State Web site.

Notes & Quotes

"When you come to a fork in the road, take it."

—Yogi Berra, baseball manager

Operating Instructions for the Business

The Operating Agreement is the key LLC document and its terms are flexible enough to meet the needs of its members. To better acquaint you with LLC law, the following is a detailed discussion of the agreement.

Choosing a Name

The name of the limited liability company must include the words "limited liability company," or more typically, an abbreviation, such as "LLC." Since the name may appear in advertising, you may want to choose one that describes your business, such a Wedding Arrangements, LLC.

Legal Eagle

You may want to reserve your name before filing the Articles. Some states will charge you to reserve the name, then hold it for a short period, such as 30 days. Remember not to use a trademarked name as part of your LLC name.

Formation and Company Purpose

The Operating Agreement formally states that the organizing members have acted to file the Articles of Organization and that the members will conduct business under the Articles unless they create amendment.

Usually the purpose statement is broadly worded to include all activities authorized under state law. However, you might want to limit the purpose statement to include only those business activities that all of the members agree on conducting. Small businesses generally focus on just one or a few business activities. If the LLC is established to sell sporting goods and attire, for instance, just say so in the purpose clause. Later, you can add contract language to allow alternative activities as the members approve and amend the agreement.

Members and Their Capital Contributions

The members' names and addresses must be listed and each member's capital contribution must be recorded (usually as Exhibit A to the agreement). Keep in mind that a prospective member is not bound by an oral promise to make a capital contribution. Therefore, a pre-formation contribution agreement should be signed by each member in order to avoid undercapitalization.

Shark Attack!

If you establish an LLC and offer memberships to outside investors, then federal and state securities laws apply, and must be strictly adhered to if you are to avoid their violation. Consult an attorney experienced in securities laws.

The capital contribution can be in cash, property, or services. If the contribution is property or service, then make sure they are properly valued, and the property is transferred to the LLC. If the property has a title, such as the title to a motor vehicle, transfer the title to the LLC.

Many small businesses underestimate their capital needs. If members can be required to make additional capital contributions, then the procedure involved must be clearly spelled out. Capital contributions cannot be returned to a member if the distribution would impair creditors. The agreement should reiterate the law, and further specify when the members may permit a distribution when assets exceed liabilities.

Members are usually issued certificates (or shares) based upon their capital contribution. The number of shares may determine voting rights and profit/loss percentage, depending on the terms of the Operating Agreement.

Members may make loans to the LLC; however, the IRS may claim that the loan is a disguised capital contribution and deny the deduction of any payment of interest by the LLC. To avoid that problem, the LLC should execute a promissory note, have a reasonable rate of interest, and make timely payments to the member/creditor.

Members' Conduct

If the members collectively manage the LLC (and we discuss the finer points of management next), then all the power to act on its behalf resides with them. Members are agents for the LLC (just as they are for a regular partnership), and could bind the company to contracts. Also, the limited liability company may be liable for a member's misconduct. The member may abscond with client funds, or negligently manage a client's affairs. For instance, one member of an LLC, let's call her Beth, was responsible for investing a client's funds. The client directed Beth to place her funds in a conservative investment portfolio. Instead, Beth speculated on the commodities futures market and lost heavily. Although the company is liable for Beth's negligence, it may choose to recoup its losses from Beth. However, if the losses were substantial, it's unlikely she'll be able to pay. Members should be reminded that they owe utmost loyalty to the LLC and must avoid any conflicts of interests. If a conflict arises, as it may in a large LLC, the member should disclose the conflict and receive member approval to proceed, or desist if approval is denied.

Accounting

Financial record keeping is critical. You should retain an accountant to set up the books and prepare at least an annual report. Large LLCs should have quarterly financial reports. Each member is entitled to review the records. Keep your financial records up-to-date and accurate so that even the most meticulous IRS auditor can't find a mistake.

Shark Attack

Minutes or a formal resolution should specifically limit a member's contract authority by requiring at least one other member's signature. This may eliminate liability for a rogue member who tries to spend much more than authorized.

Profit and Loss

Profits and losses are usually allocated according to the number of shares a member is issued. For instance, let's say Al owns 100 member shares and Betty owns 200 shares. If the LLC profits for the year are $90,000, then Al is entitled to $30,000 and Betty to $60,000. The members determine whether profits are distributed or retained by the company and allocated to each member's profit account.

Loss of Members

Eventually a member will want to retire or will die. Some states specify that the LLC must dissolve when a member leaves or dies. To use the statutory language, this is called an act of disassociation. Unless the agreement specifies otherwise, some state laws permit the member to give notice 30 days prior to leaving. Actually, the agreement should specify a longer period, at least three to six months, so that the LLC can make the necessary financial adjustments.

The agreement should permit the company to disassociate (expel) the member for wrongdoing, such as stealing client funds. Any financial loss should be deducted from the departing member's payment.

The agreement also should provide the terms by which the member's interest or the deceased's share is purchased. The LLC may purchase the interest based upon the member's capital and retained profit accounts, or upon a mutually agreed upon pre-established figure. When either one of these valuation methods is used, the member loses any goodwill generated by a going business, that is, neither method considers the value of the company name, reputation, etc. The LLC may purchase the interest

Shark Attack!

Don't skimp on the appraisal! Small businesses are notoriously hard to value. A business appraiser whose expertise involves your particular business activity is crucial so that everyone may be treated fairly.

Legal Eagle

If you have drafted the Operating Agreement without consulting an attorney, be sure to have it reviewed by an attorney to ensure that it is complete and follows state law.

based upon an appraisal of its fair market value. Any purchase should include a payout period that the company can afford, and the retiring member or the deceased's heirs can accept. Term life insurance can substantially fund a deceased member's buyout.

Adding a Member and Making an Amendment

If your corporation wants to add a member, it requires unanimous approval of the members, unless the agreement provides otherwise. You should consider a majority or super-majority (⅔ or ¾) vote to avoid the disgruntled member's blackball. The agreement must specify the means by which the members may amend it. Change happens.

Termination of the LLC

If the LLC dissolves by member vote, bankruptcy, or other cause specified in the agreement, then the members collectively, some appointed members, or the managers conclude the business, pay the creditors, and distribute the net assets to the members. The members are allocated the net assets according to their shares unless the agreement provides otherwise. Articles of Dissolution are then filed with the Secretary of State.

Managing the LLC

And now for the most important, and complex, part of the Operating Agreement: The rules governing how you'll manage the LLC. You have several options every step of the way. The members may act as the LLC managers, as do partners in a regular partnership. Or the members may elect managers, which is similar to combining corporate directors and officers. Typically, small LLCs operate on the partnership model.

Large LLCs may require a manager, a chief operating officer, or several managers (an arrangement much like that of a corporation's board of directors and officers), and their duties must be clearly specified in the agreement. Often the equivalent of an abbreviated corporate bylaws is used. The members elect the manager or managers, and retain the power to remove them from office, with or without cause. It is especially important that any removal action fully comply with the procedural requirements (notice, quorum, etc.).

When the members manage, the agreement should specify ...

➤ That meetings be called by a certain percentage of the members.

➤ That notice be given of the date, time, and place of a meeting.

➤ The appointment of proxy to vote in behalf of a member.

➤ The voting rights of each member.

➤ The quorum and number of votes required to pass a resolution.

➤ Alternatives to meetings.

LLCs are be required to have annual meetings as do corporations; however, periodic meetings are also important to keep all members informed and to record decisions in the minutes. The agreement may permit any member or specify that a certain number of members may call a meeting. If there are five or fewer members, then one should be allowed to call for a meeting. With a larger membership, one member's problem may not need much collective attention, so requiring a percentage of members makes more sense. Always follow the procedure requiring notice of a meeting, because a member who didn't know about the meeting and wasn't present could later claim no knowledge of a decision that binds him or her. As alternatives to formal meetings, The agreement could permit unanimous consent to a written resolution, or a telephone conference-call meeting.

Each member is entitled to vote according to terms of the agreement. The number of votes each member can cast is usually determined by his or her number of member shares (usually according to member's capital contribution). As an alternative the agreement could specify equal voting rights among the members. Typically, LLC meetings require a quorum of 51 percent member voting shares, and resolutions require a majority of the share votes cast to pass. Members may be permitted by the agreement to delegate substitutes *(proxies)*, but this is seldom practiced in small LLCs.

Moving Forward

After the LLC is formed, you need to remember to operate according to the Operating Agreement. Perhaps this is self-evident, but more than one LLC has moved blithely forward, completely ignoring the dictates of the agreement.

If you are a single-member LLC, always separate your personal business from the LLC business. LLC creditors may attack your protected status (no personal liability) if they can demonstrate that you continually ignored the LLC as an entity when you conducted your business. To avoid this problem, I suggest that you ...

Legalese

Proxy is the authority given by one person (for example, LLC member) to another to serve as a substitute for a specified purpose, particularly voting.

➤ Establish a bank account for the LLC.

➤ Ensure against obvious risks.

➤ Use the LLC name on all contracts.

➤ Document all important LLC transactions.

➤ Conduct all required meetings and prepare minutes as specified in the Operating Agreement.

➤ Keep good financial records.

➤ File any reports required with the Secretary of State.

➤ Sign all contracts as: "Ima Owner, member and agent, for None Company, LLC."

Notes & Quotes

"The income tax has made more liars out the American people than golf has. Even when you make a tax form out on the level, you don't know when it's through if you are a crook or a martyr."

—Will Rogers, humorist

If you have a multimember LLC, never discount the importance of good minutes and financial records. Disgruntled members and disassociated members search for miscues.

Filing the annual reports with the Secretary of State maintains your LLC status. Loss of that status can make you personally liable for business debts (same as a partner in a regular partnership).

Taxes Matter

A limited liability company is not taxed, but simply files an informational return just as a partnership does. Each member is taxed on his or her share of the distributable LLC income, even if it's distributed. The share is determined by the Operating Agreement provisions regarding profit and loss. For instance, if an LLC had $90,000 in taxable income, and member Al owns 100 shares and member Betty owns 200 shares, then Al reports $30,000 of income on his 1040, and Betty reports $60,000 on hers—whether or not the income is received.

A limited liability company can elect to be taxed as a C corporation by filing the form 8283 with the IRS; however, this is seldom done because the members wish to be taxed personally.

Helpful Sources

Most state Secretary of State Web sites contain the Articles of Organization. Books and software are available for drafting the Operating Agreement. The Association of Limited Liability Companies has a Web site: www.llc-usa.com. Some state law firms have Web sites that discuss limited liability company formation and operation, as well as the tax elections. Your local library may have books on LLCs, too.

The Least You Need to Know

➤ Limited liability companies are formed by members.

➤ The LLC must file Articles of Organization with the Secretary of State.

➤ The Operating Agreement specifies the members' capital contribution, voting, and profit share.

➤ Members are not personally liable for LLC debts.

➤ Each member is taxed on his or her allocated share of the LLC taxable income.

Chapter 5

Going Solo as a Sole Proprietor

In This Chapter

➤ Making choices on your own

➤ Your financial option, now and in the future

➤ Understanding your tax options

Remember the first dollar you made on your own? Perhaps now you want to relive that experience on a grander scale by going into business for yourself. You will be overworked and probably underpaid (at least at first) but so what? It's what you want to do, so go for it. In this chapter, we'll show you how.

You and Your Choices

Before you even open the doors to your new solo venture, you have a few decisions to make, including what type of solo businessperson you want to be. Here are your options:

➤ Sole proprietor

➤ Corporation

➤ Limited liability company

A sole proprietor has the distinct advantage of being his or her own boss. And there is little paperwork, unlike the corporation that requires filing Articles of Incorporation and keeping minutes. You get to keep the profits, but must report your business income on your 1040. But first, let's review what it means to be a corporation or a limited liability company. After that I'll tell you all about being a sole proprietor. Then you can decide for yourself what's best for you.

Notes & Quotes

"I don't always follow the crowd, because nobody goes there anymore. It's too crowded."

—Yogi Berra, baseball manager

Legal Eagle

Insure yourself! Before you begin business, consult with an insurance expert about liability, casualty, business continuation, and workers' compensation insurance.

The Corporate You

If you decide to incorporate, you'll be the only shareholder, but you won't be personally liable for the corporate debts, unless you personally guaranteed them. Banks will insist on a personal guaranty, so may the landlord if you rent, but the ordinary creditors take their chances on your corporate success.

All corporations—including those that have just you as a member—must file Articles of Incorporation with the Secretary of State to begin business, and file annual reports with that office. A corporation must have bylaws, and keep records of its meetings (even if it's just with yourself). All this does take time and money.

As a shareholder, you may elect to be taxed directly on the corporation's taxable income. This is called an S corporation. Or, the corporation can be taxed on its income, and you will be taxed only if you receive dividends. This is called a C corporation. (Review Chapter 3, "The Inc. for You, or Sharing with Others," for a refresher course in corporate options.)

LLC and You

Limited liability company (LLC) ownership may be a choice; however, not all states permit a single-member LLC, so consult a local attorney. Limited liability company members are not personally liable for the business debts. If you are the sole member, however, you will be required to guarantee loans and a lease but ordinary creditors will be paid out of the business coffers, not your pocket. As an LLC, you will be taxed personally, just like a sole proprietor, because the IRS ignores the LLC status for a sole-member company. (See Chapter 4, "The Limited Liability Company Limits Your Liability," for more about LLCs.)

You Alone Isn't Always Lonely

As a sole proprietor, you are the owner, but you aren't really alone. You may have employees. Advisors can provide their expertise in accounting, law, borrowing, and insurance. Then there are family and friends, all wishing for your success.

You hang out your sign and begin. Actually, like most businesses, you need to check with the city or county government to determine if any licenses must be obtained for your business. The state department of revenue may require you to obtain a sales tax identification number. For instance, Joe Jones, whose carpet cleaning business is called Clean Carpets R Us, may need to file a Doing-Business-As (d.b.a.) certificate with the local government (and perhaps the state). Finally, if you run your business from your home, make sure that you comply with local *zoning* laws.

Here is a brief checklist of local government agencies you may need to contact as you set up your sole proprietorship:

➤ Planning (zoning)

➤ Building code

➤ Health department

➤ Tax assessor

➤ Public works

Legalese

Zoning is the local regulation of land usage, creating such designations as residential, commercial, industrial, and agricultural zones.

Some local governments are more user-friendly than others are, of course. Check with an owner who in the same business; he or she may save you time and later complications. I also suggest you have a friendly chat with a bureaucrat to avoid violating municipal law. An ounce of prevention is a significant weight.

And not only do you own your business, you also manage it. You set your own work hours, but you know you must be a hard taskmaster to make a profit. You'll have no co-owners or board of directors to either help you or second-guess you. You decide what products to make or services to sell. You make the hiring and firing decisions. Owning a business is both a burden and a joy, but it is yours to make of it what you will.

Financing for Now and the Future

Money is rarely abundant, but you'll need some cash to start up and maybe credit to help you prosper. Here are some possible resources for your initial investment:

➤ Your cash and assets

➤ Loans from family and friends

➤ Commercial loans

Clearly, how much money you have will define how much you can invest. Remember, most financial advisors suggest that you have a savings account balance equal to three month's personal expenses before you invest. If you're starting up your business as a part-time venture, and you continue on salary at your regular job, then you might fudge a little on this rule, but not much. Optimism abounds when you begin the enterprise, but customers usually aren't breaking down your door the first day.

You may choose to sell some of your assets, such as your investment portfolio. But don't touch that tax-deferred IRA or 401(k) retirement plan. Any tax-deferred money you take out will be included as taxable income in the year withdrawn, and the IRS will tack on an additional 10 percent penalty.

Shark Attack!

Make sure you handle loans from family members with care. The IRS may contend a loan is a family gift and deny an interest payment deduction. Execute a promissory note with a reasonable rate of interest, and make payments on time.

Friends and family may rally around you. A beloved rich aunt or uncle might simply give you some of the money to get started, with no strings attached. You might even want to hint that any gifts of $10,000 or less per year are free of gift tax. (Good luck with that approach.) More realistically, they might be willing to lend you some money, and at an interest rate considerably below prime.

Banks require collateral and often a cosigner to guarantee the loan's repayment. The collateral usually comes from you, unless family or friends are willing to put up something. Likewise, the cosigner will likely be a family member or friend.

Collateral may require you to take out a second mortgage on your house. (If you're married, you'll need to get his or her consent.) If misfortune befalls your business, foreclosure may not be far behind. This is a risk, but nothing succeeds without some risk, so proceed— but you are forewarned. If you have an investment portfolio, you may use it as collateral. Household goods may be considered as a last resort, but the lender will value them at less than 50 percent of their fair market value.

Tax laws may not permit you to use a tax-deferred IRA or 401(k) as collateral. Please consult your tax advisor. Remember, banks repossess collateral if you don't keep up with the bank payments.

Be realistic about your initial business financial needs and about your ongoing needs. Project your financial needs and develop a cash flow plan with the help of an accountant or financial advisor. This may include obtaining a line of credit from the bank. Underestimating cash requirements is almost always a sure ticket to bankruptcy court.

Closing Out for New Beginnings

When you retire or depart this earthly vale, the sole proprietorship ends.

If you die, your estate will sell the business assets and pay your debts. The balance goes to those named in your Last Will and Testament, or to your heirs, if you have no will.

If you retire, you sell the business assets. You should consider hiring a business broker to help negotiate a favorable contract with the purchaser; a going business may command a premium payment and the broker's expertise is usually well worth the fee.

Since the sale of a business is a tax maze, hire a tax accountant to lead you through its complexity and save you money.

Taxes Matter

This section could be subtitled "Look Ye to Schedule C" (for a sole proprietor). You need to look at ways to put as few bucks in Uncle Sam's pockets as possible. I am here to help.

Timing

Sole proprietors are usually on a *cash basis* method of accounting. However, if you primarily sell merchandise, then you will be on *accrual method accounting*, at least, for tax purposes.

Take Calvin Cash, for instance. He services computers as a sole proprietor. When Cal gets paid he records the receipt as income; when he pays a supplier, he records the expense. He billed a customer in December 2000 and received payment in January 2001. He reports the payment for 2001 taxes. Likewise, Cal purchased supplies in December 2000 for use in early 2001; he deducts the expense for 2000.

Here's another example: Alice Accrual sells appliances at her store. Alice reports income when she has earned it, and expenses when due. Alice sold a refrigerator to a customer in December 2000, and received payment in January 2001. She reports the income when earned, in 2000. Alice ordered a freezer from the manufacturer and received it in December 2000, but she mailed the check in January 2001. The cost of the appliance is recorded when she was contractually obligated to pay, which was in the year 2000.

Legal Eagle

Shop around for a lender. Select one that will provide a flexible line of credit at a reasonable rate. Also, choose a lender that has loan officers who are knowledgeable and sympathetic to small businesses. Too often bank employees are ill-informed and inexperienced in small business needs.

Legal Eagle

Cash basis taxpayers can time income and expenses to delay income (report in next year) and accelerate expenses (report in current year). Keeping track of your tax situation allows you to properly time income and expense, and keeps your tax bill lower.

Calvin Cash usually wants to postpone income (and pay the tax on it later), so he often mails bills out to customers in early January for work he performed the previous December. He may reduce his taxes by buying supplies or services in late December for use next year. Calvin is careful not to prepay for more than one year's supplies, because the IRS may insist that he expense it (write it off) over the next year.

Deductible Expenses

Use Schedule C of your 1040 as a checklist. Some common deductions include ...

➤ Advertising.

➤ Vehicle costs.

➤ Depreciation.

➤ Employee wages and fringe benefits.

➤ Interest on loans.

➤ Professional services.

➤ Office expenses and supplies.

➤ Travel and meals.

➤ Utilities.

➤ Casualty losses and thefts.

This is not an exhaustive list; I have highlighted only a few of the deductions. The IRS has several pamphlets that help you better understand the tax law, which you may order or download from the IRS Web site.

Here's a way to make your business work for you when it comes to taxes. Say you decide to give to the local Little League. One option is to deduct the contribution on your personal tax return as a charitable expense. However, you could use the contribution as a form of business advertising if the league puts your business name on its team hat or on an outfield wall (most leagues will do this). Using the contribution as a business expense will reduce your self-employment income and can be taken as a deduction even if you cannot itemize.

Here's another option: If you commute to work and back, that mileage is not deductible; however, if you drive from one work site to another, that mileage is deductible. Keep a written record of your business miles because the IRS auditor might ask for it. Most sole proprietors just deduct the standard mileage rate set by the IRS (the 1999 rate was 31 cents per mile). As an alternative, you can *depreciate* the vehicle (according to the percentage of business use) and deduct the gasoline expense. Parking fees are deductible; parking fines and speeding tickets are not.

Another way to reduce your tax burden is through depreciation. You buy a computer for your business. The computer can be depreciated (written off) over five years according to IRS tables. The first-year depreciation in the five-year write-off is 20 percent; if the cost was $10,000, then your depreciation is $2,000. The second year depreciation is 32 percent of the original cost, or $3,200, and so it goes until the entire price is written off.

Legalese

Depreciation allows the tax-payer to deduct the cost of certain assets, such as machinery or equipment, over the useful life of the asset. For intangible assets like patents and copyrights, this is called amortization.

In my previous example, you could have written off the entire $10,000 price of the computer in the year purchased. That can significantly reduce your taxes.

If you have an office in your home, you may depreciate part of the cost of the house and deduct certain other expenses, such as a portion of the real estate taxes, mortgage interest, and utilities. Self-employed persons are allowed the deductions if the office is used regularly and exclusively as either ...

➤ The principal place of conducting business

➤ A place of business used by customers or clients.

For example, perhaps you could run your business out of your home from a specific room. The room contains your office furniture, files, computer, and other office supplies and equipment, and the room is used solely as an office. The room comprises 10 percent of the house's square footage. You can deduct 10 percent of what would be the depreciation for the entire house, plus 10 percent of the taxes, mortgage interest, and utilities.

Paying Your Employees Saves You Money

Employees' compensation, including fringe benefits, are deductible. For tax purposes, you are considered self-employed, so what you pay yourself is really income from the business, not a deductible expense. Likewise, your medical expense as a self-employed person is deductible from gross income (permitting you the choice of itemizing or taking the standard tax deduction on your 1040).

If you have a teenager, you can fill his or her incessant desire for more pocket money and receive a deduction for employee expense. Your son or daughter becomes your

Shark Attack!

Depreciation taken for the home office could require you to recognize capital gain on the sale of the home. The capital gain exclusion on a residential sale would not apply to the portion of the gain allocated to the home office.

Notes & Quotes

"There is time for work. And time for love. That leaves no other time!"

—Coco Chanel, businessperson

employee and is paid according to work performed. Money is transferred from your business to your dependent (not as a gift but for services rendered). Thus, you are teaching independence and self-reliance. No FICA (social security and Medicare tax) need be paid by you for the teenager's labor (nor withheld from the teenager's pay).

More Deductions to Consider

If you travel overnight on business, the expense of travel by plane, train, or auto is deductible, as is the lodging. Meals are limited to 50 percent of their cost. If you usually pick up the meal tab for customers, keep the receipts, and be sure to talk some business.

Make sure you carry proper insurance on the business. High winds, fire, and thieves can take a toll on your assets. If the insurance proceeds don't cover all of the loss, then you may be able to take a deduction for the underinsured portion. Ironically, however, a casualty loss could become a taxable gain if you are paid more than the fair market value or the tax value of the asset. Reinvesting the insurance proceeds in property of the same kind—rebuilding a destroyed warehouse, for example—can avoid this taxable gain. Consult with your tax advisor.

This brief list of your deductions is not exhaustive. Read Chapter 6, "Taxing Matters," for more discussion of tax law. Remember that expenses must be reasonable and relate to the business, and you must keep receipts.

State and Local Taxes

State and local tax collectors are nearly as keen as the IRS to ensure that they receive their due. These taxes could include ...

➤ Property taxes on real estate.

➤ Personal property taxes on inventory and equipment.

➤ City and state income taxes.

Consult your city or county tax office for the local taxes and the department of revenue for state taxes. Property taxes may be significantly reduced through an appeal of the local assessor's valuation; big businesses do it all of the time and save a bundle. Tax planning must include these costs. Fortunately, the payment of these business-related taxes may be deducted on your income tax return.

Helpful Sources

The Small Business Administration has an excellent Web site (www.sba.gov). The IRS has its forms and pamphlets on its Web site (www.irs.ustreas.gov). The local Chamber of Commerce and the National Federation of Independent Businesses are interested in helping your small business. Talk with other small business owners; they can be an excellent source of free advice.

The Least You Need to Know

➤ Incorporating your business is an alternative to sole proprietorship.

➤ The sole proprietor is liable for the business debts.

➤ Financing the business is usually limited to your cash and collateral.

➤ An office in your home can provide tax deductions.

➤ Employing your teenager can save both of you taxes.

Chapter 6

Taxing Matters

In This Chapter

➤ Choosing the best tax plan for you

➤ Establishing a relationship with the IRS

➤ The audit: your chances, your responsibility

➤ Don't forget the state!

➤ Helpful sources

To recap what we've covered so far, if you're sole owner of a business, your choices of an entity are sole proprietorship, corporation, or limited liability company.

If you are one of several co-owners, your choices include partnership, registered limited liability partnership, limited partnership, corporation, or limited liability company.

This chapter examines the federal income tax implications of your choices, and then proceeds to a more depressing discussion about the state tax bite. If you want a quick view of the federal tax, just read the overview and the tax discussion at the end of the four previous chapters.

Taxing Choices for You to Make

Unfortunately, the tax laws determine many business decisions, including your choice of business entity. However, you enjoy saving taxes, so this is the place to begin. What

follows is a brief summary of the tax law. Please read the entire chapter for a more thorough discussion.

Sole Proprietor

You just fill out Schedule C (self-employed business) and Schedule SE (self-employment tax, which includes social security and Medicare) and attach it to your personal 1040. All your business income and expenses are reported on Schedule C, then the net income or loss is carried forward to your 1040.

You have some ability to manipulate income and expense if you report on the cash method of accounting (income reported when received and expenses deducted when paid). Delay sending out your December customer bills until January, and pay your own January bills in December.

I suggest using Schedule C as a checklist of possible deductions. Your tax advisor may happily surprise you with a few more.

Partnerships and LLCs

Your partnership, limited partnership, or limited liability company reports its income and expenses on its form 1065. You receive a form K-1, which specifies what your distributable share of each item of income is. You record the income on your own 1040 and pay whatever tax is due; the entity just files an informational return.

Take this example: Al Able and Betty Blue are equal partners in a two-person law firm. The partnership reports ordinary income of $200,000 and capital gains of $20,000. Al's (and Betty's) K-1 records $100,000 of ordinary income and $10,000 of capital gain income. In other words, each partner reports his or her share, whether or not it is actually received.

Corporation C or S

Small corporations (75 or fewer shareholders) may elect S corporation tax status. The corporation files an information return (1120S) and sends each shareholder a K-1. Shareholders pay the tax on the distributable income just as partners do in a partnership. Although there are minor differences between partnership and S corporation tax, those need not trouble us at this time.

Any corporation is taxed on its own income as a C corporation, if the corporation doesn't qualify for S status (it has more than 75 shareholders) or the shareholders don't elect S status, then the corporation is taxed under C status. The corporation files a form 1120 and reports and pays the tax on its taxable income. If the corporation pays dividends, then its shareholders report the dividends received as taxable income.

Clearly, this brief overview of the three general types of business entities and their tax matters doesn't give you enough information. Read on for the real meat of the matter!

IRS and You in Business

Albert Einstein once said, "The hardest thing in the world to understand is the income tax." I'm sure that you can appreciate Einstein's frustration. I don't think I can lower your level very much, but here goes. (I am excluding sole proprietorship, because I thoroughly discussed it in Chapter 5, "Going Solo as a Sole Proprietor.") Here are the some of the tax elements you should consider as you form your new small business.

Restriction on Ownership

Partnerships must have two or more owners. The limited liability company (LLC) may have one member (and the member is taxed as a sole proprietor) or several members and they are taxed as partners are.

The S corporation must have no more than 75 shareholders and is limited to individuals, estates, and certain trusts and must have only one class of stock; the shareholders must all elect to be taxed under S status. The C corporation may have one or more shareholders and different stock classes.

Choice of Tax Year

Partnerships and LLCs have the same tax year as the majority of partners or members. If the partners (members) are individuals, then the partnership or LLC tax year is a calendar year, just like the individual partners.

The S corporation is restricted to a calendar year, unless the IRS approves a different year for business purposes. Some S corporations created before mid 1980 have non-calendar (fiscal) years. The C corporation is not restricted to a calendar year, and its choice of fiscal or calendar year is selected when its first return is filed.

Contribution of Property to Entity

Generally, a partner's or member's capital contribution of property is not taxable to the contributor (nor the entity) when contributed. If you contribute land to the

partnership for an interest in the entity, you will not be taxed; there are some exceptions to this, including the situation where the mortgage on the land exceeds your tax investment (basis), which is usually your initial cost less any depreciation. Please consult a tax advisor before contributing property.

Shareholders who contribute property (other than cash) are at risk for being taxed on their contributions. So never do this without talking to a good tax advisor. To avoid taxation the law requires the contributing shareholder(s) receive stock in the exchange and control 80 percent of the stock after the transfer. For example, shareholders Al and Betty contribute debt-free land in forming the corporation, and each receives 50 percent of the common stock in return. No tax would result from that transfer, because both transferors received in return at least 80 percent of the stock. However, if shareholder Charlie later transferred property for 10 percent of the stock, he will be taxed, because he did not own 80 percent of the stock after his transfer. However, the corporation is not taxed on receipt of the contribution.

Organizational Costs

The start-up expenses of any entity must be amortized over 60 months. For instance, corporation Alph incurs legal costs, accounting expenses, and filing fees in forming the corporation; these expenses can be deducted at $\frac{1}{60}$ per month.

Operation: Making Tax Laws Work for You

Once you get your business up and running, you have to consider certain operational aspects that can have an impact on your tax profile. Taxes are paid on profits, so every deduction you can find saves you money.

Taxation of Owners

Each partner, LLC member, and S corporation shareholder reports his or her share the entity's distributable taxable income (1065 K-1 or 1120S K-1) on his or her 1040. However, an S corporation that had previously been a C corporation may incur a tax in very limited circumstances. Personal tax rates are progressive and the highest marginal rate is 39.6 percent.

A C corporation pays the tax on its income; the highest marginal rate for it is 38 percent. C corporation shareholders pay a tax only on dividends received.

Timing of Taxation

A partner or LLC member reports his or her share of the taxable income in the same year in which the entity's tax year ends. If the partnership or LLC has a calendar year, then the owner reports the distributable taxable income from that year. For example, Alpha LLC has taxable income of $100,000 in 2000. Member Al reports his distributable share of the income in 2000.

S corporation shareholders usually have the same calendar tax year as the entity; therefore, the income is reported in that year. For example, Alpha Corporation has taxable income of $100,000 in 2000. Shareholder Al reports his distributable share of the income in 2000.

C corporation reports its income according to its tax year (calendar or fiscal); shareholders report dividends in the tax year received.

Allocating Income Among Owners

Here is how the different entities allocate income to their owners:

> ➤ **Partnership.** Allocates profits and losses to the partners according to the Partnership Agreement.

> ➤ **LLC.** Allocates profits and losses among its members according to its Operating Agreement.

> ➤ **S corporation.** Allocates its profits and losses according to each stockholder's pro rata shares owned.

> ➤ **C corporation.** Shareholder reports income only when he or she receives a dividend.

Consult your tax advisor about the effect of your entity choice on your personal taxes.

Character of Income

A partner, LLC member, and S shareholder reports his or her share of all forms of income, including ordinary or capital gain. The character of the entity income passes through to the owner. For example, Alpha LLC has $100,000 ordinary income and $50,000 of capital gains; Alpha member Al owns 20 percent, so he will report $20,000 of ordinary income and $10,000 of capital gain on his 1040. If a shareholder of a C corporation receives a dividend, then it is taxed on his or her 1040.

Limitation on Deductible Losses

A partner or LLC member is allowed to deduct his or her allocated entity loss up to the amount of his or her capital investment (and for a partner, up to his or her share

of a regular partnership's debt). For example, Partner Pete has invested cash of $20,000, and his share of the partnership debt is $10,000; he may deduct a partnership loss of $30,000. But please read further in this section.

An S corporation shareholder may deduct his or her share of the corporation's loss up to the amount of his or her investment and his or her personal loan to the corporation. For example, Alpha, Inc., shareholder Al invested $20,000 in the corporation and lent it $10,000. Al may deduct a corporation loss of up to $30,000. But please read further in this section.

What the tax code giveth, the tax code taketh away. Under the tax law at-risk rules, any tax loss that exceeds the owner's investment may not be deducted. In the two prior examples, the owner can deduct up to his or her investment ($20,000); any loss not taken in a year may be carried forward for future years.

With the enactment of passive loss rules applicable to partners, members, and S corporation shareholders, tax loss deductions were further limited.

Even if you pass the at-risk rules, the tax code will not allow you to deduct the loss against any other income except income from another partnership, LLC, or S corporation. For example, shareholder Al can take up to his $20,000 deductible loss in a year if he has passive income from a similar entity (such as distributable income from a partnership, LLC, or S corporation).

Fringe Benefits

Medical and dental insurance, term life insurance, and child care reimbursement are fringes that are usually excluded from the employee's taxable income. Unfortunately, partners, LLC members, and S corporation shareholders who are also employees cannot exclude such fringe benefits; however, an S corporation shareholder/employee who owns 2 percent or less of the stock is entitled to an exclusion. C corporation shareholders who are also employees can exclude fringe benefits, too.

Sale of Ownership Interest

If a partner or LLC member sells his or her interest, the gain may be taxable partially as ordinary income and partially as capital gain, usually according to the entity's capital and ordinary income assets. Taxing as a capital gain is preferable because of the lower marginal rate. Loss is determined by the same procedure. I urge you to use an accountant to figure what part is ordinary income and what is capital gain. There is no way to explain the tax result in less than one chapter, and I would not wish that on any reader. However, I can say that the shareholder who sells his or her stock at a gain will receive capital gain treatment on the entire gain.

All in the Family

To paraphrase Leo Tolstoy, happy families are all alike, but some are happier in a partnership. The family partnership is frequently suggested as a tax shelter, spreading the income among all members, including those dependents in the lowest tax bracket. Tax law does not permit a family member to be recognized as a partner unless the member either …

➤ Made a significant capital contribution from his or her own funds,

or …

➤ Materially contributes his or her services to the partnership.

Shark Attack!

Take care if you form a partnership with any family member. The IRS scrutinizes all family partnerships, so be forewarned and clearly comply with the law.

Think of it this way: Your daughter has just graduated from college and wants to work in the family partnership business. If she works for the company and significantly contributes to the business, then she can be treated as a partner. However, if you transfer a partnership interest to your preteen who neither pays for it, nor works in the business, then forget treating her as a partner for tax purposes.

Federal gift and estate taxes should not be ignored. Please read Chapter 26, "Let the Tax Code Work for You," for essential information about this important aspect of tax planning.

IRS Looks at Your Business: Preparing for Your Appearance

Let's say you receive an audit notice from the IRS. Revulsion and fear set in. The IRS is like the police officer driving behind you in traffic; you may not be speeding, but you still know the cop is there.

The grand inquisitor is ready for you, so be thoroughly prepared to win your case by following these simple tips:

➤ Make certain that you and the auditor agree on the issues to be resolved in the audit.

 ➤ Know all the facts and bring all the proper documents and records.

➤ Research the relevant tax law (or have an advisor do it for you).

➤ Prepare a list of points that support your case.

➤ Understand what points the auditor may use against your case.

➤ Prepare for the tax consequences of each point at issue.

➤ Determine where the auditor might compromise rather than litigate.

Legal Eagle

The IRS reports the following statistics for 1996 returns:

	No. of Returns	Percent Examined
Sole proprietorship	1,770,700	4.13
Partnership	1,653,100	0.59
S corporation	2,290,900	1.04
C corporation	2,608,600	2.67
Individual	118,362,600	1.28

The IRS spends most of its audit time on large businesses and businesses that operate primarily with cash transactions, since that is where the tax underreporting occurs.

The audit process begins with the ill fortune of your return being chosen. The IRS might simply send you a letter detailing the proposed corrections, and seek your agreement. If your math skills resulted in an error, by all means check the IRS calculations, and if they're correct, agree with the IRS. Be sure to promptly pay any deficiency because interest stops accumulating as soon as your payment clears. If you disagree with the IRS, then provide a detailed list of your reasons and the records to support your position (or the law, if that is at issue).

If the IRS requests an interview, prepare for the interview using the list I gave you earlier. After the interview, you will receive their findings. If you agree, arrange for payment and move on. If you disagree, you'll receive a 30-day notice letter to request an appeal conference, whether or not you later decide to go to court. The initial auditor has little authority to settle legal issues, so an appeal will be necessary for those cases. (If you do not respond, the IRS will send you a formal notice of deficiency.)

The Appeals Conference is typically held at the IRS office. The Appeals officer is highly trained, has several years of IRS experience, and holds a CPA. Most appeals require you to prepare a letter stating the facts, issues, and your legal authority. If the tax controversy involves several hundred or thousands of dollars, use a tax accountant or tax lawyer to prepare the letter. The Appeals officer has considerable latitude in settling any issue, and will certainly consider whether the case is worth pursuing in court.

If you settle every issue at Appeals, you don't need to do anything further, other than pay up if that's the agreement you made. However, if there are unresolved issues, the IRS will send you a deficiency notice (90-day letter). At this point you definitely need a lawyer, because a lawsuit is in your future.

You have the right within 90 days of receiving the deficiency notice to petition the tax court. The tax court will set a hearing in a large city near your home. The trial is by judge alone. If you lose, then you must pay any tax plus accumulated interest. You are entitled to appeal this ruling to the federal circuit court if you believe the decision is wrong.

If you do not choose the tax court route, then, in order to take your case to court, you must pay the tax and file for a refund. After the refund is denied by the IRS, you may sue the IRS for the tax in your local U.S. district court or the court of federal claims (in D.C.). The district court case is heard by a jury, while the claims court trial is heard by judge alone. If you win, celebrate, for justice has been done! If you lose, you may appeal the ruling to the federal circuit court.

Notes & Quotes

"The Tax Collector's letters are invariably mimeographed, and all they say is that you still haven't paid him."

—William Saroyan, writer

States and Cities Want Their Share, Too

Uncle Sam may grab the most taxes, but his progeny are not far behind. State and city income taxes, sales and use taxes, and personal and real property taxes all do their damage to your bottom line.

Shark Attack!

Don't neglect to check the laws in every state in which you conduct business because each state might lay claim to your income (at least the portion generated in that state). Just advertising in a state will not require payment, but having a physical presence (an office with employees) will be a sufficient connection for an income tax.

Notes & Quotes

"The thing generally raised on city land is taxes."

—Charles D. Warner, business-person

State Income Taxes

State laws vary so much that it is difficult to generalize. Most states will tax the business income at about the same rate and in the same manner as the federal government does, but there are some notable exceptions. Not all states apply the tax on taxable income (gross income less deductible expenses). Some states tax the gross income, or have a variant of net income tax. And not all states recognize S corporation tax status. To find out about taxation in your state, go to your state's Web site for the department of revenue or equivalent agency; most states now have their forms and pamphlets online for you to download. But I strongly suggest you consult your tax advisor—you will be money ahead.

Some cities also tax business income (including the self-employed).

State Sales and Use Taxes

Forty-five states and the District of Columbia have a sales tax on retail sales to consumers. The use tax is imposed as a complement to the sales tax. If a consumer purchased goods outside his or her home state for use at home, then the consumer owes a use tax to the state where he or she lives. Some states require its taxpayers to report out-of-state purchases and compute the use tax on the income tax form. For instance, if you live in Indiana and buy your car in Kentucky, you might owe Indiana a use tax payment.

Retailers are required to collect the tax and forward the proceeds to the state department of revenue. The current controversy involves collecting the sales tax on e-commerce retail sales. As of this writing, there is a moratorium on collection. Stay tuned for future developments.

You may be able to apply for a state sales tax exemption to be used when you purchase your business supplies. Consult your state department of revenue.

Local Property Taxes

Local governments tax business inventory and equipment (personal property tax) and land/buildings (real property tax). The taxes are based on the value of the property to be taxed. Numerous exceptions and exemptions often make property taxes baffling to the small business owner. I would suggest scrutinizing your tax bill, then consulting someone who specializing in property tax appeals. Many appeals are successful in reducing the tax. Most large companies routinely protest their property tax, so go ye and do likewise.

Helpful Sources

Go to your state Web site where you'll find most tax forms as well as the state tax code. Other helpful sites include: the IRS Web site at www.irs.ustreas.gov; the Government Printing Office (where you'll find tax laws) at www.access.gpo.gov; links to other tax sites at www.taxsites.com; and a CPA tax site at www.aicpa.org. Remember that Web sites do change. Many local law and accounting firms also have Web sites, and your local library has tax books (but some of them may be dated since tax laws can change quickly).

The Least You Need to Know

➤ A partner, LLC member, or S shareholder is taxed on his or her share of the entity's distributable income.

➤ A C corporation shareholder is taxed on dividends received.

➤ Tax-free fringe benefits are available to C corporation shareholders only if they are also employees.

➤ Properly prepare for an audit and you will save taxes.

➤ The Web provides a wealth of tax information.

Chapter 7

Hiring a Lawyer, Accountant, and Other Advisors

In This Chapter

➤ Getting the best legal advice

➤ You and your accountant

➤ Protecting your business, financially and from an investment perspective

➤ Reaching out to fellow small businesspeople

Business is a team sport, so begin yours with a strong, supportive team of advisors. Some of the team members will be paid, while others will provide solid advice for free.

Your team will be made up of men and women with expertise in different aspects of business and tax law. Their knowledge and guidance can be invaluable. However, do not forget for one moment that you are in charge. No one on your team should tell you what to do. People on your team can offer options and discuss consequences, but only you can determine what your best business decision is. So you will have to do some homework to be as competent as possible in taking charge.

In this chapter we'll talk about how to put together a good team and what kind of experts you should sign on. Here are the possible team members you may need to recruit, perhaps not all at once, but at some point along the way: lawyer, accountant, insurance broker, real estate or leasing broker, computer consultant, financial planner, other business owners.

Your Lawyer's Assistance

You need a lawyer on call. You're probably thinking that any lawyer who writes a book like this will, of course, suggest that you get legal advice—just professional courtesy. Well, perhaps there is some truth in this allegation, but the greater truth is that you are operating in a business system that is dominated by the law.

Here's a brief list of legal services you should consider:

What a Lawyer Can Do	Example
Draft organization documents	Articles of Incorporation
Prepare business documents	Buy-Sell Agreement
Advise on tax decisions	S vs. C corporate tax status
Write contracts	Purchase agreements
Draft employment documents	Employee handbook
Advise and litigate	Sue deadbeat debtors
Plan your estate	Last Will and Testament and living trust

Notes & Quotes

"A man who *is* his own lawyer has a fool for a client."

—Anonymous

You can do it yourself, if you choose. Drafting a contract or setting up your corporation saves you the legal fees, which may be a considerable sum for a tight budget. However, the money you save does come at a cost. Time is money, and your time may be better spent on running your business. Plus, there is a risk that your legal document may be insufficient if challenged. The contract that you draft may have dozens of loopholes.

You can find a lawyer in the Yellow Pages where you'll see dozens of attorney listings. Lawyers often list their primary areas of practice, such as business, employment, or tax matters, for example. If you choose this route, ask the lawyer for a reference of three or four business clients to contact. Then call the references to confirm the lawyer's expertise, billing practice, and timely service.

I suggest that you discuss your selection with your other advisors, because they often have experience using attorneys and know the ones who best suit your needs.

Check with the state and county bar association or licensing agency to determine if any justifiable complaints have been filed against your prospective attorney.

Interview your prospective attorney. Does he or she seem more interested in fees than in your business? Does the lawyer appear to be in a hurry, too busy to talk with you, or does he or she take the time to answer your questions thoughtfully and completely? After all, this is your business.

Discuss the costs with your attorney. If your lawyer is drafting a simple contract then he or she should be able to quote a fee. If the lawyer will be involved in a lawsuit, then the lawyer should be able to estimate the filing and related costs, and quote you an hourly fee; however, litigation is not susceptible to a very precise quote of all the costs involved so discuss the fee with your advisors. If they think it is too high, then consider another attorney.

Your attorney should be willing to take calls from you without exorbitant fees. Often you just need to know whether legal services are necessary. If in doubt, call. Reliable attorneys will frequently suggest a solution that you can implement without an attorney. The best legal advice is always practical, and frequently costs very little.

Legal Eagle

You may want to draft a contract or other legal document by using a standard form or legal software, then have the draft reviewed by a lawyer. You put in the terms most important to you and the lawyer makes sure that the document is legally sufficient. And you save legal fees!

Accounting for Your Money

You must have an accountant because you must have a clear picture of your business financial position—and a bookkeeper can't do more than provide bare numbers.

Here is a brief list of accountant services:

➤ Set up the books

➤ Provide monthly, quarterly, and annual financial statements

➤ Project future earnings

➤ Suggest cost savings

➤ Prepare the tax forms and suggest tax deductions and credits

➤ File a protest for property tax valuations

Shark Attack!

Any attorney who has been suspended for misconduct in the past may have reformed, but I suggest that you look elsewhere.

Begin at the beginning and have an accountant set up your books the right way. I have had too many clients who fight a losing battle with the IRS because they don't have good financial records. You probably know a small business owner who handles his or her own books to save money, or has a relative do them in his or her spare time. The financial picture is going to be fuzzy from the very beginning if you don't hire a professional.

Once the accounts are properly established, if you don't want to pay the accountant to keep the records, then at least have an experienced bookkeeper do it for you. The accountant can then review the books and provide periodic summaries to let you know how the revenues and expenses are lining up. If the accounts receivable are not being collected promptly or you are losing a discount by not paying your bills in a timely manner, the accountant will be able to point this out. Your cash flow can improve, and making early payments can save you money.

What is in the past (financially speaking) may be prologue to the future (financial success). If your financial records are properly set up, then you will have a firm base to project future growth. Your accountant should be able to advise you on the financial aspects of business proposals. If you want to expand into another market, product, or service line, the project revenue must at least meet projected costs. Nothing is certain, but sound financial planning is a must.

Business taxes seem to come in incessant and innumerable forms. We often focus on federal income taxes, which do snatch too much of our business profits. If you have an accountant prepare your business (and personal) returns, he or she can spot tax savings hiding in the labyrinth of the Internal Revenue Code. Large companies hire accountants to discover the breaks and keep Uncle's share down. You should do likewise.

If your business owns inventory, equipment, or real estate, the state or local assessor will hit you with a property tax. If your accountant doesn't advise on these taxes, ask him or her to suggest someone who does. Your accountant may suggest that you protest the valuation, or show you deductions not previously taken. If your accountant's fee is less than the taxes saved, then you're ahead (and the fees are deductible).

Small accounting firms may fit your needs better than the larger, more expensive firms, but the big eight (or whatever mergers have reduced them to) are catering more to small businesses. Check with other small business owners to find out who they use, or if you are a member of a business association, choose an accountant it recommends. If you have a specialized business, such as Web site development, choose an accountant who is familiar with your business.

Insuring Against the Risks

Your business may be underinsured, and most certainly you have less life insurance than you need. Risks are part of life and business; some just have to be endured, like a tax increase, while others may be insured against, like fire or casualty.

Your insurance agent or underwriter can advise you on policies for …

➤ Medical and dental health for you and your employees.

➤ Disability.

➤ Death.

➤ Property damage.

➤ Liability.

➤ Workers' compensation.

➤ Business continuation.

Most employers provide some health insurance for their employees (and the self-employed). Costs are high and coverage varies considerably. You need to find an insurance company that you can trust to pay the medical expenses. Compare costs. Consult your business association to see if it participates in a plan that is available to member companies.

If you or an employee becomes physically disabled, you don't want to rely solely on Social Security. Consider disability insurance to protect future earnings. Finding an affordable policy is the key, so consult with a good insurance broker who will suggest options that are affordable.

Group term life insurance should be part of any employee fringe benefit. The cost is relatively low; the premiums paid by the employer are a deductible expense, and coverage up to $50,000 is not taxable to the employee. If there are business co-owners, you should have a life insurance policy to fund the business Buy-Sell Agreement.

Fire, theft, tornado, and assorted calamities could strike with unerring accuracy. You can't afford not to protect yourself. You need an affordable policy for the reasonable risks, and an insurance agent who will ensure that all of your assets are continually reviewed to assess their value. Insuring a building at its original cost, not for its replacement cost, may be a fatal mistake.

Legal Eagle

Accountants specialize just as attorneys do. Accounting firms may have one partner who provides your financial reports, while another may prepare small business tax returns.

Notes & Quotes

"Sometimes the light at the end of the tunnel is an oncoming train."

—Lou Holtz, football coach

And don't forget to discuss business continuation insurance with your underwriter. While the destroyed building is being rebuilt, probably very little business can be conducted. To cover this forced inactivity, consider purchasing business continuation insurance to replace some of the revenue lost and enable you to continue paying key employees.

Employees do the darndest things, like running red lights and smashing into another car, or slipping on the shop floor and breaking a leg. Your company may be liable in either event. The law requires the employer to be financially responsible for employee negligence while on the job. Likewise, the workers' compensation laws make the employer liable for workplace injuries, even if the employee or fellow employee's negligence caused the injury.

The insurance agent who takes care of your personal insurance (such as auto and life insurance) may be just the person for you, but not the one for your business. Shop around. Check with other small business owners or your business association. Insurance premiums can be a huge expense, so choose wisely.

Banking on You to Succeed

Your business probably will need to borrow money, and bankers (or other lending institutions) have the line of credit that may tide you over when there are cash-flow dams.

Unfortunately, many bankers view you as the supplicant, risking their money on a speculative adventure. Contrast this attitude with bank credit cards. Credit worthy or not, credit card companies are ready to let you realize your every desire with plastic.

Find a banker who specializes in small business loans, and has been with the bank for some time. And find a bank that wants your business. After all, you are paying interest for the privilege of using the money, and probably putting up collateral, and personally guarantying the loan. Your banker should be more than a cash machine. The banker should work with your accountant to determine your cash needs, for now and in the expandable future when you double or treble your business.

Brokering the Realty

If you work out of your house and intend to continue with your home office, you need read no further. However, for the rest of you who are planning to work in a different location, consider hiring a commercial real estate broker to help you purchase or lease your business home.

The commercial real estate broker can assist you in …

➤ Finding the building and negotiating a purchase agreement.

➤ Finding the right location and negotiating a favorable lease.

Buying a building for your business is a huge investment. You need to determine if it is in the right location and if it can be bought at the right price. Negotiating over the price and terms of the contract may be difficult. Some of us are blessed with the ability to cut a great deal; others shy away from confrontation. Certainly if you are the latter, consider hiring a real estate broker to help you.

The broker should know the going price of property. You could save more than the broker's fee if you obtain a price that is considerably less than the initial listing. The broker will help you draft a contract that is favorable to you. For example, it may be typical that the buyer pay the second half of the semiannual installment of property taxes after the closing; your broker may convince the seller that the best way to close the deal is to pay the entire year's property taxes. Or the broker may convince the seller to reduce the price because you will need to extensively remodel the building, and you have only so much money.

Notes & Quotes

"A bank is a place where they lend you an umbrella in fair weather and ask for it back again when it begins to rain."

—Robert Frost, poet

Legal Eagle

You might want to ask your banker for a recommendation of an attorney or accountant. Particularly in smaller communities, the bankers get to know who works and who doesn't.

If you may want to lease, keep in mind that the rent per square foot may be just part of the cost of leasing. The landlord might want additional rent as a percentage of your gross sales. Negotiating that percentage downward can mean a great savings on future revenue. If the landlord is eager to have you as a tenant, the landlord might be willing to foot some of the renovation costs. The landlord's lease was no doubt drafted by the landlord's attorney. Even so, your broker should be able to negotiate more favorable terms for you. For example, the landlord might exclude all its liability for *anything* that goes wrong in the building after you occupy it. However, your broker would probably insist that the landlord be liable for its own negligence, so if its employee causes a power outage, the landlord would be responsible for your lost sales.

You and the real estate broker will enter into a contract, which will specify the broker's duties and fee. Check with other business owners or bankers to see if the fee is reasonable and the broker is reliable.

Computer Sourcing

We live in the computer age. I am writing this book on a computer, and it will be edited through e-mail attachments. Some of us can use word processing and that's about all, while others are maestros at the computer. If you lean toward the former, or are in the middle of the computer pack, then you should consider seeking advice from a computer expert.

You need computers to run your business, from writing business letters to controlling inventory, and from sending e-mail to conducting e-commerce. Unless you have a talented computer whiz on staff, and can keep that whiz kid challenged, you should consider hiring a computer consultant. The changes in hardware and software are rapid and mind-boggling. You have a business to run, so let an expert advise you on obtaining the best computer equipment and software, at a favorable price, that fits your needs.

Running a Web site is common for many businesses, and you, too, may need one to gain new customers and retain old ones. E-commerce changes the marketing and selling of goods and services, and you can't ride its wave unless you have expert advice. The Web site must be easily accessed, attractive, and functional. A site must be interesting, which means more than a listing of your products and services, but too many pictures make downloading a chore. If the customer is going to buy from you, the sales process must be quick and painless, and the merchandise must be what the customer wants. Moreover, the site must be updated frequently.

You should seek referrals from other business owners who have used a computer consultant they believe is really good. Bugs are inevitable in any system, so find out if the consultant who is recommended stayed around to squash the bugs as they appeared. Advice is what you are buying from the consultant, and the other business owners will tell you if they got their money's worth. Heed their advice.

Investing the Cash

You need to plan for your success. Then, when you succeed and start showing a profit beyond what you ever expected, you should start success planning. The money you have made should be working as hard as you are. Here's where a financial planner can help.

A financial planner should help you ...

➤ Invest your spare cash.

➤ Review current and projected future financial needs.

➤ Recommend estate planning.

Most banks aren't generous with their interest on savings accounts or CDs. Some stocks have spectacular ascents, and often, equally dramatic descents. You run a business that requires your full attention, so let an expert advise you on the best way to use your money. But set guidelines. If you just want a reasonable return, not a killing in the market, then make that clear to your investment advisor, and put it in writing.

The financial planner should examine your income and expenses and suggest ways to increase the former, and decrease the latter. You may have a spouse, several children, and a few pets who depend on you. If you have dependents, the advisor should suggest life insurance to protect them from your loss. An Individual Retirement Account (IRA) or pension contribution should be part of any financial plan; the sooner you begin, the more money will be available upon retirement.

Years have a way of moving into decades, and we get older a lot quicker than we thought possible. Most of us don't even have a Last Will and Testament. The financial planner won't draft your will or living trust, but he or she will suggest you see a lawyer, and do it now. If you have not properly planned your estate, the state will dictate who gets what. Enough said.

Legal Eagle

Computer consultants often speak a variant of English that is understood only by other consultants. If your consultant is one of this breed, avoid him or her. You must know what you are getting for your money and how it will be integrated into your business.

Notes & Quotes

"Money is like an arm or a leg—use it or lose it."

—Henry Ford, businessperson

Virtually anyone can be a financial planner, so beware of labels. Your attorney may be able to suggest a planner that he or she has worked with, or another business owner may be able to refer you to one. Discuss the planner's fee. If it is based upon other products or services you buy, then go elsewhere because he or she is selling, not advising.

Retired Pros Playing for You

Being retired doesn't means being retiring. Small business owners who have retired are often eager to impart their wisdom to beginners. They have been through the good times and bad. Business war stories can be more than just reminiscing; they can contain valuable advice. In the computer age, we often look down on those who relied on the typewriter. But technology isn't everything—people problems really haven't changed all that much, and selling still requires getting the interest of a buyer.

Retired businesspersons are in your neighborhood, often sitting next to you in your house of worship, or are members of a local civic organization. There may be a local association of retired business executives that you can contact for their services. Get to know them, and don't be hesitant to talk business. Your problem may be one that they can solve.

You may receive some excellent advice for free, which is always the right price. But consider paying a modest retainer. That will make you feel better about asking the person for help. Or, if the person will not take a fee, suggest making a contribution to his or her favorite charity.

Helpful Sources

You can obtain a great deal of valuable information on your own. The federal government Web sites are good sources. For example, the Small Business Administration (www.sba.gov) provides various pamphlets related to starting and operating a business. The Equal Employment Opportunity Commission (www.eeoc.gov) is an excellent site for employment law guidelines. Tax information is readily available from the IRS (www.irs.ustreas.gov). If you want to trademark your product, visit the Trademark Office (www.pto.gov). State and local governments have Web sites that you can visit to look up a law or municipal code, or find the appropriate forms and related instructions you need to obtain a license.

Many law firms, accounting firms, insurance companies, and real estate brokers have Web sites that can help you. Several companies have developed software that you can use to develop business plans, design Web sites, and manage your finances.

And don't forget your local library. Books can advise you for no cost but the time invested to read them.

The Least You Need to Know

➤ Choose a lawyer who can prevent problems and draft documents, at a reasonable fee.

➤ An accountant should set up your books and provide periodic financial statements.

➤ Protect your assets with adequate casualty and liability insurance.

➤ Computer consultants can improve your bottom line.

➤ Seek the advice of retired business owners who have the experience.

Part 2

Beginning Your Successful Business

Location, location, location. This is the mantra of real estate agents who want you to buy what they are selling. For some businesses, this does make sense. If your business depends upon walk-in customers, you need to select a good location. But if customers buy your goods through e-commerce, then buying or leasing in the high-rent district makes no sense.

You will also learn about buying an existing business or becoming a franchisee. Either choice requires you to closely examine the fine print and the financials. It's like buying a house—you need help to look it over, because you don't want to end up tossing your savings into the money pit.

Raising money to finance your venture may come easy, but more likely will be a struggle. Banks are eager to lend money to people who don't need it, and investors may be reluctant to part with their money, so you need to know about your capital options and how to obtain the most money at the least pain to your business. Your business idea will only prosper if it's sufficiently fertilized with cash.

Chapter 8

Buying an Existing Business: Traps for the Unwary

In This Chapter

➤ What type of business is right for you?

➤ Exploring the ins and outs of acquiring a business

➤ Making the offer and negotiating the deal

➤ Financing the purchase and understanding tax matters

Some people want to start their own business—begin from scratch and vault to success. But maybe you're different: Perhaps you want to buy an existing business. That option does have certain advantages. An existing business has customers, assets, and employees. Its financial information can help you project its future under your management. It's like buying an existing house, rather than constructing a new one. If that's what you think might work for you, read on. In this chapter, we'll show you how to increase your chances of making a successful deal on the purchase of an existing business. (Also, read Chapter 11, "Finding the Right Location: Realty Bites in Leasing or Buying," for more on buying and leasing property.)

Selecting the Right Business for You

You may be a newcomer, eager to be self-employed and to be your own boss. Or, you may already be in business and are looking to expand your current business, buy out a competitor, or diversify. You must examine your motivation to move from where you are now to the next phase.

Notes & Quotes

"About 750,000 new small businesses are created every year, according to the Department of Labor."

—*The New York Times Almanac 2000*

If you're a newcomer, then like any novice, you need to spend a great deal of time (and some money) to determine if the new business you choose truly fits your personality and finances. You must examine in minute detail not only the target business but also its particular industry. For example, if you are considering the purchase of a small clothing store, check out the competition. An outlet mall just a few blocks away may mean a short-lived business for the small store.

If you're currently in the same business as the company you want to acquire, you're in very good position to judge the value of that company. You know the territory, so you need only examine this company and how it will fit into your current business.

But if you want to diversify, then you probably will be a novice at evaluating and running any new business. Your success in your current business doesn't always transfer to a new one. Many large businesses have diversified to their regret.

Before buying a different kind of company find out the answers to these questions:

➤ Is the company in a good location for its market?

➤ Will the customers be there for you in the future?

➤ What reputation does the company have with its customers and suppliers?

➤ Are the company's physical and human assets sufficient?

➤ If this company is to join yours, how will it fit in?

This is not an exhaustive list, but it does ask crucial questions.

Realtors emphasize location, location, location, and for good reason. Although e-commerce sales are increasingly making the large brick-and-mortar business locations less important, most small businesses still sell to local customers. A good business corner where customer traffic is substantial does count for money in the cash register. Buy a fine restaurant in a deteriorating part of the city and you will not have many customers to serve.

You'll also have to earn customer loyalty on a continuing basis. Price may move them, or good service may keep them coming back for more. Visit the company as a customer and see how you're treated. If you're satisfied with how the company dealt with you, chances are that company's customers will likely stay. But if your visit was unpleasant, walk away—unless you consider yourself a turnaround expert—because there won't be many customers for you to count on when you take over.

The company's purchase price will consist of its physical assets and *goodwill*.

A company's physical assets are relatively easy to value. Unfortunately, the employees you inherit are not. If your visit to the company as a customer uncovered poor management but you buy the business anyway, you can hang out a sign proclaiming *Under New Management* to let customers know you're making changes. However, you may be pleasantly surprised at finding a well-run organization with good employees. Keeping them when you take over must be job one.

Legalese

Goodwill is an intangible business asset that relates to the company's ability to generate income in excess of the normal rate of return for its physical assets due to superior management, marketing skill, and products.

The business media often comment on the clash of corporate cultures that occurs when two companies merge. One company may have casual dress every day, while the other requires its employees to wear business suits and dresses. Attire may seem a superficial criterion to make a judgment of corporate fit, but then, maybe not. If you own a fast-food restaurant, then acquiring another one should not cause much of a clash. But what if you decided to diversify into fine dining? Your experience in one business may not translate well into another.

Using a Business Acquisition Team

You better not enter the acquisition fray without a good supporting team. The members of your team should include …

➤ A business broker.

➤ A certified Public Accountant.

➤ An attorney.

➤ A financial advisor.

If you know the company you want to buy and what to pay for it, then you don't need a business broker. However, if you're searching for the right business at the right price, and need someone to help you negotiate the deal, then consider a business broker. He or she will charge a fee, which may be a percentage of the purchase price, usually about 2 to 7 percent. You might find the house of your dreams by driving around the city or checking the ads, or you might not; just don't count on finding a business without a broker.

The business broker should be familiar with the type of business in which you're interested and be able to determine a fair price for the company.

It's your cash (or the bank's money that you must pay back) and you need to know what you're paying for. That means getting accurate financial information. Your accountant should be familiar with small businesses, and it would be a plus if he or she has some experience in the company's particular industry. Small businesses are notoriously bad at keeping good financial records, so an accountant who knows that and can make the adjustments necessary to give you an accurate picture is worth the fee.

You provide your attorney with the price, payment terms, and other options, and your attorney should draft your contract to purchase the business. Make sure that you fully understand the contract. Have your attorney replace any legalese with real words.

Both the accountant and the attorney should be familiar with the tax laws regarding the purchase of the business. Even a straightforward purchase of the business assets requires tax allocations.

Your financial advisor can suggest ways to finance the purchase, and should be able to help you obtain the necessary funds at an affordable rate.

Examining the Financials Closely

You must fully understand the financial condition of the company you consider buying. The best financial information should include ...

➤ CPA-certified balance sheets for the current year and two prior years.

➤ CPA certified-income statements for the current year and two prior years.

➤ Federal and state income tax returns for the past three years.

➤ State sales tax reports for the past three years.

Since you have not yet made an offer, the prospective seller may be reluctant to disclose this information, especially if you're a potential competitor. You may want to sign a statement affirming that the information is deemed confidential and you will not disclose it to anyone or use it for any purpose other than evaluating the company for possible acquisition. The accounting and tax information should provide a more complete picture than just one or the other.

The balance sheet lists the assets at their book value (purchase price) and the liabilities; the information is stated as of a particular date: for example, December 31, 2000. The income statement provides information about the company's revenue and expenses for a stated period: for example, January 1 through December 31, 2000. Certified financial information means that a CPA has prepared the information using generally accepted accounting practices, and thus should be reliable. However, many small businesses do not have the reports certified, so your accountant should closely scrutinize them.

My client was interested in buying a tavern. We asked for the seller's financial information and he offered three options: income tax returns on which he underreported his sales; his sales tax report, on which he likewise underreported; or his little black book, which was the true record of sales. I advised my client to avoid buying his company. There is no guarantee that the prospective seller is not cheating on his tax returns, but if he tells you that his sales are $100,000, and he reported only $50,000 last year, then walk, because he is either lying to you or to the IRS. If you buy the corporate stock, then you may inherit its tax problems.

Looking for Any Legal Problems That May Arise

Before you sign on the dotted line of a purchase contract, find out everything you can about potential legal trouble that could end up costing you money down the road. There are a number of problems to look out for, from liens against the property to toxic waste violations, from unpaid taxes to ongoing lawsuits. In this section, I'll tell you about the kinds of problems to look out for.

Shark Attack!

Avoid buying the seller's stock. A stock sale benefits the seller, but at considerable risk to the buyer if unexpected or undisclosed seller debts appear after the closing when the seller is long gone. Stick to purchasing the company's assets only.

Titles and Liens

The seller may tell you that he or she owns all assets free-and-clear. For any asset that has a title to it, such as real estate or motor vehicles, you should ask to see the title.

Search for mortgages on real estate or secured interests on personal property, including equipment, accounts receivable, inventory, and fixtures. Your attorney can order a title and lien search through a title insurance company to determine if the seller owns the real estate, and if there are any *mortgages*, mechanics' liens, or other encumbrances that would reduce the value of the property by the amount of the mortgage or lien.

Legalese

A **mortgage** is placed on real estate for the property to serve as security for the payment of a debt. A financing statement records a debt against the personal property (collateral for a loan).

Your attorney can order a search of the state Secretary of State's files and the county recorder's files to see if any of the seller's personal property has been used as collateral (whether a financing statement was filed against the collateral), which would, likewise, reduce the value of the property.

Company Leases

The company may have leases for real estate and equipment that you could assume. Your attorney should determine if the leases can be assigned, and review the specific provisions so that you could discuss any unfavorable terms with the lessors in advance. The lease obligations become the new tenant's responsibility. If you're thinking about renting or leasing real property (such as an office), contact other tenants to determine if the landlord is responsive to their needs.

Zoning

Zoning laws limit the owner's use of its real estate. A client wanted to purchase a store from a company; however, the property had never been rezoned from residential to commercial. The prospective seller assured us that rezoning would be no problem, so my client conditioned the purchase on the rezoning at the seller's expense.

Toxic Waste

If you are buying real estate, there are three letters you should remember: EPA. Your prospective seller may own land contaminated with toxic wastes. If you buy that property, you run to risk of being responsible for any cleanup, possibly at the cost of several million dollars. Always have an environmental survey performed by an environmental engineering company to determine if there are toxic wastes. Most lenders require an environmental survey as a condition to obtaining a loan.

Lawsuits

If you are buying the company's stock, rather than its assets, then you will inherit its liabilities, which could include outstanding lawsuits. Some lawsuits are frivolous and will go away; others, however, can end up costing a bundle. You should insist that the present owner disclose all lawsuits and have your attorney review all pleadings, motions, and other related documents. Again, you must know what you are buying.

Taxes

Uncle Sam and his state nieces and nephews are a determined lot; they want to see the tax money. If the company you are buying is a taxpayer (C corporation, or any unincorporated association taxed similarly), you must have your tax advisor review its tax returns. If you buy the corporate stock, then you get its tax liabilities, too.

Shark Attack!

If the environmental survey turns up evidence of dangerous environmental wastes, do not buy the property, unless you're willing to risk the future of your business.

When to Keep Contracts with Suppliers and Employees

Contracts with suppliers, like leases, should be reviewed by your attorney to determine if they are assignable and for their important terms. If you buy just the company's assets, you probably will negotiate a new contract with the suppliers unless the old contract is particularly favorable.

You may want the company's employees to stay with you. Most employees are simply at-will, which means that they can be retained or terminated at any time. However, the company may have several employees with written contracts that last for several years. If you want to keep the employees under those terms, fine; but if not, then buy only the company's assets, or have the seller renegotiate the employee contracts.

Service Warranties and Trademarks

The retail business often provides its customers with service warranties. If you take over the business, then you may be obligated to honor those warranties or face irate customers. The prospective seller should disclose this potential liability and adjust the purchase price accordingly.

Sometimes a name really does say it all. If your targeted company has an important trademarked name, then make sure that the sale includes its assignment to you. Likewise, if there are patents, copyrights, or licenses that are essential to success of the business, ensure that they are assigned as part of the sale. If you're buying a tavern, for instance, you'll need the liquor license that goes along with it.

Franchisor Approval

If you are buying a business that is a franchisee, then your lawyer should review its agreement, and your accountant should examine the financial arrangement. Franchises, as discussed in the next chapter, are often very successful (fast-food restaurants, for example), but the franchise agreement may be long term, costly, and inflexible. The franchisor must approve the assignment of any franchise.

Making the Offer and Negotiating the Deal

If you are satisfied that there are no significant obstacles to making an offer, you might then want to send a nonbinding Letter of Intent to Purchase to the seller. The letter should indicate your desire to make an offer and determine if the prospective seller is interested. The letter may contain …

➤ A list of assets you want to buy and at what price.

➤ A list of licenses, permits, and so on, that would be transferred.

➤ A list of documents your lawyer and accountant need to review.

The letter should clearly state that its purpose is to determine if the parties agree in principal on the sale, and that it is not a contract offer. Your lawyer would draft the contract offer after the seller has tentatively agreed to the deal.

Once the parties have generally agreed, then your attorney should draft the Purchase Agreement.

You must decide whether you are going to purchase ownership of the business, such as stock in the target corporation, or purchase the company's assets. Purchasing the stock in the corporation also buys its liabilities, so I would suggest you buy the business assets instead. The following discussion involves a contract to buy the assets and the terms that are usually included.

The Purchase Agreement to buy assets should usually contain the following terms:

➤ Assets being sold and the allocation of the purchase price

➤ Adjustment of sale price for contingencies

➤ Terms of payment

➤ Bulk sales law compliance

➤ Seller's representations

➤ Seller's covenant not to compete

➤ Conduct of business before closing

➤ Closing date

Creating a Purchase Agreement

The Purchase Agreement should list the assets bought and allocate the purchase price for each asset according to its fair market value. The list includes real estate to be conveyed; tangible property, such as equipment, trade fixtures, and inventory; customer information and important records; any real estate or equipment leases or contracts to be assigned to the buyer; and intangible personal property, such as patents, copyrights, trademarks, and licenses.

You need to allocate the purchase price among the assets for tax purposes. As a buyer you want to allocate as much of the price as possible to depreciable assets, such as equipment and fixtures, and as little as necessary to property that cannot be depreciated, such as land and goodwill.

If you're buying inventory, the contract should have a tentative price, which then would be adjusted based on a complete inventory at some designated time prior to closing.

The purchase may be for a cash sum due at closing, which would be reduced by any earnest money you paid at the time of the offering. Or, the agreement may permit you to make periodic payments over a specified term, with interest. I would suggest that you make two payments, even if you can pay the entire amount at closing. You might get hit with customer claims for refunds or warranties that you may feel obligated to honor, or creditor claims against inventory under the bulk sales act. If, by the second payment, perhaps in six months, a problem has arisen, then an adjustment in the payment would be required by the contract.

Shark Attack!

Be as accurate as possible! The IRS may review your purchase price allocation, so be prepared to demonstrate the fair market value for each item. You will need to report the allocation on IRS form 8594.

Under the state bulk sales act a company selling all or most of its assets is required to notify its creditors before concluding the sale. The seller's creditors may proceed to collect before the seller trots off with the sale's proceeds. As the buyer, you should receive a list of the seller's creditors, then notify each creditor of the impending sale. If you fail to comply with the law, then the creditors not notified may assert a claim against the assets that you bought.

The seller should state in the Purchase Agreement that ...

➤ The corporation (or other type of entity) is in good standing as a corporation, and its board and shareholder authorize the sale.

➤ All assets are owned and conveyed free of liens.

➤ All financial statements are accurate.

➤ All leases and contracts are assignable.

➤ There are no pending lawsuits.

➤ All material facts have been disclosed to the buyer.

Legal Eagle

Know what you're buying. Seller representations are important and should be included in the contract, but you should rely on your own examination of the representations; for example, have your accountant review the financial information.

Covenants

You don't want to buy a retail store or restaurant from your seller, and then have the seller open a competing store in the same neighborhood. A covenant (promise) not to compete would eliminate this problem. If your customer base resides within a radius of 10 miles, you should prohibit the seller from opening a competing business within that radius for a reasonable time after the closing, such as three years. Courts will enforce the covenant if it is reasonable in time and distance.

The seller should agree to continue his or her same business practices until closing. You don't want the seller to make any detrimental changes, such as selling all the most marketable inventory, or issuing discount coupons that you would be forced to honor.

The closing date is stated to fix the time of payment and transfer of assets to the buyer.

If this is a new business that you are buying, you may want to have the seller stay on for a few months to help you. Include a provision in the agreement specifying the services to be rendered, and the compensation to be paid, for the period of time you need for the transition.

Financing the Purchase

You need to come up with the money for the deal. Your current business retained earnings (undistributed profits) may be sufficient to fund the purchase, or your own personal assets, or you may be able to convince a bank to lend you the money. The seller may be willing to permit you to make monthly or annual payments, which may come partially from the income of your newly acquired business. Please read Chapter 10, "Raising Money When You Need More Than You Have," for a complete discussion of raising money.

Taxing Matters

If you are buying the ownership of the company (corporate stock), then you inherit all its tax attributes. The seller's depreciation schedules for its equipment and buildings are now your schedules. Its accounting method and elections are now yours, too. The tax status (S or C corporation) is now your status. And you guessed it, the corporation's tax liabilities are now your problem, too.

If your corporation is purchasing the stock of another corporation to merge or own the seller's corporation as a subsidiary, then you have entered the tax world known as corporate reorganization. Its complexities are beyond the discussion of this book. Consult a tax advisor who is an expert in this arcane area of the law.

When you purchase the assets, you need to perform the price allocation, as previously discussed. The depreciable assets are then yours to write down, using the tax cost (*basis of property*) that you have determined. The IRS provides depreciation tables.

Legalese

Basis of property is usually the acquisition cost; for depreciable assets, such as equipment, the basis is reduced by depreciation. Basis is used to determine gain or loss on the sale of property by subtracting the basis from the sale price.

Closing Means Beginning

The closing on the purchase of a business or business assets requires close attention to the following:

➤ Payment, which may be by cash for the total amount, or the initial payment for several installments

➤ Transfer of title to all titled assets (vehicles, as an example)

➤ Bill of sale for nontitled assets, (inventory, for example)

➤ Assignment of leases, and contracts

➤ Transfer of patents, copyrights, franchise documents, and so on

➤ Stock certificate transfer, if you are buying the business

If you're making periodic payments to the seller, then the seller will probably insist on taking a mortgage on any real estate and a security interest against personal property, so you will sign documents related to that collateral. Likewise, you will sign a promissory note for the debt.

Helpful Sources

Read *The Complete Idiot's Guide to Buying & Selling a Business* by Ed Paulson (Alpha Books, 1999). And there are several other excellent books on the market that discuss business purchases and have forms for you to use as a guideline to help your attorney draft an agreement; several may be in your local library or can be purchased at a bookstore or on the Web. The IRS Web site (www.irs.ustreas.gov) provides the tax forms and related instructions for the asset allocation.

The Least You Need to Know

➤ Spend the time necessary to buy the right business for you.

➤ Use your accountant to examine the seller's financial statements.

➤ Search for liens against the assets to be purchased.

➤ Draft a contract that fully protects your interests.

➤ Allocate the purchase price to assets that you can write off.

Chapter 9

Franchising for Success

In This Chapter

➤ An overview of franchising laws

➤ Choosing the right franchise

➤ The franchisor disclosures duly noted

➤ Your franchise agreement is written by the franchisor

➤ Solutions to franchisor problems that can arise

➤ Helpful sources

Every Saturday morning, children across America spend their TV time watching cartoons sponsored by fast food chains. My children can even spot a McDonald's among the urban clutter of buildings as we drive the interstate. You may be interested in joining thousands of businesspersons who become franchisees in a variety of businesses, such as learning centers, office and home cleaning, and convenience stores, and make a good living in the process.

An Overview of Franchising Laws

A franchise is a contract arrangement giving the franchisee the right to use the franchisor's trademark, logo, goodwill, and marketing expertise to sell goods or services. Franchises fit into two basic forms:

1. An entire business franchise
2. A product distribution arrangement

If you want to become a fast food restaurant owner, for example, then your franchise agreement will be just one entity in the entire business franchise. You'll have one product to sell under the franchisor's trademark.

If you're in a retail business that sells several product lines, it's possible to have a franchise distribution arrangement with one or more major dealers to sell their products in a specified market. For example, you might own a bicycle shop that sells several competing brands for which you've become a local franchisee. Many auto dealers are also franchisees.

As the franchisee, you own your own business and thus can decide what form of business organization to operate under, including as a corporation or limited liability company. In addition, you would operate according to the franchise agreement, which can be expensive and restrictive.

A good franchise offers you not only a recognizable name to operate under, but also a proven plan to run the business and help from the franchisor if you have problems. Your company will run the same operation as several hundred other franchisees. For instance, a Subway in Indianapolis runs similar to a Subway in Seattle.

Legal Eagle

According to *The New York Times Almanac 2000*, the top five franchises by number of franchises in 1998 were ...

Franchise Name	Total Franchises
Kumon Math & Reading	19,667
McDonald's	16,319
7-Eleven convenience stores	14,549
Subway sandwiches	13,395
Jani-King cleaning	7,038

If you crave freedom, and don't want big brother (franchisor) looking over your shoulder, then a franchise is probably not for you. Deviation from the standard practices is not usually encouraged in franchises because similarity and standardization provide customers with confidence in the product offered. The cost of your new franchise may be an important consideration. The franchise fee, which may be a substantial advance, could range from as little as $500 to as much as $45,000 or more. National franchises, for instance, usually command a significant initial fee. In addition, the franchisor will be entitled to a percentage of your gross sales, and may require you to purchase its equipment, goods, and supplies.

Many franchisors do not require that you have prior experience in the business, and will train you and your employees, but this, too, usually comes at a price to you. You may also have to pay a fee for national or local advertising, and you'll probably be restricted in the merchandise you can sell. Fast food restaurants sell the franchisor's food, period.

The franchisee, like any business owner, bears the risk of loss in the business; but in a franchise, this risk is often reduced by the sale of a known product or service that generates sales by the name alone. On the down side, you'll be limited to operating in a particular area and may not be allowed to move without the franchisor's permission. Also, you may not be able to transfer your business to anyone other than the franchisor or someone approved by the franchisor.

Choosing the Right Franchise

Before you sign a franchise agreement or pay any money, ask yourself the following questions:

➤ Am I suited for this type of business?

➤ Am I compatible with the franchisor?

➤ Does the franchisor have strong name recognition?

➤ Does the business have strong growth possibilities?

➤ Will the franchisor find me a suitable business location?

➤ Will the franchisor help with financing?

➤ Does the franchisor have a good record of successful franchisees?

➤ Is the franchisor selective in awarding franchises?

➤ Have I understood all the fees and costs?

➤ Does the franchisor have an excellent training program?

➤ Has the franchisor disclosed everything required by law?

➤ Is the franchise agreement fair?

➤ Has the franchisor answered all my questions?

It's your money and future, so it's important to thoroughly investigate the franchise. Unpleasant surprises can cost you a bundle.

You should follow the adage: *Know thyself.* Only you can determine if the franchise business is the type of business that you truly will enjoy. However, enthusiasm will not conquer all, so you need to take inventory of your skills and personality. If you are not a people person and the franchise is service oriented, then consider hiring someone who revels in customer contact, or look elsewhere for a business that requires less interaction by you with the public.

Know Who You're Dealing With

You and the franchisor will be partners—not legally but operationally. You must be able to work effectively with the franchisor. If at the initial stages of your discussions,

you have to fight through the franchisor's bureaucracy to get answers or your calls aren't returned for several days, then don't buy into the franchise. Can you trust their word? What is their business background? And obtain all the franchisor's audited financial information. Avoid a financially weak franchisor. You need to believe in your franchisor and its vision for its (and your) future.

The franchise's name need not be a household word, but it helps. You are going to invest a lot of money to use the franchise's trademark, so it should be well established and have an excellent reputation for quality products and services. In this instance, the advice to invest in what you know and like is sound.

Rely on the Franchisor's Expertise

The franchisor should share with you its plan for business development, nationally and locally. Franchisor growth and market share are important to your success. If you are going to be one of the first franchisees in your area, you need to know that others will follow, not as competitors, but for increased name recognition.

Location, location, and location. The good convenience store franchisors, for instance, know where to locate their stores for the maximum of traffic and sales. Your franchisor should help you select an appropriate site or may already have a location in mind. Carefully consider the franchisor's advice.

You need a good financial plan. The franchisor has experience with determining a franchisee's financial needs, and you should insist that it provide you with a typical franchisee budget. If money is in short supply, the franchisor may be willing to lend you some of the money up front.

Reputation and Cooperation Count

Insist that the franchisor provide you with a complete list of franchisees in your area, and be sure to contact them. Think of them as the franchisor's customers—if they are well satisfied and successful, then it's likely that you will be, too. Don't forget to ask the franchisees if the franchisor has been responsive to their business challenges. If the franchisor hasn't helped when financial, customer, or other problems have arisen, don't invest in that franchise.

In addition, if the franchisor isn't very selective in awarding franchises, then the quality of the total franchise will suffer. Just as your reputation will depend on the quality of your employees, the franchise's reputation will be enhanced by its selectivity. The franchisor should thoroughly examine your credentials, and, if it doesn't, then reconsider.

You should thoroughly understand all the fees and costs associated with the franchise. Do a reality check with other franchisees to compare the franchisor's claims. You don't need any surprises on what you owe the franchisor, because money will be tight for some time after you begin.

Many franchisors assume that you have no prior business experience, so they will train you in general business matters as well as the specific franchise business. Contact other franchisees to see if they received the help that they needed. If there were any deficiencies, then the franchisor should readily agree to improve the training. The franchisor should have a strong commitment to continued training and education. The franchisor should be willing to at least bear part of this cost.

You are making a substantial investment, so the franchisor should disclose as much about itself as required by law, and readily do so. If you don't receive this information then avoid this franchisor. Federal and state law disclosure requirements are discussed below.

Read the Fine Print

The franchisor's attorneys draft the franchise agreement. The franchisor has developed the business that you want to join, so it's understandable that the franchisor wants to protect itself and control the arrangement. Yet its terms should not be oppressive. Equally as important is the operating relationship between the franchisor and franchisees. The franchisees should tell you if the franchisor always insists on the letter of the contract

> **Notes & Quotes**
>
> "What has not been examined impartially has not been well examined. Skepticism is therefore the first step toward truth."
>
> —Denis Diderot, writer

rather than the spirit. A franchisor that always insists on its rights to the detriment of an embattled franchisee should be avoided.

After you have read all the franchisor's information and discussed with the franchisees all your concerns, you should have several questions for the franchisor. Don't hesitate to ask, and follow up with other questions until you fully understand everything about the arrangement. The franchisor's answers should be straightforward and responsive. Walk away if they are evasive.

The Franchise Disclosures Duly Noted

Most franchise arrangements come within the dictates of the Federal Trade Commission (FTC) disclosure requirements. If you are a prospective franchisee, the franchisor must give you an offering circular (disclosures) at the earliest of your first in-person meeting, or 10 working days before you sign a contract or pay money to the franchisor. Several states also regulate franchise arrangements, and the franchisor that makes an offer in those states has to comply with state law as well.

➤ **Experience and History.** You need to know as much about the franchisor as possible. Examine its business history and finances. If the franchisor has a short history in the business or has a long history of rocky finances, then beware, because you will be in the same boat with the franchisor as captain. Get to know its major players; if you have doubts about its honesty or the franchisor seems to talk a better game than it plays, then keep your money and run to the nearest exit. Check out its business plan and confer with franchisees to confirm that the plan is being followed.

➤ **Current and Past Litigation.** If the franchisor is knee-deep in litigation, particularly with several franchisees then, likewise, depart. However, most large franchisors get sued for a lot of reasons, some of which are not important. Your attorney can help sort out the legitimate claims from the frivolous ones. However, if the franchisor is in bankruptcy, definitely have your attorney investigate the filing. Some times a bad market glitch causes a temporary problem that bankruptcy reorganization and time can resolve, but maybe not.

➤ **Fees, Fees, Fees.** Franchise fees and other costs must be detailed in a financial statement, and you need to check with other franchisees to see if this statement reflects their experience. This is particularly true for the franchisor's estimate of your initial investment beyond the fees paid to it. Costs vary from city to city. What you would pay for rent and employees in New York City will be more than what you'd pay in Indianapolis. Err on the side of a conservative budget, because running a business almost always costs more than you predict.

➤ **Understanding Your Restrictions.** You may be closely tied to the franchisor's products and services. The franchisee is often obligated to buy its equipment from the franchisor and use the franchisor's services.

➤ **Territorial and Product Limits.** You may be restricted to selling only the franchisor's products or have a limited sales territory. Talk with other franchisees about these limits. If they receive shoddy products or inefficient services from the franchisor, or the franchisor's merchandise is poor quality, then you will not be successful. If your sales territory is not exclusive, then another competing franchisee can take away customers. And know the territory—another bicycle sales store at a busy intersection may be one too many.

➤ **Obligations.** The disclosure circular lists the franchisee's obligations, but don't rely on this list. Always read the contract and fully understand your obligations, because any contract you sign is binding. Likewise, the disclosure circular lists the franchisor's obligations. This list is only as good as the franchisor who follows it (and the contract). The only realistic way to determine if the franchisor meets its obligations is to confirm it with the franchisees. For example, if you are obligated to pay an advertising fee, which often you are, then ask the franchisees if the advertising has been effective.

➤ **All Necessary Financing.** If the franchisor offers you financing, the circular will disclose its terms and conditions. This will enable you to compare the franchisor's terms with other sources of financing. Check with other franchisees to find out how they financed their investment and operations.

➤ **Trademarks and Confidential Information.** You are going to use the franchisor's *trademark* (or service mark). Check with the U.S. Trademark Office in Washington, D.C., to determine if the mark has been registered. If not, then it's possible you may not be protected in using the mark in your state. Do your own quick market survey with friends and acquaintances to find out if they have heard of the company's name. This may not be scientific, but it can tell you if the name is recognized. If not, then count on a ton of advertising dollars to gain that recognition.

Legalese

A **trademark** is a word, name, or symbol that is used in commerce to identify a product. Pepsi and McDonald's are trademarked and cannot be used without the owner's permission. The franchisor's trademark is licensed to the franchisee for use during the period of the franchise agreement.

➤ **Franchisee Participation.** If you bought this book, you are unlikely to be a passive investor in the franchise. But be aware that most franchise arrangements will require you to be an active manager, completely involved in the business. So if your role is largely passive, then you better ensure that hiring a manager will do.

➤ **Details on Resolutions.** You want to control the destiny of your franchise business, so examine very closely any restrictions on your ability to do the following: Renew the franchise for additional periods at minimal cost; terminate the franchise upon *just cause* (make sure the franchisor can terminate only under just cause); resolve disputes with expedition and minimal costs; and freely transfer your franchise to a business successor or buyer.

Legalese

Just cause means good cause. The franchisor would be required to prove that the termination of the agreement was reasonable due to franchisee misconduct.

➤ **Celebrity Promotions.** Famous people endorse many products, from autos to shoes, and do so for a sizeable fee. They also endorse franchises. The FTC requires these celebrities to disclose their compensation and the extent to which they are involved in management or control of the franchise, as well as any money they have invested in the business. Your hero or heroine may just have lent his or her name, so be a little skeptical about these endorsements.

➤ **Claiming What You've Earned.** Most franchisors do not make earnings claims. However, if the franchisor does make claims about your potential earnings, the FTC requires the offering circular to disclose the factual basis and assumptions made. Compare this claim with the experiences of other franchisees who operate under circumstances similar to yours. A self-laundry outlet may do very well near several apartments, but less well in an affluent neighborhood. Remember, the franchisor wants to sell you the franchise, so expect a little exaggeration.

➤ **List of Outlets.** The franchisor must list all operating franchisees, as well as those that are nearly ready to open for business. The franchisor who has several operating franchisees in your area has developed a track record that you can check. You should use this list to contact franchisees in your state. Even a simple "How are things working out?" can help you decide to go ahead or to look elsewhere. The franchisor must also include a list of canceled or terminated franchises that occurred within the last three years. Too many of these should provide sufficient warning.

➤ **Financial Statements.** The franchisor is required to provide you with two years of audited balance sheets and stockholders' equity, as well as the cash flows for the last three years. While the FTC doesn't require a specific franchisor net worth, your accountant should be able to advise you as to its adequacy.

While the FTC requires all this to be disclosed, it does not verify the information. That is your job number one.

➤ **Keeping Copies.** The FTC circular requires the franchisor to provide you with copies of all contracts you are expected to sign. Turn these over to your attorney for his or her review.

Legal Eagle

Share all information with your business advisors. Hire an attorney who is familiar with franchise arrangements and an accountant who is properly skeptical of earnings claims. Fraud occurs in franchise arrangements just like it does in stock offerings.

Your Franchise Agreement

Expect your Franchise Agreement to run more than 50 pages. The franchise's attorney drafts the agreement in the franchises best interests, so hire an attorney who is well versed in franchise law and sufficiently aggressive to negotiate a more favorable agreement. Your franchisor may tell you to sign the contract, or walk. This may be an effective way of getting what it wants from you—your signature on the contract. Some well-established franchisors can dictate the contract, but others sometimes are more flexible.

Study the proposed agreement in conjunction with the FTC offering circular; if the contract has terms that conflict with the FTC requirement, then make sure the contract is corrected. While we can't talk about each and every provision you'll find in a franchise agreement, we can have a look at some of the most common ones.

Shark Attack!

Don't confuse sales with profit. You may sell a lot, and pay the franchisor based on this figure, while your profit is what remains after all your costs (including what you should be paying yourself as an employee and investor).

➤ **Fees, Payment Schedule, and Advertising.** What you owe and when it has to be paid should be at the top of your list of things to review. The initial fee is just that. Your ongoing fees (royalties) may be based on gross revenues, not your profit.

Advertising should help you in your market. The advertising may be directed to a majority of franchises in other markets, yet you are paying a fee; your agreement should allow you to use a portion of your fees specifically as you desire in your market.

➤ **Audits.** Since the franchisor will receive a percentage of your gross revenue, you will be expected to provide sales information. The franchisor will want the right to audit your books. If an audit occurs it should be at the franchisor's expense unless there is a substantial difference between what you report and what your records show. Likewise, the franchisor must agree to keep your financial information confidential.

➤ **Purchase Requirements.** You may be locked into buying the franchisor's goods and services. Consider requiring the franchisor to warrant the quality of the merchandise and agree to sell at a fair market price. You should get what you paid for at a fair price.

➤ **Sales Territory.** If you're locked into a sales territory, make sure that its market is not oversaturated with other franchisees. And ensure that the franchisor cannot unilaterally reduce your territory. Likewise the franchisor should be precluded from establishing a franchisor-owned company in your territory to compete against you.

➤ **Consents by the Franchisor and Obligations.** Several provisions of the agreement may require the franchisor's consent. Add a provision that would require the consent not be unreasonably withheld or delayed. Time is of the essence.

Understand both your obligations and rights as a franchisee. Make sure that there are no ambiguous or vague terms that could later come back to haunt you. Try to visualize how each of your duties or your rights will affect your business. If you are not satisfied with certain provisions, then propose changes. Reasonable requests to remove onerous terms should be honored.

➤ **Trademark Usage.** You must be given (licensed) the right to use the franchisor's trademark or service mark. You are paying to operate under that name. The franchisor should warrant its ownership and its federal registration and should indemnify you for your damages and related costs if a third party sues you for trademark infringement.

➤ **Default.** The agreement will specify numerous ways it is possible for you to default (breach the agreement), but list very few franchisor defaults. Make sure that only the most serious defaults by you—such as defrauding the franchisor—permit automatic termination. Lesser defaults, such as a failure to timely provide financial information, should permit you a period of time to cure (fix) the wrong before termination. For franchisor defaults, consult with other franchisees to determine what continual problems they have, then specify that, in your case, the franchisor must cure such defaults within 30 days, or you have the option to terminate the agreement.

➤ **Term and Renewal.** The agreement will specify the duration of the franchise, such as five or 10 years. You should negotiate a provision giving you the right to renew the franchise for an unlimited number of times as long as you are not in default. This may come at a modest fee, which should be negotiable.

➤ **Arbitration.** You don't want to litigate every substantial disagreement. Consider a clause requiring the parties to submit their disputes to an independent arbitrator, who has the experience in franchise law to interpret the agreement. The arbitration should occur in your city, use impartial arbitrators, and provide a method of assessing costs.

➤ **Termination.** The franchisor should not be able to terminate the arrangement except for just cause. You should be given adequate time to cure any defaults, except perhaps the most serious ones. Usually the franchisor will insist on its right to terminate if you fail to operate the business, understate gross revenues, don't pay the royalties and fees, or compete with the franchisor.

➤ **Covenants Not to Compete.** If the franchise is terminated or not renewed, the franchisor may want you to stop operating your business altogether and not continue under another name. The agreement may, therefore, contain a *covenant not to compete*. Understandably, the former franchisor would not want you, by then a former franchisee, to compete with a new franchisee. You, on the other hand, want to keep the option open and delete the covenant.

➤ **Transfer.** The franchise is usually not freely transferred (assigned) by you to another franchisee. The agreement will require the franchisor's approval, or at least, the franchisor's first option to buy back the franchise. If approval is required, you should include language to the effect that it "would not be unreasonably withheld." If the franchisor has first option, require that it be exercised in a timely manner. Your transferee will be required to assume the existing franchise agreement or the latest version and payment of a transfer fee. You should include a provision permitting your spouse or heirs to operate the franchise if you die or are disabled.

➤ **Entire Agreement.** The agreement may conclude with a provision stating that it contains all the contract terms between the franchisor and franchisee. This clause excludes all separate oral or written terms. If the franchisor has made any promises or claims, insist that they be included in the agreement or an addendum thereto. Otherwise, these side agreements are not enforceable in court.

Notes & Quotes

"It's still embarrassing. I asked my caddie for a sand wedge, and 10 minutes later he came back with a ham on rye."

—Chi Chi Rodriquez, golfer

Solutions to Franchisor Problems That Can Arise

Problems occur in all relationships. Good communications between the franchisor and you are vital to maintaining a productive relationship. If you have a problem, contact the franchisor and explain your difficulty. Emphasize that it is a mutual problem because anything that affects your sales reduces the franchisor's income and diminishes its reputation.

On the other hand, don't blow up and threaten a lawsuit unless the franchisor has clearly violated the agreement, and you have totally exhausted attempts to get the franchisor to correct the problem. A lawsuit is expensive and may destroy your business. It should be the last resort.

Consult with other franchisees—your problems may be theirs, too. Negotiating with the franchisor can be enhanced if more of you speak out. If the franchisor is faced with several common concerns, then it is more likely to respond to a group of franchisees than it might to a single franchisee's complaint.

Finally, heeding the old adage "disagree without being disagreeable" will go a long way in helping you to resolve problems. Light, not heat, is better.

Helpful Sources

Visit the Federal Trade Commission Web site (www.ftc.gov) for franchise disclosure requirements. Most states have Web sites with the state franchising laws. There are a number of books and magazines on franchising, which are available at your bookstore or library. You may want to contact the American Association of Franchisees and Dealers at P.O. Box 81887, San Diego, CA 92138, or the Association of Small Business Development Centers, 3108 Columbia Pike, Suite 300, Arlington, VA 22204.

The Least You Need to Know

➤ The franchise is a contractual arrangement for the franchisee to sell goods and services using the franchisor's name.

➤ You must take the initiative to thoroughly investigate the franchisor's business.

➤ Federal and many states laws require the franchisor to disclose significant information to you before you sign the contract.

➤ Your franchise attorney should review the agreement and negotiate more favorable terms for you.

➤ Join or create an association of other franchisees for mutual support.

Chapter 10

Raising Money When You Need More Than You Have

In This Chapter

➤ Money makes your business go 'round

➤ Risky business: Borrowing from family and friends risks the relationship

➤ A borrower be: Bank and government loans

➤ Understanding the law

Your parents probably constantly reminded you that money doesn't grow on trees, and now you're painfully aware of that fact because you realize your business can't get started or grow without money, which, for most of us, is a scarce resource. This chapter contains no magic formulas of alchemy to convert dross into gold, but it does provide several valuable suggestions on how to obtain initial and working capital. For good or ill, you must be a seeker of capital.

Figuring Out How Much You Need

No book can tell you how much money you'll need to start and run your business. You have to determine that with the help of your accountant and business advisors.

Your business plan may be as detailed as you desire. Consider it your blueprint for building and operating your business. Begin by creating an accurate business plan, which should include ...

➤ A description of your business.

➤ A marketing plan.

➤ A financial plan.

➤ A management plan.

The nonfinancial sections of the plan should describe your company and what it intends to sell or service, and how you intend on becoming successful. There are several books that can help you develop the plan, such as *The Complete Idiot's Guide to Being a Successful Entrepreneur* (Alpha Books, 1999), by John Sortino.

The financial section of the plan should contain …

➤ Current and projected sources of funding.

➤ A start-up budget.

➤ An operating budget.

➤ An equipment and supply list.

➤ A balance sheet.

➤ A profit and loss statement.

➤ A cash flow projection.

If you're starting a business, then the sources for all this financial information may be an accountant familiar with your particular business, other small business owners who have the experience, or a franchisor who will provide a model budget for the franchisee.

Your start-up budget should include costs you'll incur before opening, such as legal and accounting fees, licenses, equipment, insurance, supplies, advertising, initial payroll, and advanced rent. Your operating budget should include all ongoing expenses, including payroll, insurance, rent, utilities, loan payments, advertising, supplies, fees, and maintenance.

The cash flow projection should pinpoint those months of slow sales or higher expenses, so that you can plan accordingly. You might want to cover these periodic cash deficits with a line of credit from a bank.

Now you are ready to determine how to best finance your initial and working capital requirements.

Determining Your Assets

Your business will require an investment of your assets. Lenders may lend, and investors may invest—as long as you, too, have a financial stake in your business. For your investment capital, you may look to your ...

➤ Personal savings.

➤ Equity in your home.

➤ Whole life insurance.

➤ Retirement savings.

➤ Salary.

> **Notes & Quotes**
>
> "With money in your pocket, you are wise, and you are hand-some, and you sing well, too."
>
> —Yiddish proverb

You may have certificates of deposit, savings bonds, savings accounts, stocks, bonds, and mutual funds, all of which you carefully invested in over the years. Each provides a return and a safety net, so you may be reluctant to risk your savings on this new adventure, and I am not suggesting that you must. In fact, I strongly recommend that you keep something in reserve for your personal or family needs, and a little for future investment in the business should it run into cash flow problems. However, if you use most of your current investments to start up your business, you'll be apt to gain a much greater return, both financially and psychologically. If you own your home, you may be able to obtain a home equity loan at a favorable rate of interest from a bank. Many lenders will lend up to 80 percent or more of the value of your home.

Your equity in the house is the difference between its current value and any mortgage on it. You may want to ...

➤ **Refinance and obtain a new mortgage.** If your current mortgage interest rate is higher than the going rate, then refinancing is probably to your advantage, particularly if the closing costs are no greater than they are for getting a second mortgage or a line of credit. Part of the loan will repay the current mortgage, and the rest of the equity loan proceeds can be used to invest in your business.

➤ **Obtain a loan for a second mortgage.** If your current mortgage rate is better than the going rate, then keep the current mortgage and take out a second mortgage to cover your equity. You may need to use all of the loan proceeds from the second mortgage, or you may need only a portion of it now. If the latter applies, then a line of credit loan should be your choice. You will be charged interest on the amount borrowed.

➤ **Obtain a line of credit for a second mortgage.** A line-of-credit is a loan that entitles you to borrow up to the amount of the loan; you may not need all of the loan proceeds at first. Compare lender rates. Your local banks, savings and loans, and credit unions may be in competition for your loan business. E-lenders are now advertising. Have your attorney review all loan documents.

You may have a whole life insurance policy with a loan option. Part of each premium that you pay builds up a cash surrender value. If you have owned the policy for several years, then the loan amount may be used for whatever purpose you wish and the interest rate is usually low. If the loan is not repaid and you keep the policy, then the loan amount and accumulated interest will be deducted from the proceeds paid at death. Consult your insurance agent about this option.

Shark Attack!

Mortgages have to be paid or you can lose your house. Enough said.

Retirement savings in individual retirement accounts (IRAs) and defined contribution pension plans, such as 401(k), may represent another source of investment funds. You may withdraw some or all of your savings after you reach age 59½, without premature withdrawal tax penalty. However, any amount that has been tax-deferred income will be taxed when you withdraw it, and for almost all 401(k) plans and many IRAs, all of it will be taxed. If you are under age 59½, then consult with your plan administrator, because the law severely restricts borrowing against your account.

If you are going to run the business part-time, then you may be able to allocate part of your current salary as partial funding for the initial and operating budget. Starting small and working out of your home may make this a viable option.

The Risks of Borrowing from Family and Friends

When depressed Dane Hamlet said "Neither a borrower, nor a lender be; for loan oft loses both itself and friend," I believe Shakespeare's character was giving sound advice for you who are contemplating borrowing from family or friends. Your relationship changes to debtor-creditor, no matter what is said. But if you must borrow, then do so from someone who doesn't need the money, and may be very tolerant about your potential inability to timely repay the loan. If you do borrow, prepare a promissory note and a repayment schedule (and adhere to it).

Better yet, your grandmother (or some other benevolent loved one) may be willing to *give* you the money, perhaps as an advance toward your inheritance. He or she can have the joy of seeing you succeed in business and reduce estate taxes all at the same time; there will be no federal gift tax on a gift to you of $10,000 or less in any one year.

The Cost of Bank Borrowing

Banks are the money stores. They have it and you need it. Banks may be a little more willing to lend today than they were years ago, but many are still reluctant to lend to small businesses. You have to convince your banker that you are creditworthy. The banker will want to examine your business plan, particularly other capital sources, budgets, and cash flow. He or she will also want an appraisal of all property to be used for collateral and a lien search to ensure that the bank will be the first creditor.

You can expect a bank loan to involve the following provisions:

➤ **Amount to borrow.** The amount you want to borrow and the amount the bank is willing to lend may differ. You need to convince the bank that you can pay the loan back on time, and if you can't, the collateral is sufficient to cover the loan, interest, and cost of collection. If you have a bank loan officer who understands small businesses, then this job will be much easier.

➤ **Interest rate.** The interest rate on your loan is usually pegged to one or more points above the prime rate offered to top commercial customers. For example, the current prime rate may be 8 percent, and your loan will be two points above that, or 10 percent. As prime rate varies during the term of the loan, so will your rate.

➤ **Payment schedule.** The bank may want to test you by offering only a short-term loan, perhaps six months, particularly if you are not putting up much collateral. Once you establish that you pay your debts on time, then the bank may be willing to extend the loan. Set the payment dates to conform to your cash flow; if money isn't there at the first of each month, then agree to make payments by the tenth.

➤ **Loan fees.** Discuss the lender's loan processing fees before you commit to the loan. The lender may be flexible about these fees, particularly if you have investigated competitors who charge less.

➤ **Prepayment.** You should insist on the right to prepay the loan without any penalties. You may find an alternative source of financing that is more attractive.

➤ **Default.** The lender is likely to insist on a variety of events that can cause you to be in default on the loan. If you fail to make your payments on time, if you file bankruptcy (personal or business), or if collateral value falls below a set amount (or other enumerated breaches), then the bank can call the entire loan in default and immediately due. There may not be much room to negotiate about the causes of default.

➤ **Collateral.** Lenders want collateral—and the more, the merrier. The collateral may be your personal assets, including but not limited to your home or other real estate; motor vehicles; household goods; and stock and bond

Legal Eagle

Negotiate what collateral is required for the loan. The lender doesn't need to be over-collateralized. You may need to retain some assets free of a lien for other loans.

111

portfolio. The lender might also consider your business assets, including the building, fixtures, accounts receivable, equipment, and inventory. The lender will obtain appraisals for all the collateral (at your expense), then conduct a lien search to ensure that it will be protected from other creditors' claims against the assets.

Upon loan closing you will execute a mortgage against the real estate and a security interest (lien) against your personal property (assets other than land and buildings). The mortgage and security interest will be released when the loan is repaid. Obviously, this collateral will not be available as security for other loans.

➤ **Cosigners and guarantors.** Your signature alone on the promissory note may not be enough. If you are borrowing as a corporation, the bank will insist on your personal guaranty, since shareholders are not otherwise personally liable for corporate debts. The lender may require your spouse to cosign the loan, which may be difficult to get if he or she has concerns about the marriage lasting. The cosigner or guarantor runs the risk that his or her personal assets could be liable for repayment of the loan.

Once you pay off the promissory note, the bank will return it. Keep the original. Burn a photocopy of the note; its smell is better than incense.

Notes & Quotes

"Banks will lend you money if you can prove you don't need it."

—Mark Twain, writer

I have used the generic *bank* to include all lenders, but don't overlook …

➤ Credit unions.

➤ Savings and loans.

➤ Commercial finance companies.

Credit unions usually offer personal loans to members at favorable rates. Savings and Loans traditionally have been restricted to mortgage loans. Commercial finance companies provide consumer and business loans. However, all these distinctions have become less rigid in the past few years.

Small Business Administration Loan Guarantees

The Small Business Administration (SBA) has a variety of loan programs for small businesses. You may qualify for a SBA-guaranteed loan from a bank. One such program is called the LowDoc program where the paperwork is minimal, and it may guarantee up to 80 percent of a loan of $100,000. Under other SBA programs, you may be able to obtain a SBA-guaranteed loan up to $500,000. Check out the SBA Web site at www.sba.gov for a more complete discussion of its loan programs and requirements to qualify.

Investors and Securities Laws

You may have to raise money by selling equity ✗ (ownership) in your company. If you choose this option, you'll have no lenders to pay back, but you will owe stockholders dividends on any profits your company makes. However, you may have to relinquish some of your control over the company. Certainly never sell more than a 49 percent interest; if you own a majority interest, then you can have the final say.

Your Investors

You might begin with co-owners who pool their investments with your own, so that partners, limited liability company members, and stockholders increase the available business capital. Each co-owner usually receives an ownership interest equal to his or her percentage of the total capital contribution. Co-owners may be required to make additional capital contributions, as the business requires, or permit the business to retain a share of their earnings. Co-owners are not a likely source if you need a substantial infusion of new capital.

Outside investors may include …

➤ **Private placement investors.** Private placement investors may be looking at your company as an alternative to the stock market, since their ownership interest will likely require you to listen closely to their suggestions. They may have other investments that generate a tax loss that cannot be used without a similar investment that produces a tax gain.

➤ **Venture capitalists.** Venture capitalists usually invest in high-growth companies, such as dot.coms. These investors expect to receive a substantial equity interest and may insist on a significant voice in management decisions.

➤ **Strategic partners.** Another company may be willing to develop a strategic alliance with your company, and provide financing in exchange for equity. The strategic partner may be one of your suppliers or customers.

➤ **Public stock market investors.** The stock market might welcome your public offering. You retain a substantial block of the stock and the rest goes on the market. If your capital demands run in the millions of dollars, then this may be your only recourse. However, this book won't go there, because this is a book for small business owners.

Federal Securities Laws

Anytime you offer to sell an investment interest in your business you should assume that federal securities laws apply. For example, if you advertise in your local newspaper that you are selling stock in your company, this activity may be an investment "offering" and regulated by federal law. This section will not make you a securities lawyer, but it will alert you to certain dangers that could result in civil and criminal suits against you.

A brief excursion into the arcane rules of the Securities Act of 1933 and the role of the Securities and Exchange Commission (SEC) is important. The SEC has several functions that may relate to your small business offering, including ...

➤ Requiring substantial disclosure for securities offerings.

➤ Regulating the securities market.

➤ Investigating securities fraud.

Notes & Quotes

"October. This is one of the peculiarly dangerous months to speculate in stocks. The others are July, January, September, April, November, May, March, June, December, August, and February."

—Mark Twain, author

The SEC protects investors by requiring registration of a securities offering, unless there is an exemption from registration. Even if an offering is exempt, such as a sale to a current officer or director, the offeror cannot defraud the investor by making materially misleading representations.

The statute broadly defines security to include virtually any investment where the investor is not actively involved in the management of the business. Investments covered by the act include ...

➤ **Common and preferred stock.** If the corporation issues only one form of stock, then it's common stock; more than one form of stock may be another type of common stock or *preferred stock;* the corporation's Articles of Incorporation specifies the rights of the various forms of stock.

➤ **Stock warrants and options.** Stock warrants and options permit the holder to convert them into corporate stock. Warrants may be issued to permit a holder to buy stock at a stated price, say $25. If the stock is worth $50, then the warrant to buy it at $25 is valuable. A company frequently grants stock options to its valuable employees as an incentive. The stock works in a similar way as does a warrant.

➤ **Limited partnership units.** Limited partners don't participate in management, so they are passive investors, and need the protection of the securities act.

➤ **Investment contracts.** Investment contract is a generic term, which encompasses any investment offer that involves investment of money, with a common enterprise or business activity, and the expectation of profits, solely from the efforts of others.

Legalese

Preferred stock is stock that gives holders priority over the common shareholders in corporate dividends and liquidation. The corporation's Articles of Incorporation details all of the preferred shareholders' rights.

Several years ago, one of my clients invested $25,000 in so-called mortgage-backed securities. The seller promised a 12 percent annual return and claimed that my client's investment was completely secure because real estate was its collateral. Local investors were impressed and gave him over $3 million, which promptly disappeared. The seller violated both the registration and anti-fraud provisions of the 1933 Securities Act.

Start with the rule that you must register each security offering with the SEC, then look for exemptions for registration. You don't want to spend the enormous time and substantial costs to register unless you are going public.

If you want to raise capital from a few private investors, then several Securities Act exemptions are available under SEC Regulation D:

➤ **Rule 504** permits you to sell up to $1 million of securities within a 12-month period to any investor; form D must be filed with the SEC.

➤ **Rule 505** permits you to sell up to $5 million of securities within a 12-month period; there cannot be more than 35 unaccredited investors; no general solicitation is permitted; and form D must be filed with the SEC; this form discloses certain financial, historical and other information about the offeror.

➤ **Rule 506** permits you to sell an unlimited dollar amount of securities; there cannot be more than 35 unaccredited investors; the offeror must reasonably believe that each prospective investor (alone or with an investment advisor) has such knowledge and experience in financial and business matters that the investor is capable of evaluating the merits and risks of the investment; form D must be filed with the SEC.

➤ **Section 4(6)** permits you to sell up to $5 million of securities to accredited investors only, not to unaccredited investors; SEC must be notified of all sales.

➤ **Rule 147** permits you to sell unregistered securities to legal residents of your home state; no resale of the securities may occur for at least nine months after the last security is sold. This exemption is for purely local securities offerings. Since this offers no protection to investors, the courts don't favor it.

115

Shark Attack!

Never assume that you have an exemption from federal registration. Always consult with an attorney who specializes in securities law *before* you make any offer.

Legal Eagle

Get all the facts, especially if you're relying on an offeree's claim to be an accredited investor. Make sure you obtain the offeree's financial statement and investment history.

Disclosure is the operative word under the Securities law. Typically, you would use the exemption under Rule 506 or Section 4(6). You need to prepare a Private Placement Memorandum for each offeree. More precisely, your attorney must draft this document, but it requires significant input from you. This memorandum should contain the following details:

➤ Description of the rights of the securities purchaser

➤ Disclosure of the use for the proceeds of the offering

➤ History of company; its products and services

➤ Balance sheet and profit and loss statement

➤ Description of company management and their holdings and compensation

➤ Description of pending lawsuits

Verify all statements because the anti-fraud rules apply even if your offering is exempt from federal registration. Don't make any separate oral or written statements that may be misleading. Clearly specify all potential risks. Require each recipient of the Memorandum to acknowledge receiving it.

Don't take any shortcuts. If you did not follow the exemption requirements, the investor can sue for a refund of the investment. Likewise, there may be a criminal case filed against you by the U.S. Attorney, particularly if there are allegations of securities fraud.

State Securities Laws

All states have their own securities laws (known as "blue sky laws") that regulate the offer and sale of securities within individual state borders. You must comply with any state securities law where you make an offering. Federal exemption from registration does not exempt your offering from state registration.

Many state securities laws are patterned after the Securities Act of 1933, with disclosure and anti-fraud provisions. State registration is usually made through the state securities commissioner (often part of the Secretary of State's office). State exemptions vary too much to be detailed in this book.

The Least You Need to Know

➤ Develop a business plan that includes a financial plan.

➤ You may have sufficient assets to invest, or for loan collateral.

➤ Try to avoid borrowing from family and friends.

➤ Be prepared to convince the bank that you can and will repay the loan.

➤ Federal and state securities laws require you to disclose significant information to prospective investors.

Chapter 11

Finding the Right Location: Realty Bites in Leasing or Buying

---

In This Chapter

➤ A broker can help you find the right place for your business

➤ Leasing and renting: negotiating the best deal

➤ The ABCs of buying property

To be or not to be, that you've already decided. To rent or to own, that's the question. Either rent or mortgage payments represents a significant business cost. The right choice can save you money. And the ins and out of renting a space for your new business are what we'll discuss in this chapter.

Using a Broker to Find the Right Place

Location, location, location. If you're in the retail or food service business, you know that customers have to find you, so the right location can add thousands of dollars to your sales. On the other hand, if your business doesn't require a high volume of customer traffic, then the specific location may not matter nearly as much; for example, visibility isn't important for a market research company.

Searching for just the right place may be time consuming. If you've ever bought a house on your own, you may recall driving around a lot and flipping through seemingly endless for-rent/for-sale ads in the newspaper. To avoid this situation, I suggest that you hire a real estate broker to help you find your location and then assist in negotiating the lease or the purchase agreement. The broker can tap into a multitude of sources to find out what properties are currently available. To maximize his or her utility to you, use a commercial broker familiar with your type of business. A broker who locates office space, for instance, may not be particularly helpful if you are looking for a shop to sell sports apparel.

Legal Eagle

The landlord or seller may pay the broker's fee. If a seller has employed a broker, then your broker may split that one fee. The landlord who is eager to rent may be willing to pick up your broker's fee; after all, the broker put you two together.

Notes & Quotes

"Never invest in anything that eats or needs repainting."

—Billy Rose, entertainer

The commercial real estate broker should help you determine …

➤ What location best suits your business.

➤ Space requirements now and in the near future.

➤ Rental period and terms or purchase contract terms.

➤ Affordable rent or a reasonable purchase price.

For instance, a client of mine wanted to relocate to an office downtown. She hired a broker who found an excellent location, reviewed the lease, and suggested changes. The landlord agreed to remodel the office to meet her specifications, and provide a moving allowance. The landlord paid my client's broker's fee.

The Way to Rent

A lease, also known as a rental agreement, is a contract between the landlord and tenant. The lease can be for month-to-month, one year, or several years; it may be renewed, or the property purchased. The lease terms are negotiable, but some landlords are more pliable than others; a prime location commands prime rent and not much negotiation over the lease terms. An eager landlord may be willing to negotiate virtually everything.

The landlord will provide you with a proposed lease, which should act as the starting point for your negotiations. If you have a broker, he or she should review the lease and advise you. Have an attorney who is familiar with commercial leases review it, too, and make suggestions. This may seem like considerable trouble and expense, but it may save you dollars and avoid disputes with the landlord.

Your lease will contain a number of stipulations that you'll need to understand before you sign on the dotted line. Be sure to read through this section to pick up the important points to consider. Your lawyer will point out the rest.

The Rental Period

You want the lease period to be long enough to accommodate your current space needs. If you're beginning in business, talk with your advisors, especially about future growth and expanding space requirements. However, if you have been in business for a while, you should have a fairly good idea of your current space needs; then add a little for possible expansion.

Request the right to renewal for an additional period(s) at your option. The landlord will want to increase rent for the additional periods, so rely on your broker to suggest what would be a reasonable adjustment. Remind the landlord that your renewal will save him or her the time and expense of finding a new tenant.

The beginning date may not be a problem for most landlords, but if your building is under construction, then the landlord's date may be optimistic. If you are moving out of your old rental or advertising a date when you will be open for business, then adherence to the beginning date is critical. The landlord should pay you a *per diem* amount for each day you cannot occupy the premises; this amount should also cover any moving and storage costs occasioned by the delay.

Rent Money

Your rent is usually a stated amount per month, such as $1,000 payable on the first of each month. In shopping center leases, there is a base rent per month plus an additional rent determined by a percentage of your gross sales. That may be all you pay to the landlord, but there may be more, maybe much more, including …

➤ **Utilities.** You expect to pay for your utilities (telephone, electricity, heating, and cooling). But you may be required to pay for a portion of the common area utilities, particularly if you are located in a shopping mall. Have your utilities separately metered. These pass-through costs are usually allocated to the tenants for them to pay on the basis of the portion of space each occupies.

➤ **Real estate taxes.** The landlord pays the real estate taxes, but the lease may permit the landlord to pass on your portion to you. Property taxes vary considerably, even in the same city. Review the landlord's tax statements to determine what you will be paying. Remember, property taxes never go down.

➤ **Insurance.** You will be required to pay for your own insurance, and the landlord may pass on the cost of his or her casualty and liability insurance. Review the landlord's insurance premiums. And remember that insurance premiums always increase.

➤ **Repairs and maintenance.** Your building, its heating and cooling, and its parking lot require maintenance and periodic repairs. The larger the complex, the greater the costs. If you are renting an older building, count on considerable repair costs. If the parking lot needs resurfacing, the lease may require you to pay your share. These are called CAM costs (common area maintenance costs). Your broker should walk through the premises to get some idea of potential problems. Check with other tenants to see what costs they have incurred.

➤ **Advertising.** If you're renting in a shopping center, count on the mall's advertising expense to be passed on. The landlord will argue that you are the beneficiary, not the landlord, but that is only a part truth if he or she gets a percentage of your gross sales. Discuss the advertising costs with the landlord, then compare what you hear with the tenant's experience. If you are the most significant

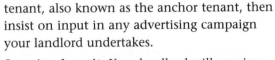

Legal Eagle

Require your landlord to estimate other costs in addition to rent, and check with other tenants for their experience. Without this, you cannot prepare an accurate budget.

Notes & Quotes

"Half the money I spend on advertising is wasted, and the trouble is, I don't know which half."

—John Wanamaker, businessperson

tenant, also known as the anchor tenant, then insist on input in any advertising campaign your landlord undertakes.

➤ **Security deposit.** Your landlord will require a security deposit, usually an amount equal to the first and last month's rent. The deposit is to protect the landlord should you breach the lease by moving out early or damage the premises (more than ordinary wear-and-tear). The lease should require the landlord to return the deposit within 30 days after you leave, and detail all landlord expenses that reduce the return of the entire amount. You may ask the landlord to keep the deposit in a separate interest-bearing account for you.

The Space

If you are renting a portion of the building, then the lease should specify your space, such as Suite 5, and include a copy of its floor plan. The base rent may be determined by the square footage, for example $10 per square foot, so double-check the landlord's calculation.

You may share space with other tenants, including restrooms, storage, and parking. Make sure that the lease specifies your rights to use each area. If parking spaces are critical to your business, put your requirements in the lease.

Consider the possibility of future expansion. You may want to specify in your lease that you have an option to rent adjacent space, if available, or move to a larger location in the building.

Condition of the Premises

Your broker should inspect the premises (or hire someone to do so). Everything should be in good working order when you occupy it. Avoid later disputes with the landlord over what needed repair by providing a list of repairs the landlord must make before occupancy, and make sure that the landlord agrees to the items and follows up by getting the work done. If the premises were damaged prior to your occupancy, make sure that your landlord knows of the damage; you don't want to have your security deposit reduced for damages you did not cause.

Usually the lease will require you to leave the premises in the same condition as you rented it, with consideration for normal wear and tear. What is normal depends on the business. If you operate a restaurant, the carpet is going to have constant use and will be well worn—expected wear and tear that you should not have to pay for when you depart.

Room for Improvement

You may be renting space that is merely a shell, waiting for the tenant's special requirements. The landlord and you will negotiate what needs doing and at whose expense. If this is your first business, then consult with experts to lay out the rental space to meet your business requirements. An office rental should be designed for efficiency; a retail rental should be designed to maximize customer service. If your office will rely heavily on computers, ensure that there is proper wiring.

Legal Eagle

Insist that all improvements be specified in the lease or an attachment thereto. Include drawings and detailed specifications, and insist that an architect or construction expert prepare and supervise the construction.

You may want to make your own improvements, in which case the landlord will insist that you get his or her approval. If you're entering into the lease, then condition your signing on the landlord's approval. You should also include a lease provision permitting you to make improvements later, subject to the landlord's approval that will not be unreasonably withheld. Improvements are usually retained by the landlord at the end of the lease. If you want to keep the shelving you installed, then provide for that in the lease.

Tenant's Use of the Property

In the absence of a lease provision restricting use, you may use the property for any legal purpose that is consistent with that type of property. Usually the lease will specify your use and limit it to that activity, such as serving food in a restaurant, providing insurance to customers in an office, and so on. You don't want the use clause to be too restrictive, however. For instance, if you think you might want to open a clothing store later, don't limited yourself in the lease to a sporting goods store. In a shopping center, the landlord may insist that your store not compete with other tenants. For example, if you sell office supplies, your lease may not allow you to sell computer software if someone else in the center already does.

Your landlord may insist on having the right to periodically inspect the premises, or enter to make repairs. The lease should specify that this occurs at reasonable times, upon notice, and will not interfere with your business activities. You should insist that the landlord include a *covenant of quiet enjoyment* in the lease.

Covering Your Liability Bases

Your landlord will require you to carry insurance to cover any damage done to the premises by you or your customers (your cook catches the kitchen on fire). The landlord will also want you to obtain casualty insurance (a customer slips on the wet floor and sues you and landlord). The landlord might set specific amounts of coverage. If so, review the requirements with your insurance agent to see if you may be able to convince the landlord to reduce the coverage and save you money. Please read Chapter 15, "Insuring Your Business (and You) Against Life's Disasters," for further discussion on business insurance.

Your landlord may also want to include a provision that excuses him or her for *any* damage to the premises. Consider this scenario under such a provision: Your landlord's employee negligently repaired your wiring and caused severe damage to your computers; the landlord would not be liable. The clause should be revised to read: "Landlord will be liable for its employees' negligent and intentional misconduct."

Complying with the Americans with Disabilities Act

You and the landlord are required under the Americans with Disabilities Act (ADA) to make the premises accessible to disabled persons (with few statutory exceptions). Your lease should include a provision stating that your premises and the common areas comply with the ADA, and that all improvements will comply with the ADA. You, or your expert, should review the ADA survey of your premises.

Assigning to Others

If you want more space than your current premises affords and you know someone who will move in, you want to be able to assign the lease to the new tenant and leave with no further liability to the landlord. If you want to sublet part of the premises because you have the room and could use the extra income, the lease usually requires the landlord's written permission. Try to convince the landlord to at least accept additional language to permit an assignment or sublease, which would read "Consent of the landlord will not be unreasonably withheld."

The Sign of Your Business

If you want customers to find your shop, make sure that the lease permits adequate signage. You need a sign outside your shop, and, if you are in a shopping center, signs on the landlord's signs. The landlord may require approval, so attach a drawing of the proposed sign to the lease.

The End of the Line

Usually you cannot cancel your lease before it ends; however, you should try to include specific provisions that would allow you to do so, for example …

➤ The premises are damaged and a portion is unusable.

➤ The premises are in a substantial state of disrepair.

➤ Road repairs make a retail store virtually inaccessible.

➤ Expected income was not reached within the stated period.

Admittedly, some of these clauses will meet with adamant refusal by the landlord. However, if fire or wind have seriously damaged the premises, then you should insist that the landlord immediately begin repairs and set a time by which the repairs must be completed.

Your premises should be *habitable* (fit for occupancy), and be sure to include that clause in your lease. The clause should permit you to notify the landlord of a problem that causes substantial interference with your business; the landlord should be required to promptly make the necessary repairs.

Road repair is the bane of retail stores. You might try including a clause permitting you to terminate the lease, or at least reduce the rent during the repairs if your income is substantially reduced.

If the landlord enticed you to rent based on projections of income, then the landlord should be willing to consider permitting you to terminate the lease, or at least reduce the rent, if your sales fall short.

Breach of Promise

The lease itself should specify the remedies available if the landlord breaches the lease. You may want to include a provision in the lease permitting you to contract for the repairs not performed by the landlord and reduce the rent accordingly. You may also want to specify that, if the landlord's breach is substantial, you can terminate the lease. For example, if you operate a restaurant and the landlord allows rats to roam the premises, causing

Legal Eagle

You should have business continuation insurance to replace income lost during casualty repairs. Please see Chapter 15 for a more complete discussion.

health code citations or a shutdown, then this should permit you to terminate the lease. In addition, you may sue for money damages for the harm done to your business.

The lease also should specify the landlord's remedies if you are in breach of the lease. For example, one tardy rent payment may not justify your eviction, but several may. If rent is computed on a percentage of the revenue and you misrepresent gross revenue to the landlord, the landlord could specify that he or she is entitled to the difference plus the accounting fees for the audit. The lease could also specify that, if you are seriously behind in your rent, become bankrupt, or significantly damage the premises, then the landlord will go to court to have the lease terminated and you evicted. In addition, the landlord may be entitled to money damages for past due rent and rent due for the rest of the lease period, as well as any physical damage to the property. If the tenant is evicted because of a breach of the lease, then the landlord has a duty to *mitigate* or lessen money damages for the breach.

Landlord Problems to Avoid

It is almost inevitable that you and the landlord will have problems. The disputes may be fairly trivial, such as parking in someone else's spot, or serious, such as needed repairs aren't being made. A good lease may reduce the conflicts, but probably not totally eliminate them. I suggest the following:

➤ Know your lease.

➤ Put your complaints in writing.

➤ Insist on a timely response.

➤ Threaten a lawsuit only as a last resort.

Don't complain until you are sure that you have the right to do so under the lease. What you believe should have been in there may not be, and the landlord will tell you so. If you are in the right, put your complaint in writing; be firm but diplomatic. A written complaint will put the landlord on written notice and will be helpful if you need to sue. Insist that the landlord timely fix the problem and set a reasonable deadline. Finally, don't threaten a lawsuit unless you intend to file; idle threats just escalate tempers.

Buying Real Estate from Acquiring to Zoning

You really need a broker to buy real estate, and that means *your* broker, not the seller's broker who will not have your best interests at heart. There are so many things that can go wrong when you buy real estate, even if it's just vacant land on which you will build.

You should rent the movie *The Money Pit,* which may be all too real for many of us who bought a house without a proper pre-offer inspection. It is also a cautionary tale for anyone who buys business real estate. Early in this chapter I talked about how the broker will help you find property; now, we'll see what else the broker can help you with once you've found a place for your business.

Mortgage Financing

Before you make an offer to buy real estate, line up your financing. Mortgage terms vary, so your broker and accountant should advise you as to the most suitable for your income. The mortgage rates vary from fixed (same rate over the life of the mortgage, such as 10 percent for 20 years) to variable (such as beginning at 7 percent, then adjusted based on a prime interest rate for commercial customers). The mortgage and mortgage note terms are usually not negotiable, but your attorney should still review them for such terms as late payment fees, prepayment penalties, and assumability of the mortgage, so you're not caught off guard later.

Get the Building Inspected

Ask your broker to recommend a building inspector and be sure you have an inspection conducted. Obtaining a termite report is just a beginning. You'll want to know about every loose nail and leaky pipe. Some problems may require minor repairs; others, like a collapsing roof or an inefficient heating or cooling system, may mean major dollars. You need to know just what you are buying and the inspection report should tell you. I discuss environment and zoning problems later in the chapter.

Find a Title Insurance Company

Your broker can help you find a title insurance company whose job it is to examine the real estate records for your real estate and insure against any defects of record. For example, if the seller has a mortgage on the property or if there is an easement for utilities, the policy will list those items. If the policy fails to disclose a defect in title, such as a judgment lien, then the title company is required to reimburse you for your loss, including paying off the lien to clear title. When you buy real estate and purchase title insurance, you pay a one-time premium based on the gross sales price. The policy will list exceptions that the title company will not insure, such as delinquent real estate taxes. Your real estate attorney should review any such exceptions before you close on the sale to determine if they are acceptable and won't diminish your marketable title. The attorney should attend closing and insist the policy be updated to the closing to ensure that no liens have been filed subsequent to the original title search. *Mechanics' liens,* liens used to pay those supplying labor or materials to improve a property, have a way of suddenly appearing at the last minute. For example, the roofer hasn't been paid for the new roof, and filed a lien against the property to collect the debt.

Recommend a Real Estate Attorney

A broker and a real estate attorney have different functions. An attorney must handle any title issues and an attorney must examine the title and is authorized to issue title insurance through a title insurance company. The broker may negotiate the deal and bring the buyer and seller together, but the attorney actually handles the settlement and all related tasks. Everyone needs an attorney for the purchase of real property.

Legalese

A **mechanics' lien** is a lien against real estate to secure payment to those supplying work, labor, and materials to improve the property.

Purchase Agreement Terms That Benefit You

You may want to outline the contract provisions that will be in your offer, and have your real estate attorney draft the final copy. If your offer is accepted, it becomes the purchase agreement. All the terms of your offer should be in writing, and it should include at least the following:

➤ **Offer.** When you make the written offer for the real estate, the seller may accept your offer, reject it, or make a counteroffer. You set the specific date and time for the seller's written acceptance, such as before 1 P.M. April 1, 2001. If the seller does not accept by that time the offer expires.

➤ **Purchase price and earnest money.** Your offer includes the price that you are willing to pay. If the seller has a broker, your broker should be willing to suggest a price that is somewhat less than the listed price, since the list price is typically higher than what the seller expects to receive. The buyer usually includes earnest money with the offer, which can amount to anywhere from $500 to $5,000, depending on the sales price. If you breach the agreement, the seller is allowed keep the earnest money, or the deposit you provide to hold the offer open.

➤ **Closing and possession.** The closing date and the date of possession are stated in the offer. There should be a *per diem* (per day) penalty if the seller delays your possession. At closing, the seller is required to deliver a fully executed general warranty deed conveying marketable title free of any liens or encumbrances, except those disclosed in your title insurance policy. Each state differs on what other closing documents are required; the attorney will list those in the agreement.

➤ **Taxes and assessments.** The contract will specify when you become responsible for the real estate taxes. States differ on the tax lien and payment due dates. You might have to pay the next installment, or the taxes might be prorated from time of closing. How and when taxes are allocated is important if you deduct the real estate taxes on your income tax return. Special assessments are typically imposed by your city for property improvements, such as sidewalks and sewers, and are paid for over several years. If such assessments were made on the property you're buying, the seller can provide you with the tax and assessment information, and the latter could be addressed in the contract.

➤ **Property lines and zoning requirements.** Any building and property improvements must not encroach on the neighbor's land. A property line survey, preferably one for which the surveyor actually pounds stakes in the ground, should be required. The seller should pay for the survey.

The real estate that you are buying must be properly zoned for your business. If you're buying a building to use for an insurance office, then its zoning will be different than that of a retail store. The contract should specify your zoning requirements, and you should confirm the zoning classification with the local planning board. Likewise, if the building is under construction or renovation, the planning commission will require permits, which the seller should have obtained, and you must confirm. If you are buying a tavern, then the building should be licensed for that purpose. Carefully check your *zoning ordinances*.

➤ **Title insurance.** We talked about title insurance earlier; the seller should pay for it. There are two types of title insurance—owners and lender's—lender's is required; owner's is optional, but recommended. They serve basically the same function, but lender's protects the lender and owner's protects the owner. Also, lender's coverage will expire when the loan is paid off. Owner's overage lasts for the length of time the owner owns the property.

➤ **Environmental survey.** You must insist on an environmental survey. Federal and state environment laws make the owner of the real estate responsible for any toxic waste cleanup expenses. Consider this scenario: Toxic materials may have been buried, or containers allowed to rust and leak on the property you're buying. Your worst nightmare is to have your property declared a super-fund site by the Environmental Protection Agency. An environmental engineer's report may be expensive, and you may have to pay for part of its cost, but that is money well spent.

➤ **Inspection.** Always have the building thoroughly inspected. If the inspection reports serious problems, the contract should permit you to cancel it and receive your earnest money. If the building is significantly damaged and cannot be repaired before closing, or if the state has begun condemnation proceedings to take all or an important part of the property, then the contract should permit cancellation. A feasibility study to determine the feasibility of the property for the buyer's intended use includes all of the above items (environmental survey, inspection, title examination, etc.) and a specified period of time the buyer has to perform these tests (30, 60, or 90 days). In the event any of the tests are unfavorable making the feasibility of the property questionable, the buyer can get out the contract and the seller must return the buyer's deposit and each is released from any further liability relating to the contract.

➤ **Nonperformance.** If the seller doesn't fulfill the conditions of the contract, such as providing a satisfactory environmental report, then you should be able to cancel the contract and the seller must return your earnest money. You may waive one or more of the conditions, such as minor problems in the inspection report, but do so only on the advice of your attorney.

➤ **Contract breach and remedies.** If either party breaches the contract—if the seller can't convey marketable title or you changed your mind about buying the property, for instance—then the non-breaching party may sue for money damages. The nonbreaching party may also sue for specific performance; this remedy permits the court to order the seller who breaches to execute the warranty deed, or the court orders the breaching buyer to make payment.

If all goes well, you and the seller will close on the sale, and you will own the real estate. Congratulations!

Helpful Sources

The federal government has several useful Web sites: Environmental Protection Agency (www.epa.gov), the Small Business Administration (www.sba.gov), and the Equal Employment Opportunity Commission for ADA compliance (www.eeoc.gov). Your local planning commission may have a Web site for zoning information. Title insurance companies and brokerages have brochures to help you. State statutes and some local ordinances may be on the Web or in your library. Your library and bookstores have several books on leasing and buying real estate, and several have forms you can use to help you prepare a preliminary draft of the lease or purchase agreement. Likewise, several software companies provide forms.

The Least You Need to Know

➤ Use a broker to find the right location to lease or buy.

➤ Don't just sign a standard landlord-written lease; negotiate terms to protect your interests.

➤ The base rent may be only part of your rental costs.

➤ Put all your lease problems in writing and respectfully request a prompt response from the landlord.

➤ Require a satisfactory physical inspection of the property for any real estate you buy.

➤ Your real estate attorney should review the title insurance policy and draft all contracts.

Part 3
Your Employees Matter

Sports analogies abound in our society, so who am I to flout tradition? You select your employee team. If your players are talented, then you will most likely win when they are properly managed. But your choices aren't unlimited and other teams don't help you with the cost by revenue-sharing. You should have an attorney and you should seek his or her advice when appropriate.

You will also learn about selecting competent employees without violating the myriad of employment laws. EEOC is a four-letter word—well, not exactly a word, but close enough. That agency administers most of the anti-discrimination laws. You don't illegally discriminate now and have no intention of doing so, but there are many traps for the innocent and unwary.

To select the best employees you probably should go through more elaborate recruiting, testing, and hiring practices than you may think necessary. For instance, you may want to use a simple lifting test to determine strength of someone applying for a dock worker position; but this test may be gender-biased if it doesn't relate to the job's usual lifting requirements.

Paying the going wage is only part of your employees' compensation package. Pensions and medical benefits may be expected, too; you need to plan for the maximum tax benefit for your compensation.

Firing an employee is never easy, but you'll probably have to do it at least occasionally. Sometimes the employee is simply not right for your business. You need to know how to terminate without creating a possible lawsuit. Read on to find out!

Chapter 12

Selecting Employees Without Violating the Law

In This Chapter

➤ Know all the major employment laws

➤ Recruiting new employees to your team

➤ Hiring the best you can get

➤ Using independent contractors instead of employees

In most cases, your business will require other people—employees—to make it go. You select, train, and pay your employees, and, sometimes, have to discipline or discharge a few. All of these employment decisions must be made within the context of federal and state employment laws. Some of the laws are fairly obvious, including the one that disallows the hiring, promoting, compensating, and firing on the basis of skin color. Other laws are more complicated, including those that require you to make reasonable accommodation for disabled employees. This chapter takes you through the hiring process. The next two chapters will focus on the details of employee compensation and personnel practices.

All the Major Employment Laws

Employment laws are not easily divisible into categories, but I am going to do so for simplicity. I'll give you a very brief summary of each law and then discuss each one in the context of your employment decisions, such as hiring employees.

Let's get started.

Illegal Discrimination

Congress and the states have enacted several laws that prohibit employment discrimination, among these are ...

➤ **Title VII of the Civil Rights Act of 1964.** This act prohibits discrimination by employers on the basis of race, color, religion, sex, or national origin. Employers are not permitted to discriminate against any persons in these so-called protected classifications when making employment decisions, such as hiring, firing, promotion, and compensation. Under this Act, almost all employees fall into one or more classifications. Title VII applies to any business with 15 or more employees.

➤ **Section 1981, Civil Rights Act of 1866.** This Act prohibits discrimination on the basis of race in contracts, which includes the implicit or explicit employment contract you make with any and all employees. Courts have broadly interpreted this law to include racial or ethnic discrimination. For example, an employer cannot refuse to hire a person from the Middle East because of his or her national ancestry.

➤ **Equal Pay Act.** This Act prohibits discrimination in compensation based on gender. An employer must compensate men and women with equal rates of pay for equal work. The real issue is the question of what is equal work. For example, an employer cannot pay a male sales clerk more than a female sales clerk performing the exact same tasks, unless he has seniority and is paid for his years of service.

➤ **Age Discrimination in Employment Act (ADEA).** This Act covers any business with 20 or more employees and prohibits discrimination against employees or potential employees 40 years old or older. Any employer decision made solely on the basis of this age category violates the law. For example, an employer cannot force an employee to retire at age 65 based on age alone; however, if the employee cannot perform the work, then that may be a valid basis for retirement.

➤ **Americans with Disabilities Act (ADA).** This Act prohibits discrimination against qualified employees who have mental or physical disabilities. The law broadly defines disability to include any impairment that substantially limits a major life activity. Employers must provide reasonable accommodation to a disabled employee

Notes & Quotes

"In 1998, the employed civilian labor force in the U.S. numbered approximately 131,500,000. It consisted of 70,700,000 men and 60,800,000 women, which included 110,931,000 Caucasians, 14,556,000 African Americans, and 13,291,000 Hispanics. The unemployment rate was 4.5 percent."

—U.S. Bureau of Labor Statistics

who is qualified to perform the job. For example, an employer cannot refuse to hire a visually impaired person whose job would include using a computer; a reasonable accommodation might to provide a special computer monitor for the disabled person. A business with 15 or more employees is covered by this Act.

Legal Eagle

Title VII of the Civil Rights Act of 1964, Section 1981 the Civil Rights Act of 1866, and the Equal Pay Act all prohibit gender discrimination in employment compensation. Title VII and Section 1981 both prohibit racial discrimination.

➤ **National Labor Relations Act (NLRA).** This Act permits employees to organize a labor union, collectively bargain, and engage in economic strikes. Employees have the right to elect a union to represent them and bargain with an employer over compensation and other contract terms, and, if the bargaining is unsuccessful, conduct a strike. An employer cannot discriminate against an employee because of his or her membership in a union. For example, an employer cannot refuse to hire an employee who strongly supports unionizing the company.

➤ **Immigration Reform and Control Act.** This Act makes it illegal for employers to hire undocumented aliens. Each employee is required to complete an INS form I-9 to ensure that the employee can work legally in the United States. The Act prohibits discrimination for national origin or for citizenship when the latter is an alien *lawfully* admitted for permanent residence. For example, an employer violates the law by refusing to hire any permanent resident alien.

➤ **State and local civil rights laws.** Almost every state has laws that parallel the federal anti-discrimination laws. Some states and local governments may have more inclusive categories, such as marital and sexual orientation discrimination.

The Equal Employment Opportunity Commission (EEOC) administers the federal anti-discrimination laws, with the exception of the National Labor Relations Act, which is administered by the National Labor Relations Board (NLRB).

Compensation

The following is a list and brief discussion of each law governing how you must pay your employees. Please read the next chapter for a more complete discussion of employee compensation.

➤ **Fair Labor Standards Act (FLSA).** This Act requires the employer to pay a minimum wage ($5.15 in year 2000) and overtime (one and one-half times regular pay) for any hours over 40 hours per week. Some employees, such as executives

135

and supervisors, are exempt from coverage under this act. The Labor Department administers the FLSA. For example, if an employee is regularly paid $8 per hour, and works 41 hours in a week, the company must pay the employee $12 for the 41st hour.

➤ **Family and Medical Leave Act (FMLA).** Employees who have worked for an employer for at least 12 months are entitled to up to 12 weeks of *unpaid* leave during any one year period because of the birth or adoption of a child, because of the need to care for a spouse, child, or parent, or because of the employee's health condition which makes the employee unable to work. For example, Jane gives birth and requests 12 weeks maternity leave, which she is permitted under FMLA. A business with 50 or more employees is covered by the Act.

➤ **Unemployment compensation.** Employees who are terminated because of employee reductions or fired because they are not compatible with their jobs are usually entitled to unemployment compensation under state law. For example, if an employer reduces the number of employees to cut costs, an employee given the pink slip can file with his or her state unemployment compensation agency for benefits. Employees who are fired for serious misconduct, such as stealing or assault, or employees who voluntarily leave their jobs without good cause are not entitled to unemployment compensation.

➤ **Employment Retirement Income Security Act (ERISA).** This Act regulates employee benefit and pension plans. An employee pension plan must not discriminate in favor of highly compensated employees, have substantial employee participation, provide for employee nonforfeitable rights in the pension, and require distribution not later than when the employee reaches age 70½. Qualified plans must conform to IRS and Department of Labor regulations.

Notes & Quotes

"The EEOC reports the following charges for fiscal year 1999: 28,819 were related to race, 23,907 to sex, 7,108 to national origin, 1,811 to religion, 14,141 to age, 17,007 to disability, and 1,044 to Equal Pay."

—Equal Employment Opportunity Commission

Health and Safety

The following is a brief discussion of the health and safety laws; later I will discuss each law in the context of employment decisions.

➤ **Occupational Safety and Health Act (OSHA).** This Act was designed to reduce workplace hazards and improve employee health and safety. Employers are required to provide a workplace free of physical dangers and meet specific health and safety standards. For example, if an employer permits employees to handle toxic materials without proper safeguards, the employer violates the law.

➤ **Workers' compensation.** Employees who are injured on the job may be entitled to state workers' compensation. The employer is usually held strictly liable for the injury, even if the employee or fellow employee is at fault. For example, if employee Jim was a little careless at work and a machine severed his finger, state law determines the amount the employer pays for the lost digit. The amount of the compensation depends on the seriousness of the injury. Each state establishes its own payment schedule.

Notes & Quotes

"Some people work just hard enough not to get fired, and some companies pay people just enough that they won't quit."

—Louis E. Boone, businessperson

Recruiting New Employees

Your first outside reading assignment, should you choose to accept it, is to scan the EEOC's *Uniform Guidelines on Employee Selection Procedures (1978)*, which can be found in the Regulations section of the EEOC Web site (www.eeoc.gov). While somewhat dated, the Regulations are a useful checklist for hiring employees.

Job Descriptions

Write a job description that provides objective criteria to measure which job applicants are most qualified. Ask your employees to help you prepare the description—they should know what the job requires. You should include in the description …

Notes & Quotes

"For it is the willingness of people to give of themselves over and above the demands of the job that distinguishes the great from the merely adequate organization."

—Peter Drucker, management expert

➤ **Essential job functions.** You need to list the core functions of the job. Ask yourself: What must be done by this employee? If you're hiring a shipping clerk, will the job require lifting and carrying boxes, and what would the typical box weigh? If you're filling a filing clerk position, does that job require typing or answering the telephone? By focusing on the functions, you can avoid the trap of excluding women as shipping clerks because they are not as strong as men or denying a person with a disability the job because he or she can't perform some non-essential function.

➤ **Qualifications required for the job.** Once you decide on the job functions, then determine what qualifications are necessary for the job. Skills: Does the job require

137

excellent typing skills? Education: Does the job require a college degree in accounting? Experience: Does the job require previous sales experience? You are looking for the best match of qualifications to essential job functions.

➤ **Nonessential job functions.** After you've determined the essential job functions, you should consider related functions that would be desirable but not necessary. If your shipping clerk makes occasional deliveries, you might want to list a driver's license as a nonessential function. Since this skill is not required, you wouldn't exclude a disabled person from the job because he or she could not drive.

Job Advertisements

Your advertisement should follow these general rules:

➤ Briefly describe the essential job functions.

➤ Indicate necessary job qualifications.

➤ Don't use phrases that could be discriminatory.

➤ Include the phrase equal opportunity employer.

You've determined what the essential job duties are, so put those in the advertisement in abbreviated language. For example, if you are hiring a secretary, you indicate that position, then state the duties: answering customer inquires over the telephone, taking dictation, and typing.

Rather than state that the job requires someone with a high school or college degree, you should specify what the duties of your accounting position entail, such as preparing profit and loss statements and corporate income tax returns. The reader should infer from the duties listed that the position requires substantial accounting knowledge; beginners need not apply.

Don't use the following words and phrases:

➤ **Young** indicates that persons age 40 or older are not desired, which violates the Age Discrimination Act.

➤ **Retiree preferred** may indicate that persons age 40 to 65 are excluded, which could violate the Age Discrimination Act.

➤ **Healthy** implies that disabled persons will not be considered, in violation of the Americans with Disabilities Act.

➤ **Salesman** should be replaced with *salesperson,* so that you would not be accused of gender discrimination in violation of Title VII.

➤ **Christian** suggests that you would not hire a person of another faith, a violation of religious discrimination provisions of Title VII; however, there may be an exception if you run a Christian school.

➤ **Single** may violate some state or local laws, and may also imply to the applicant that women with children need not apply, violating Title VII.

➤ **Fluent in English** may discriminate against persons because of their national origin, violating Title VII, Section 1981, and the Immigration law; however, if this is an essential job skill (proofreading manuscripts written in English) there may be an exception.

Do use the phrase *equal opportunity employer*. The reader gets the message that you do not intend to violate the law with your hiring practices.

Also, consider where to place the advertisements. You want to broaden your pool of potential applicants. Use a city newspaper or radio station that is read or heard by a large audience. Advertising cost is a factor, but most want ads are not expensive. You can obtain a diverse workforce by extending the advertisements beyond the suburban papers.

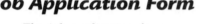

Legal Eagle

If an employer's workforce is made up entirely of one race, the EEOC takes the position that employee recruiting must extend to other races through the media that they read, watch, or listen to.

Job Application Form

The job application form you ask potential employees to fill out should ...

➤ **List essential job functions and qualifications**. The list of job requirements should clearly communicate your expectations, so no applicant can later successfully claim that you misrepresented the position.

➤ **Obtain basic applicant information.** The application form should ask for the applicant's name, address, telephone number and require the information necessary to decide if the applicant is the best person for the job. The application should list the position applied for, the education of the applicant along with any special skills, employment history, special training, entitlement to work in the United States if the applicant is not a U.S. citizen, and starting date.

➤ **Consent to background investigation and reference check.** This is to avoid any claim that the applicant's privacy was invaded, since he or she voluntarily consented. The former employers will be more candid if the applicant has consented to the reference check.

Note what you should *not* ask: age, health, number of children, marital status, race, religion, national origin, or gender.

Before You Hire

Once you have the job applications in hand, you begin the process of interviewing potential candidates, then double-check the information that they provide.

Shark Attack!

Resumé inflation, or padding a resumé with false achievements and awards, is unfortunately all too prevalent. If the applicant's resumé looks too good, you'd better confirm every claim.

Interviewing

You must prepare for the interview by reviewing the job requirements. Develop questions that focus on the applicant's ability to perform the duties, for example ...

➤ What were your duties in your previous secretarial position?

➤ Why should we hire you for this job?

➤ How have you handled unhappy customers in your prior job?

➤ How have you motivated people in your other jobs?

These open-ended questions permit a broader, more informative discussion than simple yes-no questions.

Just as your application form should not ask discriminatory questions, your interview should be free of these unlawful inquiries, too. A few illegal questions that I have heard, or had reported, are ...

➤ Are you pregnant?

➤ Do you have small children at home?

➤ How old are you really?

➤ What country are you from?

➤ Are you on any medication?

➤ Have you ever been arrested?

➤ Are you near retirement?

Investigating the Applicants

What you don't know about an applicant may hurt you—or one of your employees or customers. Be skeptical. Before you hire a person, check him or her out thoroughly. To avoid a claim by the applicant that you are invading his or her privacy, get a signed consent specifically permitting you to contact former employers, schools, references, and law enforcement agencies.

Legal Eagle

One question you may want to ask—and that is legal for you to ask—is, "Have you ever been convicted of a felony?" The answer to this question is particularly important if the felony were theft (and the job involved handling money), or rape (especially when you have female employees), or child molestation (especially when the applicant may be in contact with young people).

Former employers may be reluctant to give you more than the employment dates. They may fear a lawsuit for slander if they say something negative about their ex-employee. Perhaps the best approach is to simply ask them if they would hire the person for the type of job sought with your firm. If the answer is "no," or if it's evasive, then you have your answer.

If education is an important job qualification, request that the applicant provide official transcripts from the universities attended and graduated. If you require accounting skills, you want to see the accounting courses that the applicant successfully completed. Don't be surprised if some applicants claim a Harvard degree when the closest they came to that college was wearing its sweatshirt.

Notes & Quotes

"Employee theft, shoplifting, administrative error, and vendor fraud continue to cost the nation's retailers nearly $26 billion annually. Employee theft made up 42.7 percent of the total losses."

—University of Florida Security Research Project (1998)

References may vary from former teachers to clergy. You assume that these people would make favorable comments, but that is not always the case. I've had former students list me as a reference (without my consent) who have dubious work habits. So talk to these folks.

Your state may permit you to obtain an applicant's criminal record, and it may be prudent to do so. Since violence in the workplace really happens, you want to know if the applicant has been convicted of a violent crime. A conviction for drunk driving is relevant if the job includes driving.

Testing and Passing

You may be interested in testing for skills or medical and drug abuse. Approach either category of tests with caution.

Skills Tests

You may want to go beyond the application and interview to determine if the employee has the skills and knowledge to perform the job; testing may be your answer. Thirty or so years ago, standard employee written tests were in vogue. Courts determined that many of these written generic tests were discriminatory, because the courts determined that they had a racial and ethnic bias. Truth is, these tests weren't particularly helpful anyway because they were pseudo-IQ tests and not related to job performance potential.

If you want to test a future employee, focus on the essential job functions and determine what skills and knowledge the job requires, then test accordingly. Depending on the job requirement, here are some skills you might test for:

Shark Attack!

Lie detector tests are illegal in almost all situations under the Employee Polygraph Protection Act. Written honesty tests also are of dubious value.

➤ Speed and accuracy of typing

➤ Software manipulation

➤ Driving

➤ Engine repair

➤ Math

➤ Writing

➤ Proofreading

You want to test for relevant skills or knowledge. A writing sample may not be appropriate for a mechanic, but it would be for a newspaper reporter. A driving test is important for a person making deliveries, but not for an editorial position, although proofreading may be essential for the latter job. Both the typing and software tests may be important for the secretary.

There are personality tests from commercial vendors, but I would suggest you use these with extreme care, particularly if they ask about religious belief, sexual preference, politics, and other touchy subjects. I suggest that you contact a Human Resource director with a larger company to see what tests that they use.

Medical and Drug Testing

Don't require medical examinations of prospective employees because they violate the Americans with Disabilities Act (ADA). If you require a medical examination of all employees, then you may make the medical exam a condition of employment *after* you make the job offer. For example, if the job requires extensive night driving, you would want to know if the applicant's sight is uncorrectable and he or she has poor night vision. The conditional hire cannot reasonably perform and he or she does not get the job. Remember, the ADA only requires *reasonable* accommodation for a disability.

You are entitled to maintain a drug-free workplace. State laws vary on your right to conduct drug testing, however, so consult with your employment lawyer. If the job involves public safety, such as driving a delivery truck, then you may be able to test for illegal drugs after you make the job offer. Condition the offer on the drug test, and obtain the applicant's consent for the test. Also, hand each applicant your anti-drug policy statement.

Hiring the Best That You Can Get

When you're ready to hire the applicant, here are some final reminders:

➤ Don't make employment promises that you can't keep.

➤ Make sure that the INS Form I-9 is completed for immigrants.

➤ Comply with state law regarding hours for under-18-year-olds.

➤ Assess applicants only on objective job-related criteria.

➤ Consider using a written contract.

➤ Give each employee your employee handbook and benefits book.

➤ Make sure that all tax withholding forms are complete.

Employment contracts and employee handbooks are discussed in Chapter 14, "Keeping or Letting Go."

Independent Contractors Instead of Employees

Independent contractors supply your company with services under contract. They are not your employees even though they might perform services that an employee could provide. Typically, they are temporary workers, contracted for a limited time or task. These contractors have worked for other companies in the past and will do so in the future. The independent contractor is employed by some other company, which supplies the person's services to you, or the independent contractor is his or her own independent agent.

The advantages of using an independent contractor include not having to be concerned about ...

➤ Tax withholding.

➤ FICA payments.

➤ Health insurance or other fringe benefits.

➤ Paid vacations or sick leave.

➤ Overtime pay.

➤ Workers' compensation or unemployment tax.

➤ Anti-discrimination employment laws.

There are disadvantages, such as lack of control over the independent contractor's time or means of accomplishing the job. The independent contractor may increase his or her charge for services to cover the absence of fringe benefits. And there is the risk that the IRS, Labor Department, or other agency may insist on back taxes or penalties for the erroneous claim of independent contractor status, some of which, such as overtime pay, are the employer's responsibility to pay.

The IRS wants you to collect its withholding and FICA, so it prefers employment status. You need to carefully structure the contract to clearly demonstrate an independent contractor relationship.

Typically, the IRS will contend that there is an employment relationship if you …

➤ Control the time and manner of completing the task.

➤ Can terminate the relationship without legal liability.

➤ Furnish the tools or a place to work.

➤ Pay according to time spent on the job, not task performed.

If you exercise substantial control over when the person does the work and how he or she does it, then you've effectively hired that person and any independent contract you've both signed won't be worth the paper it's written on. So, how do you avoid this improper employee classification? Specify in the contract what services the person is to perform, but not how he or she performs it. You can set performance deadlines, but don't require office hours. Contract payment is based upon satisfactory performance of the tasks, not on time spent. And you sign the contract along with the independent contractor.

Helpful Sources

A wealth of employment information is available on Federal Web sites. The EEOC site is www.eeoc.gov; the Department of Labor's is www.dol.gov; IRS site is www.irs.ustreas.gov; the National Labor Relations Board's is www.nlrb.gov; and the Department of Justice site is www.doj.gov. Many of the Web sites provide downloadable pamphlets. Also, visit your state civil rights and department of labor Web sites for state laws and regulations. Cornell University has a good employment law Web site: www.law.cornell.edu. There is software available with employment forms and checklists, and your bookstore and library have recent books on employment law.

The Least You Need to Know

➤ Use the federal and state anti-discrimination laws as a checklist of what *not* to do.

➤ Employee recruiting should focus on the essential job functions.

➤ Independent contractors can save you money, but you must design the relationship to demonstrate independence from your control over the time and means of accomplishing the task.

Chapter 13

Money and Other Matters in Employee Compensation

In This Chapter

➤ Understanding the laws of compensation

➤ Salaried vs. nonsalaried employees

➤ Establishing an attractive pay package

➤ Creating happy endings with pensions and deferred compensation

You do get what you pay for, and employees are no exception to that rule. But you have choices in the way you structure your company's compensation that will benefit the employee at the expense of the IRS and allow you to exist and thrive at the same time. You'll also find that you must comply with certain anti-discriminatory laws. Furthermore, tax law and employment laws are intertwined, sometimes with straightforward rules, other times with confusion and complexity. Sound complicated? We'll make it easier for you in this chapter.

Compensation Overview

Money, in the form of salaries and wages, matters. Your employee usually looks first to his or her take-home pay. With any luck, this check pays the bills and allows for a little savings. Although each employee also wants the maximum of medical insurance coverage at the minimum of cost to him- or herself, as well as a myriad of other benefits, the one overriding employee question is "How much am I making?" One of your tasks as an employer is to redirect this thinking a bit, so the employee does focus on what you pay for medical coverage, group term life insurance, education reimbursement, and pension contributions. It is your cost and the employee's benefit.

In structuring a compensation package for your employees (and yourself), you should consider …

➤ **Salary and wages.** Each employee receives an hourly wage or salary, but this figure doesn't include the FICA (Social Security and Medicare) portion you pay, nor does it include the *FUTA* (Federal Unemployment Tax), nor the workers' compensation premium (covers workplace injuries). All of which add up.

➤ **Medical insurance.** Medical insurance appears to be on an ever-increasing upward cost spiral. Containing costs while maintaining sufficient coverage has to be one of your top priorities. Employees usually take coverage for granted in large companies. Many small businesses cannot afford such generous coverage. As a small business owner, you know that this cost could almost literally drive you out of business if you didn't contain it. If your employees complain, you need to remind your employees that the coverage the employer pays for comes tax-free to them.

➤ **Other fringe benefits.** "Fringe benefits" is really an odd phrase to represent a number of employee benefits. Some, like paid vacations and holidays are pretty much expected, and group term life insurance is frequently provided, too. You could also provide your employees with free or reimbursed parking, discounts on the purchase of your products, subsidized eating facilities, dependent care, educational assistance, or moving expenses. These, too, come at a cost. However, many are tax-free to the employee.

➤ **Pension plans and ERISA provisions.** Many small businesses provide some pension benefit. Often the business will provide a 401(k) plan, to which the employee contributes a percentage of his or her salary, such as 4 percent, which the employer then matches. The employer contribution is tax deferred (meaning the employee doesn't need to pay tax on it right away), and the employee's salary is reduced by his or her contribution, thus reducing the employee's income tax. The challenge is not just to come up with the money, but to comply with the pension laws, collectively known as ERISA (Employment Retirement Income Security Act). Congress, in its infinite wisdom, requires both the IRS and Labor Department to establish ERISA regulations.

Legalese

FUTA tax provides funds that the states use to administer unemployment benefits. States may reduce the unemployment tax on employers who experience stable employment.

Notes & Quotes

"Pay your people the least possible and you'll get from them the same."

—Malcolm Forbes, businessperson

➤ **Employment anti-discrimination laws.** You must observe federal and state anti-discrimination laws. Some are more obvious than others. For instance, you can't pay a man more than a woman for the same job if they both have the same employment background. And you can't discriminate in pay or in hiring because of race, religion, national origin, age, or disability. Other employment laws are more difficult to discern. For example, you must continue health insurance coverage for an employee who is on a medical leave.

Minimum Wage and Overtime Requires Punching the Clock

When the labor market is tight, you probably won't have to worry about complying with the minimum wage law. Unfortunately for your bottom line, you'll pay more to attract your employees, even those who work part-time in your fast food restaurant or as a custodian in your clothing store, typically low-pay jobs. The minimum wage for the beginning of the year 2000 is $5.15 per hour, but it will increase, as Congress periodically revises it.

Notes & Quotes

"The average hourly wage in 1998 was $12.77, and in the lowest paid wage category, retail trade, it was $8.75."

—U. S. Bureau of Labor Statistics

Coverage

In the 1930s, Congress enacted the Fair Labor Standards Act (FLSA), which requires most employers to pay minimum wage set by law, and overtime for all work over 40 hours per week The Wage and Hour Division of the U.S. Department of Labor administers this law.

There are some exceptions to FLSA coverage for your small business and its employees. While the law states that a business is not to be covered by FLSA if its sales are under $500,000, it extends coverage to all employees involved in interstate commerce. Since your business likely receives mail, makes telephone calls, or handles goods moving from one state to another, your business is likely covered by the Act.

However, certain employees may be exempt from coverage:

➤ Executives and certain managers

➤ Professionals

➤ Outside salespersons

➤ Certain computer-related employees

Minimum wage is not the issue for these employees; it's overtime. You and your executives may work as many hours as you mutually agree upon without receiving overtime pay. If your lower-level managers spend about 80 percent of their week administering their department, supervising two or more workers, making personnel decisions about the employees, such as hiring, firing, or promotion, and you pay them at least $250 per week, then they are not covered by the overtime law. However, describing an employee as a "manager" without the supervisory authority and pay described in the prior sentence will not exempt that employee from the FLSA overtime provisions.

Professionals, such as accountants, lawyers, and doctors, whose primary duties include work requiring advanced education, are also not covered by the FLSA overtime provisions.

If you employ outside sales personnel who regularly work away from your place of business while making sales or taking orders, and who spend no more than 20 percent of their time doing work other than selling, then the overtime provisions don't apply to them, either. Usually, you'll pay outside salespersons by commission, and commission work for these employees has no minimum wage requirement.

> **Shark Attack!**
>
> Don't underpay! Your state may have a minimum wage law that requires a higher minimum wage and provides greater employee coverage than the FLSA. You must check with your state department of labor for this information.

The FLSA exempts computer system analysts, programmers, and software engineers who earn at least $27.63 per hour.

Overtime

If your employee is covered by the overtime provisions, as are most clerical and factory workers, then you must keep an accurate record of the time each employee works. The FLSA requires you to pay a nonexempt employee at least one and one-half times his or her regular wage for all hours worked over 40 hours in one week. A week is generally defined at any seven-day period, and each workweek stands alone. For example, if Frank Factory worked 45 hours in week one, and 35 hours in week two, you would pay Frank for the five extra hours in week one. You are not required to pay overtime for any hours worked over eight in a single day, or for weekend work, unless the total hours for the week exceed 40.

Employee work time includes any time that you control the employee's activities. If your employee agrees to come in early or stay late to finish work, then the employee is on the clock, even if not literally so. Generally, the time employees spend changing clothes before or after work, eating a meal, or commuting to work is not covered; however, there are exceptions. For example, if you require an employee to come in after work hours to repair faulty equipment, then the commuting time would be part of his or her work time.

An employer cannot avoid paying overtime by providing an employee hour-for-hour compensatory time off for previous overtime work. However, an employer may rearrange a particular workweek, for example, 10 hours per day for four days. Also, an employer may be able to arrange for comp time in a single pay period. For example, Jane gets paid every two weeks; she works 44 hours the first week, and works 34 hours the second week. The employee is given an hour and one-half of time off for each hour of overtime worked.

Shark Attack!

You must keep accurate records to show the Wage and Hour Division. If an employee claims he or she worked overtime and was not paid for this work, you hold the burden of proof to prove him or her wrong.

Pay Practices to Avoid Lawsuits

Federal and state laws prohibit pay discrimination when not based on valid criteria. For example, you cannot pay a Catholic less than a Methodist, or an African American less than Caucasian just because they are who and what they are. However, you can pay more for an employee who is more efficient than other employees, or holds a graduate degree. The federal laws prohibiting employment discrimination were thoroughly discussed in the previous chapter, and all apply to pay as well.

Pay for purposes of the anti-discrimination laws include all forms of compensation.

Notes & Quotes

"I'm against a homogenized society because I want the cream to rise."

—Robert Frost, poet

➤ **Wages**. If the hourly wages of your female clerks are typically less than the males, then you must be able to justify each employee's differential or you may be violating Title VII of the Civil Rights Act of 1964 and the Equal Pay Act. It would be difficult to show that all of the females were less efficient or less educated, but you may be able to prove that all the men were hired before the women. Be careful, however; hiring discrimination may be the cause of this discrepancy.

➤ **Fringe benefits**. Review your medical insurance plan. The Pregnancy Discrimination Act (amending Title VII) requires that pregnancy-related conditions must be covered on terms equal to non-pregnancy-related conditions. Or your medical insurance policy may not be able to exclude HIV-infected employees, because the Americans with Disabilities Act covers that illness. Your pension plan can't require women to contribute more than men simply because they are going to live longer, statistically speaking. ERISA has certain nondiscriminatory provisions to protect low-paid employees. Even paid holidays may need to be reviewed; not everyone celebrates Good Friday.

Your Pay Package: Salary and Fringes

Your pay package is important to every one of your employees, and to you. You need to review your options.

Salaries

As I previously indicated, each employee tends to focus on his or her salary (or hourly wage). More is better, right? Or is it? For your more highly compensated employees, the answer is not so clear. Look at the tax rate for a single and a married employee (2000):

Single	Married	Percentage Rate
$ 0	$ 0	15
26,250	43,850	28
63,550	105,950	31
132,600	161,450	36
228,350	288,350	39.6

Each employee may be paying a lot of his or her salary to the IRS, which Uncle surely must appreciate. The employee can reduce the tax bite somewhat by contributing to a 401(k), which reduces the salary by the contribution. However, I suggest using a deferred compensation plan. Deferred gratification can save taxes, which to many of us is supremely gratifying.

For instance, if your employee is in the 36 or 39.6 percent marginal tax bracket, then perhaps offering a deferred compensation package is the way to go. For example, Hal Highbracket enters into an employment contract that provides an annual salary of $120,000; $100,000 is to be paid each year and $20,000 in annual installments paid after Hal retires, when he is in a lower tax bracket.

The deferred compensation plan would not be currently funded (no money deposited in the plan) because it would be immediately taxed to the employee; therefore, there is a risk of nonpayment by the employer. However, under limited circumstances, the plan could be funded without immediate tax to the employee, if the money were held by a third party and if it were subject to forfeiture, such as if the employee breaches the employment contract. Professional athletes often use deferred compensation to reduce their tax burden.

Fringe Benefits Plans

Congress wants to encourage you to provide fringe benefits to your employees so it has made your costs tax deductible and your employees' benefits excludable from their gross income for their tax purposes.

These benefits do cost you, and a few, such as medical insurance, cost a great deal. And some fringes benefit certain employees more than others. Some of your employees would prefer cash to any fringe benefits, and the tax law permits you to give employees a choice.

If you adopt what's known as a cafeteria plan, your employees may choose between cash and nontaxable benefits. Cafeteria plans provide the flexibility to allow each employee to tailor his or her pay package to fit individual needs. For example, if you have a plan that costs, per employee, $200 for group term life insurance, $2,000 for medical insurance, and $300 for dental insurance, the employee can choose to use those benefits or take the cash they're worth instead. A married employee who's covered by her husband's medical insurance might take the $2,000, instead, but she has to remember that the cash is taxable.

Notes & Quotes

"The average pay for a male college graduate age 55 to 64 in 1997 was $86,818, and for a female the same age was $40,203 (which would put an average married couple in the 31 percent marginal tax bracket); however, the average pay for all male college graduates was $66,393, and $41,626 for women."

—U.S. Bureau of the Census

Employee flexible spending plans are a variant of the cafeteria plan. The employee agrees to a reduction in salary to cover expenses, such as dental, that the employer can pay without the employee recognizing it as gross income. In essence, the employer pays or reimburses the employee for the nontaxed benefits up to the amount of the salary reduction. Use it or lose it. If the employee doesn't spend all of the money, the employer retains it. You can't include long-term care insurance benefits in either the cafeteria plan or the flexible spending plan, but you can provide it separately.

Fringe Benefits

Typical nontaxed employee fringe benefits include ...

➤ Medical and dental insurance.

➤ Long-term care insurance.

➤ Group term life insurance.

➤ Child or dependent care.

➤ Educational assistance payments.

Notes & Quotes

"$3,925 was the per capita expenditure for health care in the United States for 1997. $2,103 for each person came from private funds (medical insurance and out-of-pocket). The total health care costs were $1,092.4 billion."

—U.S. Department of Health and Human Services

➤ Employee discounts.

➤ Moving expense reimbursement.

Let's take a closer look at each of these fringe benefits and how they impact both you and your employees.

Health Insurance

Most employers who provide medical or dental insurance pay for a portion of the cost and the employee pays the rest. For example, if the employee's premium is $2,400 annually, and your company pays 50 percent of the premium, the $1,200 paid on the employee's behalf is not taxed to the employee; the employee pays $1,200, which he or she might be able to deduct from his or her own tax return as an itemized deduction (Schedule A, 1040).

Small businesses with 50 or fewer employees often establish a medical reimbursement plan. Your company would purchase medical insurance with a high deductible, perhaps as much as $2,000, which means the employee would be liable for the first $2,000 of his or her medical expenses. Then you would make a contribution to each employee's medical savings account (MSA) that the employee could use to reimburse him- or herself for medical expenses. The employee does not pay taxes on your company's contribution to the MSA.

Your older employees may be interested in long-term care insurance. The insurance covers the retired employee's expenses in a nursing home. Your company payment of the premium (or a portion) is not taxable to the employee. If the employee enters a nursing home, then not all financial benefits paid by the insurance may be excluded from his or her gross income. In 2000, the maximum benefit exclusion is $200 for each day the employee receives long-term care.

Group Term Life Insurance

Most of your employees need more life insurance. An inexpensive way to increase coverage is to provide group term life insurance. Your company can provide coverage up to $50,000 of group term life insurance without the employee having to pay any taxes on the premium. For each $1,000 of coverage in excess of $50,000, however, the employee must include an IRS-determined amount in his or her gross income.

For example, if your company provides an executive aged 40 with $100,000 of coverage, the first $50,000 coverage is tax-free; the next $50,000 of coverage has a formula for inclusion: $.10 per $1,000 coverage per month, or $50,000 ÷ $1,000 × $.10 × 12 (months) = $60, which is reported as income by your employee.

Shark Attack!

Watch your tax bottom line! Business owners are not considered as employees for the tax exclusion of fringe benefits unless the entity is a C corporation. For example, any fringe benefit payment to a partner or to a 2 percent or greater shareholder/employee of an S corporation is nondeductible to the business and is taxable to the owner.

Child and Dependent Care

Your company can provide child and dependent care to enable your employee to work. The value of such services paid for by the employer can be excluded from the employee's gross income up to $5,000, or a lesser amount if a spouse earns less than this amount. On-site child care facilities may be important to your employees.

Legal Eagle

Your employee's out-of-pocket child care expenses may qualify for a child care tax credit, which could be as high as 30 percent of $4,800, or $1,440, which is set by the tax law. The amount of the credit depends on employee's adjusted gross income and number of children in childcare.

Educational Assistance

Your company may provide each employee up to $5,250 for undergraduate education tuition, fees, books, and supplies. Usually, undergraduate expenses paid by the employee are not deductible for the employee. For example, if your company pays the tuition of $500 for an undergraduate accounting course, the employee does not have to include this as gross income; however, if you had no such plan and the employee paid his or her own tuition, this would be a non-tax-deductible expense. An educational assistance plan is a way to improve your employees' skills at no tax cost to the employee.

Employee Discounts

Your company may sell its products or services at a discount to your employees. The discount may be tax-free if the discount is …

➤ No greater than the gross profit for sale of a product.

➤ No greater than 20 percent of the customer price for services.

For example, your store sells an employee a refrigerator for $700, the customer price is $800, and your markup, or gross profit, is $150. The employee's discount is $100, which is less than the $150 gross profit, so the discount is not taxable to the employee. If the employee purchases a service contract for $80 and the customer pays $100, the discount is 20 percent and, therefore, also not taxable to the employee. Any discount in excess of the qualifying amounts means that the employee must pay taxes on the excess, because it is considered income. Your company could also provide a no-additional-cost service form of fringe benefit to its employees. For example, if you operate a hotel and permit employees to stay without charges when there is an available room, then the value of the hotel room is received tax-free by your employee.

Legal Eagle

Your employee may be entitled to either a Hope scholarship credit or a lifetime learning credit. Either tax credit is available to low and middle-income individuals for higher education expense. For example, the Hope credit may be up to $1,500 per year for the first two years of postsecondary education. You can obtain information about these credits at the IRS Web site.

Moving Expenses

You may pay for or reimburse your employee for his or her job-related moving expenses, and the payment is tax-free to the employee. Moving expenses include moving household goods, personal effects, and employee and family member travel expense to the new residence (lodging and mileage, but not for meals). If the employee incurs greater expense than your reimbursement for these moving expenses, the excess is a deduction from the employee's gross income (Schedule 3903, Form 1040).

Other Fringes

This discussion of fringe benefits isn't exhaustive by any means. In fact, here's another list of possible "extras" you can offer your employees:

➤ Lodging and meals furnished for the employer's convenience

➤ Employee achievement awards

➤ Athletic facilities provided to employees

➤ Employee transportation to work

➤ Child adoption expense

And you criticize Congress for not being generous!

Pensions and Deferred Compensation to Delay Taxes

Social Security may be there for your employees, but they won't be happy existing just on what it will pay them after retirement. Nor can they count on saving for retirement, because most of us spend up to our income (or beyond with the help of plastic). That leaves the pension as a significant source of retirement income. Fortunately, the tax code permits the employee to defer paying taxes on your company's pension contribution until he or she withdraws it. Your company deducts the contribution as you pay it into the pension plan.

Plan Types

The two typical pension plans are …

➤ Defined benefit plan.

➤ Defined contribution plan.

The defined benefit plan was typical for large industries. Joe or Jane would work for General Motors for 40 years, then would receive a stated benefit for the rest of his or her life (or the spouse's life). They could count on the check arriving each month, and could budget accordingly. GMC had its actuarial staff compute the payments over the recipient's retirement, then fund part of the payment and pay the balance from a portion of each new car it sold. Your business probably won't use a defined benefit pension plan.

Notes & Quotes

"Retirement is when you settle back and see which gets collected first—pensions, annuities, Social Security, or you."

—Roberts Orben, writer

The defined contribution plan specifies the amount that your company and the employee will contribute. A separate account is maintained for each employee, and benefits are based upon the amounts contributed and income that accrues in the employee's account. The 401(k) plan is a defined contribution plan, as is a profit-sharing plan, stock bonus plan, and employee stock ownership plan (ESOP).

Plan Requirements

To be a qualified plan, and thus tax-deferred, the plan must meet certain requirements. You should hire a plan administrator, such as an insurance company, to set it up for you, so I'll give you only a cursory treatment of this complex law. Basically, you'll have to concentrate on the following aspects of the plan:

Legalese

Vesting in a defined contribution pension means that the employee has a nonforfeitable right to the amount of the contribution. For example, if the employer's contribution has been $10,000 and the employee is 60 percent vested after five years service, then $6,000 is his or her vested portion.

➤ **Nondiscriminatory**. The plan may not discriminate in favor of a company's highly compensated employees, but may determine contributions proportional to pay.

➤ **Participation and coverage**. All employees who are age 21 and have worked for the company for one year are eligible to participate in the plan. The plan generally must cover at least 70 percent of your employees.

➤ **Vesting**. The employee is always *vested* in his or her contributions, which means he or she has a right to that money when he or she decides to withdraw it. He or she also must be vested in the company contributions according to certain requirements, say 100 percent after five years of service or a set percentage after three years and 100 percent at seven years of service.

➤ **Distribution**. Each employee must withdraw a minimum distribution amount (set by the IRS) when he or she attains age 70½ (and may begin withdrawal at age 59½). Any tax-deferred amount (and accrued income) is taxable to the employee when withdrawn.

Notes & Quotes

"The question isn't at what age I want to retire, it's at what income."

—George Foreman, boxer

Contributions to the employee's defined contribution plan cannot exceed either $30,000 or 25 percent of the employee's total compensation, whichever is less. Check with the IRS, because this money limit is adjusted to the consumer price index changes, and, therefore, will increase.

Since the 401(k) plan is typically used by small businesses, I will spend a moment discussing it. The employee may elect to receive up to a maximum $10,500 (in the year 2000) in cash, which is taxed as salary or wages, or to have the employer contribute up to that amount in a defined contribution pension plan. The plan may also permit the employee to reduce his or her salary (taxable income) with his or her own contribution. For example, your company agrees to match your employee's contribution up to 5 percent of his or her salary, which is $40,000; each of you contributes $2,000 to the 401(k) plan, and each contribution is tax-deferred until withdrawn. Under the employee's salary reduction agreement, his or her salary is reduced to $38,000.

An option for employers with 100 or fewer employees is a Savings Incentive Match Plan for Employees (SIMPLE), which can be in the form of a 401(k) plan. Or an employer may contribute to an employee Individual Retirement Account (IRA) in an amount equal to the lesser of $30,000, or 15 percent of the employee's earned income; this is known as a Simplified Employee Pension Plan (SEP). For a more complete discussion of the SIMPLE and SEP, as well as the Keogh (self-employed) plan, profit-sharing, stock bonus plans, and various IRAs, please read Chapter 23, "Wave of the Now: The Net or Home."

Helpful Sources

Visit your government Web sites. The Department of Labor (www.dol.gov) provides information about the Fair Labor Standards Act and ERISA. The Equal Employment Opportunity Commission at www.eeoc.gov discusses various anti-discrimination laws. Tax law is covered at the IRS web site: www.irs.ustreas.gov. For Social Security benefits, go to www.ssa.gov. Financial planning Web sites are a useful source of retirement and employee benefit information. Check out your state department of labor Web site. Your bookstore and library have numerous publications explaining employee benefits.

The Least You Need to Know

➤ The Fair Labor Standards Act requires a minimum wage of $5.15 per hour (as of year 2000), and one and one-half times regular pay for each hour worked over 40 hours per week.

➤ An employer cannot discriminate in compensation based on gender, race, religion, national origin, age (40 and over), and disability.

➤ Medical insurance premiums paid by the employer are tax-free to the employee.

➤ Employer pension contributions to a qualified plan are tax-deferred to the employee, who is taxed upon withdrawal.

Chapter 14

Keeping or Letting Go

> **In This Chapter**
>
> ➤ Creating meaningful employee handbooks and contracts
>
> ➤ Maintaining private employee files
>
> ➤ Establishing a safe and conducive workplace
>
> ➤ Working with workers with disabilities

Decisions. You have hired your employees and established their compensation, but now for the really difficult task—management. You need to develop an employee handbook to guide employee conduct and specify employee benefits. You need to avoid violating anti-discrimination statutes when you discharge or discipline an employee. That's what we'll discuss in this chapter.

Put It in Writing

"Put it in writing" is especially good advice for employers. Every employer should have an employee handbook, which is a handy reference for employment policies and employee benefits. Most small businesses do not have written contracts for their employees; the employees are at-will and may be terminated at any time for any legal reason, which you should state in the employee handbook.

Employee Handbooks

Prepare an employee handbook, and then give it to each new employee. The handbook communicates your employment rules and the employee's benefits. You can prepare a draft of the handbook, and then have it reviewed by your employment attorney. The handbook should be well-written and concise. I would suggest the handbook include ...

➤ **An introduction.** The introduction should include a brief history of your business and its products and services. You should also welcome your new employee as a member of your team.

➤ **Hours.** Your handbook should define normal business hours and include a reminder that employees may be requested to work overtime (for which they will be compensated at one and one-half their hourly pay for any hours over 40 in a week), as required by the Fair Labor Standards Act.

➤ **Pay.** Explain how the criteria for an employee's initial pay is established. Then discuss the procedure involved in receiving raises, including performance reviews. Since you are a small business, pay increases usually depend on business success and you need to emphasize the correlation between an employee's efforts and company success. If you intend to offer bonuses, explain how you'll determine who gets them and how much they'll be.

➤ **Benefits.** List and explain all the employee fringe benefits you provide, such as paid vacations, paid holidays, medical insurance, group term life insurance, pensions, unpaid leaves, and others that you intend to make available. Indicate what is required to qualify for each benefit, such as one year of service before participation in the pension plan. Any benefit mandated by law, such as the Family and Medical Leave Act, should be clearly explained.

➤ **Policies.** You should periodically review your employee's performance for purposes of retention, promotion, and wage increases; that evaluation permits the employer and employee to discuss successes and problems and construct goals. Address any absence and tardiness issues. Prohibit the use of alcohol and illegal drugs at work; you may offer a substance abuse treatment program to help your employees if it seems to be a pervasive problem. You may have

Notes & Quotes

"You can dream, create, design, and build the most wonderful place in the world, but it requires people to make the dream a reality."

—Walt Disney, cartoonist

Legal Eagle

Benefits, particularly medical insurance, can be costly. The handbook should state that you, as the employer, may modify these benefits at any time, so you won't be tied to a disastrously expensive plan.

a smoke-free workplace (or specify smoking areas). You should clearly state that sexual harassment will not be tolerated and may be a cause for dismissal; the handbook should specify the procedure in making sexual harassment complaints, usually through the immediate supervisor or director of human relations (or to you, the owner).

➤ **Grievance procedure.** An employee may have a compliant, legitimate or not, and should have a procedure beyond talking to his or her immediate supervisor to help resolve this grievance. This process permits an airing before the complaint festers into a disciplinary problem or legal action. If your business is large enough, you may want to establish a director of human resources to resolve all grievances.

➤ **Discipline and discharge.** Specify the kind of conduct that may result in discipline and discharge. The list should be representative and not exhaustive, such as making a false statement on the employment application, theft, excessive absences or tardiness, fighting, sexual harassment, insubordination, unauthorized release of confidential information, use of drugs or alcohol at work, and incompetence.

Shark Attack!

Clearly state in the handbook that an employee is employed *at will*, and termination may occur with or without cause. You don't want to be sued for a failure to prove the termination was with cause, so a broad employer's right-to-terminate clause is important.

The handbook should clearly state that you, as the employer, may amend it at any time and thus the handbook is *not* an employment contract. Emphasize the point by including a clause to that effect on a receipt the employee signs for the handbook.

Employee Contract

If your company does not have a written contract for your employees, I suggest that you consider providing written contracts, at least to your key employees. This is particularly important if you want to protect confidential information and prohibit the employee from competing with you when he or she leaves.

A simple employment contract should include ...

➤ **An introduction.** This should indicate the parties to the contract (company and employee), when and where you execute the contract, and should specify that it is an employment contract.

➤ **Period of employment.** If the employee is a new hire, then the period of employment should be relatively brief, for example six months to one year;

163

however, the period may be longer for a valued employee. This clause provides a degree of employment stability; however, the period of employment would be subject to early termination under its contract provision.

➤ **Pay.** You may specify pay based on a salary or hourly wage. You can refer the employee to the employee handbook for the fringe benefits. If the employee is to receive a fringe benefit beyond what he or she would receive under the handbook—such as the use of a company car—then specify this additional fringe in the contract.

➤ **Employee duties.** Specify the job and general duties for the employee. Since small businesses often have employees with overlapping duties, use a generic job description, followed by the phrase "and other duties assigned by the president or employee supervisor."

➤ **Confidential information.** Your business has customer lists, business plans, financial data, pricing lists, and trade secrets that must be protected. The employee should agree to refrain from disclosing this information to any outside person while employed and for a reasonable time thereafter.

➤ **Covenant not to compete.** The employee should agree not to work for any competitor during employment with your company. Further, the employee should agree not to work for any competitor for a specific period after the employment contract terminates. Courts will enforce this covenant if it is reasonable in time and distance. For instance, most courts will accept a two- or three-year covenant. Courts will allow the covenant to extend to any territory reasonably necessary to protect the employer, while not unduly interfering with the employee's reemployment. For example, if you have a salesperson whose territory is the southern part of Indiana, then the covenant for that territory can be enforced, but not one for all of Indiana.

➤ **Termination.** You may want to include the termination language from your employee handbook in the contract, listing various causes for termination, such as sexual harassment. Rather than litigate the issue of discharge for cause, you could provide for arbitration by an independent third party empowered to determine the facts and render a decision.

Needless to say, have your employment attorney review any employment contract you draft before you or your employees sign it.

Review Performance Periodically

You, or your supervisors, should conduct a performance review of each employee every year. You and your employee should use this as an opportunity to communicate mutual expectations. While the written evaluation can be useful to justify discipline or discharge, this should not be the primary purpose. Both the supervisor and employee should discuss improving the latter's performance, and how they each can best accomplish this goal.

Standard performance evaluation forms include documentation of ...

➤ **Quality of work.** You know quality work when you see it (or if you don't, your business will surely fail). Each employee should know what is expected and then respond accordingly. Your sales employee should generate repeat customers eager to buy from you. Your service employee should make your customer feel that your employee will drop everything to provide excellent and timely service. Your employee must know what is to be done and how it's done—then do it. This is the heart of your business. All else is really incidental.

➤ **Dependability.** "Dependable" is a rather old-fashioned word, but carries a message about the employee. Can you count on the employee to be there and on time? Does the employee follow instructions? Is the employee willing and able to work independently without constant supervision? Has the employee met his or her deadlines?

➤ **Attitude.** Customers and other employees appreciate genuine enthusiasm. My wife's first obstetrician called every patient his favorite; each one believed him because he meant it. Each employee is a team member, and the team is most successful when all have a caring attitude. The lack of these attributes can quickly poison your business.

➤ **Organizational skills.** If your employee approaches his or her work in a haphazard way, throwing everything together at the last minute, then he or she needs guidance in developing organizational skills. Your employee should be able to effectively plan his or her workload to complete the task.

➤ **Relating to others.** worthwhile is accomplished alone in a business. An employee who is successful in completing a task relies on other employees. If your employee can't enlist that help, then you need to examine the cause of this reluctance. The employee should be able to deal with confrontations when they occur and manage them diplomatically and successfully.

➤ **Communication skills.** "What we have is a failure to communicate" can apply to any business. The employee should have good oral and written communication skills. No one can effectively manage by mumbling.

Notes & Quotes

"Fairness, justice, or whatever you call it—it's essential, and most companies don't have it. Everybody must be judged on his performance, not on his looks or his manners or his personality or who he knows or is related to."

—Robert Townsend, businessperson

The evaluation form should also include a way for your employee to respond. Your employee should be able to include a self-evaluation of his or her performance: the employee's strengths and weaknesses, and what the employee needs to do to improve, and what the supervisor or you can do to help. The employee must be permitted to write a response to the evaluation, particularly if the performance was rated as unsatisfactory. Some forms use an alpha or numeric rating system for each category. I believe a narrative format is more helpful for most small businesses. A letter or number grade is much less informative.

Notes & Quotes

"I didn't say that I didn't say it. I said that I didn't say that I said it. I want to make that very clear."

—George Romney, business-person

Shark Attack!

Don't gloss over a bad employee performance on an evaluation form. If you then later fire the employee, you can be sure that the employee's lawyer will introduce the "good" evaluation in a wrongful termination lawsuit.

Employee Files

You must create a file for each employee, the contents of which should include his or her ...

➤ Job application.

➤ Employee contract (if any), confidentiality agreement, and covenant not to compete (if any).

➤ INS I-9 form for immigrants.

➤ IRS W-4 for tax withholding.

➤ Employee handbook receipt.

➤ Employee benefits.

➤ Performance evaluations.

➤ Compliments and complaints.

➤ Awards.

➤ Disciplinary actions.

➤ Attendance record.

Two words—"document" and "facts"—should guide you in maintaining an employee's file.

Document the good with the bad—just be fair. If an employee's misconduct warrants a written reprimand, put a copy in the file. Nothing will lose a wrongful discharge case quicker than contending the employee deserved to be fired and then not providing the court with any evidence of poor performance or disciplinary infractions.

Include facts only, not conjectures or allegations, in the file. A note from a supervisor alleging that the employee appeared to be intoxicated better have enough detail to warrant that conclusion, such as smelling alcohol on the employee's breath. Otherwise, if the employee proves he or she was under the influence of prescribed medication, you may be liable for defamation of character (slander or libel).

Keep the employee's file confidential. Assign some-one to maintain the file, then limit access to those persons who need to know (the business owner or employee's supervisor). In many states, employees have a right to review their files; if your state permits this and the employee wants a copy of a particular item, then make a copy for the employee— keep the original. No one else should have access to the file, except by court order.

When Employees Go Bad

Some employees need closer supervision than oth-ers. An employee may be chronically tardy or rude to customers or co-workers. An employee may have substance abuse or anger control problems. An employee may be incompetent. All these prob-lems are your problems, and they usually won't go away.

Discipline

Your employee handbook will state particular causes for discipline. If an employee hits a co-worker or customer, steals, uses illegal drugs at work, or commits sexual harassment, this would result in immediate discharge. The handbook could include a provision for progressive discipline for less serious misconduct.

The progressive discipline process involves, usually in this order …

1. Oral warning.
2. Written warning.
3. Suspension without pay.
4. Termination.

Shark Attack!

The Americans with Disabilities Act limits what you can do with medical information and the files are strictly confidential. Keep the medical files you have on these employees separate from person-nel files, and you should limit access to a designated person in the company.

Legal Eagle

The employee handbook should contain several references to em-ployment at-will. You may want to add the following language: "The employee and the company may terminate employment at any time. The employee should give the employer two weeks notice prior to termination."

The handbook should emphasize that this procedure is optional, and the company reserves the right to skip one or more steps, or discharge an employee. You should emphasize that this is a process to help to employee improve his or her conduct and retain employment with the company.

Progressive discipline isn't required, since most employees are employed at-will, but it may be useful as evidence in a subsequent wrongful termination case. You can

demonstrate your willingness to help the employee improve, and the employee's inability or obstinate refusal to change.

Discharge

Firing an employee isn't easy. You may have a sense of failure, even if the employee proved incompetent, although a sense of relief can easily be imagined. But there may be more to the drama. The employee may turn around and file a complaint with the EEOC or state civil rights commission, or sue for wrongful termination.

I suggest that you treat every termination as a potential lawsuit. Your documentation of misconduct or incompetence in the employee's file will help convince the EEOC or a court that the firing was justified. Your evaluations should reflect poor performance, if that was the cause for the discharge. If you wait until the lawsuit is filed to prepare your case, then you're too late.

Any time you discharge an employee, briefly review the anti-discrimination employment laws. For example, if the employee is disabled and unable to perform the work with reasonable accommodation, make sure that you document your efforts to make those accommodations. If the employee is discharged for sexual harassment, prepare an investigative file with signed statements from the complainant and witnesses.

If the employee has an employment contract and you terminate it prematurely, consult your lawyer to determine if you are breaching the contract. A well-drafted contract will allow you latitude in terminating the contract for just cause as specified in the contract, such as making false statements, misappropriation of company funds, sexual harassment, disclosure of confidential information, and so on. You must prove your termination was justified by producing appropriate evidence, such as fraudulent sales reports prepared by the discharged employee.

Many states prohibit employee discharge for certain public policy reasons, such as when the employer retaliates against employees who filed a complaint with an agency over alleged public safety violations. For example, if your employee filed a charge with the Food and Drug Administration that your pharmaceutical company has allegedly falsified reports, and you fire that employee, you can count on a wrongful discharge lawsuit.

If you decide to fire an employee, prepare a termination letter. The letter enumerates any compensation owed to the employee, health continuation benefits under federal law, and any severance package you offer. The severance package, which is optional (unless required by the employment contract), may include additional pay or continued payment of health insurance premiums for a period after termination, and an agreement not to contest any employee application for unemployment compensation. In return for the severance package, you may want to have the employee release any claims regarding employment and termination, including the claim of employment discrimination in violation of the Age Discrimination Act, Title VII, or other employment laws. Carefully draft this waiver (or have your attorney do so). I suggest that you use language similar to *ADEA waivers* for early retirement. As you recall, by signing the waiver the employee agrees not to later file an ADEA complaint against the employer.

The Rights of Ex-Employees

Your ex-employee and dependents may be entitled to continued health care insurance under your company policy according to the Consolidated Omnibus Budget Reconciliation Act, more under-

Legalese

The **ADEA waiver** permits employees upon retirement to waive any alleged ADEA violations, but the employee must be advised to consult an attorney, allowed at least 21 days to consider the agreement, and permitted to revoke within seven days after execution of the agreement.

standably referred to as COBRA. The length of coverage varies from 18 to 36 months, depending upon the cause of the termination. The employee must pay all the premiums for this coverage.

Your ex-employee may be entitled to state unemployment compensation. The employee files a claim and the agency determines if he or she is eligible. The determination may be appealed within the agency and a hearing held. Unless the employee committed a serious violation, such as sexual harassment or theft, the law typically permits the ex-employee to receive the compensation. Your unemployment tax rate probably will be increased only slightly, at the worst, so fighting the claim may not be worth the time and cost involved.

To soften the blow of a discharge, you might suggest to the employee that he or she resign. If possible, you could offer to help the employee find a new job, and provide a favorable reference. Sometimes employees who don't succeed for you may be very successful in a different environment. A friend hired a paralegal for his law firm; this was her first job and she insisted that he double-check everything, which he wasn't particularly happy about doing. She moved to a more structured firm and succeeded.

Sexual Harassment Is Serious Business

Your company must have a written policy against sexual harassment and then enforce it, even if federal law does not cover you because you have fewer than 15 employees. Sexual harassment violates Title VII of the Civil Rights Act of 1964. Sexual harassment can involve a request for sexual favors or creating a hostile workplace environment. The EEOC and courts will find sexual harassment exits if …

169

➤ The conduct is gender-related.

➤ The victim has not consented to sexual advances nor participated in perpetuating a hostile work environment.

➤ The conduct has affected the victim's job.

Sexual harassment is actionable whether the harasser is of the opposite sex or the same sex; both males and females can bring sexual harassment charges.

Sexual harassment exists if an employee is threatened with adverse employment consequences, including the prospect of being fired or demoted if he or she doesn't perform sexual favors; or if the employee is offered job benefits in return for sexual favors. The latter form of sexual harassment is referred to as *quid pro quo* ("something for something"). Usually it is the employee's supervisor who commits this form of harassment, but courts will hold the company liable for any adverse employment effect on the victim.

The hostile workplace environment exists when verbal or physical conduct of a sexual nature has the purpose or effect of creating an intimidating, hostile, or offensive environment at work. This may include unwanted and offensive sexual contact, solicitation, or innuendoes. The employer will be liable if it knew of the offensive conduct and tolerated it, or should have known (complaints were lodged with supervisors and nothing was done to correct the hostile environment).

Your sexual harassment policy should contain ...

➤ A statement prohibiting sexual harassment.

➤ A procedure to file complaints.

➤ Discipline procedures for the harasser.

Legal Eagle

Thoroughly investigate any claim of sexual harassment. If harassment if found, then the harasser should be punished; if no harassment is discovered, then the alleged harasser should be clearly exonerated in your findings.

The employee handbook should inform a harassment victim that he or she can complain to the supervisor or another designated person within the company. This alternative allows the alleged victim to choose, which is important if the supervisor or designated person is the harasser.

The employee handbook should let the harasser know that misconduct could result in discipline or discharge.

Consider training your employees to be aware of how their conduct may affect others. What may seem like a cute off-color story or a funny racial joke to some people may be deeply offensive to others.

Safety on the Job

You want a safe environment for your employees, so the workplace should be free of physical danger. But injuries do occur, and the injured employee may be entitled to compensation.

Occupational Safety and Health Act (OSHA)

OSHA was enacted to reduce workplace injuries by creating a safer environment. OSHA requires employers to eliminate hazards likely to cause death or serious injury. For example, I had a client who was employed to rewire a steel plant; the employer permitted high voltage wire to be strung everywhere, including bare wire across water puddles—an electrocution waiting to happen. OSHA has established safety standards for certain work environments or industries. You can visit the OSHA Web site (www.dol.gov) to view some of these standards.

Usually, OSHA will not inspect your business unless an employee has complained, there has been a serious injury or death, or the workplace is inherently dangerous (for example, produces toxic chemicals). If OSHA cites your company for a violation, then you may contest the citation with the OSHA, and that decision is subject to court review.

Legal Eagle

If your company handles toxic chemicals or workers are exposed to certain hazards, such as noise or air pollution, your workers' compensation insurance carrier should suggest ways to conform to the OSHA regulations and make the environment safer.

Workers' Compensation

Workers' compensation is a state law that provides income and medical expenses for employees who are injured or develop illnesses that are work-related. For example, if your employee slips on a wet floor at work, or drills a hole in his or her hand rather than the metal, or suffers a respiratory illness because of poor ventilation, the employee is eligible for workman's compensation.

Most small businesses buy workers' compensation insurance to cover their potential liability, although state law may allow your company to be self-insured; however self-insurance is too risky for anyone except large companies. If your employee is injured at work, your company is strictly liable and the employee will be compensated according

Legal Eagle

Insist that your workers' comp insurance carrier inspect your business and suggest ways to reduce risks of employee injury; then follow its advice. You will save money on the premiums and make the workplace safer.

to a fixed state schedule of benefits. For example, if your employee negligently cuts off his little finger on the left hand, the schedule will indicate the money benefit for that specific injury. The employee's or fellow employee's negligence is not a defense to liability; however, if the injured employee was intoxicated or deliberately inflicted the injury, the company may use that as a defense.

Your injured employee cannot successfully sue your company or another employee who caused the injury; the sole remedy is the benefit from workers' compensation.

Workers with Disabilities

Congress passed the Americans with Disabilities Act (ADA) to prohibit discrimination against persons with disabilities. Employers violate the ADA if they discriminate in employment practices based upon a person's disability. This includes all employment decisions, such as hiring, firing, discipline, compensation, and promotion. A person is considered disabled under the ADA, if he or she …

➤ Has a physical or mental impairment that substantially limits one or more major life activities; or

➤ Has a record of being disabled; or

➤ Is regarded as being disabled.

Legal Eagle

Disability under the ADA does not include the illegal use of drugs, homosexuality, sexual behavior disorders, or compulsive gambling.

Disability is broadly defined. Examples of life activities covered by the ADA include walking, talking, seeing, hearing, breathing, and learning. Mental and psychological disorders are also considered disabilities. AIDS is covered by the Act, too. A temporary condition, such a pulled back muscle, would not be covered, but a severe and permanent back injury that limits the employee's activities would be. If the person has a record of a disability, such as a persistent mental illness, then he or she is covered. Likewise, a person who the employer perceives as disabled is covered. For example, a salesclerk who was disfigured by an automobile accident may be regarded as impaired if customers refused to buy from that clerk.

ADA requires the employer to make reasonable accommodations to enable the disabled to work. This may include making the workplace accessible, modifying equipment, and changing work schedules. For example, you may have to redesign the computer workstation to accommodate a wheelchair-bound employee.

The disabled person with reasonable accommodation must be able to perform the essential functions of the job, but the employer does not have to restructure the job. For example, if the dockworker is required to lift packages on to a conveyor belt, and that is an essential job function, you don't have to eliminate the task even though it would exclude a disabled person from getting the job.

Further, the employer is not required to accommodate a disabled person if it would place an undue hardship on the employer. For example, if your software development business is located on the second floor of an older building with no elevator, you may assert that the substantial cost of installing an elevator would be an undue hardship (excessive cost) to your small business. Obviously, General Motors could not claim undue hardship in a similar situation.

Labor Unions

Most small businesses are not the target of union organizing attempts, but you should know the rudiments of the National Labor Relations Act (NLRA) just in case.

The NLRA gives employees the right to act together to form or join a union, present employees' grievances, bargain for a labor agreement, go on strike and picket the employer. Employees protected by the Act are most nonmanagement personnel, usually hourly employees.

If 30 percent of the employees file union election authorization cards with the National Labor Relations Board (NLRB), then the agency will conduct a secret ballot election. Meanwhile, you can voice your position: You may oppose the election, for example, and contest union organizer claims of low pay or poor working conditions by favorably comparing their jobs with those of your competitors. You may point out that unions control employee grievances and employees may have to pay substantial dues. What you may not do is …

Legal Eagle

Federal tax law may allow an employer certain tax credits for hiring disabled workers and tax deductions for removing barriers to access.

Notes & Quotes

"Approximately 16 million out of 102 million employees are unionized in the United States."

—*The New York Times Almanac 2000*

➤ Fire or discipline employees for organizing.

➤ Increase or decrease compensation during the election period.

➤ Ask individual employees how he or she will vote.

➤ Threaten to move the company if the union wins.

These illegal acts are called unfair labor practices. If your company violates the law and the union loses the election, the NLRB may order another election, or if there has been serious employer misconduct, certify the union as the exclusive bargaining representative for your employees.

If the union wins and is certified, then you have to bargain with it for a labor agreement. Once the union is in, obviously you lose some control over employment decisions. The best way to avoid unionizing is to treat your employees fairly and respond immediately to workplace complaints. Arbitrary conduct is an invitation to a union.

The Least You Need to Know

➤ Every employer should prepare an employee handbook.

➤ Employees should sign an agreement not to disclose confidential information.

➤ Document all employee misconduct.

➤ Every employer must have a policy prohibiting sexual harassment.

➤ Employers are strictly liable for employee workplace injuries.

Part 4

Running the Business

You're already a risk-taker or you wouldn't be in business. But, to the extent that it's feasible and affordable for you, you want to minimize those risks. Your insurance dollar can be stretched only so far. Insure against those risks that can destroy your business, like your building being blown away by a tornado.

In this part, you'll also learn about the fine print in contracts that take away what the large print gives you. Knowledge of the basics of contract law may help you get the best deal when you negotiate with a supplier or customer.

Negligent employees can cause a business measurable harm, such as an employee rear-ending another driver; some of these risks you can insure against, while others, like an allegedly defective product, may result in a lawsuit. You need to know the limits of your liability.

Yogi Berra, that eminent baseball sage, observed that the other team could make trouble for us if they win. How true, particularly in a law court. You don't want to go to court, but if you must, then you'd better know the basics of litigation. I'll take you through the courts. Truth often doesn't emerge in a trial unless it's enticed.

Chapter 15

Insuring Your Business (and You) Against Life's Disasters

In This Chapter

➤ Covering insurance basics

➤ Why your business needs liability protection and how to save time and money if your business is interrupted

➤ Protecting your employees with life and health insurance and saving premium costs

➤ Understanding your tax liabilities and responsibilities

Risk. You determine how much risk you are willing to assume, then buy insurance to cover the risk you want someone else to take. The someone else is, of course, an insurance company. Its share of the risk costs you a premium—the greater the risk, the higher the premium. In this chapter, we'll spell out the basics of insurance for the small business owner.

Insurance Basics from A to Z

The insurance industry is based on determining risk. You must consider your business risks and what you want to cover. Some risks are insurable at a reasonable premium, such as life insurance for your employees and insurance to protect your business, including liability and casualty. Some coverage is necessary to hold on to employees, such as health insurance, which can start to get pricey. And some risks come with a high premium, including insurance against environmental claims.

Once you apply, you'll receive a contract that includes the following …

➤ Effective date.

➤ Basic duties and rights.

➤ Contract terms.

➤ Cancellation.

➤ Insurer's nonpayment.

➤ Riders.

You are the insured; the insurance company is the insurer. The type of insurance—life insurance or casualty, for example—indicates the general purpose of the insurance. Coverage denotes what the policy protects; liability insurance, for instance, protects against the legal responsibility imposed on the insured because of an injury to the person or property of another.

Let's take a look at each part of the insurance process and contract now.

Application and Effective Date

The application becomes part of the policy when accepted by the insurance company. Any material misrepresentations that you make, such as health condition in a life insurance application, may be grounds for voiding the policy. The insurance coverage begins when the policy says so. If the policy is purchased from an insurance company agent, then coverage usually begins when the premium is first paid, or may be conditionally begun, subject to acceptance by the insurer's home office.

Basic Duties and Rights

The insurance company and the insured are parties to a contract and all the duties and rights that the contract provides. Both parties must act in good faith. You must disclose everything that is required for the insurance company to evaluate the risk, such as any toxic materials your business produces. Once the insurance company has accepted the risk, it must pay if the risk occurs, unless the policy provides an exception; for instance, fire insurance doesn't cover arson by the insured.

Contract Terms

The insurance contract will specify what the policy covers. The policy may provide exclusions from coverage; for example, a life insurance policy might exclude a suicide within one year of the effective date. (I will discuss coverage and exclusions from policies later.) The policy may specify certain deductible amounts by the employee, such as the first $20 of any doctor's office visit.

Each state regulates the insurance policies sold within the state, so state-mandated provisions may vary. For example, if the state requires what's known as a notice-prejudice claim, then the insurance company cannot reject a claim that was filed late unless the delay financially harmed the insurance company.

The insured must promptly notify the insurance company when an insured event occurs (let's say a fire) and then file proof of the claim—say, fire damage to building and contents. The policy may be what's called an occurrence claim policy, which provides coverage when the insured event occurs even if the claim is made later. For example, if you had a fire on April 1, 2000, when policy A was in effect, but filed the claim with Company A after you switched to Company B, then Company A remains liable under an occurrence policy. Contrast this with a claims-made policy, which covers only claims actually made during the time the insurance was in force. In the prior example, you would have to file the fire damage claim before policy A expires.

If you have multiple policies that cover the risk, then each insurer is liable only for its proportionate share. You can't collect for more than 100 percent of the damage.

Any dispute may be subject to appraisal and arbitration. For example, if your insurance covers the fair market value of your building that is destroyed by fire, and there is a disagreement as to its value, then an appraiser may be selected to resolve the difference. Any disputes over the insurance contract may be resolved by an independent arbiter, rather than through a lawsuit (although that may come later).

Cancellation

You can cancel an insurance policy at any time, but the insurance company can cancel under limited circumstances. You have to notify the company to cancel, and you may be entitled to a refund of any premium paid in advance and not yet earned, such as canceling a six-month casualty policy after only two months.

The insurer may cancel only according to the terms of the policy. For example, if you fail to pay your premiums, the insurer can cancel the policy

Legal Eagle

Since the insurance policy terms are not usually negotiable, courts generally interpret ambiguous provisions in favor of the insured. However, make sure that you understand all the important terms; seek the advice of an independent insurance agent.

after giving you due notice. State laws may govern notice and cancellation rights. If a policy has a stated period, such as five years for a term life insurance policy, the insurance company could refuse to renew the policy for an additional period.

Insurer's Nonpayment

An insurance company may raise a defense to payment under the policy. The insured may have misrepresented a fact on his or her application—if the business claimed to be a retail store, for instance, when it was a print shop with toxic materials. The insured may have lacked an insurable interest (legal right to insure against a risk), such as offering a life insurance policy on a friend. Misconduct by the insured may be grounds for nonpayment, including, say, arson by the insured of his or her own building.

Since the insurance company must act in good faith, the insured is entitled to prompt consideration of any claim, and notice of claim denial with an honest and complete explanation of the reasons for the denial. If the denial is made in bad faith, including denial of a health insurance benefit for the sole purpose of saving money, then this wrongful conduct may be the basis of a lawsuit.

Riders

The policy provides basic coverage. If you want additional benefits, you may be able to supplement the coverage with a rider. If you have a property damage policy, you may want a rider to include consequential loss coverage, such as loss of use of the property being replaced. For example, you have a fire insurance policy that covers rebuilding the structure; you may want a rider to cover lost income while the store is being rebuilt.

Property Coverage That Is Adequate

Property insurance covers direct loss to real and personal property. If you decide to purchase property insurance, here are some factors to consider:

➤ **Property covered.** Review the policy to ensure that it covers all the property you intend to cover. If the policy covers the building, does that coverage include its contents, including fixtures, equipment, inventory, and other personal property used by the business? If there has been an addition to the building since the original policy was signed, then add that to the policy coverage. If property is located off the business premises, then consider a floater policy, which would cover equipment and inventory at a trade show or in transit, for instance.

➤ **Perils covered.** Your basic coverage for fire insurance, for example, covers the perils of direct loss by fire and lightning, and certain types of smoke damage. You may purchase an extended coverage policy that insures against wind damage, hail, explosion, riot, and damage to vehicles owned or operated by the business. However, a basic policy may not cover such perils as theft. An "all risk or open perils" policy covers any kind of damage to the covered property that results from any cause not specifically excluded by the policy.

➤ **Amount of coverage.** You should insure at 100 percent of the loss. If you want to reduce your premium, then increase your deductible. That way, you'll be covered totally if you lose your whole building to fire, but won't have to pay as much to protect small losses, such as the theft of inexpensive equipment. Make sure that the policy covers the replacement cost of the destroyed asset, not just its current value. The current value of a building is almost always less than the cost to rebuild.

Legal Eagle

Consider combining your property insurance with liability coverage; the combined policies may be cheaper than buying a policy for each. Also, consider dropping collision insurance on older company cars that won't cost much to replace.

Shark Attack!

Don't forget to protect your rental property. If you're a tenant, your insurance should include the contents of the building you are renting, such as your equipment and inventory. Your lease may hold you liable for negligence that damages the building, so consult your insurance agent for advice about coverage similar to an owner's policy.

Liability Protection That Can Save Your Business

You may be liable for your employee's conduct, including most accidents and injuries that occur on company time and on company premises. Liability insurance usually involves two forms of coverage: bodily injury and property damage.

The comprehensive general liability policy is the standard business liability insurance policy. Should the insured become liable for damages to a worker or customer, the insurance company promises to pay all sums. Check the definitions in your policy for …

➤ **Bodily injury.** Bodily injury is usually defined as injury, sickness, disease, or death sustained by a person during the policy period. The injured party is compensated for his or her out-of-pocket expenses, such as medical expenses, lost income, pain and suffering, and physical injury, such as loss of use of an arm.

➤ **Property damage.** Property damage means destruction or damage to tangible property during the policy period, or the loss of use of the property from the damage. For example, if your employee causes an automobile accident that damages another person's car, then the policy will cover the cost of the other party's car repair plus rental cost for a replacement during the repair time.

➤ **Occurrence.** Occurrence is the accident causing the injury or damage. This includes negligence, but likely will exclude intentional misconduct. For example, if your employee runs a red light and hits another car, this is negligence and you would be covered; however, if an argument ensued and your employee punched the other person, this is intentional and not typically covered by the policy. Please read Chapter 17, "Employee Negligence and Other Harmful Behavior."

➤ **Coverage limits.** Coverage limits involve the amount of money the insurance company is obligated to pay for each occurrence and for the policy year. For example, your liability policy may state that the insurance company will pay $250,000 for each occurrence, and $1 million total for the policy year. You will be liable for any amount of a lawsuit judgment or settlement that exceeds this coverage. Be careful: Being under-insured can be dangerous to your business.

Business Interruption and Other Worries

You can insure against almost any risk—if you are willing to pay the premium. Property and liability insurance coverage is imperative, while other types of coverage may be less compelling. There are some other kinds of insurance coverage you may want to consider.

Business Interruption

A fire or tornado may destroy your building, and with it your business income. Customers can't buy from you if your inventory is gone with the wind. Your property insurance covers the loss of the building and its contents, but doesn't compensate for the loss of your income. The interruption insurance may also cover the cost of moving into a temporary rental. However, if you can get back into business within two to four weeks, then this insurance may cost more than it's worth.

Burglary and Theft

Thieves may break into your store, shoplifters may steal your merchandise, or employees may defraud you. Crime is a fact, and it may hit your business. Losing a little to shoplifters may be just a cost of doing business, but burglars that steal all your computers can be expensive indeed. You could add a rider to your property insurance to cover this peril.

Product Liability

If you manufacture a product, then your company may be liable for injury or damage caused by a defective product. The potential risk depends on the product's potential for harm. For example, a defective drug could cause death or serious injury to a number of users. This insurance is expensive because there is a great deal of product liability litigation these days. Please read Chapter 17 for a more complete discussion of product liability.

Legal Eagle

If employee theft is a great concern, consider purchasing a bond to cover employees who handle most of your money. If a theft occurs, the bonding company reimburses you for the loss.

Employment Practices

Employment discrimination complaints, particularly sexual harassment claims, can hit any employer. The costs not only include compensation to the victim, but also the legal fees and employee lost time in investigating and defending the claim with the EEOC and in the courts. This insurance may be expensive if you have a large number of employees. If you purchase the insurance, make sure that the protection covers the ordinary risks involved in employment claims. Please read Chapter 12, "Selecting Employees Without Violating the Law," and Chapter 14, "Keeping or Letting Go," for more about employment practices.

Legal Eagle

A manufacturer will be liable to a consumer for any product in a defective condition unreasonably dangerous to the user. A defect may include manufacture, design, or failure to warn.

Environmental Damage

If your company manufactures toxic chemicals or produces toxic waste as a byproduct, and toxic materials spill into a local creek or pollute the ground water, then your company may be liable for a very expensive cleanup. Perhaps there are toxic wastes on your property left by a previous owner, or you sent your wastes to a dumpsite that the EPA later declares to be a Superfund cleanup site. Again, you could be liable for the cleanup costs. Generally, pollution is excluded in the standard liability policy, although courts may interpret this exclusion against the insurance company in limited cases. A rider to cover pollution liability is very expensive, but may be worth considering if your potential risk is significant.

Directors and Officers

Corporations frequently offer some indemnification or insurance to protect its directors and officers from claims made against them in their official capacity. A shareholder lawsuit may claim that a director or officer harmed the corporation by his or her conduct or by a decision. For example, a shareholder suit may allege that the director was negligent in evaluating a business the company purchased. The cost of the litigation, as well as any settlement or damages, may be covered by a directors and officers liability policy. Most small businesses would not need this insurance.

Life and Health Insurance to Protect Your Employees

Providing life and health insurance for you and your employees is almost a given. The cost of group term life insurance is reasonable and should be part of any employee benefit. Health insurance is costly but necessary and disability insurance should be considered, too, particularly if the business is your sole or primary source of income.

Life Insurance

There are two basic forms of life insurance: whole life and term. Whole life insurance can continue for an indefinite period with a fixed premium and stated coverage as long as the policy owner continues to pay the premium. Whole life builds up a cash value according to the policy schedule. Whole life has several variants, such as single premium policies, universal life, and variable life, which may include flexible premiums and investments controlled by the insured. I recommend term life insurance because it provides the greatest coverage for the least cost.

Term life insurance lasts for a specific period, say five years. Term policies do not have a cash surrender value, since the premium pays for the insurance coverage only. Most term policies continue the same

Notes & Quotes

"Death *is* nature's way of saying Howdy."

—Anonymous

coverage for the period, such as $100,000 for five years; however, some policies decrease coverage as the insured gets older. Your policy may allow you to pay a higher premium for coverage to increase with the cost of living. You may establish a group term life insurance policy to cover all your employees (and you) for a specific amount, or vary the coverage, such as twice an employee's annual salary.

Health Insurance

Health insurance policy coverage truly seems to follow the adage that the big print gives, and the fine print takes away. Basic coverage health insurance usually includes payments for hospital expenses, surgeon's fees, diagnostic charges, anesthesia, operating and delivery room costs, and medicine. The basic policy may include outpatient care, emergency room treatment, nursing care, prescription drugs, and eyeglasses. Most plans have a deductible (say, $200), then will pay a certain percent of costs covered by the policy, usually 80 percent; the insured pays for everything else, although, if he or she has major medical, then that policy may pay for the costs not paid by the basic policy. Read the fine print to determine what care is covered and what is excluded.

Legal Eagle

The insurance policy should include a provision for continued insurance coverage if the insured employee is totally disabled, and may not be able to continue paying the premiums (or be employed).

The employer and employee usually share the costs of the premiums; an employer may pay all the cost of a single plan since one employee's health insurance premiums may not be that expensive, and pay a portion for a family plan. The health insurance providers may be ...

➤ Blue Cross/Blue Shield organizations, which typically provide a broader selection of coverage, including that provided the HMOs and the PPOs.

➤ Health maintenance organizations (HMOs).

➤ Preferred provider organizations (PPOs).

Legal Eagle

Assign someone in your company to assist your employees in disputes with the health insurance company. That person must be patient and persevering. Insurance companies are masters at delay and denial.

The latter two are managed care organizations, not insurance companies. Both negotiate fees with health care providers and limit the choice of doctors and hospitals. The primary care physician must refer his or her patient to a specialist for the HMO or PPO to pay for that service. Because both organizations emphasize cost control, they scrutinize all treatments and will not pay for treatment they deem unnecessary. Therefore, the HMO and PPO premiums usually cost less than the Blue Cross/Blue Shield organizations.

Disability Insurance

Disability insurance provides coverage for the loss of income when illness prevents you or an employee from working for an extended period. Personal expenses continue, and may increase, while there is no payroll check coming to the disabled person. The disability policy typically requires a waiting period, often three to six months, before the insurer begins payments. The protection covers a person who, because of an injury or accident, is unable to perform the regular duties of his or her job. Social Security benefits may be available to a disabled person, too.

Taxing Matters

Income taxes do matter, so here is a quick review of benefits that are tax-free to your employees:

➤ Health insurance premiums paid by the employer

➤ $50,000 coverage of group term life insurance

➤ Life insurance proceeds paid to a beneficiary

➤ Workers' compensation benefits

A casualty may allow the business owner to take a deduction for the uninsured portion of the loss. The tax allows you to take the lesser of the decline in fair market value or the property's adjusted basis (cost less depreciation), but the latter if the property is totally destroyed.

For example, let's say that your business owned a delivery truck that was worth $20,000 before an accident, and worth $12,000 after the accident, so the decline in value was $8,000. The $8,000 loss must first be reduced by the insurance proceeds, say $6,000, which results in a deductible casualty loss of $2,000. However, if the truck's adjusted basis (cost less depreciation) was less than the $8,000 decline in value, then you must use the adjusted basis figure. The tax law limits your deduction by taking the lower of the decline in value or adjusted basis.

Ironically, you can incur a casualty that creates a gain for tax purposes. You may have a taxable gain if the insurance proceeds are greater than the adjusted basis (cost less depreciation) in the property.

Consider this example: If your warehouse is destroyed by a tornado and the insurance company sends you a check for $200,000, your adjusted basis is $100,000 and you have a casualty gain of $100,000 ($200,000 insurance proceeds less $100,000 adjusted basis).

Fortunately you can postpone gain recognition by reinvesting the amount received in property of a like kind, such as putting $200,000 into buying another warehouse. If you reinvest less than the amount you receive, then there will be partial gain recognition on your tax return.

Legal Eagle

Have your tax consultant run the figures on an involuntary conversion, such as a casualty (tornado, fire, theft) to your business property. A mistake in the amount you need to reinvest may be costly. The tax law gives you up to two years from the end of the casualty year to reinvest.

Saving Premium Costs

Ben Franklin was right when he said that a penny saved is a penny earned. Insurance is a big-ticket expense, so you need to search for savings. You should …

➤ **Insure against the big losses**. The big losses can destroy your business; the little losses are just financial pinpricks. Covering every loss is not practical, and the small losses you insure against actually may cost you more per dollar of coverage.

➤ **Increase your deductibles.** The higher the deductible, the lower the premium. For example, determine what you can afford out-of-pocket when your vehicle is damaged in an accident, then adjust the deductible accordingly.

➤ **Choose the right insurance agent and aim for loss prevention**. The right insurance agent can analyze your business operations and advise you how to reduce the risk of loss. A simple suggestion, like installing a sprinkler system or an alarm system, can prevent a loss that could be costly and it can reduce the insurance premium. Further, your insurance agent should get you the best coverage at the lowest cost; expect nothing less.

Helpful Sources

Read *The Complete Idiot's Guide to Buying Insurance and Annuities* (Alpha Books, 1996), by Brian H. Breuel. Your library may have one of the reference books published by insurance rating services, such as *Best's, Moody's,* or *Standard & Poor;* you can check out the financial stability of your insurance company. There are a number of insurance Web sites, such as National Association of Insurance Commissioners: www.naic.org; or the Insurance Corner: www.insurancecorner.com; or the federal site: www.gsa.gov/staff/pa/cic/acli/index.htm. Your state insurance commissioner may have a Web site worth visiting, too.

The Least You Need to Know

➤ Use an insurance agent or broker who knows your business.

➤ Know what risks you need to insure against.

➤ Read the insurance policy with care to understand what it does and does not cover.

➤ Business interruption insurance is important if a fire or other casualty would shut you down for several months.

➤ Buy group term life insurance for your employees; it offers up to $50,000 coverage, is tax-free to employees, and is relatively inexpensive.

Chapter 16

Contracts That Are Binding

In This Chapter

➤ Forming a solid contract

➤ Interpreting the vague and ambiguous

➤ Remedies for breach

Contracts are the fuel for your business. Most contracts are oral, though some are written and most contracts are performed, though some are breached. You need to prepare contracts that clearly state both parties' intent, without unduly cluttering the contract with verbose legalese. This chapter is intended to help you do just that.

In Search of a Solid Contract

A contract is a promise or set of promises for the breach of which the law gives a remedy, or the performance of which the law in some way recognizes a duty. Actually, most of us know a contract when we see one, mainly because it says "contract" or "agreement" right on it. But I'm not sure that we always know a contract when we hear one. Oral contracts are usually no less binding than written ones, but their precise terms may be much more elusive.

The essence of each contract involves certain rights and duties. The contract rights (benefits) for one party correspond to the duties (obligations) of the other party. For example, Purchase Company promises in a contract to pay Seller Company $100,000 (duty), and Purchase would receive the deed to Seller's real estate (right). Conversely, Seller agreed to convey the deed to Purchaser (duty) and will receive his or her payment (right). Each contract you enter can be viewed as rights or benefits you receive and duties or obligations you must perform.

Contracts are either bilateral or unilateral. Bilateral contracts involve an exchange of promises of future performance. In the previous example, Purchaser and Seller exchanged promises: Purchaser to pay $100,000, and Seller to convey the deed to the property at a date set in the future. Most contracts are bilateral.

However, if one party makes a contract offer, and the other party accepts by immediately performing the contract, then this is a unilateral contract. Say Ms. Customer orders a #100 widget from Supplier Company, who ships the order in response to her contract offer they've just made a unilateral contract.

Notes & Quotes

"Man is an animal that makes bargains; no other animal does this—one dog does not change a bone with another."

—Adam Smith, economist

Legalese

Common law is judge-made law, as contrasted with the contract law consisting of federal and state constitutions, statutes, and administrative agency regulations. Common law in your state may have developed over decades and is governed by the principle of precedent, or what courts have previously ruled on a legal question.

How does all this matter to your business? Contract law requires you to ask two questions:

1. Do we have a contract?
2. What are the terms of the contract?

Neither question is as simple as it appears, and answers to either may have an important impact on your business. Contracts are not made to be broken, but some are breached; you need to know your rights.

Contract law has two sources: Uniform Commercial Code, Article 2, for sales of goods, and *common law* for all contracts not involving sales of goods, such as employment, insurance, and real estate. I will discuss the differences as they appear in this chapter.

Forming a Solid Contract

Every contract your business enters into requires four elements for its legal existence:

1. Offer
2. Acceptance
3. Consent
4. Consideration

In addition, the parties to the contract must have the legal capacity to enter into the contract, and the contract has be to legal. Also, a few contracts—real estate contract and sales of goods worth $500 or more—must be in writing to be enforceable. This writing requirement is called the Statute of Frauds. Let's take a look at what goes into the creation of a contract.

Offer

You (the *offeror*) make an offer to another company (the *offeree*) to enter into a contract, and the offer specifies the proposed contract terms. If the offeree accepts the offer, a contract is formed. If the offeree rejects the proposal outright, no contract is formed. If the offeree suggests different terms, he or she creates a new offer. Only when both parties agree is a contract formed.

The offer by the offeror should ...

➤ Convey the offer to a specific offeree (Company B).

➤ Have a definite subject matter (10 pounds of cotton).

➤ Set a time for acceptance (by 1 P.M., April 1, 2000).

If you send a purchase order to a supplier, or conversely, a customer comes into your store and orders your merchandise, either conveys the offer to the other party. The offeror intends to make a contract.

The terms of the offer must contain terms sufficient to form an enforceable contract; too vague or ambiguous an offer may not be sufficiently clear to be accepted and have identifiable terms.

Acceptance

The offeror should establish a deadline for the offeree to accept, preferably in writing. If the offeree doesn't accept the terms within the time limit, then there is no contract. An acceptance that materially varies from the offer also is considered a rejection. However, a minor variation in the terms such as an alteration of just few days for the time of performance may result in a contract if it involves the sale of goods. Therefore, you may want your offer to contain a requirement that acceptance must be according to *all* the terms of the contract.

You may revoke your offer at any time before the offeree accepts. However, if you are a merchant selling goods and provide the customer with a firm offer, which is a written promise to keep the offer open for a specified period, then you cannot revoke before that time has expired. For example, let's say you make a written offer to sell a riding lawnmower for $1,500 and you include in the offer your promise to keep the offer open for two days. You then cannot revoke the offer before the two days are up. Another exception is referred to as detrimental reliance. For example, you told a

Legal Eagle

Write your contracts in plain, good English. You can use a form contract as a starting point, but too many contain unnecessary legalese. Say what you intend. A simple list of offeror and offeree rights and duties will usually suffice.

prospective employee that if she moved to your city at her expense, then you would hire her; you have made a nonrevocable offer if she relies on your offer to move to your city, but if you end up not hiring her, then she can sue you for her expenses and lost salary.

If you are the offeree, make sure that you understand all of the offeror's terms. If you don't understand a term, then have the offeror clarify it and amend the written offer to reflect the clarification. Don't sign a contract that doesn't contain all of the important terms of the contract, because if it's not in the contract the court may refuse to enforce it. This is particularly true if this so-called external term contradicts a term in the written agreement, or if the contract contains a zipper clause that specifically states that the parties agree that there are no terms outside the agreement.

Legal Eagle

A prospective buyer could enter into an option contract with a seller to make the offer irrevocable for the period of the option. For example, the prospective buyer could give the seller $5,000 to keep the seller's offer to sell Blackacre open for 30 days. In essence, the option contract buys time.

An acceptance may be conditional; therefore, the contract would exist only if the stated condition occurred. For example, if you are buying a building, you would want to condition your purchase upon evidence that the seller owned the property free of liens (as shown by title insurance) and satisfactory evidence of the building's structural soundness. Once you receive that evidence the seller has removed the conditions, you can proceed to contract.

Consent

Each contracting party must consent to the agreement voluntarily. You may pay more for a good or service than you want, but if you weren't forced or defrauded, then your agreement was consensual. In a lawsuit, a party may ask the court to be excused from performance because of a lack of consent, which means the party may seek to prove one of three charges:

➤ **Duress** means that one coerced another into signing the contract. In fact, an act may be legal in itself, but so overcomes the other party's free will to amount to duress. For example, if a boss tells an employee that he will fire her if she doesn't sell her house to him, then this is duress even though he may be able to fire her under employment at-will. In most business transactions, this would be difficult to prove, unless one party is so strong that it can literally cram down the contract on the small party. In that instance, the court may not enforce a completely unfair and one-sided contract, but these are rare cases.

➤ **Undue influence**, which means that one party uses a dominant position of trust to unfairly persuade the other party to enter into a one-sided contract. For example, if an attorney persuaded a client to sell him property at a very advantageous price, then this misconduct may amount to undue influence because the client is apt to trust that the attorney (whom the client hired and pays) will act in the client's best interest. However, it takes proof that a buyer completely dominated a seller in order for a court to determine that selling an item at a very low price came about through undue influence.

➤ **Misrepresentation** is the most common of claims. One party misrepresents material facts that then become the major inducement for the other party to contract. If the misrepresentation is intentional, then it is fraud. For example, you contract with Bill Builder to add on to your store after Builder claims to have built several additions like yours. However, Builder had never built any addition before and thus has materially misrepresented his skills. The misrepresentation would permit the innocent party to rescind the contract.

➤ **Mutual material mistake of fact** involves both parties making a false assumption about a material term in the contract. For example, both the buyer and the seller believe that the land is suitable for growing crops, but later both discover that the land was polluted prior to the contract and all the top soil must be removed. The basis of the contract was the assumption that the land could grow crops, which was a mutual material mistake.

If the party proves duress, undue influence or misrepresentation, then the court may refuse to enforce the contract and may award damages to the injured party. Please read the section on contract remedies later in this chapter.

Consideration

A contract requires consideration, which is a legal term for a bargained-for exchange of benefits between the parties. Courts usually do not examine the adequacy of the consideration, only its existence. The focus is on the exchange of something of value, not whether the buyer paid too much or the seller got too little from the contract.

However, consideration can exist without the bargained-for exchange under certain limited circumstances. Specifically, a contract without consideration is valid if the contract involves the other party's reliance on your promise for the following:

➤ **Charitable pledge.** If you pledged $10,000 to a local charity for a building project, which it undertakes in reliance on your promise, then you are contractually bound even though you haven't received any tangible benefit for the contribution.

➤ **Contract guarantee.** If a parent or spouse guarantees a contract in writing, then the guarantee is enforceable even though the guarantor received nothing of value.

➤ **Promissory estoppel.** Promissory estoppel protects a party who spends money or gives up time or energy relying on the other party's promise. Courts won't allow the promissor to later claim lack of consideration as a way to void the contract. For example, a franchisor promises to grant you a franchise to sell hamburgers if you buy a building and pay the franchisor for training. In this case, the franchisor requested that you change your financial position in reliance on its promise of a job. If the franchisor claims it received no benefit from your conduct, thus no consideration, you respond by asserting promissory estoppel (the franchisor is stopped from denying the existence of consideration).

Legal Eagle

A unilateral, or one-party, mistake generally cannot excuse performance, unless the mistake was so obvious to the other party that it would be unfair to enforce the contract, such as a typographical error that obviously understates the price by 50 percent. The court can reform the contract to reflect what terms the parties intended.

Capacity and Legality

Any party to a contract must be of legal age—18—and have the mental capacity to understand his or her contractual rights and duties. Any underage minor can disaffirm (avoid) the contract within a reasonable time after becoming age 18 by returning the consideration received. For example, if you sold a motorcycle to a minor, the minor buyer can return the cycle in the same condition as purchased and receive his or her money back. A person who lacks mental capacity can likewise disaffirm the contract personally or through his or her guardian, and thus the contract is *voidable*.

An illegal bargain involves a contract term or performance that is criminal, civil wrong, such as fraud, or against public policy. The subject matter of the contract may be illegal, such as the sale of marijuana, or the purpose may be illegal, such as hiring a goon to attack another performer or creating a price-fixing agreement in violation of the federal antitrust laws.

An illegal contract is unenforceable. However, if a term of the contract is illegal but can be separated from the rest of the contract without materially changing the contract, then the contract itself, minus the illegal provision, may be enforceable. For example, if the contract violates the state usury law (illegal rate of interest), the court may be able to amend this to a legal rate and otherwise enforce the contract.

Legalese

Voidable means the contract exists until the person disaffirms, while void means the contract cannot be enforced. A contract with a minor or mentally incapacitated person is voidable, unless that person has a guardian, in which case the contract is void.

Statute of Frauds Writing Requirement

The Statute of Frauds has nothing to do with fraud. Instead it is a requirement that certain contracts have to be in writing if you want to enforce them. For business contracts, these terms include ...

➤ Contracts for the sale of land.

➤ Broker commission contracts.

➤ Contracts that cannot be fully performed within one year.

➤ Suretyship or guarantee contracts.

➤ Contracts for the sale of goods worth $500 or more.

For instance, a contract that requires producing a television program for two years cannot be fully performed within one, and must be in writing to be enforceable. However, some contracts with a stated period of over one year may not come within the Statute of Frauds, such as a two-year insurance contract for fire coverage, because the property may be destroyed within one year.

Legalese

A **surety** or **guarantor** is a person who agrees to be responsible for the debt of another.

A suretyship or guaranty requires a written document to hold the *surety* or *guarantor* liable. For example, if you sell a car to a young person with little credit history, you will want to have the parents sign a written guarantee that they will pay if their child does not. You may also want them to cosign the promissory note for the loan or a sale on credit.

The Statute of Frauds requires a writing; that it contain enough terms to indicate that it's a contract; and that it be signed by the person against whom the contract is being enforced.

The writing can be handwritten or typed; a faxed document with a signature and an e-mail document with a digital signature would be considered a "writing." The document must have enough terms to show that it is a contract, such as the names of the parties and the services to be performed or goods sold. The defendant in a lawsuit may assert that the contract did not comply with the Statute. Then it's up to the plaintiff to show that the defendant's signature or its equivalent appears on the writing. However, if the defendant receives a memo confirming the oral contract and did not object within 10 days, the court will waive the signature requirement.

Further, if you specially manufacture the goods for the party who orders them, then the court may also waive the writing requirement. For example, if you made business cards to order for a customer, complete with the customer's logo and address, and the customer refuses to accept delivery because you had no written contract, you can enforce the contract. If a customer has accepted part of any shipment, the Statute of Frauds applies only to the part not yet accepted.

Legal Eagle

Always put it in writing. If you have an oral order for goods costing $500 or more, fax or mail the written confirmation with the details of the order. If the buyer does not object within 10 days, you have an enforceable contract.

Interpreting the Vague and Ambiguous

Too often our contract terms are not clearly expressed or are capable of having more than one meaning. This fault may land you in court, and require a judge to interpret what you probably meant at the time you formed the contract. Read Strunk and White's *The Elements of Style* (Macmillan, 1973), a handy little book that emphasizes clarity. Then write your contract according to its principles, or insist your lawyer do so.

If the court or an arbitrator must interpret your contract, he or she will hear evidence as to what you and the other party intended. However, that testimony may be colored by the self-interest required to win the case. Or to put it tersely, the other party may lie.

The court may use one of several methods to interpret what the parties intended, including the following:

➤ **Plain meaning of ordinary words within the context of the entire contract.**
   This first approach is often referred to as the "dictionary interpretation." Almost literally, the court goes to the dictionary to ascertain what the term means. This approach may be more applicable when contracts are written in plain English,

but may be less helpful if the contract is poorly written. Nonetheless, you need to know that a court may take you at your word, at least as it's commonly understood.

➤ **Performance of the term under this or past contracts.** The court may look to performance under this contract or under past contracts to interpret a term. Said another way, actions speak louder than words. For example, if you are halfway through the current contract and have accepted a discount for each payment made within 10 days, then you really have indicated to the other party that the discount exists, even if not expressed well, or at all, on paper. Likewise, if you have a new contract, and past practice under similar contracts required you to pick up the goods at the seller's place of business, then the term "delivery" will continue to mean that you'll pick up the goods at the seller's business—unless your new contract expressly requires delivery at your business location.

➤ **Trade usage.** Trade usage recognizes that businesses in a specialized area of commerce use special terms among themselves. The court will recognize this usage.

➤ **Gap fillers.** The Uniform Commercial Code (UCC) for Sales has provision for absent terms, or gap fillers, for contracts where none of the foregoing methods apply. For example, if the parties haven't expressly or indicated price or implied one, then the UCC gap filler states that price is the reasonable value at the delivery location. Likewise, if the parties haven't indicated a delivery location, the UCC specifies that delivery will be at the seller's place of business or where the goods are located.

➤ **Construed against the party writing the contract.** Finally, the court may construe the contract against the party who drafted it and created the vague or ambiguous term. This is particularly appropriate when the contract is a standard form and the party drafting it insists upon its wording.

Notes & Quotes

"In Paris they simply stared when I spoke to them in French; I never did succeed in making those idiots understand their own language."

—Mark Twain, writer

Legal Eagle

Make sure you're clear on your terms every time you sign a contract. Review each contract renewal. Compare the expressed terms with each party's practice. If you do not want to continue the same way, then clearly express the change in the new contract.

Shark Attack!

If you make a written contract offer, read the acceptance of its terms by the offeree because he or she might add terms. These additional terms may be enforceable if you do not timely reject them (or if they materially alter the contract). You could insist in your offer that your contract must be accepted without alteration.

On Time and It Works

If your company sells cars, carpet, or canned carrots, each sale involves certain warranties. Any contract, whether with a consumer or supplier, requires both parties to fully perform the contract according to its terms, and the failure to do so may result in a lawsuit.

Warranties

Contracts for the sale of goods may contain express warranties and become part of the bargain between the seller and buyer. The express warranty may be created by a description of the goods in the contract or by a sample or model. Most expensive products, such as cars, riding mowers, and computers have a written express warranty detailing the expected quality of the product. Some products contain a simple warranty, such as "100 percent cotton" or "will not shrink if washed according to instructions." A written warranty is not required, but if given, cannot be disclaimed by language like "as is" or "no warranties." Once given, the express warranty exists.

In addition, the federal Magnuson-Moss Act creates certain warranty rights for consumers. For any consumer product costing $15 or more, the Act requires consumers to be informed of …

➤ Who is entitled to warranty protection.

➤ Which parts of the product are warranted.

➤ What can be done to correct a defect in the product.

➤ When the warranty becomes effective.

➤ From whom the consumer can obtain warranty performance.

The Act does permit a disclaimer of consequential damage for the defective product that damages a consumer's other property. For example, a defective coffee pot may explode and damage a nearby toaster; the damage to the toaster was consequential and liability disclaimed by the coffee pot manufacturer.

Defective products that harm persons or damage property may breach an express or implied warranty; the manufacturer may also be liable under negligence or products liability; please read Chapter 17, "Employee Negligence and Other Harmful Behavior," for further discussion.

If you sell consumer goods, your buyers also receive an implied warranty of merchantability that the goods sold are of at least average quality and fit for ordinary usage, are adequately packaged and labeled, and conform to any promise made on the label. Many consumer product recalls involve defects, such as metal in margarine, loose engine bolts, and baby swings that collapse. The contract includes this implied warranty and the consumer can sue for a defect, unless there is an effective disclaimer.

Sometimes the implied warranty can be disclaimed if the seller conspicuously does so, for example, by putting a disclaimer in boldface print and using the phrase "as is" or "seller disclaims warranty of merchantability." Courts construe such disclaimers narrowly and usually will not enforce the disclaimer when personal injury results from the defect.

If a seller knows that the buyer is relying on the seller's expertise to select goods appropriate for the buyer's requirement, then there may be an implied warranty of "fitness for a particular purpose." For example, if you own a ski shop and a novice skier relies upon you to select the appropriate skis for his or her size and skill, by your selection alone and by implication, you are warrantying that the skis are fit for the customer's intended use. Courts in some states are reluctant to allow the seller to disclaim this warranty.

In addition to any warranties of quality, the UCC requires from the seller an implied warranty of good title to the goods sold and that there are no liens or security interests against the goods.

Legal Eagle

Despite the implied warranty of good title, if you are buying equipment that carries a substantial price tag, always do a search with your Secretary of State UCC file for any financing statements (liens) against the equipment. If any are filed, the creditor who filed has a claim against the property.

Performance by the Parties

Contracting parties are required to follow the terms of their agreement. Of course, they may amend the original contract. Any amendment may require additional consideration by the party seeking the change, such as additional money or additional services. Under the UCC sale of goods, however, the modification may be valid even without additional consideration if requested in good faith, such as if a seller delays delivery because his or her supplier failed to get the goods delivered on time. Under the UCC, the seller is obligated to timely deliver goods that conform to the terms of the contract. Unless the contract indicates otherwise, the goods are to be delivered in a single lot, and title passes when delivery occurs. The buyer is then required to accept and pay for goods that conform to the terms of the contract. The buyer has the right to inspect the goods before acceptance and reject nonconforming goods. However, if the buyer fails to inspect the goods in a timely manner or if he or she uses the goods, the courts may deem that behavior is acceptance under the UCC. If the buyer rejects nonconforming goods, then the buyer must give timely notice of the rejection and specify the particular defects. Thereafter, the buyer must follow the seller's reasonable instructions as to the disposition of the rejected goods.

Legal Eagle

If the other party to your contract indicates he or she might not perform, the UCC permits you to demand assurance of performance. You send a letter to the other party requesting a definite assurance (promise) that the other party will timely perform. If the other party repudiates the contract or fails to respond to your request, then you can treat this as a contract breach.

The buyer may revoke acceptance if the seller assured the buyer that the defects would be fixed, or the defect was difficult to discover.

If one party has not fully performed, there is a contract breach, unless the buyer permits the breach (as buyer would if he or she accepted late delivery of goods). Remedies for a contract breach are discussed later in this chapter.

Third-Party Performance

A contract may involve performance by a third party, which is called contract delegation, better known as subcontracting. Some contract performance is typically delegated; construction companies frequently subcontract to others. Contracting parties may delegate part or all of the performance unless one of these conditions exist:

➤ The contract specifically prohibits delegation

➤ Delegation materially affects the other party's expectations

While delegation is expected in construction contracts, it may not be in other areas of business, particularly in personal service contracts or where the manufacturer's expertise is expected. For example, if you hire a carpenter to remodel, you would not want me as a substitute carpenter. If you contract with Eli Lilly to supply your medication, you don't want the company to delegate production to some fly-by-night drug manufacturer. If the proposed delegation substantially alters the bargain, then neither party is allowed to delegate.

Excusing Performance

Sometimes contract performance, or at least timely performance, may be excused by the law. One of the traditional excuses is the *doctrine of impossibility*. Impossibility involves some force of nature, such as a tornado that destroys the seller's manufacturing plant or a fire that destroys a building ready to be sold. In some cases, impossibility may only excuse timely performance, but only postpone the date, such as when a severe snow storm delays delivery.

The law may excuse performance that is impractical, but requires evidence that …

➤ The nonperforming party was not at fault.

➤ An event has occurred that the parties had not contemplated when they made the contract.

➤ The nonperforming party did not agree to assume the risk of the occurrence.

For example, a builder agrees to construct a high-rise building and substantial subsurface testing showed only minor impediments. However, once construction began, the soil proved nearly impossible to hold the high-rise and the project had to be abandoned. Contract performance may be excused because of the unforeseen difficulty rendering the project impractical to complete.

In addition, the parties may have agreed upon conditions affecting performance that change after both parties sign the contract. The occurrence may increase or decrease a party's duties, or terminate the contract. For example, a franchise contract may require the franchisee to pay a higher fee as the gross sales increase, or an employment contract may permit termination if the employee discloses trade secrets to a competitor.

Legalese

The doctrine of impossibility, particularly regarding forces of nature, is often referred to as "acts of God."

Drafting Checklist

You may want to draft your own contracts, then have your attorney review the draft. Most contracts contain the following:

➤ **Parties.** The parties to the contract must be identified, ABC Corporation, an Indiana corporation (seller) and Able LLC, an Indiana limited liability company (buyer).

➤ **Recitals.** In this section the parties indicate their intent to contract and the general purpose of the contract. The seller intends to sell pickup trucks to the buyer.

➤ **Consideration.** This section specifies the subject matter of the contract, what the parties are exchanging. For example, the seller shall deliver 10 #222 pickup trucks to the buyer for the sum of $225,000.

➤ **Conditions.** Either party may state conditions of contract performance. One such condition might be that the buyer has to provide a valid *letter of credit* to the seller before the seller ships the first installment.

➤ **Performance.** This section may provide the details of performance, such as delivery by lots, delivery time and location, and payment. For example, "seller will deliver five pickup trucks on April 1, 2001, and five to be delivered on May 1, 2001, at buyer's place of business, and with payment after inspection but no later than 10 days from delivery."

Legalese

A **letter of credit** is usually issued by a bank, agreeing to honor a draft and check of its customer.

➤ **Term.** The contract may involve a specified period, such as "Seller will provide warranty service on pickup trucks for a period of one year from date of last delivery, after which the contract terminates."

➤ **Assignment and delegation.** If the parties want to exclude *assignment* or delegation, then they should specify that condition, otherwise the law may permit either if there is no material effect by assignment or delegation.

➤ **Remedies.** The parties should indicate what constitutes a breach, such as nonpayment or late delivery of defective trucks. The method of computing damages may be included. Certainly, there should be a provision for payment of attorney fees to the nonbreaching party, otherwise each party pays its own fees.

➤ **Integration.** This section specifies that all the terms of the parties' contract are included in the written agreement. If you have any oral or written promises made by the other party, make sure you write them into the final written agreement or the integration clause will exclude them.

➤ **Severablity.** If one section of the contract is declared by the court to be unenforceable, the rest of the contract shall remain and be enforceable.

➤ **Signature.** If either contracting party is an entity, such as a corporation, then the person is signing the contract on its behalf, such as Jan Jones, as President, ABC Corporation.

Please review the various contract forms in Appendix B, "Basic Business Forms," for further suggestions.

Remedies for Breach of Contract

A party may breach the contract if it fails to perform its end of the bargain. If its performance is incomplete, defective, or repudiated, the nonbreaching party may sue for the contract breach.

A contract party may cancel a contract if the other party fails or refuses to perform, or may sue for a contract breach and request money damages or other forms of relief. The goal of contract remedies is to place the nonbreaching party in as good a condition as the party would be in if the contract had been property performed.

Money Damages

Money damages are the most typical remedy sought. Courts calculate damages by estimating how much money it would take to make the nonbreaching party whole—in essence, substituting money for performance.

The measure of damages could be the cost to complete the contract—for example, if you contract to have your lawn landscaped for $5,000 and pay in advance, but the landscaper failed to plant some bushes worth $500 that you had paid for, the damages are $500 in your favor.

The court could also calculate damages based upon your lost profit. Let's say someone hired you as a caterer to furnish a party with food, but your client backed out at the last minute. In addition to paying you for your time and expenses, a court may also demand that the client pay you $1,000 for the profit you would have made had you been allowed to perform.

Legal Eagle

Punitive damages—damages in excess of what it would cost to make the nonbreaching party whole—are usually available only when the breaching party has committed fraud.

Consequential damages—damages to make up for a loss that extends beyond the immediate contract—may be awarded in certain contract breaches, often as a result of nontimely performance. If time is important, you must tell the other party *prior* to performance of the possible consequences, such as the need for additional expenses or lost revenue. For example, you contract for construction of your retail store and the builder promises completion on a certain date. If you inform the builder (preferably in writing) that you will lose approximately $5,000 in sales for each day that you are not open, then you have set the stage for consequential damages if the construction is not complete on time.

Equity Remedies

Under certain special circumstances, money damages may not provide an adequate remedy for the nonbreaching party. In such cases, the court awards what is known as equity. Equity may permit the three following outcomes:

➤ **Rescission.** Rescission allows the court to cancel the contract because of unjust benefit or harm to one party. Grounds for rescission may include misrepresentation, mutual mistake, duress, undue influence, or incapacity. For example, you contract to buy shelving for your store but the seller misrepresented its load-carrying capacity so you can't use it. You can sue for rescission and get your money back.

➤ **Reformation.** Reformation permits the court to change the contract to reflect what the parties intended but did not adequately express in the written contract, or to modify an illegal term in the contract. For example, you intended to buy 100 reams of typing paper, which was what the seller intended to sell; however, due to an unnoticed typo the contract read *1000* reams. The court can reform the contract to read what you intended. (But don't count on court intervention, so read and understand what you sign.)

➤ **Specific performance.** Specific performance may be available when the other party refuses to close a sale for real estate or for unique goods, including antiques and collectibles.

Your Agent May Bind You to a Contract

You may have an employee who has the authority to contract on behalf of your business. For example, your office manager has the authority to order office supplies and your company buyer has authority to purchase goods for sale at your retail stores. These employees are agents for your company.

Your company will be bound to any contract your agent agrees to if the agent acts within his or her express authority. For example, if you authorize your office manager to buy up to $500 of supplies with ABC Company, then you will be obligated to pay for the order within those parameters.

Your company may also be liable for any contract your agent agrees to if the agent acts within his or her apparent authority. In other words, your conduct may lead a seller to believe that your agent has the authority to contract, when, in fact, the agent has no such authority, or has exceeded his or her express authority. For example, your office manager has $500 express authority but has bought from ABC Company for several months. On one occasion, your manager orders $600 in supplies. Even though your manager's $100 over the limit, you may be bound because it was reasonable for ABC to assume your manager has the authority to purchase and did so within his or her authority.

The Least You Need to Know

➤ Important contracts should be in writing and contain all the terms agreed upon between the parties.

➤ Contracts should be written in clear, precise English.

➤ Courts may award money damages for a breach, require the party to perform the contract, or rescind or reform the contract.

Chapter 17

Employee Negligence and Other Harmful Behavior

In This Chapter

➤ Protecting your business from employee negligence

➤ Understanding the law about products liability

➤ Battery, libel, and other intentional torts

➤ Legal remedies from A to Z

Your employees can cause you some grief. Running a red light, leaving the bolts loose on the engine you sell, or punching an irate customer may leave your business vulnerable to a costly lawsuit. And then, sometimes things just happen. You implode a building to raze it, only to see bricks flying to places they shouldn't. Or your employee detains what appears to be a shoplifter, only to discover no pilfered goods. In this chapter, we'll discuss the kinds of behavior, activities, and events that could leave your new business open to lawsuits and other litigation—and show you the best way to protect yourself and your company.

Employee Torts and Your Liability

You, as an employer, may be liable for the *torts* (wrongdoings) of your employees that cause physical harm. The legal doctrine holding the employer liable is called *respondeat superior,* or "let the master answer." Under old common law, the employer was referred to as the master, and the employee as the servant. The law will hold the employer liable if there was …

1. An employer-employee relationship.

2. The employee was acting within the scope of his or her employment.

3. The employee committed negligence and certain other torts.

Let's take a closer look.

Employment

In order for you to be held responsible for the actions of someone who works for you, you must actually employ that person, which means that you control the employee's conduct when he or she is in the workplace. This control may involve setting working hours and providing office space and equipment. You also pay this person based on the number of hours he or she works, and withhold his or her taxes in accordance with federal and state tax laws.

Your legal relationship with an employee is different from the one you have with an independent contractor. For example, if your lawyer runs a red light while on the way to work on a specific aspect of your case, you will not be liable because your lawyer is an independent contractor in private practice. Torts caused by independent contractors will not generally impose liability on those who hire them under that designation—unless the contractor's activity is inherently dangerous, such as handling highly toxic materials. Another circumstance under which you could be held liable for a tort committed by an independent contractor is if you hired an independent contractor to remodel the workplace to conform to OSHA safety requirements but the company was negligent, and the defective repair injured one of your employees. The law requires you to ensure the workplace is safe, and are not excused from that obligation by hiring another company to perform your duty. This is often referred to as a "nondelegatable duty."

Legalese

Tort is a civil wrong, a breach of a legal duty that causes harm or injury to another. Torts include negligence, products liability, battery, and strict liability (I'll tell you about that a little later), among others.

Scope of Employment

The employee's conduct is within the scope of employment if …

1. The employee's act is the kind he or she is employed to perform.

2. The tort occurs during, or close in time with, the employee's work time.

3. The tort occurs during an action triggered by a purpose meant to serve the employer.

For example, you hire Ima Employee to make deliveries and while on her route during the workday, her inattention causes an auto accident (she was exiting a fast-food place with her lunch in hand so she could eat while continuing her rounds). Under this circumstance, your company would probably be held liable for that employee's negligence, even though it involves a minor deviation from regular work. If the employee is clearly furthering her own personal interest and substantially deviates from her job, however, then you probably wouldn't be held liable. For example, if Ima went considerably off her route to visit a boyfriend, then she would not be within the scope of employment.

Legal Eagle

If your employees work outside the office, state in writing exactly when they are working and when they are off the clock. Doing so may limit your liability for employee detours for personal reasons. This policy can be placed in the employee handbook.

Employee Negligence

If the employee was negligent and acting within his or her scope of duties, then the employer is liable for the employee's negligence. For example, if your employee negligently repaired a customer's brakes that then failed, totaling the car and injuring the customer, both you and the employee are liable for the employee's negligence.

You may also be liable for certain intentional torts committed by the employee within the scope of employment and foreseeable from the nature of the employment. For example, you hire a repossession man, Steve Gettum, and Steve punches the debtor to recover the goods. You're liable for the battery, which was excessive force, but may be foreseeable due to the nature of the job and the kind of pressure a repo man often has to provide to recover a car from someone who doesn't want to give it up.

Likewise, your company may be liable for the employee's misrepresentations to a customer, especially if you keep the benefit of the misrepresentation. For example, ABC Company's salesperson claims that the product kills all household germs, but the best the spray may do is to drown a few. ABC is liable to a customer who sues because the spray didn't kill the bugs in his house because the company knew or should have known of the misrepresentation, but nevertheless kept the proceeds

Shark Attack!

The references you give concerning a former employee are a potential source of defamation litigation, so make sure that any information provided is truthful. And avoid making disparaging remarks.

207

from the sale. An employer may also be liable for slander or libel committed by one of its employees. For example, if your personnel manager responds to an employment inquiry by saying falsely that a former employee was discharged for sexual harassment, both you and the personnel manager may be liable for slander.

Negligence Can Hurt

Negligence is the top tort. In essence, negligence is the failure to exercise the reasonable care of any ordinary, prudent person in a given situation. To prove negligence, the injured party (plaintiff) must show that …

1. The defendant owed the plaintiff a legal duty of due care.

2. The defendant's conduct was unreasonable under the circumstances.

3. The defendant was the direct and proximate or foreseeable cause of the incident.

4. The plaintiff suffered personal injury or property damage.

Legal Duty

There are several circumstances under which you owe others a duty of care. For example, if you own a store, you owe your customers a duty to keep the premises reasonably safe, and that duty exists the moment the customer enters the store. If you manufacture a product, you owe a duty to consumers that the product is reasonably safe from harmful defects, and the relationship between you and your customer exits from the moment the customer purchases your product. Your delivery person owes a duty to all other drivers and pedestrians to drive reasonably. A childcare worker owes a duty of care to his or her ward; a railroad owes this duty to its passengers; and a hotel owes this duty to its guests.

If you or your employee puts a customer in peril, then you may owe what is known as a "duty to rescue." If you run a fitness center and discover that the treadmill is broken, then you owe a "duty to rescue" your customer from the danger by either repairing the treadmill or removing it from the gym room floor.

Another example of when you owe another a duty is if you voluntarily assume a certain responsibility to that person. For example, if you volunteer to drive a diner who's become ill at your restaurant to the hospital, then you are obligated to do it. Though you had no duty to help this person, once you decided to help you have to do it in a reasonably careful way. It must be performed reasonably.

You also have a duty to reasonably control your employees and their behavior. For example, let's say your restaurant has valet parking and one of your employees hits the accelerator rather than the brake while trying to park a car and causes a crash. Your duty to control that employee's conduct makes you liable to the customer who trusted your valet. Or say you hire a security guard without checking for felony convictions (and the employee has several). Should the employee violently assault a customer, you will be liable for negligently hiring and placing the employee in a situation where he or she could continue to assault people.

Unreasonable Conduct

Another aspect of negligence is what is known as "unreasonable conduct." In deciding this standard, courts compare the actions of the accused wrongdoer to the actions of a reasonably prudent person under the same or similar circumstances. It's not necessary that the businessperson protect others against all potential harm, but only that he or she act in a reasonably careful manner. If a businessperson meets this standard, then he or she does not have to protect others against all risks of harm. Indeed, no business can ensure the complete safety of its customers. The question then is, "How would a reasonable person behave?"

For instance, we are all admonished in state driver manuals to observe the conditions of the road. Freezing rain makes driving more treacherous, so a reasonable person would take notice and drive more carefully. If you own a store, it's up to you to take care that nothing slippery finds its way onto the floor, and a reasonable store owner would make sure that his or her employees periodically check the aisles for such potential problems. If your restaurant has a tricky step leading to the restaurant, it's your duty to put up a sign warning patrons. If you don't, you could be liable for any injury that occurs.

Keep in mind that circumstances may dictate what is reasonable care. For example, the court will not hold the care you provide in an emergency situation to the same high degree as care you give in a calmer moment.

Causation

The defendant's conduct must be the direct and proximate *cause-in-fact* of the plaintiff's injury or property damage. Being a direct cause of an accident means that there is a direct connection between your conduct and the event. For example, if you tossed a lit cigarette into a trash can containing gas rags, and a fire started and spread to a nearby building, then you would be the direct cause of the damage to that building.

Legalese

Cause-in-fact, or direct cause, is an act or omission without which (but for) an event would not have occurred.

Proximate cause involves a less direct, but nonetheless foreseeable, consequence of conduct, and the connection between the conduct and injury is strong enough for the law to impose liability.

209

For example, if your sidewalk remains icy even after you shovel it, it's reasonably foreseeable that a pedestrian could slip and fall into the road where a car could hit him or her. Although the driver of the car could be seen as the direct cause of the accident, you would be the proximate cause—and liable—because of your failure to properly shovel your sidewalk.

In some cases of negligence, it may be difficult to prove exactly what caused the injury or damage. The law of *res ipsa loquitur* ("the thing speaks for itself") permits a plaintiff to prove causation under two conditions: 1) if the harm would not have occurred without someone's negligence and 2) the instrumentality causing injury was under the defendant's exclusive control. For example, if you're able to prove that a soda bottle contained a ring or other foreign object, you've proved negligence on the part of the bottling company because a properly prepared bottle of soda would not contain such a foreign object.

Personal Injury or Property Damage

The final element of negligence is damage or injury. Unless a person suffers damage or injury, he or she cannot sue for damages. For example, under most circumstances, simply driving recklessly does not cause injury and therefore is not actionable. Therefore, if your employee drove through a red light but just missed an oncoming car, the driver of that car has no action against you or your employee.

Defenses to Negligence

Even though the plaintiff may have proven all four requirements for negligence, the defendant may partially or wholly defeat the claim with a defense. The two typical defenses are comparative negligence and assumption of the risk.

Shark Attack!

Be careful! Some states recognize the tort of negligent infliction of emotional distress, so that the near-miss accident which causes identifiable emotional distress, such as nightmares, shaking, and agoraphobia may result in liability to you.

Who's More at Fault?

Comparative negligence apportions the damages between the person injured and the wrongdoer and/or among all people involved in the accident. For example, let's say your driver was speeding when he or she hit the plaintiff's car. But the plaintiff had suddenly turned right into the intersection without heeding a clearly marked stop sign. Both defendant and plaintiff can prove the other negligent. If the plaintiff was comparatively negligent and contributed 20 percent of the damage, then the court will reduce the plaintiff's recovery by that 20 percent. However, a few states practice what is called *contributory negligence,* which denies all recovery to a plaintiff who is in any way responsible for causing his or her own accident. If the plaintiff in the earlier situation lived in such a state, he or she would not be able to recover damages for his or her injury.

Assuming the Risk

If the plaintiff voluntarily assumes the risk of harm from the defendant's negligent conduct, then the plaintiff cannot recover. Assumption of the risk requires proof that the plaintiff knows and understands the risk, and the plaintiff voluntarily accepts the risk.

Legal Eagle

Some states deny any recovery to the plaintiff if the plaintiff was negligent. Almost all states have switched to comparative negligence.

For example, if a consumer attempts to repair a defectively manufactured toaster while it's plugged in, then the consumer has assumed the risk of the electric shock. Or if a customer trudges down an aisle that's clearly marked "Danger: Wet Floor," then the customer assumes the risk of slipping.

Products Liability: Defects That Cause Harm

The tort of products liability involves a defective product, where there is a defect in design, manufacture, or improper instructions or warnings. When a consumer is injured by a product, the injured party may be able to use one of several tort and contract theories of liability, including negligence (which we've already discussed), strict liability and products liability (often linked), and breach of contract warranty (which we discussed in the previous chapter).

Strict Liability and Products Liability

Product liability law holds the manufacturer liable for a defect in a product that makes the product unreasonably dangerous, proximately causes harm, and has not been substantially changed since manufacture.

The defect may be in the manufacture of the product or in its design. An example of a manufacturing defect would be engine bolts in a car that are too weak to hold the engine in place. A design defect might be something like a lawnmower that doesn't have an effective safety guard over the opening. If the mower flipped out a stick that impaled its victim, the manufacturer is liable. Defective warnings also may be the basis of products liability. Manufacturers and other suppliers of products have a duty to warn users of any risks in using the product, unless the risk is commonly known. For example, a drug manufacturer must warn consumers that a drug may cause drowsiness and warn the user not to drive after taking the drug.

You may even have to warn consumers about the effects of their potential misuse of the product. For example, a manufacturer of an electric hedge trimmer should warn the consumer against using the trimmer after a rain or during an early morning dew, even though an increased danger of electrocution might seem obvious. However, even if a product is arguably defective, consumer misuse may be a defense to the tort, such as when a consumer who was aware of the defect assumes the risk of using it or negligently uses it. For example, if the user decided to use a power mower to trim a hedge and trims a vital body part in the process, then the user's misuse is a defense that the manufacturer could use to protect itself against liability. Likewise, it would be a defense if the user ignores the trimmer warning, goes ahead and operates it in wet weather, and is electrocuted. Also, it would be a defense if the car owner continues to drive the car after notification that the engine mount bolts are defective and could cause the engine to fall off the car.

Intentional Torts from Battery to Libel

At times we can do some pretty dumb things. Unfortunately, our less-enlightened conduct may cause harm to others, and when it does we or our company may have to pay up. The following is a discussion of our tort rights and wrongs.

Assault, Battery, and False Imprisonment

Once upon a time there was a very, very angry pro basketball player who took out his wrath on a photographer by kicking him in the private parts (or thereabouts). The basketball player realized the error of his ways and sought to make amends for his transgression by the usual means of offering money because he knew he had committed the tort of battery.

Now, you're not likely to have to worry about controlling pro athletes in your line of business. But you may employ folks with anger management issues. In fact, probably all of us have our flash points. However, you need to know what conduct—yours or your employees'—may result in your company being liable.

Notes & Quotes

"When angry, count to four; when very angry, swear."

—Mark Twain, humorist

➤ **Assault.** Assault is a voluntary and intentional threat of immediate harm, or an attempted battery that missed its target. You don't touch, but come mighty close. For example, if one angry dude waves a baseball bat close to the other's head and threatens him with an instantaneous headache, this is an assault. Likewise, if the dude threw the bat at his intended victim but missed, this is an assault.

➤ **Battery.** Battery is a voluntary and intentional harmful or offensive touching. The basketball player intentionally struck the photographer. Although the blow may have hurt or was simply embarrassing, either qualifies for battery since the tort involves a wrongful touching. Battery can also involve an indirect touching, such as throwing the basketball at the photographer.

➤ **False imprisonment.** False imprisonment is wrongful confinement. Alleged shoplifters often claim this tort against shop owners who detain them until the police arrive. In order for the store to be liable for this tort, the security guard must have confined the suspected by the use of physical force, or threat or assertion of legal authority *without justification,* and the suspect had no reasonable means of escaping detention. For example, a novice security guard sees a teenager acting *strangely,* so the guard grabs the teen's arm and takes her to a holding area. The guard insists that she empty her purse, and if he finds nothing, the guard has no *reasonable suspicion,* so you and he will be liable for false imprisonment.

Shark Attack!

Don't detain a suspected shoplifter unless you're pretty sure of the charge. Most states have a statute permitting shop owners to detain a suspected shoplifter for a reasonable period for investigation, if there is a reasonable suspicion. Insist that no detention occur unless the guard can state that he or she saw the theft (or heard an alarm go off).

A property owner can use reasonable nondeadly force to protect property. Certainly, a security guard can use reasonable force to detain a suspect if detention is warranted. The gist of all three torts is the concept of *wrongfulness.* For example, the security guard who threatens a touching or touches, and then detains the suspect, may do so if there is a reasonable suspicion of theft by the suspect. This, however, would not excuse a male guard from frisking a female suspect except in the most unusual of circumstances; for example, she had a weapon.

Trespass and Conversion

Tort law recognizes the owner's right to use his or her property without improper interference. Trespassing is a wrongful, intentional intrusion upon someone else's real

Legal Eagle

If young children come to your store, ensure that there is nothing left on the property that is both dangerous and interesting to explore; posting "No trespassing" signs will not protect you.

estate. The trespass occurs with the intrusion; if any damage is done, then that adds to any court award. For example, your neighboring business parks its vehicles on your property despite your request to the contrary, and often hits your newly planted trees; this is a trespass. A trespass occurs when the property owner withdraws permission to be there.

Generally you are not liable for an injury to a trespasser unless you intentionally harm him or her (such as rigging a spring gun to shoot any intruders). However, you may be liable for an injury to a young child who trespasses because he or she is attracted to something dangerous on your property, and cannot appreciate the danger. The doctrine of attractive nuisance is established to hold the property owner or tenant liable for negligence. Trespass by the youngster is no defense, nor is comparative negligence or assumption of the risk; however, the company will not be liable if it is not negligent.

When someone takes your personal property without your permission, that is conversion. The person may steal it, or simply borrow it without permission for a while. The shoplifter who steals your merchandise, or the teenager who hot-wires your delivery van for a joyride, is committing conversion. The thief can be liable for the actual value of the property stolen, while the joyrider is liable for the loss of use. However, if a customer mistakenly takes another person's overcoat, then promptly returns it to the owner upon discovery of the error, this is not conversion.

Strict Liability

What you do *on* your property may affect others *outside* your property. You may enjoy the smell of leaves burning on a crisp autumn evening but your neighbors may not. Strict liability may involve …

➤ Defective products that injure.

➤ Wild animals or pets with a vicious propensity to injure.

➤ Ultrahazardous activities.

I've already discussed defective products earlier, so let's get right to vicious animals and ultrahazardous activities. Most businesses don't have wild animals about the premises, but a few have guard dogs. However, I knew of one company that kept a pet lion on the premises; if Leo the lion escaped and injured anyone, then the owner would be liable. Likewise, owners are liable for any guard dog that mauls or bites a customer (adult trespassers may assume the risk if you post a notice about the guard dogs).

The law may permit certain commercial activities that are abnormally dangerous but useful, for instance, manufacturing toxic chemicals or imploding a building to raze it. If foreseeable harm results from the ultrahazardous activity, then the business may be liable. For example, if the imploding building unexpectedly throws bricks on cars parked a significant distance away, then the company is strictly liable for the damage. However, if, despite adequate warning, a person parks his or her car too close to the site and a brick hits the car, the owner of the car may have assumed the risk.

Notes & Quotes

"Give a man a fish, and he can eat for a day. But teach a man how to fish, and he'll be dead of mercury poisoning inside of three years."

—Charlie Haas, writer

Nuisance

Tort law divides nuisance into private and public nuisances. Private nuisance involves an activity that substantially and unreasonably interferes with another's use and enjoyment of his or her land. The interference must be more than a minor annoyance. The usefulness to society of the other party's conduct and its arrival on the scene first are factors in determining if the activity is unreasonable.

A neighboring business that uses a blaring P.A. system to attract customers may be committing the tort of nuisance. Likewise, the neighboring restaurant that improperly stores its garbage near your retail store is committing a nuisance. However, if you are considering moving your store to a rustic country scene, the farmer with his odorous manure came first and you won't win a nuisance lawsuit.

The tort of public nuisance involves an unreasonable interference with a right common to the general public. Municipal ordinances may prohibit certain conduct, such as burning trash in open containers. A violation of the ordinance would be a public nuisance. If a person can prove harm, then he or she may sue to stop (abate) the nuisance and collect damages. For example, if the neighboring tavern permits intoxicated customers to urinate on the public sidewalks or have brawls, you may sue for nuisance.

Defamation

Tort law recognizes that one's reputation, privacy, and emotional well-being can be protected.

Libel and slander are the two defamatory torts. Libel is written; slander is oral. Both involve a false statement communicated by one person to another. In essence, the false statement lowers the

Notes & Quotes

"A slander is like a hornet; if you cannot kill it dead with the first blow, better not strike it at all."

—H. W. Shaw, writer

215

community's estimation of the person, or deters others from associating with him or her. Often libel and slander involve false statements asserted as fact, such as a public claim that a certain person has been convicted of a crime, is sexually immoral, unprofessional in business, and others. For example, your newspaper accuses a local builder of using shoddy materials. If this is true, the builder will lose his or her case for slander if he or she brings it forward. However, if it isn't true, the newspaper will be liable to pay for the damage caused to the builder's business. If your human resources manager responds falsely to a reference inquiry about an ex-employee by saying that the ex-employee was fired for stealing, then your ex-employee has a case against you for slander.

Invasion of Privacy

Most of us cherish our privacy, and we hope others respect our right to be left alone. Unfortunately, there are those who would intrude. The law of invasion of privacy is relatively new, and is continuing to develop. Courts have recognized the invasion of privacy when there is ...

➤ Wrongful appropriation of a person's name or likeness.

➤ Wrongful, offensive intrusion on private matters.

➤ Public disclosure of private facts.

The use of a person's name or photograph in an advertisement without permission is invasion of privacy. For example, if a prominent baseball player is displayed in a beer commercial without having given his consent, then the beer company and the advertising agency would be liable. So-called identity theft—wrongful use of Social Security number or photo ID—may be the tort of invasion of privacy, too.

Legal Eagle

If you are using any person's name or photo in an advertisement or video production, obtain his or her consent in writing.

A wrongful, offensive intrusion may involve such misconduct as an illegal search of the victim's home, use of a long-range listening device to invade the home, or persistent and unwanted communication. A debt collector may violate federal law by harassing a debtor by frequently calling at work or calling at all hours of the night; if the harassment is intrusive, it may also be an invasion of privacy.

The public disclosure of private facts about a person may be a tort if the disclosure is considered highly offensive to a reasonable person and is not a matter of public concern. For example, if a personnel employee disclosed that another employee was using her health benefits in a detox unit for drug abusers, this would be invasion of privacy.

Intentional Infliction of Emotional Distress

Extreme and outrageous conduct can inflict serious emotional harm. One of the local radio stations had a "fat person of the day" contest. One nominee was outraged, as she should have been, and threatened a lawsuit—the radio station quickly settled. The intentional misconduct must be shocking to the reasonable person. If a debt collector contacted neighbors claiming the debtor is a deadbeat, or took out an advertisement to that effect, then the collector may have committed the tort.

Rude behavior by an employee is intolerable but does not amount to a tort. However, if an employee refuses to serve another person because of race, nationality, or gender, that may violate federal or state public accommodation laws, and this misconduct may be the tort of intentional infliction of emotional distress.

Wrongful Contract Interference and Product Disparagement

Hiring an employee away from your competitor, snagging its customer, or disparaging its product may be standard practice, but could be a tort.

For instance, wrongful interference with someone else's contract is a tort. The contract interference may be between a company and its employees, or a company and its customers or suppliers. The tort requires proof that there was a valid contract between two parties, which the third party knew of, and the third party intentionally caused one of the two parties to breach the contract to advance the financial interest of the third party.

For example, let's say you have a valid, written contract with a key employee and a competitor who knows about the contract entices the employee to leave you. The resulting broken contract permits you to sue your ex-employee and to sue the competitor for the tort of contract interference.

Another example: Your company has a supply contract with a customer and it is to continue for another year. A competitor convinces the customer that it can provide a better deal, so your customer breaks its contract and goes with the competitor. If the competitor knew about your contract and convinced the customer to breach, then you can sue the customer for breach of contract, and the competitor for tortious contract interference.

Competitors may legitimately compare their products, but the tort of product disparagement occurs when financially injurious falsehoods are made about a product. The tort involves publishing lies

Notes & Quotes

"Honesty is the best policy—when there is money in it."

—Mark Twain, writer

about a competitor's product that defame the quality of the goods. If the competitor can prove financial loss because of the improper publication, such as sales figures showing that customers refused to buy the product, then the tort exists. For example, if your company manufactures a toothpaste and a competitor takes out an ad that falsely claims your toothpaste causes tooth decay, you may sue for product disparagement if your sales drop after the ad runs.

Remedies for the Injured

The goal of every plaintiff is to persuade the judge or jury that the defendant committed a tort, and the plaintiff is entitled to a remedy.

Damages

An injury invites compensation. The plaintiff may prove economic loss, such as lost wages, out-of-pocket expenses, medical bills, and loss of property value. There may be noneconomic personal injury, such as pain and suffering, mental distress, and physical impairment. To the extent that the plaintiff can quantify the loss, the judge or jury can order compensatory damages.

For example, your driver negligently hit another motorist; the car was totaled for a cost of $10,000; the motorist lost $5,000 in wages while recovering; medical bills were $20,000; the jury determined that his back injury caused him considerable pain to the tune of $50,000. All these mount up and you (and your insurance company) are liable for the tab.

Some intentional torts, such as assault, battery, false imprisonment, and defamation also invite an award of punitive damages, in excess of expense. Juries may give punitive damage verdicts to punish serious misconduct. However, some state statutes may limit punitive damages and judges may reduce punitive damages awards that are excessive.

For example, your personnel employee erroneously told a prospective employer that an ex-employee was fired for sexual harassment. The ex-employee lost a job opportunity because of this slander; the court may award lost wages and punitive damages because of the misconduct.

Equitable Remedies

For certain torts, money damages may not be adequate to correct the harm. You may want the court to stop the defendant's tortious conduct. The remedy is an *injunction*. Usually the wrongdoing involves some continuing harm, such as a continuing trespass or nuisance.

For example, your neighbor continues his obnoxious ways of littering his yard with garbage. Money damages alone are insufficient, so you want, and likely will receive, an injunction ordering the neighbor to clean up the yard and stop further trashing.

Helpful Sources

Cornell Law School has a valuable Web site that includes a discussion of tort law: www.law.cornell.edu. Likewise, visit www.findlaw.com. You may want to check the Web sites of your local law school, as well as your state Web site for statutes. The Consumer Product Safety Commission has a site discussing product defects: www.cpsc.gov. For the other side's check out the American Trial Lawyers Association site: www.atla.org, and the law firm of Alexander, Hawes & Audet at www. consumerlawpage.com.

The Least You Need to Know

➤ An employer is liable for an employee's negligence while working.

➤ Negligence occurs when a person's unreasonable conduct causes injury or property damage.

➤ A manufacturer is liable for a product that is unreasonably dangerous and hurts a consumer.

➤ An employer may be liable for false imprisonment if a security guard wrongfully detains a customer without reasonable suspicion of a theft.

➤ A party may collect money damages necessary to compensate for a tort injury.

Chapter 18

Suing or Being Sued: Basics of Litigation

> **In This Chapter**
>
> ➤ The lawsuit, from suit to nuts
>
> ➤ Understanding the uses of Small Claims Court
>
> ➤ Appealing to a higher court
>
> ➤ Arbitration and other alternatives to litigation

Suing or being sued seems to be a rite of passage for many businesses. Things happen. About 90 percent of all lawsuits do *not* go to trial, but the whole procedure may be vexatious and costly. You need to know the basics of litigation to prepare for the almost inevitable, and that's what we'll show you in this chapter.

Where to File Your Lawsuit

What follows in the section is a brief civics lesson, which may seem a little dry. I make no apology. If you paid close attention in high school government, you may skip this part.

Court Systems

We have two court systems: state and federal. Each state has its own courts, as does the federal government. Each court system is divided into three levels:

1. The trial court, including the state superior court at the state level and the U.S. district court at the federal level.

2. An intermediate appellate court or court of appeals at both levels.

3. The highest appellate court, including the Supreme Court, either state or federal.

All cases start at the trial level, and the party that loses at the trial level may appeal to the next level. Most cases stop at trial level, but a few get to the highest court if they present unique questions of law.

Federal Courts

The federal courts have limited jurisdiction, which means they can hear only certain cases. All other cases are tried in state courts. A federal court has jurisdiction over the following cases involving …

➤ The United States Constitution.

➤ Federal statutes or administrative law.

➤ A suit between a plaintiff and defendant who live in different states.

Your business is not likely to be entangled in Constitutional issues, so let's look at the other three.

Business law is replete with federal statutes and federal administrative law. Just pick any three letters and you have a federal agency that affects your business, from the IRS to the EPA. The federal courts have jurisdiction over any litigation based upon a federal statute or federal administrative regulation.

Two examples may suffice. Let's say an employee claims discrimination. Ultimately, the employee may sue in U.S. district court alleging a violation of Title VII of the Civil Rights Act of 1964—a federal statute. Or a company begins selling stock to investors. The Securities and Exchange Commission might sue on the basis that there had not been proper registration with the SEC under its statute and regulations, largely a matter of administrative law.

Notes & Quotes

"There were 265,200 civil cases filed with the 89 U.S. district courts in 1997, and only 3 percent went to trial."

—Office of the Clerk of the U.S. Supreme Court

Diversity jurisdiction in the federal court requires that: 1) the plaintiff and defendant are legal residents of different states, and 2) the amount sued for is at least $75,000. (No federal law need be involved.) The litigation, for instance, could be over a contract dispute or a serious auto accident. Here's an example: Your Indiana company contracts with a software supplier in California and the software doesn't work, but the seller refuses to fix it. The costs of the software and damages amounts to over $75,000; therefore, you may sue in federal court.

In addition to the general jurisdiction of the U.S. district court, the federal government has specialized courts, such as the tax court, bankruptcy courts, and court of federal claims.

A party that loses in district court may appeal to the regional court of appeals, such as the going from the U.S. District Court for Southern Indiana to the U.S. Court of Appeals for the Seventh Circuit. The ultimate appeal is to the U.S. Supreme Court, but few cases get that far. Of the 7,692 civil and criminal cases appealed to the Supreme Court in 1997, only 91 ended up with written decisions by the Court.

State Courts

State trial courts have general jurisdiction over both civil and criminal cases. Some courts are divided into those two categories, as well as into other courts with special jurisdiction, such as divorce, juvenile, probate, and small claims courts (for minor civil cases). You can determine which court is appropriate for your case by contacting the court clerk in the county where you are filing a lawsuit and giving him or her the basic thrust of the suit.

Each state has appellate courts to review trial court decisions. The appellate courts do not allow the parties to re-litigate the facts, but only discuss alleged errors of law, such as an erroneous jury instruction given during the trial. Usually, courts of appeals will reverse a trial court only when there has been a substantial error of law that could have affected the outcome.

For example, a party might have lost an automobile negligence case at the trial court because the judge instructed the jury that the defendant was liable simply if he or she caused the accident. This instruction is substantially misleading because it omits the other elements of negligence, such as the requirement that defendant acted without reasonable care. Therefore, the erroneous instruction might have led the jury to reach an unfair verdict, and this error allows the appellate court to reverse the decision.

Civil Procedure: Complaint to Trial

You have been harmed, either financially or physically. Your discussions with the other party to resolve the matter have been unsuccessful and thus you feel you have no recourse but to take the case to court. Or maybe you're on the other side, accused of causing financial or physical harm. Either way, you need to know all the steps involved and how you can help your lawyer to win the case.

The Lawsuit Begins

A lawsuit begins with a claim of injury, usually economic or physical. The path of a typical lawsuit for the plaintiff is as follows:

Notes & Quotes

"Law is not justice and a trial is not a scientific inquiry into truth. A trial is a resolution of a dispute."

—Edison Haines, lawyer

➤ **Harm done,** such as a breach of contract or a personal injury. Not all harm results in a lawsuit. Sometimes you just walk away the wiser. However, if your business has been significantly damaged, then you may want to consult an attorney about your legal rights.

➤ **Consultation with an attorney.** Most attorneys charge by the hour, so you may want to ask at the beginning what the attorney's hourly fee is. Your lawyer may be able to give you only the roughest of estimates as to what this may cost. Keep in mind that most litigants pay their own legal fees, so be prepared—your lawyer's time is your money. If there is a contract dispute, bring the contract and all related papers. If there is personal injury, bring all the medical information. You need to disclose all the facts, good, bad, and indifferent, because your lawyer needs to know the strengths and weaknesses, for surely your opponent will dwell on the latter.

Legal Eagle

Your lawyer is bound by the Rules of Professional Conduct to keep your information confidential unless you authorize its disclosure.

Legalese

The **Rules of Civil Procedure** govern all civil litigation; the federal and state rules are very similar.

➤ **Informal investigation by the attorney and paralegals.** Your lawyer may assign a paralegal or investigator to further look into the facts of your case. For example, if the issue involves an accident, the paralegal may visit the accident site and take pictures. Your lawyer may have to interview witnesses or research the law. All of this you pay for, so ask your attorney to keep you apprised as to the progress (and expense).

➤ **Settlement attempt.** After all this, you and your lawyer will discuss whether to demand full compensation for the wrong done to you, to propose a compromise to the other party, or to sue. It's your call. Your lawyer can advise you, but no lawyer can accurately predict the outcome of a lawsuit. However, a lawyer with knowledge of this area of the law and trial experience can give you some idea of your chances and the costs involved.

If, at this point, you and the other party are unable to come to terms, the lawsuit goes forward when the injured party files a complaint in the appropriate court. Then the defendant files an answer to the complaint, and pretrial motions begin according to the *Rules of Civil Procedure*. Let's take a look at the next stages of the lawsuit.

The Lawsuit Pleadings

If you are suing, then you are the plaintiff, and the other party is the defendant. This is simple enough; however, bring in third parties and things get a little more confusing, but more about them later.

Filing the Lawsuit

The complaint begins the lawsuit, as long as you file it in the appropriate court, meaning one that has jurisdiction over the issue you're litigating and is the proper venue. The proper venue means the court that is convenient for the plaintiff and defendant; if the two parties live in different places, proper venue is usually either the residence of the defendant, the location of the injury, or the location of the property at issue. The complaint sets out the facts and legal claim for which you are seeking a remedy. Most complaints contain the following:

➤ The names of the plaintiff and defendant

➤ A statement of the nature of claim, such as breach of contract

➤ The court jurisdiction

➤ The facts alleged that result in remedy

➤ The remedies sought

The Rules of Civil Procedure permit notice pleading, which means that you provide simple allegations of fact necessary to put the defendant on notice. If the defendant contends not to understand, then he or she can file a motion requesting a more definite statement. Usually a brief statement of who, what, when, where, and how will suffice.

Here's an example of a statement from a plaintiff involved in an auto accident: On April 1, 2000, at the intersection of East and South Street, Notown, Indiana, the defendant drove through a red light in a negligent manner and struck the plaintiff's automobile, which was legally proceeding through the intersection. This caused damage to the plaintiff's vehicle and bodily injury to the plaintiff. The statement (also called the complaint) may or may not specify the amount of damages requested. The complaint and a summons will then served upon the defendant, usually by mail (certified may be required) or by personal service (civil sheriff or process server). The summons notifies the defendant that he or she has 20 days (or whatever the Rules prescribe) to file an answer, or the plaintiff may seek and receive a default judgment.

Shark Attack!

Don't procrastinate. If you receive a complaint and summons, take it to your attorney immediately. If you don't respond to the complaint in a timely manner, you'll lose the lawsuit automatically through what's called a default judgment.

You may request a jury trial in the complaint, or the defendant may do so in the answer. In some cases jury trials are not available—such as a request for an injunction only—but if money damages are sought, then a jury is usually allowed. Whether you want a jury trial may be another matter; follow your attorney's advice.

The defendant must file an answer, responding to each of the facts alleged in the complaint. The defendant can admit or deny each claim, or admit or deny in part each claim, or in good faith claim a lack of knowledge or information. For example, the defendant in the earlier auto accident example may admit driving the car in question but deny running the red light or hitting the plaintiff's car.

If the defendant has any affirmative defenses against the plaintiff's complaint, then these need to be included. The affirmative defenses are listed in the Rules of Procedure, and include failure of contract consideration, fraud, illegality, payment, release, and statute of frauds, among others. Comparative negligence—that the plaintiff bears some responsibility for his or her injury—is an example of an affirmative defense used by the defendant.

The Art of the Countersuit

The defendant may want to countersue the plaintiff. If the defendant's claim arises out of the same transaction or occurrence, then the defendant may be required to file a compulsory counterclaim against the plaintiff as part of its responsive pleading. For example, if the plaintiff claims breach of contract, the defendant may respond by denying that he or she breached the contract, and then sue the plaintiff for his or her own breach of that same contract in a countersuit. However, if the defendant has a claim against the plaintiff in an unrelated matter, such as the breach of a different contract, the court may allow a permissive counterclaim.

If a counterclaim is filed, then the other party must file an answer to it.

Three's a Crowd: Third Parties and Cross Claims

At times the plaintiff and defendant aren't the only ones who should join the parties. For example, the auto accident may involve multiple drivers, or the contract may involve more than two people or entities.

I once had a client who was a subcontractor on a building project. The developer didn't pay the mortgage company, so the mortgage company sued. My client and several subs weren't paid, so they filed mechanics' liens against the real estate, and then joined the lawsuit. In the end, the litigation involved nine parties, each of whom filed complaints, answers, counterclaims, answers to counterclaims, cross-claims, and answers to cross-claims. The pleadings alone cost a few trees in paper. The cross-claim brings in a new party. For example, the defendant in an auto accident may claim a third party caused the accident, such as a driver who rammed into the defendant's car and caused the defendant to hit another car. This new party must then file a counterclaim in a timely manner.

Movers and Shakers: Motions

Lawyers are fond of their motions. The most typical motions filed with the court include …

➤ Motion to dismiss.

➤ Motion for judgment on the pleadings.

➤ Motion for summary judgment.

The first two generally allege lack of jurisdiction or a failure to state a claim for which the court can provide a remedy. For example, unless a case involves a federal issue or diversity, a judge would grant a motion to dismiss due to lack of jurisdiction if the plaintiff filed the suit in federal court. Or if the complaint alleged no negligence by the defendant nor harm to the plaintiff, then there is no valid claim and the court would grant the defendant's motion to dismiss.

> **Legal Eagle**
>
> Make sure you follow proper procedure. Any motion must be filed with the court and a copy sent to the other party. The judge usually permits oral or written argument before deciding the motion. Even if a motion is granted, the losing party may still be able to continue the lawsuit by amending the complaint.

Any party may file a motion for summary judgment (a motion that alleges there are no genuine issues of fact), and that the moving party (the party making the motion) is entitled to a judgment as a matter of law. This motion requires sworn statements (affidavits) and other evidence, such as depositions and interrogatories (questioning of those involved) in its support. The moving party must convince the judge that there is, in essence, nothing to litigate; but if there are any facts in dispute, the judge will deny the motion.

For example, if Al Aged, age 50, was fired and he sued under the Age Discrimination Act, the reason for the firing is a factually disputed question and thus summary judgment would not be appropriate. However, if Al were age 38 at the time he was fired, the judge would grant the summary judgment to the defendant because the Act only protects employees age 40 and above.

Pretrial Discovery

The Rules of Civil Procedure for both federal and state courts permit plaintiff and defendant extensive pretrial discovery to gain information and evidence from the other party or third parties, such as witnesses. Any party may obtain discovery regarding any matter that is relevant to the litigation, and not privileged. Some of the discovered information, such as that discovered in a deposition, may be used in the trial as evidence, while other information will help build your case, or if not, at least let you know how tenuous your case really is.

Pretrial discovery may include ...

➤ **Written interrogatories.** These are questions sent to the other party or parties to the lawsuit. The questions usually are brief, simple, and fact-based. For example, in a contract dispute, you may ask the defendant if he or she signed a contract with you on a specific date, and did he or she receive advance payment for services to be rendered.

➤ **Depositions.** Depositions are sworn statements by witnesses and parties made in the presence of attorneys. The witness is asked questions and responds accordingly. If the witness is another party to the complaint, then his or her attorney will be there to ask rebuttal questions, and perhaps object to the questions posed. Any objections are usually noted on the transcript. Deposition is somewhat like a witness examination and cross-exam at trial, except you usually have access to the questions ahead of time so that you can prepare.

➤ **Production of documents or things.** Both the plaintiff and defendant bring forward all documents and physical evidence relevant to the case.

➤ **Requests for admission of facts.** You may ask the opposing party to admit the truth of the statements submitted. Any matter admitted under such a request is established as true for purposes of the trial. For example, a plaintiff can ask the defendant to admit that the machinery causing her injury had not been inspected for defects for six months prior to the injury.

Pretrial Conference

After discovery and before trial, the attorneys meet with the judge in a pretrial conference. The purpose of the conference is to clarify the issues, review the facts and documents, and explore settlement possibilities. The judge will ask the parties to exchange witness lists. Judges differ on how much they are willing to push attorneys for settlement.

Legal Eagle

Always be willing to settle if the terms are right. Settlement should always remain an option, except in the most unusual cases. This does not mean that you take whatever is offered, but that you keep an open mind. This is business, not a personal vendetta.

Trial

The trial between two parties generally follows this format:

➤ **Jury selection.** During jury selection, the attorneys ask potential jurors questions to eliminate unsuitable jurors, a process called *voir dire*. Attorneys want sympathetic jurors, so questions will seek to find those kindred souls who might see the case from the plaintiff's perspective. Each side has a number of preemptory challenges, usually three, that allow them to dismiss a juror without cause. Of course, the attorney may be able to convince the court that the potential juror should be dismissed for cause, such as bias or knowledge of one of the parties.

➤ **Opening statements.** Each attorney is allowed to make an opening statement concerning the facts he or she intends to prove. This gives each lawyer an opportunity to provide that party's version of the facts. The jury, or judge if trial by judge alone, better understands the nature of the case.

➤ **Presentation of evidence.** The plaintiff has the burden of proof, usually by the preponderance of the evidence, which means that the jury thinks it more likely than not that the event took place as alleged. The plaintiff begins with its witnesses and tangible evidence. The defendant has the right to cross-exam each witness and object to the plaintiff's questions or tangible evidence. The court will rule on the objections as they are made. After the defendant's cross-examination, the plaintiff may ask each witness further questions to rebut unfavorable responses in cross-exam. Then the defense presents its case in the same way, and will try to undermine and rebut the case presented by the plaintiff.

➤ **Closing arguments.** After both sides have finished, then each presents a closing argument. Each attorney summarizes the evidence presented, and emphasizes the evidence that supports his or her case and the shortcomings of the opponent's case.

➤ **Jury instructions and verdict.** The judge instructs the jury as to the applicable law and tells the jury its role is to evaluate the facts. The judge emphasizes that the jury must render its verdict based upon the evidence introduced in the case. Once the jury has reached

Legalese

The process of jury selection is called **voir dire** ("look-speak"). It is pronounced *vwah deer*.

Shark Attack!

Unless you're an attorney, don't try handling a lawsuit on your own. The Rules of Civil Procedure and the Rules of Evidence are quite complicated—and go far beyond the scope of this one chapter.

Notes & Quotes

"You can observe a lot just by watching."
—Yogi Berra, baseball manager

229

a decision, it renders a verdict in favor of one party, and specifies damages, if any, to be paid to the plaintiff. This concludes the trial. (If there is no jury, the judge issues the verdict.)

➤ **Post-trial motions.** The losing party may file a motion requesting a new trial or a motion for judgment notwithstanding the adverse verdict by alleging that the jury verdict was wrong as a matter of law. The judge may grant the motion if he or she is convinced that the jury was in error. If the motion is not granted, then the losing party may want to appeal.

➤ **Appeals.** Either party may appeal a judgment. The party appealing (appellate) requests a transcript from the trial. The other party (appellee) files a responding brief. The appeals court (usually three members) reads the trial transcript and briefs, and hears oral argument. The appellate court will not reverse unless there was a substantial error of law that could have affected the outcome of the trial.

Notes & Quotes

"The people can change Congress, but only God can change the Supreme Court."

—George W. Norris, politician

Small Claims Court

You may want to handle a small collection matter, contract breach, or rental dispute yourself. Check with your local small claims court. Often the court has a brochure to help you through the process. The steps usually involve filing the complaint and serving it on the defendant, going to trial, and collecting the judgment if you win.

Filing the complaint usually consists of filling out a simple form. You briefly state the facts and the amount of damages to which you are entitled. Your request for damages cannot exceed the court's authority, which varies in each state from $2,000 to $15,000.

The complaint must be served on the defendant, usually by certified mail or by a court process server. In many states the defendant doesn't have to file an answer; the defendant just shows up, or doesn't appear, in which case you can obtain a default judgment.

The trial is informal, but that doesn't mean you don't have to follow the rules of evidence. The plaintiff presents his or her case with testimony and tangible evidence. In most instances, the defendant will not have a lawyer, but assume the worst and make sure that you have all the necessary documents, and don't use sworn statements instead of live witnesses.

Open your case with a short summary, then you and your witnesses will testify and present tangible evidence. Make sure that you discuss testimony with each witness before the trial and organize the tangible evidence in proper sequence. The court wants your evidence to be clear and concise, because the judge may be hearing dozens of cases that day.

The defendant may cross-examine your witnesses and object to your evidence. The defendant may present his or her own witnesses and evidence, which you may cross-exam and to which you may object.

At the conclusion, briefly summarize your case and ask the court to award you the requested damages.

The court may rule right away or send you its order later. In some states, you cannot appeal the court's decision; check with the court clerk. If you win, you still must collect the judgment. Please read about this process in Chapter 20, "Extending Credit and Collecting from a Reluctant Debtor."

Alternatives to Litigation

Lawsuits can be time consuming and expensive. In recent years, legislatures have enacted statutes that allow parties to use alternative methods of dispute resolution: *arbitration* and *mediation*.

The arbitrator acts as a judge and will render a decision. The arbitrator may be an attorney, but that is usually not required. If the parties agree to abide by the decision, and do so, then the dispute ends with arbitration; however, if one party reneges on the agreement, the other party can file a lawsuit to enforce the award. Prepare your arbitration case just like a trial; however, the rules of evidence may not be so strictly applied.

Legalese

In **arbitration** the parties formally submit their dispute to a person (arbitrator) whose decision is binding. In **mediation,** the parties seek outside help (mediator) to assist in persuading the parties to settle their dispute.

If you choose mediation, the mediator's role is to help the parties evaluate their positions and clarify the issues. Often the mediator is not an attorney. The mediator may hold private sessions with each party to determine what the party's true position is on each issue and what compromises are acceptable. Through this process the mediator attempts to inject a note of realism and engender a willingness to settle the dispute. The mediator may suggest settlement terms, often based upon experience. If the parties cannot resolve their differences through mediation, then there is recourse to arbitration or litigation.

Helpful Sources

I recommend reading Brent W. Terry's book, *The Complete Idiot's Guide to Protecting Yourself from Everyday Legal Hassles* (Alpha Books, 1995). Your state Web site may contain the Rules of Procedure and the Rules of Evidence. The federal rules can be found at the Cornell Web site: www.law.cornell.edu. Many federal and some state courts have their own Web sites. Alternative dispute resolution can be found at the American Arbitration Association Web site: www.adr.org.

The Least You Need to Know

➤ A lawsuit begins with the filing of a complaint alleging facts and requesting damages or other court action.

➤ The plaintiff has the burden of proving his or her case.

➤ You can handle your own case in small claims court.

➤ Arbitration and mediation may be a viable alternative to suing.

Part 5

Protecting Your Business Assets

Your business name may be your most valuable asset. Have you trademarked it? Aspirin is a household name, but once was a trademarked name and now the owner is long since forgotten. Don't let that happen to your business.

In this part, you'll also learn how to avoid claims of deceptive advertising and deceptive sales practices. Consumer protection laws range from lending to collecting. You can refuse a credit sale because a person is not creditworthy, but not because he or she is over 80 years old.

When you sell on credit you need to ensure payment, and one way is to obtain a security interest, or lien, on the debtor's collateral, which you can repossess for nonpayment. If the debtor files personal bankruptcy, there may be little you can do, but little isn't the same as nothing.

Not everyone goes downtown to a business. Some of us stay home and work from there. Computer commuting saves gas. Which brings up the next subject— e-commerce. The new way of doing business still requires observing the old laws, with some distinct twists that warrant your attention.

Chapter 19

Consumer Rights and Your Responsibilities

In This Chapter

➤ Designing accurate and appealing ads

➤ Sales practices that are on the up and up

➤ Keeping your consumers safe and sound

➤ Understanding credit protection laws

We are all consumers and most businesses want to do what is right for their customers. Most do. Some don't. The consumer protection laws are written for the minority of businesses that try to make a fast buck at the consumer's expense. No doubt you run a fair business, but even you can inadvertently violate a consumer protection law. This chapter alerts you to the major laws so that you can properly serve your customer as you intend—honestly.

Advertising Without Misleading

Customers love quality at a bargain price, so you have to convince them that you provide both. Advertising is the means to do just that. Although you certainly do not intend to deceive any potential customer, it's possible that consumers may misconstrue your ad. This section will discuss what the Federal Trade Commission (FTC) deems deceptive advertising, so that you can avoid any possible claims that your ad campaign violates the law.

While not all advertising comes within the authority of the FTC, many ads do, including the use of newspapers, electronic media, and the Internet. The FTC usually focuses on national advertising, and leaves local deceptive ads to the state and local governments. The latter agencies usually follow the FTC guidelines.

Deceptive Advertising

The FTC requires advertising to be truthful and nondeceptive, fair, and accurate, with evidence to back up its claim.

An advertisement is deceptive if it is likely to mislead a reasonable consumer, contains a material misrepresentation, or omits material information. An advertisement is unfair if it causes or likely will cause significant consumer injury that the consumer could not reasonably avoid. Deception may occur when the ad claim takes on an appearance of authenticity, that is, makes specific and concrete claims.

The FTC focuses on the advertisement's effect on the consumer. The relevant questions it asks, and you should, too, about the ad are ...

➤ Are consumers likely to reach false beliefs about the product or service?

➤ What are the consumer's expectations for the product or service after the ad?

➤ What would the typical consumer's response be to the ad?

Notes & Quotes

"Trickery and treachery are the practices of fools that have not wits enough to be honest."

—Benjamin Franklin, inventor

Shark Attack!

Never mislead or deceive with your advertising. Deceptive advertising may be the basis of a contract breach for misrepresentation or a tort action for fraud.

The FTC looks at the ad from the perspective of the average consumer. For example, if an advertisement claims that it can kill numerous household germs, and then, in the fine print, lists dozens it does not affect, the ad is clearly deceptive.

An ad that misrepresents the product by implication is also deceptive. For example, an ad showing a windup toy dog strolling down a street implies that the toy dog is able to "walk" for a relatively long distance, such as a block or so. If the dog requires re-winding every five feet, you've created a deceptive ad.

Omitting important facts is also prohibited because what the ad doesn't say may be very misleading and deceptive. For example, an ad for a weight-reduction pill that guarantees a consumer will lose weight but fails to mention important side effects, such as vomiting and headaches, is likely to be deemed misleading.

If the advertisement makes any factual claims, such as a restaurant ad that states that a majority of food reviewers recommends the restaurant, then there must be evidence to support the assertion. If the ad claims the scientific community supports the diet pill, then there must be evidence of reliable studies to confirm the claim.

On the other hand, vague generalities and obvious exaggerations are not likely to mislead. For example, if you claim that your business serves customers better than any competitor in town, this is considered simple "puffing" and not deceptive advertising.

FTC in Action

The FTC will look closely at claims about health and safety, as well as any claims that consumers have trouble evaluating for themselves. For example, an advertisement for a bicycle helmet may claim that the helmet protects against serious head injuries. That's a difficult concept for the average consumer to evaluate if something goes wrong. The FTC indicates that it will consider the following in acting against an advertisement:

➤ The scope of advertising campaign

➤ The extent to which ad represents a pattern of deception

➤ The extent of injury to the consumer's health, safety, or finances

> ### Notes & Quotes
>
> "Joe Camel is dead. He had it coming."
>
> —Bruce Reed, politician

The FTC will likely defer to state or local consumer protection agencies if the advertising is local. Often, a state attorney general has a consumer protection office, as do many municipalities. The Better Business Bureau can help resolve disputes, too. The FTC looks to the impact of the deception; the greater the potential for serious injury or widespread financial injury is, the higher the priority for FTC action.

If the FTC receives significant complaints about a deceptive or unfair advertisement, then it will investigate and may issue a formal complaint to the alleged offender. If the company agrees to settle by modifying or withdrawing the ad, then no further action may occur.

However, if there is no agreement, the FTC may conduct a hearing to determine if the company violated the law. An administrative law judge conducts the hearing according to agency administrative rules. Please read Chapter 22, "ABCs of Administrative Law," for more about administrative law.

If the FTC proves deceptive or unfair advertising, it may order the company to cease and desist, and may impose daily fines for future violations. It may order corrective advertising, in which the company must admit its earlier ad was misleading. The order may be reviewed or enforced through the federal courts.

Your Ads

Here's the positive advice I can give you about creating advertising for your company:

➤ Be truthful; your ads must be factually accurate.

➤ Avoid the word *free* unless there are absolutely no strings attached.

237

➤ Double-check all pricing information.

➤ Don't mislead when you compare your product to those of your competitors.

➤ Have sufficient goods available to meet demands from the ad.

➤ Test the ad on some customers before you run it to be sure a term or description isn't open to easy misinterpretation.

Deceptive Sales Practices to Avoid

States have enacted statutes that prohibit certain deceptive sales practices. A few of the violations include ...

➤ Bait-and-switch advertising.

➤ Claiming that a product or service is on sale or available when it isn't.

➤ Claiming a used product to be new.

➤ Claiming that a product requires replacement or repair when it doesn't.

➤ Claiming an endorsement of a product or service, when none exists.

What You See Is Not What You Get

Bait-and-switch advertising involves a company offering a very low price for an item to bring customers into the store, but then discouraging the customer from buying it or claiming that the item is unavailable. The low price is the bait, and the salesperson does the switch.

For example, Finest Furniture Company advertised a dining room table for $399, but when the customer appeared in response to the ad, the salesperson, as instructed by the boss, criticized the advertised model as poorly made and pitched a more expensive $799 model. This is the classic bait-and-switch technique.

If you advertise or mark an item as "on sale," the sale price you set must be less than its usual price. Likewise, for any advertised item, you must have sufficient quantity in stock to meet a reasonably expected demand.

Sale Away!

If your company tags an item as on sale for $59.99 when the usual price is $55.00, then this is a deceptive sales practice. If a company advertises VCR players for $111.11, but has only a few in stock (particularly if it then tries to switch customers to a higher priced item), this, too, is a deceptive practice. Many of the consumer complaints to the FTC involve auto repair shops billing customers for a new auto part when it's used, or making unwarranted repairs, all of which are deceptive practices.

Endorsing the Truth

If a company claims an endorsement, say from *Consumer Reports,* when there is none, it violates the law. It might be helpful to briefly review the FTC endorsement and testimonial guidelines. These are posted on the FTC Web site (www.ftc.gov). Product or service endorsements must reflect the honest opinions, findings, beliefs, or experience of the endorser. If the advertisement represents the endorser as using the product, then the endorser must have been a bona fide user at the time the endorsement was made.

Notes & Quotes

"There is only one valid definition of business purpose: to create a customer."

—Peter Drucker, management expert

For example, Ima Smiley must use the toothpaste that she endorses. If an expert endorses the product, then his or her qualifications must in fact give that person the expertise represented. For example, the endorser of an automobile's engineering designs should have engineering qualifications associated with cars, not a chemical engineering degree.

In sales, the Biblical golden rule should apply. Treat your customers as you would want to be treated—and they will return.

Soliciting by Phone, Delivering by Mail

In addition to deceptive practice statutes, many states have laws restricting telemarketers' activities. These laws vary, so you need to contact your state consumer protection division. Federal law prohibits telephone solicitation using an automatic telephone dialing system or prerecorded message.

Many state laws permit a buyer who purchased merchandise at his or her residence to cancel the sale by written notification to the seller within three business days. For example, if Hal Homeowner buys a vacuum cleaner from a door-to-door salesman, Hal has three days to cancel the sale. If you receive unordered merchandise through the mail, then you can refuse delivery or treat the unsolicited merchandise as a gift. For example, if you didn't order the multivolume set of Lord Byron's *Complete Poems* but received one in your mail complete with a bill, you may either return or keep the unordered merchandise without cost to you. (However, keep in mind that you won't be able to do so if you're a member of a book or music club and simply fail to return the monthly selection slip.)

A company that sells over the telephone or takes mail order sales must ship the product within the time stated or advertised, inform customers when the orders cannot be shipped on time, and issue a refund within a specified time when an order is cancelled.

Please read Chapter 23, "Wave of the Now: The Net of Home," about use of the Internet for advertising and sales.

Consumer Safety Laws

Two federal agencies are responsible for the health and safety of many consumer products: the Consumer Product Safety Commission (CPSC) and the Food and Drug Administration (FDA).

Protecting Consumers

The CPSC has comprehensive regulatory authority over about 15,000 consumer products, including toys, clothing, appliances, furniture, and playground and sports equipment. Regulations apply to any company that manufactures, imports, distributes, or sells any consumer product covered by its law.

The Consumer Product Safety Commission issues mandatory safety standards for some products (such as bicycles), bans certain products (such as lead-based paint), and helps develop standards for other products. CPSC maintains a clearing house of information on the risks associated with consumer products.

Legal Eagle

CPSC has a small business ombudsman to assist you in answering questions about compliance with its laws. The CPSC Web site is www.cpsc.gov.

According to CPSC, small businesses must report to the CPSC when …

➤ One of its products has a defect or creates a substantial risk of injury to the public.

➤ One of the manufacturer's consumer products has been involved in three or more personal injury lawsuits in a two-year period.

➤ Toys involve incidents of children choking on them.

Medication and Foodstuff Protection

The FDA protects consumers from purchasing and using adulterated or misbranded food and drugs. The Food and Drug Administration regulates food additives and medical and other health devices. If your company is involved in any of these areas, it would be worthwhile to visit this agency's Web site at www.fda.gov. Federal and state laws regulate information provided on consumer product labels and packages. The statutes require accurate information about products and a warning of possible dangers from their use. For example, packaged-food labeling must include nutritional facts, and limit the use of such terms as "fresh" and "low fat." The FDA, Agricultural Department, FTC, and Department of Health and Human Services are all involved in these areas, as well as some state agencies. If your business includes packaging consumer goods, I recommend visiting all these agencies' Web sites for more specific information.

Credit Where Credit Is Due

Most businesses extend credit to their customers in one form or another. You need to know the consumer credit laws, which include the following:

➤ Equal Credit Opportunity Act (ECOA)

➤ Fair Credit Reporting Act (FCRA)

➤ Truth in Lending Act

➤ Fair Credit Billing Act (FCBA)

➤ Electronic Fund Transfer Act (EFTA)

➤ Fair Debt Collection Practices Act (FDCPA)

Notes & Quotes

"Total consumer credit outstanding in 1998 was $1,308.4 billion, up from $796.4 billion in 1990."

—*Federal Reserve Bulletin*

Applying for Credit

When a customer applies for credit, a business cannot discriminate on the basis of sex, race, marital status, religion, national origin, age, or receipt of public assistance. The Equal Credit Opportunity Act (ECOA) law applies to any company that regularly extends credit, including retail and department stores. For example, the ABC store would be violating the law if it required married women to have their husbands co-sign any loan. The law doesn't prohibit you from refusing credit based a customer's finances—you just can't discriminate based on nonfinancial factors.

The Fair Credit Reporting Act (FCRA) is designed to ensure that consumer credit reporting companies furnish accurate and complete information. If you deny a customer credit because of a credit report, then you must notify the customer of the name and address of the credit-reporting agency.

Legal Eagle

Always notify your customers or potential employees if you use a credit report to deny them employment or take any other adverse action based on that report, as per the FCRA. You'll also need to provide the name and address of the reporting agency to your customers.

Under the FCRA, the consumer has a right to receive a copy of his or her credit report from a credit reporting agency, to know who received the credit report in the last year (or two years if employment related), and to receive a free copy of the credit report if credit was denied on the basis of information in the report. Any consumer has the right to dispute the accuracy of the information in the report, and to add a summary explanation if the dispute is not satisfactorily resolved.

Full Disclosure

The Truth in Lending Act is primarily a credit disclosure law for personal loans and installment sales involving $25,000 or less. It also covers real estate mortgage loans. The purpose of the Act is to allow consumers to comparison shop among lenders. If you extend credit to a consumer, then you must conspicuously state the annual percentage rate (APR) of the loan and the total cost of the loan. For example, if a customer purchases an appliance on a retail installment contract, the agreement would state "10 percent APR, and total cost of payments for the life of loan is $1,100." The APR includes all the direct costs, including interest, and all indirect charges imposed for the credit offered, such as the cost of a credit report. A violation of the disclosure requirements may permit the consumer to sue for compensatory and punitive damages, as well as attorneys' fees.

Any loan that results in obtaining a second mortgage or refinance loan on a consumer's residence requires a three-business-day right to rescind. For example, a company that sells aluminum siding and obtains a second mortgage on the residence for the financing, must allow this three-day rescission right.

Many consumer leases are also covered under amendments to Truth in Lending. The Act regulates consumer leases involving a contractual obligation of $25,000 or less and the lease exceeds four months. Any advertisement and lease must disclose the total amount due; the number and amounts of lease payments; determination of residual value and realized value; and whether an extra charge is imposed at the end of the lease term. A new car lease is a typical application of the statute.

Laws that limit the rate of interest that can be charged are called usury statutes. State statutes may limit the rate of interest that can be charged on a loan or retail installment sale. Laws vary, so consult your state statutes.

Billing, Credit Cards, and the EFTA

Billing mistakes on credit card statements and electronic fund transfer accounts, including debit cards and ATMs, do occur. The Fair Credit Billing Act (FCBA) establishes a procedure for correcting those credit card billing mistakes. The credit card customer must notify the issuer (the credit card company, not the store from which he or she bought the item) within 60 days from the billing. The issuer is then obligated to investigate any alleged errors. If the error is confirmed, the charged item is deleted; however, if the issuer denies the error, than the consumer may request documentation of the disputed transaction.

Credit card holders are liable for no more that $50 per card when unauthorized charges are made before the issuer is notified. A stolen credit card is the most typical example of limited liability. However, if a holder lends another person his or her credit card, and that person misuses it, the holder is liable for all charges.

The Electronic Funds Transfer Act (EFTA) covers automatic teller machines, point-of-sale (debit) cards, and electronic funds transfers. The consumer must promptly notify the issuer that the card is lost or stolen to minimize responsibility. If notice is given within two days, then the liability is $50; over two days and up to 60 days, the liability is $500; over 60 days the liability may be unlimited. If there are any errors on the EFT statement, the customer must report the error within 60 days, and after the timely reporting the issuer must investigate and report its conclusions to the customer.

Debt Collection

The Fair Debt Collection Practices Act (FDCPA) applies to debt collection companies and collection attorneys and prohibits certain abuses; they are liable for their misconduct. The Act does not apply to creditors who are collecting their own accounts.

The Act requires a collection agency to include a validation notice whenever it initially contacts a debtor for payment. The notice must state that the debtor has 30 days within which to dispute the debt and to request a written verification of the debt.

FDCPA specifically prohibits the collection agency from using the following tactics:

➤ Contacting the debtor at his or her place of employment if the employer objects

➤ Contacting the debtor during inconvenient or unusual times

➤ Contacting third parties other than the debtor's parents, spouse, or financial advisor

➤ Harassing or intimidating the debtor, such as posing as a court official

➤ Contacting the debtor after the debtor has notified the agency that he or she refuses to pay, except as to advise of a possible lawsuit

Again, a creditor is not covered by the Act as long as the creditor does not use its own name. Please read the next chapter about creditor collection methods.

Helpful Sources

Federal Web sites are very useful: Federal Trade Commission (www.ftc.gov), Consumer Product Safety Commission (www.cpsc.gov), Food and Drug Administration (www.fda.gov), Health and Human Services (www.hhs.gov), Small Business Administration, which has great links (www.sba.gov). Visit your state consumer protection Web site. Some local governments have a consumer affairs Web site. Consumer Union, the publisher of *Consumer Reports* magazine has a Web site, both free and subscription (www.ConsumerReports.org).

The Least You Need to Know

➤ A deceptive advertisement, according to the FTC, is one that is likely to mislead a reasonable consumer.

➤ Federal law requires anyone who sells a product that has caused three or more serious personal injuries within two years to report this to the Consumer Product Safety Commission.

➤ Truth in Lending requires installment sales retailers to notify the consumer of the annual percent rate (APR).

Chapter 20

Extending Credit and Collecting from a Reluctant Debtor

This chapter could have been titled "Creditor's Rights." If you extend credit, your risks and rights are important to your business success. Accounts receivable receipts don't mean much until they are turned into cash. We'll also look at the downside—your debtor's bankruptcy and see if anything can be collected from the bankrupt. Also, we'll explore the ins-and-outs of credit as it applies to your small business.

Getting Paid: The Options

Getting paid for your work or selling your goods is always a supremely gratifying moment. Your customer may hand you several portraits of Andy Jackson, General Grant, or Ben Franklin. Or you may get plastic in the form of a credit or debit card. Sometimes, your customer will have the bank electronically transfer the money.

Cash

Cash is good. But our currency isn't copy-proof, so you may want to use one of those handy devices, such as a special pen, to determine the real from the fake. If you get a stack of hundreds from a customer and it totals more than $10,000, then under federal law you must report this transaction to the IRS on Form 8300. The feds have suspicious minds.

Credit Cards

MasterCard, Visa, and the rest charge you for the privilege of allowing your customers to use their cards. The charge may range from 3 percent to 5 percent of the sale. You must follow the credit card issuer's rules, such as checking the expiration date of every card and getting approval for certain purchases. In most cases, even if the cardholder doesn't pay his or her bill, you'll still get your money, (which is why you're willing to pay the fee to the credit card company). However, if the customer claims your merchandise was defective and refuses to pay on that basis, you'll be the one who'll have to answer that charge directly.

Checks

Taking personal checks is always risky business. The customer may have insufficient funds to cover the check, the account may be closed, or someone, other than the customer, with the proper authority to do so might have to sign the check. I would suggest taking the following precautions:

➤ Accept only local checks.

➤ Accept only checks that display the preprinted customer name and address.

➤ Require that customers sign personal checks in your or your clerk's presence.

➤ Confirm all business checks with business owners if you don't know who has the authority to sign.

➤ Don't accept checks larger than the purchase price and give cash back.

➤ Don't give a cash refund until the bank has cleared the check and you've received the money in your account.

➤ Verify large checks with the bank.

➤ Ask to see photo identification.

➤ Stamp the back of the checks "for deposit only" and promptly deposit them.

Despite your precautions, bad checks may bounce up. If so, check first with the bank to see if the customer now has a balance sufficient to honor the check. If the customer does, run—don't walk—to the bank and cash the check. Second, call your customer and give him or her the chance to correct what may well have been a simple mistake. If you don't succeed at this point, write your customer a brief letter requesting payment and suggesting a lawsuit if prompt payment doesn't occur. Finally, if you still don't receive valid payment, file a lawsuit in small claims court. Many state laws will permit damages of three times the amount of the check, plus court costs and attorneys' fees. Or turn the check over to a collection agency and let them have a go at it.

Notes & Quotes

"Some people use one half their ingenuity to get into debt, and the other half to avoid paying it."

—George D. Prentice, businessperson

Legal Eagle

Get two signatures on an unknown customer's check. If you don't know the customer but do know someone with whom he or she's shopping, have the known customer endorse the check as well. That way the companion would be secondarily liable if the customer's check bounces.

You can request prosecution, but unless the bad-check writer is a notorious crook, the police may decide they have more important priorities.

Keep in mind that the customer may have stopped payment on the check, causing it to bounce. If that's the case, then try to determine the problem and resolve it. For example, the customer may have changed his or her mind about buying the merchandise. The simplest resolution may be for you to ask for its return.

Another alternative you should consider, particularly for checks involving significant amounts, is to require a cashier's check issued by a bank, or have the customer get his or her check certified by a bank. In certifying a check, the bank is guaranteeing that the funds are on deposit, and your risk is shifted to the bank.

Promissory Notes

Cash, checks, and credit cards are the most common ways consumers pay for the goods they buy. An alternative is a promissory note. By accepting an I.O.U., you are, in effect, financing the customer's purchase. In return, your customer agrees to pay you on or before its due date, with interest, according to the terms of the note you both sign. The promissory note is typically used by the businessperson who sells on credit, such as for large equipment; the businessperson may want to sell the note at a discount to a finance company.

The customer, known as the maker of the promissory note, is primarily liable for the note. If you sell the note to a bank or finance company (usually at a discount of its face value), then you, as endorser of the note, will be secondarily liable; you pay the bank or the finance company if the maker does not.

If one maker is good, a co-maker (co-signer) may be better, because you would then have two persons who are primarily liable. Remember that the Equal Credit Opportunity Act prohibits discrimination based on race, gender, and so on, so don't insist as a matter of practice, for example, that all wives get husbands to co-sign.

Securing the Loan with Collateral

A promissory note is just a promise to pay. The maker's word may be good, but better yet is the maker putting up some collateral you can seize if the maker defaults on the loan.

Statutory Liens

State law may protect creditors in certain transactions by creating a statutory lien, which is a claim or right against certain property, and which may be satisfied from the proceeds of the sale of the property. The statutory lien is different than a mortgage lien, which the mortgagor and mortgage company agree to. The two most typical liens involve property improvements: mechanics' lien against real estate and an artisan's lien for repairs to personal property.

If your company installs a roof, constructs an addition to a house, re-paves a driveway, or otherwise improves real estate, you may be entitled to a mechanics' lien against the property if your customer doesn't pay you. You must file the lien in a timely manner and the law may require you to foreclose the lien within a year of filing. Most states require the filing within 60 to 120 days from completion of the work. Usually, the homeowner, developer, or business that you file against will pay after receiving notice. If not, your recovery in the foreclosure can include attorneys' fees and court costs.

For example, if an artisan repairs personal property and the computer repair company or the auto service station has a possessory lien against the customer's property for work performed, the customer must pay for the services rendered before receiving her property. The lien is terminated once the repairperson voluntarily returns the property to the owner.

Mortgage

A mortgage is a lien on real estate created because of a loan. The property owner (mortgagor) borrows money from and executes a mortgage to the lender (mortgagee). The mortgage is then recorded in the county recorder's office where the real estate is located. The real estate becomes a form of collateral for the lender. If the borrower breaches the terms of the loan, then the lender can sue to foreclose on the mortgage and have the property sold.

Notes & Quotes

"I like players to be married and in debt. That's the way you motivate them."

—Ernie Banks, baseball player

If you're providing services or selling property to a customer who will sign a promissory note, then you may want to take a mortgage on business or personal real estate as collateral. The customer may already have a first mortgage, so make sure there is enough equity (value about the first mortgage) to cover his or her debt to you. You must have a title search done, usually by a title insurance company, which would disclose ownership and any liens. If the information is satisfactory, then have the customer sign the mortgage and promptly record it with the county recorder. Retain the mortgage (promissory) note in your files.

Security Interest in Personal Property

A security interest on tangible and intangible personal property is similar to a mortgage on real estate—the creditor wants protection against default. If you are a creditor, you'll want to look at the value of the debtor's business assets, then take the appropriate steps to include some of those assets as collateral for the loan or credit sale. Collateral typically includes equipment, machinery, inventory, fixtures, accounts receivable, and notes receivable. The Uniform Commercial Code (UCC), Article 9, Secured Transactions, is the state statute that covers security interests; many states have a slightly different version of this Article.

As a creditor you take the following steps to create and perfect (file) a security interest:

➤ Appraise collateral to determine its value.

➤ Search the UCC files at the Secretary of State or County Recorder.

➤ Prepare a security agreement, which the debtor signs.

➤ Prepare a financing statement, which the debtor signs.

Shark Attack!

Choose with care the collateral you accept against debts owed to you. If the proposed collateral has a prior filed financing statement, then yours would be second in line; use other collateral that is not covered because two financing statement is one too many.

➤ File a financing statement with the Secretary of State or County Recorder.

➤ Prepare a promissory note, which the debtor signs.

You should search the office where another creditor might have filed a financing statement against your proposed collateral. Where you search depends on how the collateral is being used by the debtor. Financing statements against equipment, machinery, inventory, and accounts receivable are filed with the Secretary of State in most states; however, financing statements filed against farm assets may be filed with the County Recorder. Financing statements against fixtures, such as shelving or lighting, are usually filed with the County Recorder. If your search shows no financing statements exist, then you proceed to the next step.

The Security Agreement

The security agreement is the contract between the debtor and the creditor. The debtor conveys a security interest in the collateral to the creditor (secured party). The security interest is like a lien against the collateral, and the security agreement provides the remedies available to the secured party if the debtor doesn't repay the loan. The security agreement usually contains the following terms:

➤ A list of all the collateral

➤ The transfer of security interest

➤ The written permission required to move the collateral, if the debtor wants to move it to a different store

➤ A provision requiring the debtor to maintain the good condition of collateral, and pay insurance premiums, and taxes on it

➤ A clause describing repossession rights and other remedies for breach

Some types of collateral may be listed generically (all the inventory located at 1 North South Street, Notown, IN) or by specific identification (motor ID number). Inventory should include the proceeds from its sale, and any purchased after the security agreement is in effect, often referred to as a floating lien.

If the collateral decreases in value, then the secured party loses some of its protection; therefore, the agreement will require the debtor to maintain the collateral, as well as pay for its insurance coverage. When the collateral is mobile, the secured party doesn't want to chase after it if repossession is necessary, thus the requirement of written permission to move it.

The security agreement provides terms for default by the debtor. Typically, the secured party is permitted to repossess the collateral even if it is necessary to go on the debtor's property to do so. The repossession may not use or threaten physical violence.

The agreement usually gives the secured party the option of retaining the collateral (and extinguishing the debt) or selling it in a public or private sale. If the collateral is sold and its proceeds are less than the debt (and cost of collection), the secured party is entitled to the difference. Therefore, the secured party can still collect the difference from the debtor.

After both parties sign the security agreement, the secured party will require the business debtor to sign a financing statement. A consumer who buys merchandise will just sign the retail installment agreement, which contains the security agreement.

The financing statement will be filed with the Secretary of State or the County Recorder, which is called perfecting the security interest. Depending on the debtor's use of the collateral, you'll file either with Secretary of State or the County Recorder. (Please review our prior discussion about a UCC search, which would be conducted at the Secretary of State's office or County Recorder's office prior to granting the loan.)

Shark Attack!

Don't procrastinate! Timely filing of the financing statement is crucial, because the first secured party to file generally has first right to the collateral.

Means of Perfection

The UCC provides two other means of perfection along with filing the financing statement with the Secretary of State or County Recorder: possession of the collateral and attachment of consumer goods, or automatic perfection.

The pawnbroker is a typical example of perfection by possession; this is often referred to as a pledge. The pledged goods have a perfected security interest as long as the secured party retains possession. If the collateral is a promissory note or certificate of deposit, then possession is the means of perfection.

When a consumer buys merchandise on installment, the agreement will create a purchase money security interest, which is automatically perfected. Few consumer credit sales involve perfection by filing a financing statement.

Legal Eagle

If collateral is moved to another state, the secured party needs to perfect in the new state, generally within four months of arrival.

Once the secured interest in the collateral is perfected, the secured party usually has a prior claim to any subsequent creditors or buyers. There are two significant exceptions. When a secured party has a security interest in inventory, a consumer purchasing merchandise in a retail store takes free of the security interest. If the security agreement included proceeds from the sale of the inventory, then the proceeds become the collateral. In addition, debtors who have purchased consumer goods might sell them to a neighbor; the neighbor who is unaware of the security interest takes the merchandise free of the interest. In neither instance is the debtor released from the debt because of the sale.

Collection Process: Letter to Collecting the Judgment

Bad debts occur despite your best efforts. Some debtors may not be worth pursuing, others may justify your time and trouble. Sometimes just a little extra effort may reward you with at least a partial payment of the debt.

Collecting Without Suing

An ounce of prevention—a credit check performed in advance of delivery the merchandise or services—may help avoid the problem of collection, but it will not eliminate it entirely. I suggest sending a follow-up bill, if the first one hasn't been paid promptly. Customers do lose statements or procrastinate. You may want to follow this with a telephone call after sufficient time has elapsed, but this may be more confrontational than you wish.

Legal Eagle

Get it in writing! When a customer places an order, you should have an agreement that clearly specifies a rate of interest for overdue amounts and the right to charge collection costs, including court costs and attorneys' fees; the latter is generally not allowed unless specified in the contract between the parties.

Sending out a collection letter may be the next step. While the Fair Debt Collection Practices Act does not apply to small businesses that collect their own debts, you should follow the basic philosophy imbedded in the statute—do not harass the debtor. Your letters should be firm and perhaps suggest a compromise if appropriate, but should not contain any threats of criminal prosecution, communication with the customer's employer, or public disclosure. You may indicate that nonpayment may result in turning over the debt to a collection agency or a lawsuit.

A collection agency may be feasible if the collection process becomes too time consuming. Obviously, the collection agency will charge you, usually a percentage of the amount collected, but 50 percent is better than 0 percent. You might want to consider hiring an attorney just to write a collection letter; sometimes the lawyer's letterhead, alone, may say enough to get you paid.

Judgment and Collection

Unless you have a right to repossess the collateral under a security agreement, you probably will not be able to convince a court to allow a pre-judgment (before the verdict) seizure of the debtor's property.

Chapter 18, "Suing or Being Sued: Basics of Litigation," discusses lawsuits, so please review that chapter, particularly the section on small claims court, which is where most creditors file their suits for payment.

Once you obtain a judgment, then you may proceed through the court to collect on it. One method is to obtain a writ (order) of execution against the debtor's non-exempt assets, have the sheriff seize the assets, and sell them at a public sale. With many consumers this may not be feasible since the exempt assets may be the only assets the debtor owns. Exemptions vary from state to state, and generally are described in the next section of this chapter. For example, if the debtor owns a few household goods and a very used car, then the writ of execution will not be productive.

Another method you might consider is a *garnishment* order against the debtor's wages or money in a bank account. The garnishment order is served upon the debtor's employer or bank. However, federal law generally restricts all garnishment orders of an employee's wage to 25 percent of disposable earnings per week.

Debtor Bankruptcy

There are some notices you just don't like to receive. One is a notice from the bankruptcy court in which a debtor has listed you as a creditor. If you are an

Legalese

Garnishment is a court order directed against the debtor's assets held by a third party (garnishee) to turn over the property to the court.

unsecured creditor, and a consumer debtor has filed under the liquidation chapter, your outlook for repayment is bleak.

The main bankruptcy code chapters for our discussion are …

➤ Chapter 12 bankruptcy, liquidation for individuals and businesses.

➤ Chapter 11 bankruptcy, business reorganization.

➤ Chapter 13 bankruptcy, wage earner plan.

In Chapter 24, "Insolvent: Coping with Bankruptcy Prevention," we'll discuss insolvent businesses. This chapter focuses on a personal bankruptcy under Chapters 7 and 13 of the bankruptcy code.

Petition, Stay Order, and Initial Proceedings

Bankruptcy law has two goals: to protect the debtor by giving him or her a fresh start free from creditor claims, and to ensure that the bankrupt's creditors are treated fairly in receiving the debtor's nonexempt property in settlement of their claims.

A bankruptcy filing under Chapter 7 may be voluntary (initiated by the debtor) or involuntary (initiated by creditors); involuntary personal bankruptcies are rare. The debtor must initiate Chapter 13, which means that no creditor can bring a bankruptcy action under Chapter 13. The bankruptcy petition is filed with the U.S. District Court where the debtor resides, and is assigned to a bankruptcy court. The petition triggers a stay (an order to stop) on all of the debtor's creditor collection efforts; this stay usually applies to creditors who are suing, collecting on a judgment, repossessing, or foreclosing against the debtor. For example, if you are suing the debtor on a breach of contract, all action in the case stops from the moment the petition is filed. Creditors can apply to the court for relief from the stay.

Legal Eagle

When the debtor owes you a bundle, consider retaining an attorney to review the petition and determine if the debtor is worth pursuing through bankruptcy. A small debt is probably not worth the effort and expense of professional advice.

The voluntary personal bankruptcy petition and supplemental forms will contain the following information about the debtor:

➤ A list of assets

➤ Identification of property claimed as exempt

➤ A list of secured and unsecured creditors

➤ Current income and expense

Once the voluntary petition for personal bankruptcy is filed, the court will enter an Order for Relief, and the clerk will mail notices to all listed creditors, indicating the time of the creditors'/debtor's meeting, and deadline for filing creditor claims and objections.

Creditors can object to the bankruptcy discharge if the debtor's petition is fraudulent, willfully conceals assets, or a discharge has previously been granted within six years of filing.

Most personal bankruptcies are no-asset estates (all exempt property), so the trustee's function is fairly minimal, since the listed debts are discharged and the bankrupt person keeps the property claimed as exempt; the trustee is appointed by the bankruptcy court. If there are significant nonexempt assets, then the trustee collects this property, liquidates it, and pays the creditors according to the priority established in the Code.

Exempt Property, Distribution, and Discharge

The bankrupt person's estate consists of all of his or her property wherever it's located. If the bankrupt party has made a gift of property to a friend or relative within a year, or if within 90 days of the petition a creditor has been paid more that it would have received in the liquidation, those assets may be included.

Federal law permits the bankrupt to keep some of his or her property in a Chapter 7 liquidation; these exemptions are up to ...

➤ $16,150 equity in a residence.

➤ $2,557 interest in motor vehicles.

➤ $425 per item of household goods, up to total of $8,625.

➤ $1,075 in jewelry.

➤ $850 in other personal items.

➤ $1,625 in professional tools.

➤ $16,150 in personal injury compensation.

➤ $8,625 cash value in life insurance.

➤ Pensions.

Shark Attack!

A bankruptcy trustee may require a creditor to repay to the trustee any money received from the bankrupt within 90 days of the petition.

Many states have opted out of the federal exemptions, so check your state law.

After the exempt property is successfully claimed, the trustee may distribute any remaining property of the bankrupt party according to a stated priority. The order of distribution is as follows:

➤ Administrative expenses—court costs, trustee and attorney fees

➤ Paternity, alimony, maintenance, and support obligations

➤ Taxes

➤ Unsecured creditors

Secured creditors may be able to repossess the collateral through the bankruptcy court or have the bankrupt party pay the secured party. A creditor is a secured party only to the value of the collateral. For example, if the debt is $10,000, and the collateral is worth $5,000, then the security interest is limited to $5,000, and the rest of the debt is unsecured.

Creditors can object to the discharge, which is a court order wiping out the debt. But certain debts are not dischargeable, such as three years back federal income taxes, property or credit obtained through fraud, alimony, and child support. Claims based on willful misconduct (such as a battery judgment) government fines, certain consumer loans, luxury items of $1,075 obtained within 60 days of the Order for Relief, and certain student loans are also not dischargeable.

If a debt is discharged, then a creditor can no longer collect it. However, the debtor can reaffirm a debt before discharge. The reaffirmation agreement must be filed and approved by the court and clearly state that the reaffirmation is not required.

Shark Attack!

Don't assume that bankruptcy laws don't change. Congress is currently considering bankruptcy amendments that would limit Chapter 7 personal bankruptcy. Please consult with your attorney about any changes.

Bankruptcy Chapter 13

Wage earners only need apply for Chapter 13. This chapter permits the bankrupt to partially pay creditors over a period of three to five years, and thereafter the debts are discharged.

Any individual who has regular income and owes fixed unsecured debts of less than $269,250, or owes fixed secured debts of less than $807,750, may petition. The bankrupt person's plan of payment is submitted to the court (creditors may object), and if approved, the bankrupt person will turn over his or her disposable income to the trustee who then will pay the creditors. Disposable income is defined as income not reasonably necessary for the maintenance and support of the debtor and dependents. Failure of the debtor to make timely payments may result in conversion to Chapter 7 liquidation.

Helpful Sources

Cornell University's Web site has a discussion of bankruptcy and creditor's rights laws: www.law.cornell.edu. The American Bankruptcy Institute Web site is another source: www.abiworld.org. Finally, use the bankruptcy lawfinder: www.agin.com/lawfind. Many trade organizations provide useful suggestions about collecting debts.

The Least You Need to Know

➤ Have the debtor's check certified by the bank if you have doubts.

➤ A security interest in the debtor's collateral may protect you in the event of a default.

➤ Send a collection letter before filing a lawsuit.

➤ You may be able to collect a judgment against the debtor by garnishing his or her wages or executing against his or her nonexempt property.

➤ Unsecured creditors in a personal bankruptcy liquidation can expect very little.

Chapter 21

TMs, SMs, Copyrights, Patents, and Trade Secrets

> **In This Chapter**
>
> ➤ Making what's yours, yours
>
> ➤ The law behind copyrighting printed or recorded works
>
> ➤ Maintaining patents and trade secrets
>
> ➤ Helpful sources for your intellectual property needs

A rose by any other name may be trademarked. Write, and it shall be copyrighted. Invent a better mousetrap and file a patent. All these go under the label of intellectual property. Your business plan may be a better-kept trade secret than our top-secret nuclear files. In this chapter, we'll explore the world of trademarks (and its cousin the service mark), copyrights, and patents so that you can hang on to your trade secrets.

Making Your Mark

Your company name is important to your business because, with any luck, customers will identify with it. If you have any doubt about its importance, think about the most identifiable names and symbols in this country. When my kids were young, they could spot the golden arches while zipping along the interstate at 70 mph. There may be some isolated soul in this world who hasn't heard of Coca-Cola, but I doubt it. While the name and symbol of your small business may not ever gain worldwide recognition, you do want to make sure that it's all yours to do with as you please.

Trademark and Service Mark

Federal and state laws permit you to trademark your products and service mark your services. Your business can continue without a trademark, but if you want to expand, especially through Internet sales, then consider a trademark.

A trademark (or service mark) is a word, phrase, symbol, or design (or combination of words, phrases, symbols, and designs) that identifies and distinguishes one from another the source of the goods or services. To simplify things a little, in our discussions in this chapter, I'll use trademark and service mark interchangeably. For example, McDonald's trademarks virtually all its "Mc" products. Nike trademarks its swoosh. Mr. Peanut is a trademarked figure to identify Planter's brand peanuts. "Winston tastes good like a cigarette should" was a popular trademarked slogan from the 1950s.

Notes & Quotes

"I am more of a sponge than an inventor. I absorb ideas from every source. My principal business is giving commercial value to the brilliant but misdirected ideas of others."

—Thomas Edison, inventor

A trademark must be distinctive enough to enable consumers to identify the manufacturer of the product easily and to differentiate among competitive merchandise. Trademarks may fall into these categories:

➤ Independent marks

➤ Secondary meaning

➤ Trade dress

Invented *trade names* may become powerful trademarks, such as Xerox, Kodak, or Pepsi. Consumers can easily identify these brands because they have become strong marks without describing any particular product. Keep in mind, though, that you can't trademark general terms, geographic terms, or personal names—unless you can give them what's known as a "secondary meaning." Steven Jobs couldn't trademark the apples he could grow in an orchard, but he could trademark the apple as a symbol for the computers he invented.

Legalese

The term **trade name** indicates a business name, and may be protected as a trademark if it's the same as the company's product.

Trade dress involves the image and overall appearance of a product. McDonald's packaging is readily identifiable. Campbell's soups can be spotted on any shelf.

Trademarks are not available for the following:

➤ An image of a living person without consent

➤ Material that is immoral, deceptive, or scandalous

➤ Disparagement of persons, institutions, beliefs, and symbols

➤ Anything similar to a current trademark if likely to deceive

Creating the Trademark and Service Mark

The trademark or service mark may be established by using the mark in commerce or registering the mark with the U.S. Patent and Trademark office (PTO). Many states have their own trademark offices. Once the mark is used for goods or services, it exists and may be protected by law, unless it conflicts with an existing mark.

Federal registration provides the broadest protection and is recommended if you are going to conduct your business in more than one state. Registration gives nationwide notice that the trademark belongs exclusively to you and cannot be used without your permission. You use the symbol ® as public notice of the federal registration. The application form and instructions can be obtained from the PTO Web site: www.uspto.gov.

Once you apply, the PTO publishes your application; if there is no objection, the office issues you a certificate of registration. To determine if there is a conflict between two marks, the PTO looks at the likelihood of confusion, that is, whether consumers would be likely to associate the goods or services of one party with those of another party. For example, another soup company using the distinctive red and white Campbell's label would confuse grocery shoppers—but not if the label were on a can of paint. You should renew your federal registration every 10 years.

Legal Eagle

Take advantage of the most up-to-date search engines. The PTO is continuing to develop its electronic search capacity, so check with its Web site before proceeding with the application.

Protecting the Mark

Make sure that you document and substantiate when you first used your trademark, perhaps with a dated invoice that displays the trademark. Continue to use the trademark on your advertising, letterhead, and invoices, and note whether it is a registered trademark or state protected, by using the trademark or service mark symbol (™ or ℠) next to it. If you don't use it, you could lose it.

Shark Attack!

A word of warning: Aspirin was once trademarked, but it became used so generically that it went into the public domain, and was no longer protected. You must rigorously enforce the TM by demanding that any infringer stop using your mark, or you will sue.

Vigorously enforce your trademark rights. If you discover another company using the mark, or infringing on your copyright, send the company a letter demanding it refrain from future use. If the company continues to infringe, then you may have to sue. If you win the lawsuit, then you could receive an injunction against the defendant and damages.

The PTO has recently issued an Examination Guide to deal with trademarks, service marks, and domain names. Please see Chapter 23, "Wave of the Now: The Net of Home," for further discussion of protecting domain names.

Copyrighting Printed or Recorded Work

Let's say you create a model business plan that could be sold to others. Or your advertising materials are unique and creative, but you want to add one superstar, say, Snoopy. On a personal level, you enjoy downloading music from the Internet. Before you do anything, think copyright.

Creating Copyright Material

Federal copyright law protects the creator of literary or artistic works. When the work is in a fixed form—such as a manuscript or piece of sheet music—there exists an automatic and immediate copyright. Copyright protection exists at the moment of creation, even if the work is never published. The creator doesn't have to affix the copyright notice to the work, although doing so and filing with the Copyright Office provides some legal advantages that we'll discuss later in this chapter.

For example, just by typing up your business plan, you've copyrighted it. It is yours and no one else has the right to publish it or use it.

To be copyrighted, a work must be original and fall within one of these categories:

➤ Literary works

➤ Musical works

➤ Dramatic works

➤ Pantomimes and choreographic works

➤ Pictorial, graphic, and sculptural works

➤ Motion pictures and audiovisual works

➤ Sound recordings

➤ Architectural works

All kinds of work may be copyrighted, including some that is slightly less than completely original, such as a compilation of short stories—the compiler would hold the copyright to that collection, as long as he or she received permission to collect the works from the original authors.

The copyright law specifically does not offer protection for an idea, procedure, process, system, method of operation, concept, principle, or discovery. For example, you may have a great idea for communicating to customers through the Internet, but you can't copyright it. However, if you write an article describing the idea, the article itself is copyrighted. Mystery writers constantly seek new ways to kill victims; writers can freely borrow the idea from others without violating copyright law. But if one writer used the words and characters of another, he or she would be infringing on the copyright and could be liable for damages.

All works created after 1978 are protected for the life of the author plus 70 years; then, unless the author's estate extends the copyright, the work reverts to the public domain.

Once the copyright material has been created, the owner has the exclusive right to do, or to authorize others to do, the following:

➤ Reproduce the work

➤ Prepare derivative works based upon the work

➤ Distribute copies of the work

➤ Perform or display the work publicly

Legal Eagle

If you create a computer program, copyright it! The Copyright Office has accepted software registration for several years.

Legal Eagle

If you hire someone to create a business plan or brochure for you, make sure that your contract is "work for hire." This type of contract allows you to own the copyright to the material the work-for-hire writer creates.

Protecting the Copyright

While the copyright is secured immediately upon creation, registration with the U.S. Copyright Office is recommended. Whether you register or not, you should affix the copyright notice upon the work using a line like, "Copyright 2000 Stephen M. Maple." The notice informs the public that the work is copyrighted. If someone uses the work without the copyright owner's permission, then the infringer may be liable for damages.

Although informal copyright has legal force, registration with the Copyright Office has certain advantages, including …

➤ Creating a public record of the copyright.

➤ Providing the necessary prerequisite to filing an infringement lawsuit.

➤ Entitlement to statutory damages and attorney fees if the copyright is found to be infringed upon.

Legal Eagle

If your business operates on an international basis, make sure to ask the Copyright Office for a pamphlet that defines your right of copyright in that venue.

Registration is a rather simple process: Complete the application form, enclose the fee, and send it back along with a copy of the work. Registration is effective as soon as you meet the requirements.

Infringement and Fair Use

Anyone who violates the exclusive rights of the copyright owner is liable to the owner for infringement. This includes engaging in authorized reproduction, adaptation, public distribution, public performance, public display, and importation.

If someone has infringed on your copyrighted work, you may sue in federal court. Typically, you will ask the court to issue an injunction prohibiting future infringement, and allowing for you to receive money damages and recoup attorneys' fees. A prerequisite for the lawsuit is registration of the copyright. Actual damages are based on the harm caused to the copyright holder by the infringement. As an alternative to actual damages, the owner can elect to recover statutory damages from $500 to $20,000, or up to $100,000 if the infringement is willful.

Copyright law does provide a limited exception to infringement, referred to as fair use. Clearly, this exception is very limited. The law permits such use for purposes of literary criticism, comment, news reporting, teaching, scholarship, and research.

Factors considered under fair use include …

➤ The purpose and character of the use, including whether it's used for commercial or nonprofit use.

➤ The nature of copyrighted work.

➤ The amount and substantiality of the portion used in relation to the whole work.

➤ The effect of use upon the potential market for the work.

You should get permission for any commercial use of copyrighted material. Even one picture of Snoopy in a large ad will violate the law. However, if you're using two pages out of a large manual for internal training purposes only, then this would likely be fair use.

Patents for Useful Things

A patent for an invention is the grant of a property right to the inventor, issued by the U.S. Patent and Trademark Office. The grant of a patent involves the right to exclude others from making, using, or offering for sale the invention.

Creating a Patent

Patent law recognizes two kinds of patents: a utility patent and a design patent. Any person who invents or discovers any new and useful process, machine, manufacture or composition of matter, or any new and useful improvement can be granted a utility patent. For example, if your company invents a new chemical compound, you can get a utility patent on it.

A utility patent is appropriate for inventions that are new, useful, and nonobvious. For an invention to be nonobvious, a person with ordinary skill in the technology involved would be able to see a significant difference between the new invention and those similar to it created in the past. This test precludes a patent for minor tinkering on a previously patented invention.

Notes & Quotes

"In 1901 there were 25,546 patents granted for inventions; 43,040 in 1950; 96,514 in 1991; 147,520 in 1998, of which 16,407 were granted to individuals."

—Patent and Trademark Office

A design patent covers an object's novel nonfunctional visual and tactile characteristics, including the shape of a product and the way that it is decorated.

The inventor must apply to the U.S. Patent and Trademark Office (PTO) for a patent. Usually a business hires a patent attorney or agent to perform a patent search before the application. The search will help identify any prior patents that may conflict with the applicant's claim. The patent application must include …

➤ A specified patentable claim

➤ A summary of the invention

➤ Drawings showing each feature to the invention

The description must be specific enough to distinguish it from other inventions. If the invention is an improvement on another product, the specification must point out the part of the original product to which the improvement relates.

Once the patent has been applied for the inventor may attach the notice "Patent Pending." The PTO assigns the application to an examiner who searches for U.S. and foreign patents to determine if the applicant's invention is new, useful, and nonobvious. The PTO keeps the information on the application strictly confidential. Once the examiner is satisfied, the PTO issues the patent.

Legal Eagle

Make sure you get your employees who invent for you to sign an agreement requiring them to assign any patents to the employer. While the so-called "shop right" may give an employer the implied right to an assignment, it is better to make the assignment explicit.

However, if the PTO denies the patent application, the examiner will issue a formal action giving specific reasons why the claims on the application are defective or are not patentable in light of prior inventions. If the patent is denied, the applicant may request reconsideration and reply to all of the examiner's objections. If there is a final rejection, the applicant can request review by the Board of Patent Appeals; if further denied, then the applicant can appeal to the federal court of appeals or sue the Commissioner in the District Court of the District of Columbia.

Protecting the Patent

The patentee (owner) has a grant that confers the right to exclude others from making, using, selling, and so on, the invention for a period of 20 years (14 years for a design patent).

A violation of the owner's exclusive right is called an infringement. The owner can sue for the infringement in federal court, and the owner has the burden of proof and must show how the defendant's device or process infringes on the patent. The defendant is liable even though he or she made a trivial change or slight improvement.

Legal Eagle

Consult your state department of commerce and industry about helping you develop and market your invention.

If the court finds an infringement has been found, it will likely issue an injunction. The court may also award damages adequate to compensate for the infringement, such as a reasonable royalty fee for the use by the infringer. The owner's lost profits, including sales that went to the infringer, may be a good measure of damages. If the violation was willful, the court could triple the damages as well as award attorneys' fees.

Trade Secrets Kept

You may have a business process or information that cannot be patented, copyrighted, or trademarked, but is important to your business success. There is no federal law that protects trade secrets, but most states have a statute that protects your secrets.

Trade secrets could include such things as …

➤ Business plans and marketing strategies.

➤ Customer lists not generally available.

➤ Databases.

➤ Computer programs.

➤ Product specifications.

➤ Recipes.

➤ Employee handbooks.

Thus trade secrets apply to both ideas and the expression of those ideas.

The subject matter of the trade secret must be kept secret, and the owner must take reasonable efforts to maintain secrecy. In addition to asking employees and customers to sign contracts saying they agree not to disclose trade secrets, you may want to keep trade secret documents apart from ordinary files, label the materials as confidential, and have a sign-out policy. The secret must have actual or potential independent economic value, such as a market survey or a recipe for special barbeque sauce.

Legal Eagle

Require your employees who have access to trade secrets to sign an agreement not to disclose the confidential information. Likewise, your customers who have access to trade secrets should sign a nondisclosure agreement. Emphasize that this provision is important and will be strictly enforced. You should indicate in the agreements what information is considered a trade secret.

State statutes impose liability only if there is a misappropriation of the trade secret. For example, if a competitor hires away one of your employees and obtains the secret information, the competitor has violated the statute. Of course, if you voluntarily disclose this information to the public, then it's no longer a trade secret and anyone can use it. Likewise, if the information becomes dated, such as a customer list that is several years old, then it is no longer trade secret information.

The owner of the trade secret may sue in state court (or federal court if there is diversity jurisdiction) for an injunction prohibiting its use, and for damages. For example, if the competitor used your secret customer list to lure your customers away, you may sue for lost profits or for whatever the misappropriator gained (such as savings due to the efficient use of your databases).

Helpful Sources

The PTO Web site provides very useful information for patents and trademarks: www.uspto.gov; the Copyright Office Web site is www.loc.gov. Information on intellectual property is available at www.legal.net. Cornell University Web site is informative: www.law.cornell.edu. Check out www.findlaw.com. State Web sites may contain information about state registered trademarks, and contain the trade secret statute. Check with your state and local governments to obtain assistance on promoting your inventions.

The Least You Need to Know

➤ Register your product name with the U.S. Patent and Trademark Office.

➤ Copyright protection begins when the written work is finished, but may be registered with the U.S. Copyright Office.

➤ Patents for inventions are protected for 20 years.

➤ Confidential information may be protected under state trade secret statute.

➤ Online trademark searches are becoming a reality.

Chapter 22

ABCs of Administrative Law

In This Chapter

➤ Agency authority from statutes

➤ Agency rules are the law

➤ Adjudicating rights and wrongs

➤ Agencies in action

➤ Small business rights

➤ Helpful sources

Few television series show lawyers arguing before administrative agencies. The criminal or civil courtroom is where the action is on television. In reality, though, federal and state administrative agencies affect small businesses more than the courts do. One brief fact: There are more federal administrative law judges than federal court judges. In this chapter, we discuss what administrative law is, and what impact it may have on your small business.

Agency Authority from Statutes

Congress creates federal administrative agencies. State legislatures, likewise, create state administrative agencies. This discussion will focus on federal agencies, but most state agencies function in very similar ways. When Congress creates an agency it provides its name, purposes, functions, and powers. For example, the law grants the Federal Trade Commission (FTC) the following powers:

➤ To create rules and regulations to carry out the purposes of the Act

➤ To conduct investigations of unfair business practices

➤ To investigate possible violations of federal antitrust laws

➤ To publish findings of its investigations

➤ To hold trial-like hearings to resolve trade disputes or antitrust issues

Most federal and state administrative agencies have Web sites that explain agency functions. You can look at the FTC Web site, www.ftc.gov, to get a good overview of its functions.

There are two basic types of agencies: executive agencies (such as the Department of Agriculture), and independent regulatory agencies (such as the Securities and Exchange Commission). Executive agencies may have several subagencies that are important regulators. Here's a list of some examples:

Executive Agency	Subagency
Treasury	Internal Revenue Service (IRS)
Justice	Immigration and Naturalization Service (INS)
Agriculture	Food Safety and Inspection Service
Commerce	Patent and Trademark Office
Labor	OSHA (Occupational Safety and Health Administration), Wage-Hour Division
Health and Human Services (HHS)	Food and Drug Administration (FDA)

Some examples of federal independent regulatory agencies include ...

➤ Federal Trade Commission (FTC).

➤ Securities and Exchange Commission (SEC).

➤ National Labor Relations Board (NRLB).

➤ Equal Employment Opportunity Commission (EEOC).

➤ Consumer Product Safety Commission (CPSC).

➤ Environmental Protection Agency (EPA).

The independent regulatory agencies are not accountable directly to the president of the United States as are the cabinet (executive) agencies. The independent agencies have officers who serve for fixed terms and are removable only for just cause.

Most agencies, federal or state, have three basic powers: legislative, executive, and judicial. The agency can adopt rules of procedure for itself and regulations that interpret or implement its statute. The agency can administer its laws, and adjudicate their violation. The next few sections of this chapter will focus on these powers and how they affect small businesses.

Agency Rules Are the Law

Agencies adopt rules and regulations to fulfill the purpose for which they are created. For example, the SEC was established to regulate the securities market, so it has issued rules defining registration requirements of securities offerings, and exemptions from registration.

Administrative agencies follow three basic steps in issuing new regulations:

➤ **Notice of proposed rule.** A federal agency that decides to create a new rule must first publish notice of the rule in the *Federal Register,* which is a daily publication. The notice states when and where the rule-making proceeding will be held, the agency's authority for making the rule, and the terms of the rule. Your state probably has an equivalent to the *Federal Register* for its agencies.

➤ **Comment period.** Following publication of the notice, the agency allows time for the public to comment. Usually the public consists of businesses subject to the proposed regulation, but often consumer groups will note the regulations as well. The purpose of this comment period is to allow interested parties to make their responses to the proposed rule understood. These comments may be in writing or oral, if the agency holds a hearing. The agency may respond by adopting, modifying, or withdrawing the proposed rule. Many trade organizations, such as the Chambers of Commerce and the National Federation of Independent Businesses, notify members of important regulations. Comments may be an important form of lobbying for or against the proposed rule.

➤ **Adoption of final rule.** The agency will review the comments, draft a final rule (or withdraw it), and publish it in the *Federal Register.* The rule is later compiled with other federal agencies' rules in the *Code of Federal Regulations* (CFR). The CFR is published on the Government Printing Office (GPO) Web site. Your state has a similar publication for its regulations. You might go to the state agency Web site, because most have their regulations on the site, or have a link to a site that does.

Legal Eagle

The *Federal Register* is online at the Government Printing Office Web site: www.gpo.gov. Some states may have their equivalent publication on the Internet. If you are in a business that is highly regulated, such as transportation, then periodic review of the federal or state register may be important.

After the regulation is adopted, it might be challenged in court. Courts generally will give deference to the agency's expertise in creating a rule. However, the rule may be challenged upon the grounds that the agency ...

➤ Exceeded its statutory authority.

➤ Improperly interpreted its statute.

➤ Failed to follow procedural requirements.

For example, if the SEC decided to regulate the sale of life insurance policies, the courts may conclude that this is beyond the agency's statutory authority, which is regulation of the securities market. Therefore, the regulation would be void. Or the IRS through the Treasury Department may attempt to issue a regulation limiting the corporations that can elect Subchapter S status; if such proposed regulation clearly misconstrues the statute, then the courts may not enforce it. Finally, if the agency did not follow its own rules regarding, notice, comment, and adoption, the rule may be successfully challenged in court.

Legal Eagle

Consider joining a trade association. Its lobbying efforts in Congress, state legislatures, and with administrative agencies may help ease a costly regulatory environment.

One final note. If the legislature broadly delegates authority to make rules or delegates to the agency the right to implement the statute, then courts are reluctant to interfere. Regulations that interpret a statute may be more easily challenged. Again, I would emphasize that any court challenge is difficult, so it is better to seek moderation from the agency; that's what the comment period can do for you.

Adjudicating Rights and Wrongs

The executive function of the agency may involve investigating and possibly charging a business or individual with a violation of its statute or regulations. In turn, the judicial function occurs when the agency acts as a judge of the alleged violators.

Investigation

Administrative agencies conduct investigations of the businesses that they regulate. Most of these investigations involve monitoring compliance with the regulations. For example, OSHA or the state equivalent conducts on-site investigations, particularly when there has been a safety complaint or a serious workplace injury. In addition to inspections, the agency may request documents or records. The federal Wage-Hour Division requests time cards, for instance, in order to verify overtime claims by employees.

Usually business owners simply sigh and comply with the agency requests. Maintaining good relations with your regulatory agency is important. However, if the request is unreasonable—if it requires that employees spend hours compiling records, for instance—then you can refuse the request.

After your refusal, the agency may seek a search warrant or use a subpoena. On-site inspection warrants are relatively easy for the agency to obtain; to challenge one is usually unproductive. The subpoena may be for testimony, or it may be for documents; the latter is called a *subpoena duces tecum*.

If you challenge the subpoena, a court may consider …

➤ The purpose of investigation.

➤ The relevance of information sought.

➤ The specificity of request.

➤ The burden of demand.

The request must have a legitimate purpose. The information sought must be adequately described and relevant to the investigation. For example, a demand for all personnel records would be not be specific enough to be relevant to an investigation of a violation of the Fair Labor Standards Act for alleged failure to pay overtime. Since the business bears the costs of producing the records, it may contend that the demand was unduly burdensome. Courts balance the agency's right to know with the business's burden of production. Most courts will defer to the agency unless the request is obviously irrelevant or onerous.

Shark Attack!

Beware of agency requests that involve a disclosure of trade secrets or other confidential information. Your attorney should draft an agreement with the agency that this information is not to be publicly disclosed. That is not always possible, but try.

Adjudication

After the investigation, the agency may begin to take administrative action against an alleged violator of its statute or regulation. Most actions are resolved by negotiation with the agency. For example, one of my clients owned a golf course that set aside one day especially for women golfers. A man complained to the state Civil Rights Commission, which then issued a complaint; we negotiated a shorter golfing time exclusively for the women to satisfied the agency.

If the negotiations aren't successful, then the agency may issue a formal complaint (or charge). The procedure may follow this order:

➤ The complaint is issued.

➤ An answer is filed.

➤ A hearing before an administrative law judge is held.

➤ A judge gives an order.

➤ An appeal to the agency's governing body (commission) is made.

➤ The final agency order is given.

➤ An appeal to the court for review of agency's order is submitted.

I am going to use the example of the National Labor Relations Board (NLRB), because it is typical of many administrative adjudications.

Let's say the NLRB receives a charge of an unfair labor practice from a worker who alleges that her company refused to promote her because she actively supported her local union. The local NLRB office will appoint an investigator who will interview the employee, employer, and any witnesses.

The NLRB local counsel will review the evidence and the investigator's recommendation. If counsel believes that there is sufficient evidence to proceed, then the NLRB will issue a formal complaint, which is much like a complaint in a lawsuit. The employer and the NLRB may decide to settle by, for instance, agreeing to promote the employee to the next job opening.

If no agreement is reached, the case will go to a hearing before an NLRB administrative law judge (ALJ). An NLRB attorney will represent the employee; the employer should have its own legal counsel. The ALJ hears the witnesses and receives tangible evidence, including documents such as written evaluations of the employee.

The rules of evidence are usually more relaxed in administrative hearings, because many agency hearings do not involve attorneys who are sticklers for the somewhat arcane rules. Of course, all evidence must be relevant. For example, if the employer tried to introduce evidence that the employee had flunked chemistry in high school, this would not be relevant to her performance at work.

The charging party begins, since she and the NLRB have the burden of proof. Witnesses will be examined and cross-examined; documents might be offered into evidence and objected to. The format is similar to a civil trial, but without the jury.

After the hearing the ALJ will render a decision. The written decision will involve detailed findings of fact and conclusions of law. The findings of fact in this hypothetical case would include a decision that the charging party was an employee of the respondent, that she had received satisfactory evaluations, that she was fully qualified to be promoted, that others with lesser qualifications were promoted before her, and that she was business agent and chief contract negotiator for the union. The ALJ would then conclude that the company committed an unfair labor practice by discriminating against her for her union activities.

Legal Eagle

Prepare with care! An administrative hearing requires the same meticulous preparation as does a civil trial. Any employer witness should go through a mock exam and cross-exam.

The losing party—the company in this case—may want to contest the ALJ's decision with the NLRB. The parties file briefs with the NLRB, which then decides whether to approve, modify, or reject the ALJ decision. The NLRB has the authority to review both the finding of facts and conclusions of law; it might draw a different inference from the facts than did the ALJ.

If either party disagrees with the NLRB order, then he or she must go to the federal court of appeals. Courts of appeals give great deference to administrative agency interpretations of their statute, but on occasion they will overturn the NRLB order. The next level of appeal would be the U.S. Supreme Court. The Court reviews a few agency orders each year.

I would add that not all agency adjudications are as formal as the NLRB. For example, unemployment claims usually involve a informal hearing before a state ALJ who listens to testimony (recorded on a tape recorder), accepts documents, and, on occasion, asks questions; rules of evidence rarely are consulted; the findings and conclusions are relatively brief.

Agency in Action: The Zoning Board

You probably won't be cited before the NLRB, but you may be involved with local or state administrative agencies. I have selected a local agency with which you are likely to have some contact: the zoning board.

Most cities and counties regulate land use and develop a comprehensive zoning plan. In essence, each plot of land is zoned for a particular use, such as single-family residential units, commercial properties, and industrial buildings, to name three. Each local government probably has a slightly different procedure and different zoning categories, but there is a great deal of similarity, at least enough so to use this as an illustration.

Pre-Hearing

Let's begin. You want to change the zoning classification on some land so you can build a new store. You probably will need an attorney or zoning expert to take you through the steps with the local planning commission. I'll try to duplicate that in this hypothetical case.

Here is how the process should work:

➤ You check the current zoning of the lot and zoning of the neighborhood.

➤ You obtain a land-use petition to rezone.

➤ You prepare a proposal.

➤ You consult with the local planning staff for pre-filing review.

➤ You file a petition with the local planning commission.

➤ The Petition is docketed and a hearing date is set.

➤ You publish and mail legal notices to the neighbors.

➤ Planning staff recommendations are prepared.

➤ You receive the staff recommendations.

➤ A hearing before the zoning board or hearing examiner is conducted.

➤ You appeal if necessary.

Many zoning ordinances permit a change if it results in the best and highest use of the property. For example, if your proposed store location is part of a changing neighbor where other stores and strip malls are coming in, then the change from single-family residential to commercial may be warranted. For a minor change in the land use, such as from a residence to insurance agent's office in the home, you could petition for a *zoning variance*.

Legalese

A **zoning variance** is the authority granted by the zoning board to modify the zoning use for a limited purpose, while the zoning on the property does not change.

It's in your best interest to convince the planning staff that a rezoning is appropriate, because its recommendation usually carries considerable weight with the zoning board. If the staff is not greatly overworked (most are very busy), you should run your preliminary proposal by the staff. They know the regulations better than anyone, and can point out required modifications as well as suggest changes they feel would be appropriate.

If the planning staff suggestions are feasible, then modify your proposal accordingly. Before you petition, discuss your proposal with any neighborhood association that would be affected by the change. A presentation at one of their meetings is an excellent way of discussing your proposal; neighbors can ask questions and you can reassure them that you will be a responsible neighbor. The voice of the people also has considerable impact on the zoning board, so get them on your side if possible.

Your rezoning petition should, of course, contain all the required information. In addition, add whatever information, such as sketches or photographs, that would likely persuade the staff and even the zoning board before either has heard one word of testimony.

If the staff recommendations are favorable, you should win, unless there is a great outcry from the neighbors and they flood the hearing chamber. If the recommendation is negative, all is not necessarily lost. Try to get one last conference with the staff before the hearing; there may be modifications on your plan that both of you can accept.

Getting a Hearing

Prepare for the hearing and make sure you know the zoning commission rules of procedure. The only rule of evidence likely to be enforced is the hearsay rule, which requires a witness to testify as to his or her own personal knowledge, not repeat what another witness has said. Have your testimony down pat. Line up your exhibits. Don't assume that the board or hearing examiner knows the neighborhood. And, if you can, use modern technology—a video camera can replace most of your testimony and be very convincing.

If you are successful, then the subsequent rezoning ordinance should not be a problem. However, if you are not successful, then consider going to the city council (or whomever is the next in the appellate line), but winning there or in court is probably going to be very difficult.

Small Business Rights

Congress, and our state legislatures sometimes acknowledge that small businesses are vital to our economy. Four federal statutes, which may have their equivalent in your state, designed to further the cause of small businesses across the country, deserve mention:

➤ **Freedom of Information Act.** This act requires federal government agencies to disclose many of their records to any person upon request. There are a few exclusions, such as filed tax forms or criminal investigative records. Many of the records may be available electronically, such as the corporate filings with the Securities and Exchange Commission.

➤ **Government-in-Sunshine Act.** This act is an open meeting law. Meeting notices and agendas are to be posted and the meetings open to the public. Decisions are to be made in open meetings. There are a few exceptions, such as criminal and litigation matters.

➤ **Regulatory Flexibility Act** and the **Small Business Regulatory Enforcement Fairness Act.** These acts require federal agencies to consider the impact any regulation has on small businesses. Agencies are to provide notices through trade journals of forthcoming regulations so that businesses can file comments with the agency. The Small Business Administration has established an ombudsman to accept comments from small businesses about their dealings with federal agencies.

The Least You Need to Know

➤ Most agency hearings are informal and the most important rule of evidence is relevance.

➤ An administrative law judge's decision is subject to review by his or her agency.

➤ Administrative agency meetings are required to be open to the public, with few exceptions.

Chapter 23

Wave of the Now: The Net or Home

In This Chapter

➤ Your domain is your kingdom

➤ What is a domain and do you really need one?

➤ Is e-commerce right for your business?

➤ Understanding Web Law

➤ Getting comfortable with your home office

Dot coms have taken over the advertising on Super Bowl Sunday; NASDAQ spends its ad bucks on the dot coms. What are we to make of all this? That is a particularly difficult question for lawyers to answer. Yesterday's statutes and court decisions don't always fit. The law simply hasn't caught up in cyberspace. In fact, this chapter may seem somewhat dated by the time the book comes out in just a few months. For that I can make only a half-hearted apology, because I am writing in a time of great transition. We know where we've been, but we are unsure where the cyberspace journey will take us.

In this chapter, I'll introduce you to the state of the Internet as it applies to the small business owner. I've even added a section on the home-based business in this chapter because I believe that e-commerce and the Internet will expand the opportunities for entrepreneurs to work from their home.

Your Domain Is Your Kingdom

A *domain name* is part of the uniform resource locator (URL), which is the address of a site or document on the Internet. Eventually, if you set it up properly, e-traffic and commerce will run through your domain.

Creation and Registration

Typically, a domain name consists of what's known as a second-level domain, followed by a dot, then a top-level domain. For example, a company may have its address as: http://www.abc.com. (the abc is the second-level domain, and the .com is the top-level domain). Here are the current top-level codes:

Top-Level Code	What the Code Stands For
.com	Commercial, for-profit organizations
.edu	Four-year colleges/universities
.gov	U.S. government agencies
.int	International organizations
.mil	U.S. military organizations
.org	Miscellaneous (usually nonprofit organizations)

Several proposed business-related codes include the following: .firm (businesses), .info (information services), .nom (personal), and .store (retail businesses). Countries have a code, such as .uk (United Kingdom) and .jp (Japan).

The domain name you choose may be registered with Network Solutions, Inc. The Internet Corporation for Assigned Names was created in 1999 to supervise the addition of new registrars, and you may register with any of these new companies.

Trademark Issues

Chapter 21, "TMs, SMs, Copyrights, Patents, and Trade Secrets," has a more thorough discussion of trademarks (goods) and service marks (services). As you recall, the most expansive protection for a company name is through federal registration with the Trademark Office. Once your name is registered and you attached the ®, a court can restrain any unauthorized use by an infringer from further use and the infringer could be liable for money damages. This trademark right is enforceable nationwide, but has limited protection internationally.

You can register a mark composed of a domain name as a trademark or service mark only if it functions as a source identifier, that is, if it identifies a company providing the goods or services.

Legalese

A **domain name** is the Internet equivalent of a listing in a telephone directory. It routes the data to your location.

The Trademark Office has established guidelines for registration:

➤ A second-level domain name is sufficient for the mark (surelock)

➤ A surname and top-level domain name *cannot* be registered (maple.com)

➤ A top-level domain name combinations *cannot* be registered (netorg.com)

➤ A domain name that is an adjective *cannot* be registered (whiter)

➤ A generic domain name *cannot* be registered (chicken.com)

➤ A geographic domain name *cannot* be registered (Indianapolis.com)

Notes & Quotes

Business Week suggested in its May 15, 2000, issue some more appropriate identifiers for domain endings: .mom (parenting), .ugh (ickiest site), .con (scam artists), .dot (women named Dorothy), and .mmm (food sites).

Notes & Quotes

"Today (July 4, 2000) there are more than 56 million computers connected to the Internet on a worldwide basis. Individuals can now access more than one billion Web pages, and an estimated three million pages are added daily. Recent studies show that on-line small business transactions nearly doubled from prior years to 40 percent between 1998 and 1999."

—Robert L. Mallett, writer

Further, advertising one's products or services is not, in itself, sufficient for a registered mark of the domain name because the advertising of that company's products or services does not constitute a service, such as "Pepsiad." The U.S. Trademark Office, in its capacity as the interpreter of the federal trademark law, have established these rules.

Network Solutions, one of the registrars, has a registration dispute policy, which may be invoked when one
party claims another's registration infringes on a
trademark. It gives preference in registration to the
owners of the federally registered trademark over anyone who holds a domain with an identical name unless the domain was obtained before the effective date
of the trademark. Further, Network Solutions provides
little protection for design marks, common law marks,
and state registrations. Please refer to my discussion of
the various "marks" in Chapter 21.

Another important trademark issue involves confusing
marks. The owner of a trademark must aggressively
defend it to maintain its distinctiveness, or lose the
mark. This includes challenging another's use of the
same or confusingly similar mark on competing prod-
ucts. While the courts have developed several standards, including the degree of similarity between the marks in appearance and customer suggestion, the likelihood of
confusion may be, I know it when I see it.

Federal law protects famous marks with an antidilution statute. This applies to domain names. This protection may include noncompeting uses, such as *grecianformula*
for a salad dressing. However, one court has dismissed an infringement claim by the
company Toys R Us against a company using the domain name "gunsareus."

Squatters, Pirates, and Tags

Cybersquatting usually refers to the practice of stockpiling domain registrations in
bulk for future resale to the public. Cyberpiracy refers to registration of well-known
names with the intent to sell the name to the brand's owner. The latter also includes
registering names that are confusingly similar to well-known brands. Generally,
courts that have dealt with the problems these tactics create have ruled against the
squatters and pirates under trademark law or unfair trade practices.

Tags are embedded commands in the source code of a Web site. When a user clicks
on to a link (often appearing as an underlined word), the computer moves to the new
site (or different text). Tags can be programmed to bring all or just part of the new
site to the browser. These links themselves are probably not a copyright infringement,
but the material drawn from the link may be copyrighted (which is for another discussion).

Linking can be programmed to reroute or cover up ads in the second site. The second
site may derive considerable revenue from its by-passed or blocked advertising. This is
an issue worthy of several law review articles, so, alas, I have no definite answer if
this happens to your site.

E-Commerce: Your Dot.Com

Does your business plan include e-commerce? Should it? Not easy questions to answer. But the best answer probably should be no if you're entering this brave new world for no other purpose than because everyone else is doing it. Despite the optimistic statistics, not everyone is selling on the Internet, nor should they. You must decide if selling through the Net will be profitable either for the bottom line or for improved customer satisfaction. The so-called bricks-and-mortar businesses can continue quite profitably.

However, if you decide to proceed, know these two things: no Web site is ever up and running on time, and Web site construction and maintenance always cost more than estimated.

Notes & Quotes

"Consumer e-commerce retail sales (e-tails) were $20 billion in 1999; they are predicted to be $143.8 billion by 2003."

—Forrester Research, Inc.

Getting Started

You must first decide what you want your Web site to accomplish. Is your Web site for increasing in-store sales or selling online, or both? If it's selling online, then my advice is to hire a professional to develop your Web site. But you must be in charge of the final product—and you must think like a potential customer.

Perhaps the most important question is this: How does my Web site make a customer's daily life easier? It could be about saving money or saving time. Convenience is the key. If a click on your site

Legal Eagle

A good domain name may help attract customers. Brevity and uniqueness are helpful. The problem is, everyone has the same idea. Trademarking your site may be vital to your future.

sells a quality product at a good price, and it's timely delivered, then you have a loyal customer. Life is more serene for your customer, and profits rise for you.

Sadly, the opposite is often the case. Navigating a Web site is often like negotiating a labyrinth. Your customer begins the search with high hopes, only to get lost on the trip. Web buyers are an impatient lot. If you lose a potential customer, it's not likely that you will ever get him or her to return.

Operating the Site

Potential customers visit Web sites to browse, to buy, and to be informed. Buying is what you want, but getting the customer in your Web store is a beginning. Customers may be drawn to your site by your advertising on other sites, through a Web search, or by word of mouth.

The customer wants something from your site, so give it to him or her. To use the current buzzwords, make your site content rich. Describe your products or services in considerable detail. Give your customers as much choice as possible. Then assure your customer that you will be there after the sale if he or she has any questions or problems.

Add something to your site that others may not have thought about—a daily quiz or crossword puzzle, or links to other sites, or a prize. Be entertaining and informative without being glitzy. Glitzy often translates into colorful graphics, which are time-consuming to download, and impatient customers will go elsewhere.

Operating the site is demanding and costly. You need to constantly reevaluate the Web site and what it's producing for you. It must give you an adequate return on your investment in profits and customer satisfaction.

Cyberlaw: New Wine in Old Skins

The domain name and its trademark-related issues are just a few of the challenges to a legal structure that never keeps up with technology. For example, contract law relies on paper documents and written signatures, neither of which exists in the same form in the digital world. Just recently the president of the United States signed a digital signature law, which treats an e-signature the same as if it were physically written on a piece of paper.

Since the law lags behind technology, the best advice is to assume that the old laws apply, perhaps with an e-law twist. Never assume that you will have any greater protection than the current law allows unless a new statute covers the legal issue. For example, if you attempt to obtain equity financing through Internet sales of your stock, the federal Securities Act of 1933 still applies and registration of the securities offering with the SEC is required (unless there is some exception from the general rule). The ability to link to other sites, maintaining personal and site privacy, and publishing on the Web are just a few of the Internet challenges American law has yet to conquer.

Linking

One of the true marvels of the Internet is linking. You are at one site, hit the link, and you are almost instantaneously at another location. Links make a Web site more useful to its customer and provide additional benefit without extra cost. There are several legal issues worth discussing, including the following:

➤ Trademark issues

➤ Copyright infringement

➤ Offensive sites

If your site has a link to the second or subsequent page of another Web site, it may appear to the cursory user that this is but a continuation of your own Web site. Also, this bypasses the other Web site's advertising page. Both might cause copyright problems, so the best practice is to link to the other site's home page and avoid the issue.

If another site has copyrighted material, then a link to that site is not a copyright violation in itself, nor are you violating the other site's copyright if one of your visitors illegally copies material from the other site. Or so it now seems. But the best practice is to obtain the other site owner's permission to link, and to clearly state on your site that you have no ownership over any material in the other site, which may be subject to copyright protection.

Sometimes you can link to controversy. Site content is likely to change, usually not dramatically, but change it will. You should periodically review the links and consider removing any that would greatly offend your users. You probably would not be held liable if you linked to controversial material, but you don't want to offend users. Certainly check out the sites before you link; whitehouse.gov is a very different site from whitehouse.com (a porn site). Then place a notice on your links that you are not responsible for the content of other Web sites. I would also suggest that you allow users to comment on the linked sites, which may rid you of potential problems.

Notes & Quotes

Most of the world wants something simple to use—press one button, and you're on the Internet."

—Raymond J. Lane, writer

Privacy: Theirs

One of the greatest concerns users have, and rightly so, is protection of their privacy. The law certainly hasn't dealt adequately with this problem. Most customers just have to take the Web site owner's word that his or her privacy is honored.

The problem isn't really with credit card numbers. Most vendors are sensitive to this issue. Clearly you need to ensure protection against misuse here. But many of us give our card numbers to retailers over the telephone, so most Internet consumers aren't overly concerned. On the other hand, the Internet is the most useful tool to obtain information about your customers. You can collect this data and use it to determine the right product mix to sell, how to advertise to your market, and retain

Shark Attack!

Don't violate your e-consumer's privacy by sharing information with other e-commerce sites. Such a violation may be considered deceptive advertising. If a customer is harmed by the disclosure, he or she may sue for invasion of privacy.

loyal customers. It's a gold mine. Be stingy; don't share it. And tell your customers that you aren't going to share any of their information with anyone outside your company. Then stick to this policy. Also, it's a good idea to have several safeguards installed so that a hacker cannot enter your database through your Web site and gain access to your client's confidential information.

Privacy: Yours

Your business information may be vital to your success. If you share that with customers or business partners, you want to ensure that it remains confidential. Trade secret law protects only what you protect. You must insist that the recipient of your information agrees in writing to maintain the confidentiality, and that the customer or business partner signs the agreement.

Many businesses are following the government's lead in using digital technology to scramble its communications so that an eavesdropper cannot steal the information. Usually the parties *encrypt* (code) the communication. Each party has a key, which is a method by which the sender encrypts the message, and the other can decode it. This sounds a lot like James Bond, but it clearly serves a necessary purpose.

Legalese

Encryption is the scrambling of digital messages in such a way that only the sender and receiver can read the message.

Often documents are sent as e-mail attachments. The recipient can read the document, and may make changes, which are then returned to the sender. I have reviewed and altered several contract proposals this way. Again, confidential communications may be an issue.

Spamming

Spamming is the sending of unsolicited commercial e-mail. It's the electronic equivalent of junk mail. Don't do it. Always ask your Web site visitors if they would like personal e-mail messages about new products or special sales. If customers have control they may be willing to grant you that privilege.

Legal Eagle

If you share customer e-mail addresses with others, you should inform the customers and permit them to remove their names from the list.

Publishing

Your Web site may contain articles written by others or generated by your own staff. Always receive permission for copyright license from the author of any article, unless an employee writes it as part of his or her duties.

Carefully read any article you publish. Misinformation, particularly about product safety issues, may cause your reputation serious harm, and if it causes harm to others, may leave you open to a lawsuit. If you have any doubt as to its accuracy, confirm, or don't publish.

Likewise, if the information misrepresents the product, then a user may claim fraud or a violation of a state deceptive sales practice statute. If the information is defamatory, you may be the object of a libel suit. Court rulings have given limited protection to Internet service providers who merely allow the information to be posted. You, on the other hand, have the right to select, and maybe edit, the material. That can make you liable for the material.

Contracts

The same basic contract law principles apply in cyberspace as it applies on paper, but the parties involved have to be more careful about a record of the terms agreed upon. An equivalent of a paper trail showing the contract terms may be important in proving the existence of a contract.

Not all contracts have to be in writing but some do, such as the Statute of Frauds writing requirement for sales of goods over $500 and certain other contracts. The Uniform Commercial Code was adopted before e-commerce so the digital world wasn't considered. A paperless contract probably will be enforceable if it can be replicated on paper; the digital signature is acceptable as an authentication of the contract. Of course, there still may be an issue of whether the electronic contract presented in court was the one that both parties agreed to. Obviously, the paper contract containing both signatures is a fairly foolproof guarantee of the contract's integrity.

Since you may be contracting with parties in other states, or even other nations, the issue of which state or country's contract law applies can be vexing. The existence of a contract, terms, breach, and remedies are all important to e-commerce sales. I discuss this issue in a later section. The parties can agree on the state of jurisdiction and include its reference in the contract. I would suggest that you consider this option.

Legal Eagle

Until the issue of paperless contracts is settled, I would suggest a paper contract with the parties' signatures on any significant contracts, certainly any that involve several thousand dollars.

Torts in Cyberspace

I can guarantee that when there is an injury in cyberspace, there will be a lawyer to argue one tort theory or another. Misinformation on your Web site can turn into a lawsuit for fraud. Or, if your instructions on the product's use causes a physical injury, then the result may be a lawsuit for negligence or product liability.

If a Web site defames a person, then a complaint for libel may follow. Or, if personal information is disclosed to a third party, then invasion of privacy may be claimed, or even the intentional infliction of emotional distress. Taking some company's trade secret information may be conversion (misappropriation).

As in contract law, the usual tort principles apply, but the issue again may be jurisdiction. The question is which state or country's laws apply, and where would any lawsuit be tried. There are no clear answers. But the victim's own state, that is, where the harm occurred, may have jurisdiction. The more persons claiming harm in a particular state, the more likely their state will assert jurisdiction, so sales records may be an important determinant. There is at least one libel suit involving a New York publisher who allegedly defamed a resident of California; the court held that California courts could try the case.

My intent is not to unduly alarm you, but to indicate that these problems have not been sufficiently addressed. Continue to operate your business on the Internet, if that's what works best for you, but make sure you have adequate insurance coverage for these risks.

Jurisdiction

While I have touched upon state jurisdiction in previous sections, it deserves further discussion here. I remind you that jurisdiction involves a state applying its laws and trying a case involving a transaction that may not have even occurred within its borders. For example, you advertise and sell a product from your Web site. Later, you get a letter from a deputy attorney general claiming that this transaction violates that attorney's state's deceptive sales practice law. How do you respond, or do you have to respond? Clearly, if your ad targeted residents from that state, then it may have jurisdiction.

Courts have indicated that the following may be considered in a jurisdiction issue:

➤ Physical presence in a state

➤ Significant minimal contacts in a state

➤ Conduct where you can reasonably anticipate jurisdiction

➤ Activities purposefully directed at a state's residents

Clearly, the state in which the company operates has jurisdiction over it. Minimum contact within a state doesn't include just establishing a Web site that may be visited by one or more of the state's residents. Again, the number of customers from that state can make a difference. Unfortunately this area of the law is still very murky.

If it's not reasonable to foresee litigation in a particular state, then the state courts may not have jurisdiction. For example, let's say that a company sold a car over the Internet to a resident of New York who, while traveling through Oklahoma, had an accident, allegedly because of a defect in the car. The seller's contact with Oklahoma is nonexistent, so it could not reasonably anticipate a lawsuit from that state.

If you direct your sales activities to a particular state, then count on it asserting jurisdiction. For example, if your site contains a contest and clearly invites residents of Indiana to participate, then that state can assert jurisdiction over the transaction. This may be true even if only one resident is harmed; however, the greater number harmed in a state the more likely the state can validly assert its jurisdiction.

Again, it's not my intention to dampen your enthusiasm for e-commerce. But it's a different legal arena from one in which a disgruntled customer sues you over a sale that occurred in your store.

Legal Eagle

Keep records of sales to each state's residents. If you made one sale to an Indiana resident, that state would have difficulty in asserting jurisdiction.

Taxes and the Net

The taxman may come to your Internet business, but from where? You know about the IRS claims on your income, but what about states where you make your sales? As of July, 2000, there is a moratorium on collecting sales and use taxes by the states. I have no crystal ball for your future, but with the varieties of state and local sales taxes, not to mention taxes in other countries, this issue cannot continue to be ignored as billions of dollars in potential tax revenues go uncollected.

This is clearly not just your problem if you sell on the Web, but it may be a shared misery if the moratorium is lifted.

Notes & Quotes

"The Net is a 10.5 on the Richter scale of economic change."

—Nicholas Negroponte, writer

Your Home Is Your Office

Barbara Weltman's book *The Complete Idiot's Guide to Starting a Home-Based Business, Second Edition* (Alpha Books, 2000) estimates that almost 3 million new home-based businesses will be established in the year 2000. You may be one. I am. My law practice has been in my home for over 20 years. Look out your window. I would bet that someone in your neighborhood has a business in his or her home. Most are part-time enterprises, but surprisingly many are full-time. Computers and the Internet have changed the way many of us work, and who we work for.

Most home-business legal issues are not unique to that business and have been discussed throughout this book; however, there are some worth a brief mention.

Zoning, Restrictive Covenants, and Licenses

Zoning laws vary considerably. Before you establish a business in your home, check with your local agency. The less intrusive your business is, the less likely that zoning laws will interfere. For example, if you are your only employee and customers never or rarely visit your house, then you really aren't bothering anyone and may be exempt from any regulation. However, if you have several employers and frequent customer visits, parking will be a problem and so may be the zoning restrictions. If the latter describes your business, then you may be able to obtain a special permit or may have to seek a zoning variance.

Your residence may have certain restrictions on use (restrictive covenants) and home office use may be one of them. If you are buying a house and intend to locate your business there, have your attorney examine all real estate documents. Likewise, your homeowner's association may have bylaws restricting business operations. Again, check the bylaws before you proceed.

Your local government may require a special license to operate a home-based business. You also need to discuss with your attorney any other licenses or permits that may be required, such as a retail sales permit or registration as a d.b.a. (doing business as).

Shark Attack!

Signage may be a problem for a home-based business. A modest sign attached to your house may be acceptable, but a big yard sign probably will not be.

Employees

Most one- and two-employee home-based businesses are exempt from federal and state anti-discrimination laws. For example, the Civil Rights Act of 1964 requires employment of 15 or more before it applies. However, many states and local governments may apply their laws with lesser numbers. Interestingly, OSHA has previously proposed workplace safety regulations for the home office; fortunately, it has not pursued this intrusive design, which does not mean that it won't in the future.

Likewise, federal minimum wage and overtime may not apply to a very small business, but if sales are substantial, then the Wage and Hour folks may claim jurisdiction. Also, many states regulate this area. Employee federal and state tax withholding applies.

Taxes and Your Home Office

If your home is your office, then be prepared to take the relevant tax deductions. Make sure that you set up at least one room that is exclusively used for your business. You can depreciate part of your house, and deduct a portion of the utilities, real estate taxes, and mortgage interest, and deduct the cost of a separate telephone line.

Your local government may increase your property tax assessment if you have a home business, or there may be a local income or sales taxes to contend with.

Shark Attack!

Don't forget to pay your quarterly estimated taxes on your business income. Pay as you go is good advice, particularly when the alternative is scrambling for money on April 15.

Helpful Sources

Read *The Complete Idiot's Guide to e-Commerce* (Alpha Books, 2000) by Rob Smith, Mark Speaker, and Mark Thompson for an excellent discussion of that topic. Likewise, read Barbara Weltman's *The Complete Idiot's Guide to Starting a Home-Based Business*. Visit many retail Web sites to understand their structure. You may want to subscribe to one or more magazines on e-commerce. The Federal Trade Commission (www.ftc.gov) discusses online sales. There is an American Association of Home-Based Businesses Web site: www.aahbb.org and American Home Business Association Web site: ww.homebusiness.com.

The Least You Need to Know

➤ Your domain name is your Internet address.

➤ Domain names may be trademarked.

➤ Get permission to link to another Web site.

➤ Important contracts should continue to be in writing and signed by the parties even though digital signatures are legal.

➤ Contract and tort cases may be tried in any state where there is significant contact with its residents.

➤ Check the local zoning and homeowner association bylaws to determine if there are restrictions on a home-based business.

Part 6

Looking Ahead and Closing Down

Every author needs a miscellaneous section, and this is it.

I make no apologies. Some of this discussion is decidedly depressing. If your business is on the verge of bankruptcy, you need to know the consequences, but the prognosis may not always be bleak. Bankruptcy Chapter 11 is there for your company to work out of its debts, and emerge stronger from it.

Business tax discussions are guaranteed to confound and confuse. I can't promise that you will enjoy reading about it, but I can promise that you could find it financially rewarding to do so.

You may be heading for retirement or just beginning your family. The business may be worth a lot more than you expected. I represent a couple who started in the tent rental business just a few years ago and now their business is booming. They know that they need to estate plan. The last will and testament is just a beginning.

Chapter 24

Insolvent: Coping and Bankruptcy Protection

> ## In This Chapter
>
> ➤ Understanding bankruptcy, before it happens to you
>
> ➤ The ins and outs of working with creditors
>
> ➤ If you have to sell the business
>
> ➤ 7 or 11, the bankruptcy chapter right for you

Bad things sometimes do happen to good businesses. If you find that your company is in trouble, remind yourself that you are a survivor, and no business is completely over until the final order in a Chapter 7 bankruptcy liquidation. Even in this darkest hour, you can begin anew. In this chapter, we'll take you through the difficult, but ultimately survivable, ordeal.

Protecting Your Personal Assets

Planning can never completely avoid all financial problems, but it can temper the results. Some of this planning comes at the very beginning when you select your business entity, while others involve business choices.

Choice of Business Entity

A sole proprietor is personally liable for all business debts. If you convert to a corporation, then you personally would be liable for only those debts that you guaranteed, including bank loans. Trade creditors could go after only corporate assets. Likewise, you could change from a partnership to a limited liability company (LLC), because members of an LLC are not personally liable for its business debts, unless they personally guaranteed them. With a partnership, you may be liable for all the debts if your partner(s) are insolvent, which is not a happy thought. In most instances, the conversion can be made tax-free, which is a happy thought.

Personal Loan Guarantees

Don't make personal loan guarantees of business debts at all is my advice. However, banks will insist, particularly if you are incorporated or are a limited liability company. Guarantee as little as possible, and ask for a limit on time required for the guarantee; if you have made timely payments for two years, perhaps the lender will remove the guarantee, but don't bet on it.

Legal Eagle

Avoid personally guaranteeing your rent, and never guarantee trade creditors (unless there is no other way to get your supplies). But if you do, make sure that the guarantee expires after no more than two years because by then you'll have shown how responsible you are.

Notes & Quotes

"Capitalism without bankruptcy is like Christianity without hell."

—Frank Borman, astronaut

If you're married, the lender often wants your spouse's signature as well, which can have distinct disadvantages. Keep in mind when asked to do this that, in most states, jointly held spousal real and personal property is exempt from creditor judgments, unless both guarantee the debt. I had one client whose wife absolutely refused to guarantee his business loan; the exasperated lender finally waived her signature. Go ye and do likewise.

Instead of asking your spouse to co-sign, make sure that your co-owners also personally guarantee the loan, because then you'll all share the liability. Of course, if their assets are nil, then you may be stuck with the tab. My advice is to become partners with thrifty, saving folks.

Pledging Collateral

Your business assets are usually fair game for a mortgage or security interest. Try to keep some business assets away from your current lenders to allow for future loans. Don't put your house up as collateral unless you absolutely have to. If you do and your loan isn't repaid, the lender may foreclose on your house. If you have some personal investments, such a corporate stock, the bank may be willing to accept this as a pledge.

Keep Adequate Insurance Coverage

It's the catastrophes that hurt. The store burns down or has a minor fire and the water damage does the rest. Fire insurance and business continuation insurance can keep you going. Your deliveryman may run a red light and smash into another car. Your business liability insurance should cover your responsibility. Insurance is one of your most important expenses. The amount of the coverage should be your main question, not should you have it.

Paying Taxes

Pay your taxes, and on time. The IRS expects those employee withholding and FICA checks to keep rolling in. If they don't, the IRS will come knocking right after you miss a payment, and their collection folks are hard-nosed. Not only is your business liable for the unpaid amounts, but you may be personally liable for a 100 percent penalty. And even bankruptcy won't relieve you of this tax debt.

The IRS may be quick with a tax lien for failure to pay withholding and FICA taxes, which may interfere with loan prospects and may result in the IRS seizing your assets. The IRS may also garnish any of your wages and attach other property. Federal law exempts few personal assets from IRS clutches.

Legal Eagle

If you must make a choice of which creditor to pay, pay the IRS, and early if necessary so that other demanding creditors don't obtain a judgment against your bank accounts before you send the check to the IRS. All this also applies to your state department of revenue.

Pre-Bankruptcy Planning

If personal bankruptcy looms ominously, then a little planning may be in order. You may recall from Chapter 20, "Extending Credit and Collecting from a Reluctant Debtor," that individuals may exempt part of their property from bankruptcy. State laws do vary on the amounts (many states have opted out of the federal exemptions), but most have several common exemptions:

➤ Personal residence

➤ Other real estate and personal property

➤ Cash value in life insurance

➤ Pensions

You may want to shift some assets to take advantage of these exemptions. For example, cash is not exempt, but cash paid to the mortgage company to increase your equity in your home also increases the exemption on that property.

You can use this strategy for any of the exempt assets. For example, if you own stocks, bonds, or mutual funds, then consider cashing them out and increasing the amount you put in your pensions. However, there are limits on annual pension contributions, and selling investments may incur additional income tax. Selling investments involves a capital gain, which is taxed at a lower rate than your other income. I am not suggesting that you defraud your creditors, but this is a legitimate way to protect your personal assets.

Arrangements with Creditors

A business that is financially troubled needs all the help it can get. I have a few suggestions that can help lessen the problem. But no solution fits every case. In Chapter 7, "Hiring a Lawyer, Accountant, and Other Advisors," I mentioned several advisors that you should have available for consultation. Now would be an excellent time to seek their advice. A good accountant can bring order to finances in disarray. A former business owner and advisor probably had hard times, too, and could suggest how you might cope.

Warning Signs

Financial problems sometime creep up on us. We are vaguely aware that things are amiss but aren't sure. Some warning signs that should alert you include …

➤ Frequently paying bills late.

➤ Creditors requiring payment on delivery.

➤ Credit cards and line of credit usually maxed.

➤ Receiving threatening letters from creditors.

➤ Lawsuits filed to collect bills.

➤ Sending in withholding/FICA taxes late, or not at all.

First Suggestion: Cut Back on Personal Nonessentials

Your personal life could be interfering with your business. If you have an expensive lease on a personal car, turn it in and rent or buy a cheaper model. SUVs are impressive at the gas pump, too. I like to eat out, but that can be expensive. We can be entertained by a rented movie just as easily as seeing its first run. Credit cards aren't necessarily created to be maxed out, and the interest you pay on them is likely sucking your business dry, so shredding them may be a good step.

Legal Eagle

Consumer credit counseling bureaus are available in most areas to help us get our personal finances in order. There are numerous books and articles, likewise, to assist.

Second Suggestion: Cut Back on Business Nonessentials

You need to carefully scrutinize every expense. Get advice from your accountant. Most businesses focus on increasing revenue, which is fine, but your goal is profit and that can come from reducing costs, too. Look hard at every budget item. I'm assuming that you have a budget; if that is not the case, or if the budget is just a piece of paper, then you may have serious problems.

You may have an expensive lease on a business vehicle or other equipment. Consider turning it in for a cheaper model. Second best may be good enough even for a successful business. Cutting back on advertising may seem counter-productive, but you'd better make sure that you are getting the best bang for the buck. It's impressive to do a TV ad, but perhaps radio or the newspaper would be more effective and much less costly. Reducing personnel may cost you customers, but you need to analyze each job to see how it can be more productive.

Bottom line: If an expense doesn't generate a profit or increase customer satisfaction, then it may cost you the business.

Working with Your Creditors

Creditors want to be paid; there is no mistaking that fact. Indeed you may be in a financial bind because one of your biggest customers suddenly turned a blind eye to your bills or a deaf ear to your phone calls. Whichever side you're on, you've got to be realistic about payment.

Legalese

A **workout** is also referred to as a composition, which is a formal contract involving the debtor and several creditors, in which each creditor agrees to take less than the total debt as payment in full.

Shark Attack!

Don't go it alone when it comes to a workout agreement. Creditor workout agreements are contracts; you need a lawyer who can effectively negotiate and draft these contracts. When you settle, you want everything settled.

If you are a debtor in financial trouble, then consider talking with your creditors. Creditors know when you're in trouble because they aren't getting paid. So suggest a debt *workout* plan. They might just go for it because then your business will be able to continue to buy from them. It's strange, but sometimes the more that you owe, the more creditors are willing to bargain, particularly if a bankruptcy filing seems like a viable alternative.

Possible solutions to feeling overburdened by debt include …

➤ Monthly payments.

➤ Lump sum payment.

➤ Partial liquidation of your assets.

➤ Creditor takes collateral.

Spreading the debt over several payments can measurably assist your current cash crunch. The payments could total more, or less, than the debt, and be paid with or without interest. You need to analyze your cash flow, or use an accountant to do so. If sales continue to be good and you can reduce expenses, then this may be the way to go. If the cash flow is a drip, then this isn't a realistic option.

A lump sum offer may be appropriate if you have the current cash, or can obtain it readily through a short-term loan or investor equity. How much the creditor will accept depends on his or her assessment of the chances of collecting on a court judgment. Small claims court is pretty fast; other courts are very slow—months can elapse even for the best cases, and that means attorney fees.

One source of a lump sum payment may be the sale of some of your assets. Obviously these assets have to be fairly nonessential to your business. Selling your tools or holding a fire sale for your inventory is unwise, except in the most extreme cases. Unfortunately, buyers can smell a bargain, and you may not get a fair price for the assets.

You could offer the collateral back to the creditor in full payment of the debt. This is a bird-in-the-hand approach to which the secured creditor might agree if the debt is not large enough to warrant a full-blown lawsuit, or if you're current with your payments and the creditor can't repossess. Remember, the secured creditor is generally protected in bankruptcy, at least to the extent the debt is equal to or less than the value of the collateral.

Making the Tough Decisions

Tough love can apply to businesses. Through no fault of your own but simple bad luck, you might have created the wrong business at the wrong time in the wrong location. Three wrongs still don't make a right, and you might want to cut your losses by closing up shop.

Closing Your Business

As I write this chapter, one of my favorite buffet restaurants is shutting its doors. It had been there for 30 years, serving good food at reasonable prices. Its customers were loyal, but are now cash-poor senior citizens. Maybe you can relate. Perhaps it's best to halt the financial hemorrhaging by closing. You will want to negotiate with your unsecured creditors over their debts. Likely they will settle for what's available. The secured creditor will repossess its collateral. The main problem is with the personal guarantees. The alternative to a successful negotiation of the debt may be personal bankruptcy, which may be of little comfort to the creditors who could be willing to compromise.

Selling Your Business

Your first question might be, "Why would anyone would want to buy a failing business?" To get your answer, check out *Business Week* or *The Wall Street Journal* for glowing articles about turnaround experts. These are the guys who take over a poorly performing business and make a success of it. Your prospective buyer may think he or she can do a better job than you can. Or maybe the buyer owns one business like yours and would like another; economies of scale (two can run cheaper than one) could work. Or it could be that your business has always fascinated the buyer. For example, your bookstore may not make much of a profit, but that could be just fine for a book lover who retired on a substantial pension.

If you are selling your business, please reread Chapter 8, "Buying an Existing Business: Traps for the Unwary." You're now on the flip side. Also read Ed Paulson's *The Complete Idiot's Guide to Buying and Selling a Business* (Alpha Books, 1999). Paulson's book provides some good pointers.

The steps I would suggest are as follows:

➤ Get your financial information organized.

➤ Appraise the value of your business.

➤ Hire a business broker to sell it.

➤ Arrange to settle all business debts.

Your accountant can help you put together the figures. You may want to gloss over some negatives, but don't succumb to temptation. The buyer could later have regrets over the purchase and want to sue you. The best charge is fraud, so be truthful. If the buyer is experienced in the business, he or she may spot savings you hadn't thought of or couldn't implement.

Legal Eagle

If your business is in great financial shape when you want to sell, you should still follow the steps that I have outlined. You just have the good fortune to negotiate in a better position.

Get your business appraised. You really don't know what it's worth on the market. A good appraisal can give you a realistic view about the selling price, and if the appraisal is shared with your prospect, may convince the buyer.

Brokers put buyers and sellers together. Consult your advisors; one or more of them has used a broker in the past. The broker may have the expertise and negotiating skills you lack. The broker's fee may be the best part of this deal if he or she finds a ready buyer.

Try to structure the purchase to obtain relief from all business debts, particularly those that you have personally guaranteed or for which you put up your personal assets as collateral. Your lender may be willing to substitute the buyer as debtor and the buyer's assets as collateral.

Dissolving the Entity

Sole proprietors simply remove the shingle and nothing needs to be filed with any government agency. Of course, the business debts have to be paid or settled, because you are personally liable for them.

If you are in a partnership, the partnership doesn't usually file any documents with any agency. However, you must pay or settle all partnership debts because each partner is personally liable for all of the debts.

If your business is a limited partnership (LP), limited liability company (LLC), or a corporation, then you must file Articles of Dissolution with the Secretary of State. The Articles require entity approval, such as board and shareholder approval for a corporation. Many states require a release from the state department of revenue before the Secretary of State can issue a certificate of dissolution (this means that you don't owe any back taxes).

You also need to file final federal and state tax returns for your business entity, such as Form 1120 if you're a C corporation, 1120S if you're an S corporation, and 1065 if you're a partnership or an LLC.

Many businesses just close and don't close out with the Secretary of State, IRS, or the state department of revenue. Take the final step and avoid some grief.

Bankruptcy: 7 or 11

Filing under Chapter 11 for business reorganizations, or filing under Chapter 7 for liquidation may protect troubled businesses. Either chapter allows you time and permits orderly dealing with your business creditors.

Chapter 7 Liquidation

I discussed personal bankruptcy under Chapter 7 of the Bankruptcy Code in my Chapter 20, so I suggest that you reread that section if your business is a sole proprietor or a partnership, because both involve personal liability.

If your business is an LLC or corporation, bankruptcy Chapter 7 will liquidate the business assets. The business property is sold, usually under the supervision of a bankruptcy trustee, and the proceeds are used to pay the business debts. Generally the unsecured creditors suffer since they are the next to the last to receive any distribution. The last, of course, are the LLC members or corporate shareholders; it's rare but could happen that the liquidation pays all the debts and has some money to distribute to the owners. Unlike the personal bankruptcy, there are no exemptions; everything goes.

The corporate or LLC Chapter 7 order frees the business owners of all debts except those personally guaranteed or taxes. S corporations rarely owe an income tax (shareholders report its income on their 1040), and the LLC wouldn't owe a tax (members report its income on their 1040). However, a C corporation may owe income taxes. The IRS may not be able to collect back C corporation income taxes, but it may argue that the shareholders or officers have aided in evading taxes. Remember that a failure to pay withholding and FICA taxes can make any corporate officer or responsible member personally liable for the tax penalty.

Chapter 11 Reorganization

Chapter 11 permits your business to continue running, usually with you at the helm; the bankruptcy term for this is debtor in possession, which means that the business owner continues to run his or her business, as opposed to the trustee in possession. Here are the typical steps under bankruptcy Chapter 11:

1. The debtor or creditor(s) files the bankruptcy petition.
2. The court stay order and creditor notification are delivered.
3. Creditors committees are organized.
4. Debtor is in possession, who continues to run the business.
5. The debtor prepares a bankruptcy reorganization plan.
6. Creditors committees accept or reject the plan.
7. The court confirms the debtor's plan or alternate plan.
8. The debtor fulfills the plan.

The debtor (voluntary) or creditors (involuntary) may file a Chapter 11 petition. The petition will include a list of creditors to whom notice is to be sent. Usually the creditors do not have to file a claim unless the debtor or other creditors dispute the debt.

An unsecured creditor committee is appointed by the U.S. Bankruptcy Trustee, usually these are the seven largest creditors. The creditor committee may examine the debtor under oath, investigate the debtor's acts, and consult with the debtor in possession who is running the business (or the trustee if he or she is in possession). Other creditor committees may be formed.

In most Chapter 11 proceedings, the debtor continues to run the business. A trustee may be appointed to run the business if the current management has committed fraud, mismanagement, or is incompetent, which is determined by the bankruptcy court. Perhaps surprisingly, a Chapter 11 debtor may receive additional loans. This may be necessary to continue the business. The lender may receive a priority position in the bankruptcy for the post-bankruptcy loan. Also, the court may permit the debtor to cancel unprofitable contracts and leases. The debtor has an exclusive right for 120 days to prepare and present a reorganization plan to all the creditor committees. The plan may alter the rights of unsecured creditors, secured creditors, and shareholders. Creditors' claims are divided into different classes, and each creditor within a class must be treated the same. For example, each unsecured creditor would receive its pro rata share of its debt.

The debtor's plan must be accompanied by adequate business and financial disclosures to the committees. The bankruptcy court will review the disclosures to ensure that they are sufficient. The creditor and shareholder committees will vote on the debtor's plan. If all accept the plan, then the court will likely approve it, and it goes into operation. However, one or more of the committees may not give approval; approval is by a majority of the creditors and by ⅔ of the amounts claimed of the debts. One or more creditor committees may propose an alternative plan.

The bankruptcy court makes the final determination. Even if the committees veto the debtor's plan, the court can still approve it, or some modification of the plan. A small business with no more than $2 million of debts may be eligible for a somewhat expedited Chapter 11, which would be quicker and less costly; attorney fees, trustee fees, and court costs are paid from the bankrupt's assets. After confirmation of the plan, the debtor, creditors, and shareholders are bound to follow it.

Taxes and Bankruptcy

As I previously have stated, taxes, whether federal or state income, sales, or property, rarely are discharged in bankruptcy.

The IRS will make an immediate assessment of the tax, interest and penalties due once it's notified of the bankruptcy petition. Any IRS tax liens could be enforced against the bankruptcy assets. It's obviously to your advantage to have paid the IRS before any other creditor.

In addition, the tax code may require the taxpayer whose debt is discharged or reduced in bankruptcy or in a creditor workout to reduce the tax basis of his or her assets accordingly. This is in lieu of recognizing income. Sounds a bit confusing. For example, if an unsecured loan of $10,000 is completely discharged, then the debtor may have to reduce the tax basis (original cost less depreciation) in an asset like equipment by that amount. This reduction may cause a greater gain if the equipment is later sold, or reduce its potential depreciation. My advice is to get an accountant to figure all this out.

Helpful Sources

Read Paulson's book, *The Complete Idiot's Guide to Selling and Buying a Business*. Check out the American Bankruptcy Institute Web site: www.abiworld.org. The complex federal bankruptcy code and tax code is on the Government Printing Office Web site: www.gpo.gov. Many law firms have Web sites on bankruptcy, which can be discovered through your search engines. Your library may have books on bankruptcy.

The Least You Need to Know

➤ Incorporating your business may protect your personal assets from business creditors.

➤ Business creditors may be willing to accept a workout, which would give them less than 100 cents on the dollar.

➤ Bankruptcy Chapter 11 may save your business by allowing you to work out a bankruptcy plan, which, if approved by the court, binds the debtor and creditors.

Chapter 25

Your Estate Plan Includes the Business

In This Chapter

➤ Creating an estate plan that takes your business into account

➤ Documents you can't do without: Wills and trusts: documents you need

➤ What you need to know about marriage and divorce when it comes to your business

➤ Deciding who takes over when you depart

Procrastinate long enough and you won't need a last will and testament. Your state has its own plan for your estate if you don't have a will. The IRS and your state department of revenue will likely receive more than their fair share of your estate if you don't properly plan your estate. This chapter discusses estate planning from A to Z.

Business and Other Assets

Are you as prepared with your estate plan as you think you are? Let's start with a brief checklist (circle the applicable answer):

    Yes   **No**   My spouse and I have current wills.

    Yes   **No**   My spouse and I have recently consulted an estate planning professional.

    Yes   **No**   I have reviewed the value and ownership of all my assets and liabilities.

    Yes   **No**   My spouse has reviewed the value and ownership of all his or her assets and liabilities.

Yes	No	I have reviewed all my business ownership agreements.
Yes	No	I have reviewed my life insurance needs.
Yes	No	I have a pension or 401(k) plan.
Yes	No	My estate will have sufficient cash to pay the debts and taxes, with enough left over for my family.
Yes	No	I have designated someone to handle my affairs when I am no longer capable of doing so.
Yes	No	I have taken sufficient steps to reduce my income taxes now, and the death taxes against my estate.

If you've answered "no" to even a few of these statements, you've got some work to do! Let's get started.

Your Personal Assets

You must inventory your assets to determine their value and ownership forms, such as property that is solely owned, jointly owned, or co-owned with a spouse, and you can find an estate inventory form in Appendix B, "Basic Business Forms."

Solely owned property is distributed to the beneficiaries named in your last will and testament. For example, if you own corporate stock solely in your own name, the stock ownership is transferred to the person(s) named in your will upon death. If you have no will, then the state *intestate* law transfers it to the heirs whom the state designates.

Co-owned property may be owned ...

➤ Joint tenancy with right of survivorship.

➤ Tenancy in common.

➤ Tenancy by entirety or community property.

You may own a bank account, certificate of deposit, stocks and bonds, real estate, and miscellaneous other property as joint tenants with right of survivorship. This means that if you or your spouse dies, the other automatically owns the property. The decedent's will has no effect on jointly owned property, unless both die simultaneously.

The bank account card you signed with the bank usually will have the phrase "joint with right of survivorship" on it if co-owned; CD, stocks, and bonds will have the

Notes & Quotes

"If a man dies and leaves his estate in an uncertain condition, the lawyers become his heirs."

—Ed Howe, writer

Legalese

Intestate simply means dying without a will. If a spouse survives a decedent and children, under state law those survivors may be required to divide the solely owned property.

phrase on its face; the real estate deed will include this phrase after the grantees' (owners') names.

Or you could co-own property as *tenants in common*. This form of ownership may occur when siblings inherit property together, such as when two sisters inherit the family farm. Or, two nonrelated persons may invest in property together. When one co-owner dies, his or her heirs or beneficiaries of the will receive it.

Tenancy by entirety and *community property* are spousal co-ownership rights. Spouses may also own property as joint tenants; many states limit tenancy by entirety to spousal co-ownership in real estate. For example, if a husband and wife co-own their home as tenants by entirety (on the deed), and one dies, the surviving spouse owns the house; the decedent's will has no effect. In the community property states, the surviving spouse owns his or her half, and the other half may be disposed of by the decedent's will or a community property agreement.

Legalese

Community property states include Arizona, California, Idaho, Louisiana, Nevada, New Mexico, Texas, Washington, and Wisconsin. Puerto Rico allows community property. Each state has slight differences in their community property laws.

Life insurance proceeds are paid to the beneficiary named in the policy regardless of any different stipulations that might appear in the decedent's will. I've been involved with several estates where the owners of life insurance policies didn't update the beneficiary clause so the benefits went to someone else, say, an ex-wife. If there is no designated beneficiary in the policy, then the will distributes the life insurance proceeds to its beneficiaries, or if there's no will, the heirs receive their share.

Pensions have a designated beneficiary who will receive the balance of the pension upon the owner's death. If married, the owner usually designates the spouse. In fact, the spouse is entitled to his or her share of the other spouse's pension unless the spouse waives it in writing. Annuities, likewise, usually have a surviving annuiant (beneficiary) named. If no surviving pensioner or annuiant is designated, then the balance is distributed as if it were solely owned property.

A person may have placed his or her property into a living trust. The trust itself designates to whom the property is transferred upon the owner's death. (There is a more complete discussion of trust law later in this chapter.)

Business Assets

You will likely be operating your business under one of these forms: sole proprietor, partnership, limited liability company, or corporation.

If you are a sole proprietor, each business asset is solely owned property, and title to all your business property is in your own name. If you have a will, the will distributes the business assets, or if there is no will, then your intestate heirs get the property.

The sole shareholder and the sole member of a limited liability company own the corporate stock or LLC membership, while the entity itself owns its business assets. Upon the owner's death, his or her corporate stock or limited liability company membership is distributed like any other solely owned property.

If you are a partner in a partnership, limited liability partnership, or limited partnership, or are a member among several members of a limited liability company, or are one shareholder among several corporate shareholders, the disposition of your interest may be controlled by the agreement that you signed. A well-drafted partnership agreement, limited liability operating agreement, or corporate stock purchase agreement will specify the rights of a deceased's partner's (or member's or shareholder's) estate to his or her interest and the corresponding duties of the surviving partners (or members or shareholders).

Usually this takes the form of a mandatory purchase of the interest by the survivors, and a mandatory sale by the personal representative of the deceased's estate, which receives the proceeds, often over several years. However, if there is no buy-sell provision, then the deceased partner's, member's, or shareholder's interest becomes part of the estate and is distributed by the will, or in its absence, to the heirs.

Avoiding Probate

We have all heard horror stories about *probate*. The squabbling heirs, the innumerable court appearances, and the greedy lawyers are part of the tale. This happens most frequently when the deceased failed to properly plan his or her estate. I don't have any magic formula for trouble-free probate, but I do have some valuable suggestions.

Probate or No Probate

First, what probate is, then what it is not. A person's estate *is* subject to probate if he or she …

Legalese

Probate is the court supervision of the distribution of a decedent's estate. State laws somewhat vary on their probate procedure.

➤ Solely owns property.

➤ Co-owns property as tenants in common.

➤ Shares in community property (in some states).

➤ Owns a pension, annuity, or life insurance with *no* named beneficiary.

Conversely, property is *not* subject to probate if she or he …

➤ Co-owns property jointly with a survivor.

➤ Co-owns property with a surviving spouse as tenants by entirety.

➤ Owns a pension, annuity, or life insurance with a named beneficiary.

➤ Has property in trust.

➤ Owns a life estate in property, such as a mother who would deed her house to a daughter, but retain for her life the right to use the house rent-free.

The majority of the estates will not require probate because the decedent co-owned property jointly with survivorship, tenants by entirety, or owned life insurance with a specified beneficiary. In addition, some states provide a simple transfer of property by affidavit (sworn statement) if the solely owned asset's value is under a specified amount, such as $25,000.

Probate Procedure

Probate may not always be avoided, so you need to know the basics of the process.

The estate is opened by filing a petition with the probate court in the county where the decedent resided. Usually the person named in the decedent's will as the personal representative (executor) files the petition, but any beneficiary in the will could also file. If there is no will, then typically an heir files the probate petition.

Many states have two different forms of probate: supervised and unsupervised. The latter typically involves opening the estate, filing an inventory (list of assets), and closing the estate with only minimal court involvement. Supervised administration requires court approval for virtually everything. Usually all the beneficiaries of an estate must agree to use unsupervised administration, since it typically does not require probate court approval for the personal representative's acts.

The petitioner requests the court to admit the will, and to appoint the person named in the will as the personal representative. After the court does so, the newly appointed personal representative notifies all the beneficiaries listed in the decedent's will and any known creditors. Most states also require a local newspaper to publish a notice to the creditors and other interested parties of the probate. The court may require the personal representative to obtain a performance bond to protect the estate from any wrongdoing by the personal representative.

If the decedent died without a will, then the state statute usually provides a priority for a near relative (spouse or children) to serve as a personal representative; the rest of the procedure is the same.

The personal representative is responsible for collecting the decedent's probate assets, and then listing those assets on an inventory filed with the court. The personal representative is also responsible for paying the estate debts and taxes from its assets. Many of these debts are relatively straightforward, such as utility bills, credit card debts, medical bills, funeral expenses. A creditor's claim may be contested, and the result determined by the court.

If the estate is unsupervised—which I advise whenever possible—the court is not involved in the personal representative's acts. However, if the estate is supervised, the court must approve any sale of assets and distribution of the net assets to the beneficiaries of the will or the heirs. In addition, the court must approve an accounting of all assets received and expenses paid; in unsupervised probate, the personal representative just accounts to the beneficiaries or heirs.

Planning to Avoid Probate

If you would like to avoid probate, my advice is to die poor. Not really. There clearly are some advantages to avoiding probate:

➤ No court costs

➤ No probate attorney fees

➤ Quicker distribution of the decedent's assets

➤ No will contest, since the will is irrelevant

➤ Possible death tax savings

Court costs are usually in the $100 to $250 range. Attorney fees may be considerable, often around five percent of the estate. Jointly owned and tenancy by entirety property become the survivor's property upon the co-owner's death. The pension, annuity, and life insurance are distributed according to the terms of their contracts. Likewise, the trust distributes its asset or pays its income according to its terms. If a decedent had a life estate, the remainder owner becomes the sole owner. For example, a widow may deed her house to her daughter (who becomes the remainder owner), retaining a life estate in it; when the widow dies, the daughter owns the house because the mother's life estate is extinguished at her death.

Will contests can be messy affairs. If there is no probate, the will has no assets to distribute, and no disgruntled heirs to attack it.

I talked about death taxes in the previous chapter. Planning, such as giving appropriate gifts during your lifetime, may avoid tax and probate. Likewise, property held jointly with a spouse is free of federal estate tax at one spouse's death.

What then is to be done?

➤ Create joint ownership bank accounts with the persons who you want to own the accounts at your death; the creation of the accounts will not in itself trigger a gift tax; only the withdrawal by the noncontributors will do that.

➤ Put your spouse's name as co-owner on all your property; there is no gift tax for transfers to a spouse; however, if your estate is $1 million or more, then a wholesale transfer may cause substantial estate taxes upon the death of the last to survive.

➤ By all means, make sure that all of your pension plans, annuities, and life insurance policies have named beneficiaries.

➤ Consider using a trust to transfer your assets at death, rather than a will (or in addition to a will). More on trusts later.

Shark Attack!

An unhappy heir may challenge the creation of a living trust by alleging the person establishing it was mentally incompetent, defrauded, or subject to undue influence. Likewise, a transfer by gift or creating a joint account can be contested on these grounds. Proof of mental incompetence in challenging a living trust is usually more difficult than for a will contest.

A word of caution is in order. Avoiding probate may be a laudable goal but, like most things, it does have its tradeoffs. Any time joint ownership is created from solely owned property there may be a potential gift-tax problem. Also, if you create a joint account with only one of several children, then the surviving child takes the entire account—a result that you may not intend. What I do advise is careful planning with your estate planning professionals.

Legal Eagle

An alternative to joint ownership may be to designate persons to which a bank account is paid on death (POD).

Estate and Gift Taxes for Life Planning

Federal tax folks are very demanding. You give property away, and you pay a gift tax. You die and your heirs inherit, they pay an estate tax. And the state revenue department wants its share, too. It's a nuisance. Fortunately, these pesky taxes do have exemptions.

You can give away up to $10,000 per person each year with no federal gift tax; this amount is doubled if your spouse joins in making the gift. In addition, up to $675,000 lifetime or estate transfers are free of federal gift and estate taxes; this figure gradually increases to $1 million in 2006. And, you can give or leave to your spouse an unlimited amount free of either tax.

The following sections discuss the federal estate and gift taxes. I am not discussing state gift taxes; however, you should know that there are a few states that do tax certain substantial nonspousal gifts. Nor am I discussing state death taxes; almost all states either follow the federal estate tax (at a much, much lower rate) or have an inheritance tax on the beneficiaries (at a fairly modest rate with near relatives generally taxed less).

Federal Estate Tax

The federal estate tax form is very simple: How much did you die owning? Send us that amount. Not really.

The estate tax computation can be summarized as follows:

gross estate – expenses = taxable estate
+ post-1976 taxable gifts
= tax base
× tax rate
= tentative tax
– federal and state tax credits
= estate tax due

Any property a decedent solely owned, co-owned, or substantially controlled is part of what is known as the gross estate. If a surviving spouse co-owned property, then only one-half of its value is included, and the other half is usually a marital deduction, resulting in no spousal property being taxed. Other co-owned property is included to the extent the decedent had an interest in the property.

Revocable living trusts, which were created by the decedent for the decedent or others, are included in the gross estate. Likewise, life insurance proceeds from a policy the decedent owned are in the gross estate. If the decedent transferred property and retained a life estate (deeded the house to the children and kept the right to live in the house), that is included. Pensions and annuities may be included in the gross estate. There are other less typical inclusions, but this constitutes the vast majority of property included in the gross estate.

Shark Attack!

An issue with the IRS is the value of property; if there is any doubt and big bucks are involved, use an appraiser who has been successful in similar estate situations. The IRS almost always will challenge small business evaluations. Your accountant may be acquainted with an appraiser.

Any debts owed by the deceased are deductible from the gross estate, including mortgage and credit card debt. Casualty losses that occur during probate are deductible. Probate fees are deductible, as are transfers to charity. Transfers to the deceased's spouse either as surviving co-owner or through inheritance can be deducted; certain transfers in trust to the spouse also count.

For small businesses, there is an additional deduction of up to $675,000; this means that a decedent can have a taxable estate of $1,300,000 without any estate tax. This additional deduction is permitted only if more than 50 percent of the estate value is the small business, and certain other restrictions may apply.

Property received by a surviving spouse outright from the deceased spouse qualifies for a martial deduction from the gross estate. The law permits one spouse to establish for the other spouse a certain type of trust, called a Qualified Terminable Interest Property (QTIP), which will also qualify for the marital deduction. This trust is often used to protect the surviving spouse from unwise decisions about his or her inherited money.

Legalese

A spousal trust, called **qualified terminable interest property or QTIP,** qualifies for a marital deduction when the spouse receives the annual income and the property is included in the spouse's estate at death; children are often the beneficiaries after the spouse's death.

Since the estate and gift taxes are unified for computation, the estate has to include any post-1976 taxable gifts. This is a good reason to file gift tax returns if a gift to anyone is over $10,000 in a year. To this total, or tax base, an estate tax rate is applied. The effective rate begins at 37 percent for estates over $675,000 and gradually increases to 55 percent for estates over $3 million. The result is referred to as the tentative tax because a unified federal tax credit and state death tax credit apply to reduce the tentative tax to the actual estate tax.

A simplified calculation on a taxable estate of $890,000 would look like this: tentative tax from the tax chart (rate 37 to 39 percent) is $302,900. The 2000/2001 federal tax credit is $220,550 and the state death tax credit from the IRS chart is $27,120, giving a total credit of $247,670. The estate tax is $55,230. You can more specifically follow this calculation, or your own, by going to the IRS forms Web site and clicking on the instructions of Form 706.

The federal estate tax return must be filed within nine months of the decedent's death. The personal representative files the Form 706. The time for filing state death tax returns varies with the state, so consult your state department of revenue.

Federal Gift Tax

Giving your property away can avoid the federal estate tax, but don't get carried away, particularly if Congress increases the exemption.

Gifts to your spouse or charity are tax-free. Immediate transfers to an ex-spouse in a divorce settlement are not subject to the tax. Gifts to your children or others are subject to the tax only if the gift is over $10,000 per year ($20,000 if the spouse joins in the gift).

A loan to a child at less than the going rate of interest is considered a gift of the foregone interest. For example, if you lent your child $50,000 at 0 percent interest and the federal fund rate was 10 percent, you gave your child $5,000, which is clearly within the $10,000 exemption; however, a larger gift loan or other gifts may exceed the exemption.

You may make total lifetime transfers that equal the federal gift/estate tax exemption equivalent ($675,000 for 2000/2001) without paying any gift tax. The downside is that those gifts that exceed the annual exemption reduce your exemption amount (actually for computation purposes it reduces your tax credit) for future gifts or for the estate tax.

For example, if for your first taxable gift you alone gave your child $90,000, there would be no immediate tax to be paid. The taxable gift amount of $80,000 has a tentative tax of $18,200; you simply apply the unified credit of $220,550 which gives you a new credit of $202,350 for future gifts and estate tax.

The donor (person making the gift) pays the federal gift tax. A gift tax return on Form 709 is required if you make any gift to a person that exceeds $10,000; the due date is April 15.

Legal Eagle

You may establish certain trust accounts for your minor children; the account can be kept in the account until the child reaches 21 years of age.

Wills and Trusts: Documents You Need

You need a last will and testament because no estate plan is complete without a will. No matter how much you plan to avoid probate, things often change before you get around to making a change. A lucky lottery number or an unexpected gift or inheritance may be in your future. A trust is certainly something that you should consider.

Dying Without a Will

When I was in the Army back in the early '70s, I prepared a will for one of the last survivors of the Spanish-American war; he was 95 at the time. He told me that he thought it was about time to make a will. I agreed.

Many of us do procrastinate about making a will, and since we are still alive everything's okay; tomorrow is soon enough. Unfortunately, tomorrow may not come for some of us. Dying can be a tragedy; dying without a will is a complication. If you don't have a will, your heirs will be specified by state statute, so property may be inherited by someone you wouldn't want to leave a dime to. Probate will be more time consuming and expensive. There may be more death taxes, too.

State statutes vary about an heir's rights, but the spouse and children usually share equally in a decedent's probate estate where there is no will; however, a second or later spouse who did not have a child with the decedent may receive less. If there are no children (or grandchildren), the spouse and the decedent's parents may share in the estate, with the surviving spouse receiving the greater portion. If there is no spouse, the children receive the entire estate. Beyond this your heirs include your parents and siblings. Close friends, stepchildren, and in-laws are not your heirs.

If you are not satisfied with the state distribution, then create a no-probate estate, or make a will.

Notes & Quotes

"Never make your doctor the beneficiary of your will."

—Anonymous

Legalese

Devisee is the modern term for a person who receives property from the will. Heir is more commonly used for a person who receives the decedent's property through intestate distribution.

Your Last Will and Testament

A typical will has three major sections: beneficiary *(devisee),* personal representative (executor), and guardian.

You can name anyone as devisee in your will. However, if a spouse is excluded (or given less than he or she would receive in an intestate distribution), then the spouse can elect against the will and receive the intestate share (usually one-half of the probate estate).

You can divide up your estate in any manner that you choose. For example, you could give one-half to your spouse, one-fourth to your children, and one-fourth to a charity. You can also make specific devises, for instance, "I devise my collection of 1961 New York Yankee baseball cards to Steve Maple."

Choose a personal representative who has good common sense; since you have a business that may be part of your estate, the person should be someone who has some business experience. The personal representative is responsible for moving the estate through the court, so he or she should be well organized. The estate's attorney

Legal Eagle

Choose your children's guardians with care. If managing money is not a guardian's strong point, you could name a bank as guardian of the property, or set up a trust to manage the children's money.

will provide the personal representative with legal advice so an attorney as executor is not necessary. For many uncomplicated estates the spouse serves as the primary personal representative and one or two of the adult children as an alternative.

If you have a minor child (under age 18) or a mentally or physically disabled adult child who is not capable of managing his or her affairs, then a court will appoint a guardian for the child when you and your spouse are no longer living. You should name a person(s) to serve should that happen. I usually suggest a person or couple who is compatible with your age and lifestyle—someone who you would want to rear your children.

The court appoints the guardian, based upon what is best for the children, but usually honors the nomination in a parent's will. The guardian is responsible for rearing the children and managing their money. The guardian will make financial reports to the court every one or two years. The guardianship terminates when the child reaches age 18, unless the child has an incapacitating disability; then the guardianship may continue for a lifetime.

I have included a sample will in Appendix B for your information. I know that you might be tempted to simply prepare and sign your own will, thus saving legal fees. But this may be a false savings if the will is not properly executed or confusingly written. There is certainly more of an incentive to contest a will if the probate estate is ample. Some attorneys charge between $150 and $300 for a simple will.

Once you have a will, you should review it every three or four years to make sure that it meets your current needs. If you marry, divorce, add children, retire, sell your business, or hit the lottery, you should review the will to determine if changes are warranted. Don't make any written changes on the will itself, because this may invali- date it.

Most states require at least two witnesses to the will. The person making the will signs and the witnesses sign, all in each other's presence. The witnesses are told that they are signing a will but they need not see its contents. The will does not have to be notarized.

If you want to make any minor changes, such as naming a different personal representative, then prepare a codicil, which is an amendment to a will. The codicil is executed in the same formal manner as the will. If you have any substantial changes, such as changes in beneficiaries, then execute a new will.

Trusts

A trust is an estate-planning document that permits a trustee to administer the assets of the grantor who establishes the trust. The trust may be established during the grantor's life, which is called a living or *inter vivos* trust. Or the trust may be established through a will upon the grantor's death, which is called a testamentary trust. The living trust may be revocable or *irrevocable*.

Legalese

An **irrevocable** living trust usually involves children or even grandchildren as its main beneficiaries. The grantors have no power to change the trust terms after it is created. The federal gift tax may apply since the creation of the trust is a gift to a third party.

The essential contents of a trust are ...

➤ Grantor (settlor) establishes the trust

➤ Trustee administers the trust

➤ Principal (corpus) is property transferred to the trust

➤ Income beneficiary receives trust income during life

➤ Remainderman beneficiary receives trust property at termination

If you want to avoid probate yet want to control your assets during your life, then the revocable living trust may be for you. You (and your spouse) may establish the trust as grantor by executing the trust document and depositing a minimum of one dollar in the trust, which is the principal or corpus of the trust. Virtually any property can be transferred to the trust.

For example, the grantor(s) may put some or all of their liquid assets into a trust, including stocks, mutual funds, CDS, and so on, by simply changing the owner from their names as individuals to their names as trustees. A residence or other real estate can be transferred to a trust by executing a new deed to the trustee.

The grantors are usually the trustees unless both are incapable of managing the trust. The trust is revocable so that the trustees can add or withdraw principal. The grantors are the income beneficiaries so they retain all the income from their investments; the tax effect remains unchanged in the grantor trust—the grantors are taxed on the income. The typically revocable trust provides for the distribution of its principal after the death of the last surviving spouse, usually to the children.

The revocable trust usually provides for successor trustees if the grantors or trustees are no longer capable of managing the trust. Frequently the successor is one of the children, but it can be a bank or other institutional trustee; the latter, of course, would charge a fee but does provide professional management.

If you have young children, then consider a trust for them to protect them if something happens to you and your spouse. The trust may be an unfunded revocable living trust, which later could be funded by the proceeds of a life insurance policy on the parents' life and from the probate estate. The alternative is a testamentary trust for each parent, which becomes effective upon death.

In either event, the children's property is held in trust until they reach a mature age. The income and the principal would be used to pay for their expenses, including college costs. The trust allows the children to be more mature when they receive their inheritance. In most states, when a child becomes 18, he or she is free of a guardianship and entitled to any inheritance. I'm not convinced that most 18-year-olds are mature enough to handle the new wealth.

Power of Attorney and Living Will

If a person becomes incapable of managing his or her financial or personal affairs, a guardian may be appointed to do so. The guardianship is supervised by the court, so everything is public, and the guardianship costs money to administer. A trust created before a person becomes incompetent is a viable alternative.

Another possibility is a durable power of attorney. The power of attorney is given to another person, typically a spouse or child. Usually, the authority under the power cannot be exercised until the grantor becomes incompetent. The power of attorney continues until death or revocation by the grantor.

A living will is a legal form directing that the declarant's life not be artificially prolonged if he or she is in a terminal condition. The living will is chosen by some to allow themselves death with dignity. If you chose to execute a living will, I suggest you give copies to your physician and to your local hospital to be included in your medical records.

Marriage and Divorce Has Its Effect

Marriage and divorce may seem unusual topics to cover in a book for small businesses. But read on.

Notes & Quotes

"In 1998, there were 117,856,000 married persons in the U.S. who were 18 or older; this represented 59.7 percent of that group. The median age for the first marriage was 26.7 for men, and 25 for women. Not surprisingly, June was the most popular month for weddings and January the least popular."

—Census Bureau, National Center for Health Statistics

Marriage

If you are a single businessperson contemplating marriage, I offer you my congratulations. This is a legal guide, so I won't go into who should, and who shouldn't, have a *prenuptial agreement,* but I would be remiss if I didn't mention the possibility of one.

Let's say a businesswoman wants to keep total ownership of her property in her name. In that case, her husband-to-be must sign a prenuptial agreement, which would waive any right to claim the business as a marital asset subject to court division. Whether the agreement provides a waiver of her husband's claim upon the death of the business owner may depend if this is a second marriage and her children are her first priority as her heirs.

Legalese

A **prenuptial agreement,** signed by both of the future spouses, spells out any aspects of property ownership during the marriage that the two can think of, and it is a legally binding. The prenuptial agreement may specify what property is to remain the separate property of each party, and what property will be marital property. The agreement usually indicates who gets what in the event of a divorce or death; typically, this involves a waiver of any claim to certain property.

Notes & Quotes

"In 1998, there were 2,244,000 marriages and 1,135,000 divorces; there were 200 divorced persons for every 1000 married persons."

—Census Bureau, National Center for Health Statistics

While the courts usually enforce prenuptial agreements, each party should have an attorney, or at least be advised to get one, and completely disclose the premarital assets. This will deter a later claim of fraud or undue influence that could render the contract voidable. I recommend that the prenuptial agreement have a signature block for both attorneys and an attachment for each party's financial disclosures.

Divorce

If a businessperson has a prenuptial agreement, all may be well for keeping the business, and keeping the court from considering it as an asset for which the other spouse should be compensated. If there is no pre-nup, then expect to pay to keep the business.

No-fault divorces are the norm, so the issues that arise are usually child custody, child support, ex-spousal support, and property distribution. I will discuss the last issue. Most courts will divide the marital property fairly evenly, maybe not 50/50 but close to it. If the business owner in my example wants to keep her business, then her spouse will get the equivalent in cash or other marital property. If there is not enough other property, that may be a big problem. However, if the marriage was relatively brief, the court could consider the business as separate property, with little or no compensation going to her husband.

Alimony may not a favorite word, but it has a place in divorces, particularly in property settlements. The advantage to the payor is a tax deduction from gross income; conversely, the payee has to report it as income. This continues to apply until the final payment is made, with one exception—if most of the alimony is paid in the first three years, the payor may have to report some of the previous deductions as income—a penalty for front-loading the alimony.

Legal Eagle

Take care with your pension during a divorce. If there is a pension involved, the spouse releasing his or her right to the pension must execute a form with the pension company; a clause in the divorce decree or property settlement agreement is insufficient.

The amount of the alimony is obviously negotiable. The payor may have to pay a bit more to compensate for tax to the payee. If there are children, perhaps there could be some minor reduction in child support, which is not deductible for the payor, and an increase in the alimony, which is deductible.

Business Successor Planning

None of us is getting any younger. (I write this as my 56th birthday is rapidly approaching.) You may have been in business for many years and now, frankly, you should consider a successor when you retire. If the business is all yours, then you may want to sell it or turn it over to your children. If the business is co-owned, then the other owners may be willing to buy you out.

Think about the following:

➤ Analyze the current status of the business.

➤ Consider the cash value of the business.

➤ Review any buy-sell agreements with co-owners.

➤ Ponder which child could take over, or perhaps which employee.

Most businesses have a life cycle. The beginning involves struggle and little value other than potential; then the company turns the corner and becomes profitable; and finally it reaches a point where success mandates expansion and change. If you are in the last stage, then it's your call about moving up or moving on. The point is—think about the business in your future.

If your business has been successful, then it may be an attractive purchase for someone. You may realize its greatest potential for growth when the business is at the point of change—to expand or regress. If your business is worth so much because you are there, then the purchaser may want you to stay on as manager, at least for a brief period. Chapter 24, "Insolvent: Coping with Bankruptcy Protection," includes a discussion on selling a business.

We've discussed business buy-sell agreements in other places. I just want to remind you to pull out your buy-sell agreement and reread it to see what you agreed to those many years ago. Then put the pencil to the paper to see how much you would get if you left right now. If you intend to stay a bit longer, this may provoke some thinking, particularly if your share wouldn't reflect what the company's worth. You may want to amend the agreement.

A family business may have an appointed successor. Everyone gets used to this succession, and responsibilities can increase with experience and success. If there is no apparent successor, then it's time to groom one. You are there to delegate and advise. Do so before it's too late.

If there is no natural successor, perhaps a key employee might be interested in buying you out. If that is a future prospect, consider offering the employee an equity interest in the business.

For example, you may offer some minority share, such as 10 percent of the common stock. I would suggest a contract that would require the employee to successfully serve for a period of time, say two years, before receiving the stock. The tax law refers to this as a restricted property transaction, and the employee reports the fair market value of the stock as income when the restriction expires, or can elect to report it as income when the contract is executed. The election may be a better choice if the company's value, and thus the stock, substantially appreciates in value.

Just something to consider.

Helpful Sources

Many banks and trust departments have excellent pamphlets on estate planning. Life insurance companies will do a thorough analysis of your estate. The library will have several books on estate planning. Modesty doesn't prevent me from recommending my book, *The Complete Idiot's Guide to Wills and Estates* (Alpha Books, 1997). The senior law Web site is www.seniorlaw.com, and the AARP Web site is www.aarp.org. Many law firms that specialize in estate planning have valuable Web sites. Your state Web site likely will include its probate code.

The Least You Need to Know

➤ Start your estate planning by reviewing your current finances.

➤ Jointly owned property with right of survivorship avoids probate.

➤ Probate is the process of administering the decedent's assets that pass through the will, or go to the heirs if there is no will.

➤ A revocable living trust avoids probate and may avoid a guardianship.

➤ A prenuptial agreement may allow the business owner to keep the business after a divorce.

➤ If retirement is in the near future, plan now for a business successor.

Glossary of Legal Terms

acceptance   The assent to the terms of an offer.

accord and satisfaction   An agreement to perform in a different manner from what was originally called for, and the completion of that agreed-on performance.

adhesion contract   A contract that is drawn by a party with greater bargaining power or designed for that party's benefit, offered on a take-it-or-leave-it basis.

admissible evidence   Evidence that is relevant and proper to be considered in reaching a decision following rules of evidence.

affidavit   A written statement sworn to under oath before a notary public as being true to the person's own knowledge, information, and belief.

affirmative defense   A defense that admits the plaintiff's allegations, but introduces another allegation that would avoid liability for the defendant.

agent   A person authorized to act on behalf of another and subject to the other's control.

alimony   A payment made to a divorced spouse by a former spouse for support and maintenance. Also called spousal support.

answer   The main pleading filed by the defendant in a lawsuit in response to the plaintiff's complaint.

arbitration   A method of settling disputes in which a neutral third party makes a decision after hearing the arguments on both sides.

assignment   The transfer of a right from one person to another.

assumption of the risk   The plaintiff assumes the consequences of injury.

attorney-in-fact   An agent who is authorized to act under a power of attorney.

attractive nuisance   A doctrine establishing a property owner's duty to use ordinary care toward trespassing children who might reasonably be attracted to the owner's property.

automatic stay   A self-operating statutory postponement of collection proceedings without a court order against a debtor in bankruptcy.

bankrupt   The state of a person or business who is unable to pay debts as they become due.

bankruptcy   A legal process that aims to give debtors who are overwhelmed with debt a "fresh start" and to provide a fair way of distributing a debtor's assets among all creditors.

battery   The intentional contact with another person without that person's permission and without justification; the unlawful application of force on another person.

bearer paper   An instrument that requires no endorsement of the payee to be negotiated.

bilateral contract   A contract containing two promises, one made by each party.

bill of sale   A signed writing evidencing the transfer of personal property from one person to another.

boilerplate   Standard language used commonly in documents of the same type.

breach of contract   The failure of a party to a contract to carry out the terms of the agreement.

bulk sale   A transfer in bulk of a major part of the materials, supplies, merchandise, or other inventory of an enterprise to a buyer, after which the seller usually closes the business.

bylaws   The regulations adopted by a corporation.

C corporation   A corporation governed by Subchapter C of the Internal Revenue Code that pays corporate taxes on its income.

causation   The direct and proximate cause of someone's injuries.

certified check   A check that has been accepted, and thus guaranteed, by the bank on which it was drawn and has been marked to indicate such acceptance.

Chapter 7 bankruptcy   A proceeding designed to liquidate a debtor's property, pay off his, her, or its creditors, and discharge the debtor from most debts.

Chapter 11 bankruptcy   A method for businesses to reorganize their financial affairs, keep their assets, and remain in business.

Chapter 13 bankruptcy   A method by which an individual with regular income can pay his or her debts from future income over three to five years.

close corporation   A corporation that has restrictions on the transfer of shares.

codicil   An amendment to a will that must be executed with the same formalities as the will itself.

common stock   Stock with no preferences for dividends or a liquidating distribution, but entitles the owner the right to vote.

community property   Property acquired by a husband or wife during marriage that belongs to both spouses equally, in Arizona, California, Idaho, Louisiana, Nevada, New Mexico, Texas, Washington, and Wisconsin.

comparative negligence   The proportionate sharing between the plaintiff and the defendant of compensation for injuries, based on the relative negligence of the two.

compensatory damages   Damages that compensate the plaintiff for actual losses resulting from the breach.

complaint   A civil pleading that contains a short and plain statement of the claim indicating that the plaintiff is entitled to relief and containing a demand for the relief sought.

conforming goods   Goods that are in accordance with the obligations under the contract.

consequential damages   Losses that do not flow directly from a breach of contract but from the consequences of it.

consideration   An exchange of benefits and detriments by the parties to an agreement.

contract implied in law   A contract that is imposed by the court to prevent unjust enrichment. Also called quasi contract.

copyright   The exclusive right given to an author, composer, artist, photographer, or publisher, to publish and sell exclusively a work for the life of the author plus 70 years.

corporation   A legal entity created under state law with the power to conduct its affairs as though it were a natural person.

counterclaim   A claim that the defendant has against the plaintiff.

covenant   A promise or assurance.

cover   The right of a buyer, after breach by a seller, to purchase similar goods from someone else.

credit-shelter trust   A type of marital deduction trust that reduces the taxation of the last spouse to die by limiting the amount in that person's estate to a sum that is not taxable, currently any amount under $675,000.

cross-claim   A claim brought by one defendant against another defendant in the same suit.

cross-examination   The examination of an opposing witness.

defamation   The wrongful act of damaging another's character or reputation by the use of false statements. Also libel and slander.

default judgment   A judgment entered on failure of a party to appear or plead at the proper time.

defendant   A person against whom a legal action is brought.

delegation   The transfer of a duty by one person to another.

deposition   The testimony of a witness, given under oath but not in open court, and later reduced to writing.

devise   A gift of property in a will.

directors   People who are elected by stockholders to manage a corporation.

discovery   Methods that allow each party to obtain information from the other party and from witnesses about a case before going to court.

durable power of attorney   A document authorizing another person to act on one's behalf with language indicating that it is either to survive one's incapacity or become effective when one becomes incapacitated.

duress   The overcoming of a person's free will by the use of threat or physical harm.

executor   A man nominated in a will of a decedent to carry out the terms of the will; a personal representative of an estate. A woman with the same function is call an executrix.

express warranty   A statement of fact or promise that goods have certain qualities.

fair-use doctrine   A rule stating that the fair use of a copyrighted work for purposes such as criticism, comment, news reporting, teaching, scholarship, or research is not a copyright infringement.

fiduciary   A person in a position of trust, such as an executor, administrator, guardian, and trustee.

firm offer   A merchant's written promise to hold an offer open for the sale of goods.

franchise   An arrangement in which the owner of a trademark or trade name, licenses others under special conditions or limitations, to use the trademark or trade name to sell goods or services.

fraud   A misrepresentation of a material, existing fact, knowingly made, that causes someone reasonably relying on it to suffer damages. Also called deceit.

327

garnishment   A procedure for a court to attach a defendant's property that is in the hands of a third person.

health care consent   A written statement authorizing an agent to make medical treatment decisions for another in the event of the other's inability to do so.

heir   A person who inherits property when there is no will.

holder   A person who is in possession of a negotiable instrument that has been issued or indorsed to that person's name or to cash.

implied authority   Authority to perform incidental functions that are reasonably and customarily necessary to enable an agent to accomplish the overall purpose of the agency.

implied warranty   A warranty that is imposed by law rather than given voluntarily. Also a warranty of merchantability and fitness.

impossibility   A method of discharging a contract that is impossible to perform, not merely difficult or costly. Also known as "Act of God."

incorporators   People who organize a corporation by filing articles of organization with the state.

independent contractor   One who performs services for others but who is not under the company who hires him or her; not an agent.

indictment   A formal written charge of a crime made by a grand jury.

inheritance tax   A state tax imposed on a person who inherits from a decedent's estate.

injunction   An order of a court to do or refrain from doing a particular act.

insanity   A defense available to mentally ill defendants who can prove that they did not know the nature and quality of their actions or did not appreciate the criminality of their conduct.

installment note   A note that is to be paid in multiple payments during a period.

***inter-vivos* trust**   A trust that is created by the settlor when he or she is alive. Also called living trust.

intestate   Dying without having made a valid will.

irrevocable living trust   A trust that may not be rescinded or changed by the settlor at any time during his or her lifetime.

issue   All people who have descended from a common ancestor.

joint tenancy with the right of survivorship   Property owned by joint tenants; when one joint owner dies the other co-owner becomes the sole owner of the asset.

judgment notwithstanding the verdict   A judgment by the judge rendered in favor of one party notwithstanding a verdict in favor of the other party.

jurisdiction   The power or authority that a court has to hear a case.

landlord   A person who owns real property and who rents it to another under a lease.

lease   A contract granting the use of certain real property by its owner to another for a specified period in return for the payment of rent.

lien   A claim or charge on property for the payment of a debt, such as a mortgage or mechanics lien.

life estate   An estate limited in duration to either the life of the owner or the life of another person.

limited liability company (LLC)   A form of business organization that has the tax benefits of a partnership and the limited liability benefits of a corporation.

limited liability partnership (LLP)   A general partnership in which only the partnership, and not the individual partners, is liable for the tort liabilities of the partnership.

limited partnership   A partnership formed by two or more persons having as members one or more general partners and one or more limited partners.

limited warranty   An express warranty given for consumer goods that is less than a full warranty.

liquidated damages   Damages that are agreed on by the parties at the time of the execution of a contract in the event of a subsequent breach.

living trust   A trust that is created by the settlor when he or she is alive.

living will   A written expression of a person's wishes to be allowed to die a natural death and not be kept alive by heroic or artificial methods.

mediation   An informal process in which a neutral third person listens to both sides and makes suggestions for reaching a solution to a contract or labor dispute.

merchant   A person who sells goods of the kind sold in the ordinary course of business, or who has knowledge or skills peculiar to those goods.

misrepresentation   A false or deceptive statement or act.

mitigate   To lessen or to keep as low as possible.

mortgage   A lien against real property for the purpose of securing a debt.

mutual mistake   When both parties are mistaken about an important aspect of a contract.

negligence   The failure to use that amount of care and skill that a reasonably prudent person would have used under the same circumstances and conditions.

nuisance   The use of one's property in a way that causes annoyance, inconvenience, or discomfort to another.

offeree   One to whom an offer is made.

offeror   One who makes an offer.

operating agreement   An agreement that sets forth the rights and obligations of the members and establishes the rules for operating a limited liability company.

option contract   A binding promise to hold an offer open.

parol evidence rule   Oral evidence of prior or contemporaneous negotiations between the parties that is not admissible in court to alter, vary, or contradict the forms of a written agreement.

partnership   An association of two or more persons to carry on as co-owners of a business for profit.

patent   A grant by the U.S. government of the exclusive right to make, use, and sell an invention for 20 years.

peremptory challenge   During jury selection, dismissing a prospective juror for which no reason need be given.

personal property   Everything owned that is not real estate.

personal service   Delivering a copy of a summons and complaint to the defendant personally.

plaintiff   A person who brings a legal action against another.

pleadings   The written statements of claims and defenses used by the parties in a lawsuit.

preferred stock   Stock that has a first right before common stock to dividends, and to capital when the corporation is dissolved.

principal   One who authorizes another to act on one's behalf.

probable cause   Reasonable grounds for belief that an offense has been committed.

product liability   Liability of manufacturers and sellers to compensate people for injuries suffered because of defects in their products.

promissory estoppel   A doctrine under which no contract consideration is necessary when someone makes a promise that induces another's action or forbearance, and injustice can be avoided only by enforcing the promise.

promissory note   A written promise by one party to pay a sum of money to another party.

proximate cause   The foreseeable cause.

punitive damages   Damages as a measure of punishment for the defendant's wrongful acts.

qualified indorsement   An indorsement that limits the liability of the indorser.

qualified terminable interest property (QTIP) trust   A marital deduction trust that gives all trust income to a surviving spouse for life, payable at least annually, with the principal passing to someone else upon the spouse's death.

quiet enjoyment   The right of a tenant to the possession of the rented property and to be undisturbed in that possession.

quitclaim deed   A deed to real property in which the grantor transfers only his or her interest, if any, in the property and gives no warranties of title.

real property   The ground and anything permanently attached to it including land, buildings, growing trees, and the airspace above the ground.

reasonable care   The degree of care that a reasonable person would have used under the circumstances then known.

relevant evidence   Evidence tending to prove or disprove an alleged fact.

respondeat superior   A rule of law that makes principals and employers responsible for the torts of their agents and servants committed within the scope of their authority or employment.

revocable living trust   A trust that may be rescinded or changed by the settlor at any time during his or her lifetime.

S corporation   A corporation governed by Subchapter S of the Internal Revenue Code in which the income of the corporation is taxed directly to the shareholders rather than to the corporation itself.

secured creditors   Creditors who hold mortgages and security interests.

service mark   A term used to describe trademark protection for services.

service of process   The delivering of summonses or other legal documents to the people who are required to receive them.

settlor   A person who establishes a trust.

sole proprietorship   A form of business that is owned and operated by one person.

specific performance   An order by the court ordering a breaching party to do that which he or she agreed to do under the terms of the contract.

spendthrift trust   A trust designed to provide a fund for the maintenance of a beneficiary and at the same time to secure it against the beneficiary who wastes money.

statute of frauds   Certain contracts must be in writing to be enforceable.

statute of limitations   A time limit, set by statute, within which a lawsuit must be commenced.

strict liability   Liability for an act that causes harm without regard to fault or negligence.

sublease   A lease given by a lessee to a third person conveying the same interest for a shorter term than the period for which the lessee holds it.

subpoena   An order commanding a person to appear and testify in a legal action.

substantial performance   A doctrine allowing a contracting party to sue the other party for breach even though slight omissions or deviations were made in his or her own performance of the contract.

surety   One who undertakes to stand behind another; that is, pay money or do any other act in the event that his or her principal fails to meet an obligation.

tenant   A person who has temporary possession of an interest in real property of another under a lease.

tenants in common   Two or more persons holding an undivided interest in property, with each owner's interests going to his or her heirs on death rather than to the surviving co-owners.

testamentary capacity   Sufficient mental ability to make a will.

testamentary trust   A trust that is created by will and that comes into existence only on the death of the testator (the person who made the will).

third-party beneficiary   Someone for whose benefit a promise is made but who is not a party to the contract.

title search   An examination of all recorded instruments that affect the title to a particular parcel of property for the past 50 or more years.

tort   A wrong against an individual, such as negligence or battery.

trademark   Any word, name, symbol, or device used by a business to identify goods and distinguish them from those manufactured or sold by others.

trade secret   A plan, process, or device that is used in business and is known only to employees who need to know the secret to accomplish their work.

trespass   The intentional and unauthorized entry on the land of another.

trust   A right of ownership to property held by one person for the benefit of another.

trust corpus   The body, principal sum, or capital of a trust.

unconscionable   So harshly one-sided and unfair that the court's conscience is shocked.

undue influence   The overcoming of a person's free will by misusing a position of trust and taking advantage of the other person who is relying on the trust relationship.

unilateral contract   A contract containing one promise in exchange for an act.

unjust enrichment   Occurs when one person retains money, property, or other benefit that in fairness belongs to another.

variable-rate mortgage   A mortgage with an interest rate that fluctuates according to changes in an index to which it is connected.

variance   An exception to the zoning regulation.

vicarious liability   Liability that is imputed to principals and employers because of the wrong doings of their agents and employees.

warranty of fitness for a particular purpose   An implied warranty, given when a buyer relies on any seller's skill and judgment in selecting goods, that the goods will be fit for a particular purpose.

warranty of habitability   An implied warranty by a landlord that the premises are fit for human habitation.

warranty of merchantability   An implied warranty, given by merchants in all sales (unless excluded), that goods are fit for the ordinary purpose for which such goods are used.

warranty of title   A guarantee that title is good, that the transfer is rightful, and that no unknown liens on the goods exist.

will   Originally, a legal instrument stating a person's wishes as to the disposition of real property at death, but now referring to both real and personal property.

writ of execution   A written order to the sheriff to enforce a judgment of the court.

zoning   The process of regulating the use of land by designating specific areas for certain uses.

Basic Business Forms

The forms in this section are useful starting points for any businessperson. Each state has its own body of law so that no form can be completely applicable for each state. Likewise, laws change. I would suggest that you consult an attorney after preparing a draft of your legal document.

General legal forms are available from several sources. On the Web, for example, you can find forms at www.lectlaw.com and www.ilrg.com. Or you can buy *Quicken Business Lawyer 2001,* which is a collection of legal forms on disk. Also, your state may have business entity forms, such as Articles of Incorporation, on its Web site.

In the meantime, I've provided some basic forms to get you started, including …

1. Partnership Agreement.
2. Shareholder Agreement.
3. Limited Liability Articles of Organization.
4. Lease.
5. Agreement to Sell Business.
6. Installment Promissory Note.
7. Estate Planning Information.
8. Last Will and Testament.

Partnership Agreement

This partnership agreement form is for a small number of active partners. I used the development of real estate as an example of a partnership "purpose." The form contains the basic terms and can be used as a checklist to determine what terms your partners agree to. Mark up the form as a tentative agreement, then submit it to your attorney for final drafting.

General Partnership Agreement
of
ABC Property Associates

This General Partnership Agreement (the Agreement) is made and entered into this _____ day of _____, 20__, by and among the persons who have executed this Agreement on the signature page hereof and all other persons who hereafter become a party hereto by executing an addendum to this Agreement (referred to collectively as the "Partners" and each individually as a Partner).

Recitals

WHEREAS, the parties hereto desire to form a partnership (the Partnership) to purchase, develop, and lease certain real property located in Any County, Anystate (the Property);

NOW, THEREFORE, in consideration of the mutual covenants herein contained and intending to be legally bound hereby, the Partners hereby agree as follows:

Name, Place of Business, and Purpose

  1.1 The activities and business of the Partnership shall be conducted under the name of ABC PROPERTY ASSOCIATES.

  1.2 The principal office of the Partnership shall be 123 America Drive, Any County, Anystate, or at such other places within or without the state as the Partners may determine.

  1.3 The purpose of the Partnership shall be to acquire, develop, lease, own, and sell the Property; to enter into agreements of purchase, lease, and sale and other undertakings as may be related to the Property; to obtain such loans, make such arrangements or rearrangements as may be necessary or desirable in carrying out any or all of the foregoing purposes; and to carry on such activities as may be necessary or incidental to the foregoing purposes.

Term of the Partnership

  2.1. The term of the Partnership shall begin on the date hereof and shall continue until terminated as specifically provided in this Agreement.

Contributions to the Partnership

3.1.   The partners shall make cash contributions from time to time to the capital of the Partnership in accordance with the respective percentages set forth in Section 4.3.

3.2.   If any Partner makes a disproportionate advance of any funds to or for the account of the Partnership in excess of his or her percentage interest in the Partnership, such advance, in the absence of a written agreement of the Partners to the contrary, shall be considered a loan to the Partnership and shall not result in an increase in the percentage interest of such Partner in the Partnership.

3.3   A capital account shall be maintained for each Partner, reflecting his or her capital contributions, allocation of net income or losses, withdrawals, and all other appropriate adjustments.

Profits and Losses and Drawings by the Partners

4.1.   The net income and losses of the Partnership shall be determined in accordance with the cash receipts and disbursements method of accounting used by the Partnership for federal income tax purposes.

4.2.   Drawings of income shall be made by each Partner from Partnership funds in such amounts and at such times as all Partners shall agree upon.

4.3.   The net income or losses of the Partnership shall be allocable to the Partners in the proportions set forth here:

James Bond	25%
Karen Kute	25%
Diane Dont	30%
Suzanne Swift	20%

Partnership Property

5.1.   All right, title, and interest to real or personal property acquired by the Partnership, including all improvements place or located on such property, and all rents, issues, and profits arising therefrom, shall be owned by the Partnership.

Fiscal Matters

6.1.   Proper and complete books and records shall be kept with reference to all Partnership transactions and property, and each Partner shall at all reasonable times during business hours have access thereto. The books shall be kept by a cash receipts and disbursement method of accounting. The books and records of the Partnership shall be reviewed annually at the expense of the Partnership by an accountant selected by the Partnership, who shall prepare and deliver to the Partnership, for filing, appropriate partnership income tax returns and such other information as may be necessary to enable each Partner to file his or her personal federal, state, and local tax returns.

Management of the Partnership

7.1. All material Partnership decisions, including, without limitation, those specified in Section 7.2. shall be made jointly unless such authority is otherwise delegated by one Partner to the others in a particular instance.

7.2. No Partner, without the consent of the other Partners, may:

(i) Do any act in contravention of this Agreement;

(ii) Do any act that would make it impossible to carry on the business of the Partnership;

(iii) Affiliate, employ, or terminate professional or nonprofessional personnel of the Partnership;

(iv) Possess Partnership property or assign the right of the Partnership or the Partners in specific Partnership property for other than a Partnership purpose;

(v) Make, execute, or deliver any general assignment for the benefit of creditors;

(vi) Assign, transfer, pledge, compromise, or release any claim of the Partnership except for full payment;

(vii) Make, execute, or deliver any deed, long-term lease, or contract to sell all or substantially all the Partnership property;

(viii) Make, execute, or deliver for the Partnership any note, bond, mortgage, deed of trust, guaranty, indemnity bond, or surety bond if such document creates any personal liability for any Partner other than that personal liability to which the Partner may have agreed in writing;

(ix) Make any expenditures or disbursement in excess of $_____$;

(x) Borrow monies to the extent such borrowing would cause the aggregate amount of indebtedness to exceed $_____$; and

(xi) Purchase or acquire real property.

7.3. An account or accounts in the name of the Partnership may be maintained in such bank or banks as the Partnership may select from time to time, and checks drawn thereon may be signed on behalf of the Partnership by any two Partners, except as provided in Section 7.2(ix).

7.4. No salaries or other compensation shall be paid to the Partners.

Dissolution and Liquidation

8.1. The Partnership shall be dissolved upon the occurrence of any of the following:

(a) The mutual consent of the Partners; or

(b) The sale, abandonment, or disposal by the Partnership of all or substantially all of its assets; or

(c) The entry of a final judgement, order, or decree of a court of competent jurisdiction adjudicating the Partnership to be a bankrupt; or

(d) The bankruptcy of a Partner; or

(e) The death of a Partner.

8.2.   Upon the dissolution of the Partnership, the Partner charged with winding up the Partnership affairs shall proceed to liquidate its assets, wind up its affairs, and apply and distribute the proceeds, after debts and expenses and subject to reasonable reserves, to the Partners or their personal representatives in cash according to their respective percentage interests in the Partnership.

Miscellaneous

9.1.   All notices, statements, or other documents required or contemplated by this Agreement shall be in writing and shall either be personally delivered to the person entitled thereto or mailed, postage prepaid, to such person at his or her last known mailing address.

9.2.   This Agreement shall be interpreted and construed in accordance with the laws of the State of Anystate.

9.3.   The Partners agree that they will execute any further documents or instruments and perform any acts that are or may become necessary to effectuate and to carry on the Partnership created by this Agreement.

9.4.   This Agreement may be executed in any number of counterparts, each of which may be executed by one or more of the Partners, and all such counterparts when executed and delivered shall together constitute one and the same instrument.

IN WITNESS WHEREOF, the parties hereto have executed this Agreement on the day and year first above written.

Partners:

_____

_____

_____

_____

Shareholder Agreement

The shareholder agreement is a form for a corporation with a few active shareholders. The shareholders agree to name specific shareholders as directors and officers. They limit the right to transfer the stock by giving the first option to buy to the existing shareholders. There is a mandatory purchase of a deceased shareholder's stock. Mark up the agreement then submit it to your attorney for redrafting.

Shareholder Agreement

AGREEMENT made _____, 20__, by and between _____ Corporation having its principal office at _____, City of _____, State of _____, hereinafter sometimes referred to as the corporation; _____, residing at _____ City of _____, State of _____; _____, residing at _____ City of _____, State of _____; _____, residing at _____ City of _____, State of _____, each of the foregoing being the owner this day of one-third the outstanding shares of the corporation, and together being the owners of all the outstanding shares of said corporation.

WHEREAS the parties desire to promote their mutual interests and the interest of the corporation by making provision to avoid future differences.

NOW, THEREFORE, it is mutually agreed as follows:

1. Each of the undersigned shareholders agrees that so long as [he/she] shall remain a shareholder [he/she] will vote [his/her] respective shares in the above-mentioned corporation for each of the following as a director so long as the said director-designee remains a shareholder of the corporation:

(1) _____

(2) _____

(3) _____

Any of the foregoing directors who ceases to be a shareholder of the corporation shall simultaneously with the transfer or surrender of [his/her] shares submit to the corporation [his/her] written resignation as a director.

2. For the best interest of the corporation, _____ Corporation and the undersigned shareholders agree to have each of the following appointed and elected an officer of the corporation so long as the said office-designee remains a shareholder and proves faithful, efficient and competent:

For President: _____

For Secretary: _____

For Treasurer: _____

Any one of the foregoing officers who ceases to be a shareholder of the corporation shall simultaneously with the transfer or surrender of [his/her] shares submit to the corporation [his/her] written resignation as an officer.

3. All parties hereto further agree that each of the aforesaid officers, so long as [he/she] remains a shareholder and proves faithful, efficient, and competent, shall continue to be employed in the additional posts presently occupied by [him/her];

inactivity because of age or ill health shall not be construed incompetence. Any one of the foregoing employees who ceases to be a shareholder of the corporation shall simultaneously with the transfer or surrender of [his/her] shares submit to the corporation [his/her] written resignation as an employee.

4. Each of the undersigned employees agree that [he/she] will devote [his/her] best efforts to enhance and develop the best interests of the corporation. Salary shall serve as compensation for services both as officer and employee.

5(a). Each of the undersigned shareholders agrees that [he/she] will not transfer, assign, sell, pledge, hypothecate, or otherwise dispose of, the shares owned by [him/her] or them, or the certificates representing the same, unless such shares shall have been first offered to the corporation at a price per share to be computed pro rata on the basis of the value hereinafter provided in subparagraph 5(c) hereof for a one-third interest in the corporation, as revised from time to time as therein provided. Such offer shall be made in writing and remain standing for a period of thirty (30) days. In the event the offeree wishes to accept the offer, it must agree in writing to purchase the entire block of shares offered and shall simultaneously make a down payment in cash of thirty (30) per cent of the purchase price. The balance of the purchase price shall be payable on the same terms as are prescribed in subparagraph 5(e) hereof for all payments after the initial payment on purchase of the interest of a deceased shareholder. In the event the offeree shall not signify its intention to purchase said shares within such thirty (30) day period, then the offeror shall be authorized to otherwise sell or dispose of his stock, which stock shall thereafter be freely transferable and no longer subject to the provisions and limitations of this agreement. The provisions of this paragraph shall not bar a transfer, assignment, bequest, or sale of shares of stock by one of the undersigned to a member of [his/her] immediate family who shall take, however, subject to all the limitations of this agreement as if he or she were a party hereto.

5(b). All parties hereto agree that upon the death of (1) _____ or (2) _____ or (3) _____, the executors, administrators, or legal representatives of the deceased shall within thirty (30) days after qualification as such sell to _____ Corporation and said corporation agrees to buy all the shares therein owned by said deceased at the time of [his/her] death. It is the desire and intention of the parties hereto that within the period above specified after the death of any one of the three principals specified in the opening sentence of this paragraph numbered 5(c), [his/her] family shall terminate all interest in the corporation, and all members of the family to whom any shares in this corporation have been or shall be transferred pursuant to permission granted by the last sentence of subparagraph 5(b) above shall at the same time sell to _____ Corporation all shares registered in their names or owned by them. The purchase price prescribed in subparagraph 5(d) hereinafter, as revised from time to time, refers to the value of a total block of shares consisting of one-third of the total outstanding shares, and if, as permitted to all principals by the last sentence of subparagraph 5(b) above, some of the shares making up the block required in the name of or owned by some member of the family other than the deceased principal specified in the opening sentence of this paragraph numbered 5(c), the prescribed purchase price for the total block shall be allocated pro rata to the actual ownership of the shares making up said block.

5(c).   The parties hereto agree that as of the date hereof a block of shares representing a one-third interest in the corporation has a value of $ _____. It is the intention of the parties to revise this figure on April 30, July 21, and October 31 of every year, and the last figure agreed upon in writing by the parties hereto prior to an *inter-vivos* offer as set forth in subparagraph 5(a) or 5(b) or before the death of one of the three individuals set forth in subparagraph 5(c) shall be conclusive as to the value of said block for purpose of this agreement. The parties hereto have included in their initial figure and intend to include in future revisions thereof an allowance for good will.

5(d).   The purchase price shall be paid as follows: <u>Thirty (30%)</u> per cent in cash within <u>30</u> days after qualification of the legal representatives of the deceased shareholder. <u>One-quarter</u> of the unpaid balance shall be paid <u>twelve</u> months thereafter; and a similar sum shall be paid every <u>six</u> months thereafter until the shares have been fully paid for; interest at the rate of _____ % on the installment being paid shall be paid with every installment. The obligation to make the <u>four (4)</u> installment payments shall be evidence by negotiable, promissory notes signed by the corporation, as maker, and endorsed by all surviving signatories to this agreement, as accommodation endorsers. Time is declared to be of the essence for such payments. The promissory notes shall provide that the maker shall have the right to prepay the whole or any part thereof without premium or penalty.

If on the occurrence of the contingencies above specified, the corporation is unable lawfully to pay the full purchase price, then such funds as are available shall be used to purchase part of the shares offered, and the corporation and its shareholders shall promptly take action to the extent necessary to make funds available for purchase of the remaining shares. If the funds shall be insufficient within the period of time hereinabove prescribed to make payments for the entire block of shares offered for sale, the parties hereto agree that then and in that event, a special joint directors' and shareholders' meeting shall be called for the purpose of dissolving the corporation, and each of the parties hereto agrees that at such meeting he or she will vote to dissolve the corporation. In lieu of voting dissolution, as above provided, the shareholders other than the offeror shall have the privilege of purchasing said shares as individuals, in proportion to their then ownership of outstanding shares.

5(e).   The last principal to survive shall be free to dispose of as [he/she] pleases of the shares owned by [him/her], free from any of the restrictions imposed by this agreement.

6. Each share certificate of the Corporation shall bear the following legend in conspicuous type:

Transfer or pledge of the shares represented by this certificate is restricted under a shareholder's agreement dated _____, 20__. A copy of the agreement, which affects also other rights of the holder of these shares, is on file at the office of the Corporation.

7. Should at any time any dispute arise between any one or more of the parties hereto with respect to his or her or their rights, obligations, duties, and requirements under and by virtue of the provisions of this agreement, except as to the valuation of stock, said dispute, except as aforesaid, shall be referred to, and consent and approval of each of the parties hereto is expressly given to refer said dispute for determination to the American Arbitration Association, whose determination and/or decision shall be final and binding upon the parties hereto, and there shall be no appeal from said decision.

8. The corporation is authorized to enter into this agreement by virtue of a resolution adopted at a special joint meeting of the shareholders and directors held on _____, 20__.

9. This agreement or any of its provisions may at any time be changed, modified, or canceled by mutual consent of all the undersigned, their heirs, executors, administrators, legal representatives, or assigns, but unless and until so changed, modified, or canceled, this agreement shall be binding upon the parties, and their heirs, executors, administrators, legal representatives and assigns, any or all of whom shall execute and deliver all necessary documents required to carry out the terms of this agreement.

10. In the event that any provision of this agreement shall be ruled invalid or unenforceable by a court of competent jurisdiction, it is the intent of the parties hereto that the balance of the agreement shall be enforced as if said invalid or unenforceable provision has not been included in this agreement.

IN WITNESS WHEREOF, the individual parties hereto hereunto set their hands and seals, and the corporation has caused this agreement to be signed by its duly authorized officers and its corporate seal affixed.

_____ Corporation

Attest by:

_____
President

_____
Secretary

_____

_____
Shareholders

Limited Liability Articles

File this limited liability company articles of organization, or your state's own equivalent form, with your state's Secretary of State. The form may be simplified in some states by just including the basic information in Articles 1 through 6. You must have an operating agreement, but you don't have to file it. Your attorney should draft your operating agreement. I haven't included that form here because state laws on limited liability corporations vary considerably, unlike partnership agreements, which are governed by fairly uniform laws in the various states.

Articles of Organization
of

_____

The undersigned, acting as organizer (Organizer), hereby forms a limited liability company under the _____ Act of the State of _____ (the Act) and does hereby adopt as the Articles of Organization of such limited liability company the following:

Article 1. Name. The name of the limited liability company shall be _____, LLC (the Company).

Article 2. Duration. The period of the Company's duration shall be perpetual until the Company is dissolved in accordance with the Operating Agreement of the Company or the Act.

Article 3. Purpose. The Company shall have unlimited power to engage in and do any lawful act concerning any or all lawful businesses for which limited liability companies may be organized according to the laws of the State of _____ including all powers and purposes now and hereafter permitted by law to a limited liability company.

Article 4. Registered Office and Registered Agent.

(a) The street address of the registered office of the Company in_____ is _____, _____, _____.

(b) The name of the registered agent of the Company at the above registered office is _____.

Article 5. Continuation of Business of the Company. Upon the resignation, expulsion, bankruptcy, or dissolution of a Member or occurrence of any other event that terminates the continued membership of a Member in the Company, or if any Member transfers all or a portion of its Interest in the Company, the Company shall be immediately dissolved, unless the business of the Company is continued by the remaining Members in accordance with Section 6.1 of the Company's Operating Agreement.

Article 6. Management. The Company is to be managed by its Members as provided in the Operating Agreement of the Company.

Article 7. Indemnification of Members, Organizers, and Managers.

(a) To the greatest extent not inconsistent with the laws and public policies of Indiana the Company shall indemnify any Member, Organizer, or Manager, if the Company has a Manager or Managers (any such Member, Organizer, or Manager, and including any responsible officers, partners, shareholders, directors, or managers of any such Member, Organizer, or Manager that is an Entity, hereinafter being referred to individually and collectively as the indemnified person) made a party to any proceeding because such person is or was a Member, Organizer, or Manager as a matter of right, against all liability incurred by such person in connection with any proceeding; provided that it shall be determined in the specific case in accordance with paragraph (d) of this Article that indemnification of such person is permissible in the circumstances because the person has met the standard of conduct for indemnification set forth in paragraph (c) of this Article. The Company shall pay for or reimburse the reasonable expenses incurred by a Member, Organizer, or Manager in connection with any such proceeding in advance of final disposition thereof if (i) the person furnishes the Company a written affirmation of the person's good faith belief that the person has met the standard of conduct for indemnification described in paragraph (c) of this Article, (ii) the person furnishes the Company a written undertaking, executed personally or on such person's behalf, to repay the advance if it is ultimately determined that such individual did not meet such standard of conduct, and (iii) a determination is made in accordance with paragraph (d) that based upon facts then known to those making the determination, indemnification would not be precluded under this Article. The undertaking described in subparagraph (a)(ii) above must be a general obligation of the person, subject to such reasonable limitations as the Company may permit, but need not be secured and may be accepted without reference to financial ability to make repayment. The Company shall indemnify a Member, Organizer, or Manager who is wholly successful, on the merits or otherwise, in the defense of any such proceeding, as a matter of right, against reasonable expenses incurred by the person in connection with the proceeding without the requirement of a determination as set forth in paragraph (c) of this Article. Upon demand by a Member, Organizer, or Manager for indemnification or advancement of expenses, as the case may be, the Company shall expeditiously determine whether the Member, Organizer, or Manager is entitled thereto in accordance with this Article. The indemnification and advancement of expenses provided for under this Article shall be applicable to any proceeding arising from acts or omissions occurring before or after the adoption of this Article.

(b) The Company shall have the power, but not the obligation, to indemnify any person who is or was an employee or agent of the Company to the same extent as if such person was a Member, Organizer, or Manager.

(c)   Indemnification of a person is permissible under this Article only if (i) such person conducted himself, herself, or itself in good faith, (ii) such person reasonably believed that the person's conduct was in or at least not opposed to the Company's best interest, and (iii) in the case of any criminal proceeding, such person had no reasonable cause to believe the person's conduct was unlawful. Indemnification is not permissible against liability to the extent such liability is the result of willful misconduct, recklessness, or any improperly obtained financial or other benefit to which the person was not legally entitled. The termination of a proceeding by judgment, order, settlement, conviction or upon a plea of nolo contendere or its equivalent is not, of itself, determinative that the individual did not meet the standard of conduct described in this paragraph (c).

(d)   A determination as to whether indemnification or advancement of expenses is permissible shall be made by any one of the following procedures:

(i)   By the Members by a majority vote consisting of Members not at the time parties to the proceeding; or

(ii)   By special legal counsel selected by the Members in the manner prescribed in subparagraph (d)(i) above.

(e)   A Member, Organizer, or Manager of the Company who is a party to a proceeding may apply for indemnification from the Company to the court, if any, conducting the proceeding or to another court of competent jurisdiction. On receipt of an application, the court, after giving notice the court considers necessary, may order indemnification if it determines:

(i)   In a proceeding in which the Member, Organizer, or Manager is wholly successful, on the merits or otherwise, the Member, Organizer, or Manager is entitled to indemnification under this Article, in which case the court shall order the Company to pay the individual his or her reasonable expenses incurred to obtain such court ordered indemnification; or

(ii)   The person is fairly and reasonably entitled to indemnification in view of all the relevant circumstances, whether or not the person met the standard of conduct set forth in paragraph (c) of this Article.

(f)   Indemnification shall also be provided for a person's conduct with respect to an employee benefit plan if the person reasonably believed the person's conduct to be in the interests of the participants in and beneficiaries of the plan.

(g)   Nothing contained in this Article shall limit or preclude the exercise or be deemed exclusive of any right under the law, by contract or otherwise, relating to indemnification of or advancement of expenses to any person who is or was a Member, Organizer, or Manager of the Company or is or was serving at the Company's request as a director, officer, partner, manager, trustee, employee, or agent of another foreign or domestic company, partnership, association, limited liability company, corporation, joint venture, trust, employee benefit plan, or other enterprise, whether for-profit or not. Nothing contained in this Article shall limit the ability of the Company to otherwise indemnify or advance expenses to any person. It is the intent of this Article to provide indemnification to Members, Organizers, and Managers to the fullest extent now and hereafter permitted by the law consistent with the terms and conditions of this Article. Indemnification shall be provided in accordance with this Article irrespective of the nature of the legal or equitable theory upon which a claim is made including without limitation negligence, breach of duty, mismanagement, waste, breach of contract, breach of warranty, strict liability, violation of federal or state securities law, violation of the Employee Retirement Income Security Act of 1974, as amended, or violation of any other state or federal law.

(h)   For purposes of this Article:

   (i) The term *expenses* includes all direct and indirect costs (including without limitation counsel fees, retainers, court costs, transcripts, fees of experts, witness fees, travel expenses, duplicating costs, printing and binding costs, telephone charges, postage, delivery service fees and all other disbursements or out-of-pocket expenses) actually incurred in connection with the investigation, defense, settlement, or appeal of a proceeding or establishment or enforcing a right to indemnification under this Article, applicable law or otherwise.

  (ii) The term *liability* means the obligation to pay a judgment, settlement, penalty, fine, excise tax (including an excise tax assessed with respect to an employee benefit plan), or reasonable expenses incurred with respect to a proceeding.

 (iii) The term *party* includes a person who was, is, or is threatened to be made, a named defendant or respondent in a proceeding.

  (iv) The term *proceeding* means any threatened, pending, or completed action, suit or proceeding, whether civil, criminal, administrative, or investigative and whether formal or informal.

   (v) The Company may purchase and maintain insurance for its benefit, the benefit of any person who is entitled to indemnification under this Article, or both, against any liability asserted against or incurred by such person in any capacity or arising out of such person's service with the Company, whether or not the Company would have the power to indemnify such person against such liability.

Article 8. Definitions. Terms used but not defined in these Articles of Organization shall have the meanings set forth in the Act.

Dated: _____

          _____
          Organizer

Lease

This is a basic lease form for a small office or retail store. Use the form as a checklist of terms to go over with your prospective tenant, then have your attorney draft the final form.

Lease

THIS LEASE, entered into by _____,
(hereinafter referred to as Landlord) and _____,
(hereinafter referred to as Tenant),

WITNESSETH THAT Landlord and Tenant, in consideration of their mutual undertakings, agree as follows: Landlord hereby leases to Tenant and Tenant hereby leases from Landlord:

[Legal description attached]

common address: _____
(hereinafter referred to as Leased Premises) and all appurtenances thereto for a term of _____, commencing on _____, 20___, and ending on _____, 20___, unless sooner terminated, and Tenant without demand or notice shall pay a monthly rental of _____
($_____), payable on or before the first day of each month in advance, at the address of the landlord set forth in this Lease, or such other address as Landlord by notice shall direct, all upon the following covenants, terms, and conditions:

1. USE, COMPLIANCE WITH LAWS. The Leased Premises shall be used by Tenant only for the purpose of a residence. Tenant shall keep the Leased Premises in a clean and orderly manner. Tenant may not use the Leased Premises in a manner that would violate law or create a nuisance.

2. SURRENDER AND HOLDOVER. Upon the expiration or sooner termination of this Lease, Tenant shall surrender to Landlord the Leased Premises, together with all other property affixed to the Leased Premises broom clean and in the same order and condition in which Tenant received them, the effects of ordinary wear, acts of God, and casualty excepted. Tenant shall remove all of its personal property prior to the termination of this Lease; any property left shall be deemed abandoned and may be kept or disposed of by the Landlord. If Tenant shall remain in possession after the term of this Lease expires, with the consent of the Landlord, then Tenant shall be lessee from month to month and subject to all the terms of this Lease.

3. ASSIGNMENT AND SUBLETTING. Tenant may not assign or sublet the Lease or Leased Premises without the written consent of Landlord.

4. ALTERATIONS AND MAINTENANCE OF LEASED PREMISES. Tenant may not make any substantial additions or alterations without the written consent of the Landlord. Tenant shall maintain the Leased Premises in the same order and condition in which Tenant received the premises. A List of Landlord improvements to be made, if any, are attached and made a part of this Lease; otherwise, Tenant leases premises in "as is" condition.

5. DESTRUCTION. If the Leased Premises should be damaged or destroyed by fire or other cause and not habitable, then either party may cancel this Lease by giving written notice to the other party.

6. TENANT'S PERSONAL PROPERTY. Landlord is not liable for the loss or destruction of Tenant's personal property.

7. INSURANCE. Tenant shall maintain a liability insurance policy for injuries on the premises in the amount of _____ Dollars ($ _____). Tenant may maintain a contents policy on Tenant's personal property.

8. CONDEMNATION. If the Leased Premises is condemned by any legally constituted authority, or if a conveyance or other acquisition in lieu of such condemnation is made, then this Lease shall terminate as of the date of possession required by the condemnor. All compensation paid in connection with the condemnation shall belong to the Landlord.

9. MECHANIC'S LIENS. Tenant may not permit any mechanic's liens to be filed against Leased Premises; however, if any mechanic's lien is filed, Tenant shall promptly obtain a release.

10. INDEMNIFICATION AND RELEASE. Regardless of whether or separate, several, joint or concurrent liability may be imposed upon the Landlord, Tenant shall indemnify and hold harmless Landlord from and against all damages, claims and liability arising from or connected with Tenant's control or use of the Leased Premises, including without limitation, any damage, or injury to person or property. This indemnification shall include Landlord's attorney fees in connection with any such claim. Tenant does hereby release Landlord for any accident, damage, or injury caused to person or property on or about the Leased Premises.

11. UTILITIES. Tenant shall pay all utilities, including but not limited to, heat, electricity, water, sewer, and telephone.

12. DEFAULT. Any violation of this Lease for a period in excess of five (5) days, or the filing of bankruptcy or other similar creditor action against Tenant, shall be deemed a default. Upon the occurrence of any default, the Landlord may, at its option, in addition to any other remedy or right it has hereunder or by law, (1) re-enter the premises, without demand or notice, and resume possession without being liable for trespass or for any damages and without terminating the Lease, (2) terminate this Lease at any time upon the date specified in the notice to Tenant, and Tenant's liability for damages shall survive such termination, (3) without terminating the Lease, relet the

Leased Premises without the same being deemed an acceptance of a surrender of this Lease nor a waiver of Landlord's rights herein.

A late fee of _____Dollars ($_____) shall be paid by Tenant if Tenant is _____ (_____) days late in payment of the rent.

13. ADVANCES AND INTEREST. If a default occurs, and Landlord exercises its option to cure the default by paying a sum of money, then such sum shall be due from Tenant to Landlord immediately, and shall bear a rate of interest of ten percent (10%) until paid.

14. ATTORNEY FEES. Each party shall pay the other party's reasonable legal costs and attorney's fees incurred in successfully enforcing the terms of this Lease against the other party.

15. ACCESS BY LANDLORD TO LEASED PREMISES. Landlord, agents, and prospective lessees, purchasers, or mortgagees shall be permitted to inspect and examine the Leased Premises at all reasonable times and Landlord to make repairs not made by Tenant.

16. QUIET ENJOYMENT. If Tenant shall perform all of the covenants and agreements herein provided, Tenant shall have peaceable and quiet enjoyment of possession of the Leased Premises without any manner of hindrance from Landlord or any parties lawfully claiming under Landlord.

17. OTHER TERMS. _____

_____

_____

_____

_____

_____

_____

18. GENERAL AGREEMENT. This Lease shall extend to and be binding upon the heirs, personal representatives, successors and assigns of the parties. All notices to be given to the parties hereunder shall be deemed sufficiently given when in writing and actually served or deposited in first-class U.S. mail, postage prepaid:

if Landlord _____

if Tenant _____

IN WITNESS WHEREOF, Landlord and Tenant have executed this Lease on _____, 20___.

LANDLORD _____

TENANT _____

Agreement to Sell Business

This is a basic form to buy/sell a small business. Since businesses vary greatly, use this form as a checklist of terms to consider, then submit the marked up copy to your attorney for final drafting.

Agreement to Sell Business

Agreement made this _____ day of _____, 20__ by and between _____ and _____ (doing business as _____) of _____ (hereinafter referred to as "Seller") and _____ (hereinafter referred to as the "Buyer").

Whereas the Seller desires to sell and the Buyer desires to buy the business of a certain _____ now being operated at _____ and known as _____ and all assets thereof as contained in Schedule "A" attached hereto, the parties hereto agree and covenant as follows:

1. The total purchase price for all fixtures, furnishings, and equipment is $_____ Dollars payable as follows: (a) $_____ paid in cash; certified or bank checks, as a deposit upon execution of this Agreement, to be held by _____. (b) $_____ additional to be paid in cash, certified or bank checks, at the time of passing papers. (c) $_____ to be paid by a note of the Buyer to the Seller, bearing interest at the rate of ____percent per annum with an option of the Buyer to prepay the entire outstanding obligation without penalty. Said note shall be secured by a chattel mortgage and financing statement covering the property to be sold hereunder, together with any and all other property acquired during the term of said note and placed in or within the premises known as _____, _____.

2. The property to be sold hereunder shall be conveyed by a standard form Bill of Sale, duly executed by the Seller.

3. The Seller promises and agrees to convey good, clear, and marketable title to all the property to be sold hereunder, the same to be free and clear of all liens and encumbrances. Full possession of said property will be delivered in the same condition that it is now, reasonable wear and tear expected.

4. Consummation of the sale, with payment by the Buyer of the balance of the down payment and the delivery by the Seller of a Bill of Sale, will take place on or before _____,20__.

5. The Seller may use the purchase money, or any portion thereof, to clear any encumbrances on the property transferred and in the event that documents reflecting discharge of said encumbrances are not available at the time of sale, the money needed to effectuate such discharges shall be held by the attorneys of the Buyer and Seller in escrow pending the discharges.

6. Until the delivery of the Bill of Sale, the Seller shall maintain insurance on said property in the amount that is presently insured.

7. Operating expenses of _____ including but not limited to rent, taxes, payroll, and water shall be apportioned as of the date of the passing of papers and the net amount thereof shall be added to or deducted from, as the case may be, the proceeds due from the Buyer at the time of delivery of the Bill of Sale.

8. If the Buyer fails to fulfill his or her obligations herein, all deposits made hereunder by the Buyer shall be retained by the Seller as liquidated damages.

9. The Seller promises and agrees not to engage in the same type of business as the one being sold for_____ years from the time of passing, within a _____ radius of _____.

10. The Seller agrees that this Agreement is contingent upon the following conditions: (a) Buyer obtaining a Lease on the said premises or that the existing Lease be assigned in writing to the Buyer. (b) Buyer obtaining the approval from the proper authorities of the transfer of all necessary licenses to the Buyer. (c) The premises shall be in the same condition, reasonable wear and tear expected, on the date of passing as they are currently in.

11. All of the terms, representations and warranties shall survive the closing. This Agreement shall bind and inure to the benefit of the Seller and Buyer and their respective heirs, executors, administrators, successors, and assigns.

12. If this Agreement shall contain any term or provision that shall be invalid or against public policy or if the application of same is invalid or against public policy, then, the remainder of this Agreement shall not be affected thereby and shall remain in full force and effect.

IN WITNESS WHEREOF, the parties hereto have caused this instrument to be executed in triplicate on the day and year first above written.

SELLER: _____

BUYER: _____

Installment Promissory Note

This installment promissory note is for a loan that you'll repay over a relatively short period of time. The loan is not secured by a mortgage or collateral in this note. State laws vary, so have your attorney review this form before the debtor signs.

Installment Promissory Note

$_____ Final Installment Due Date: _____

For value received, the undersigned promises to pay to the order of _____ the sum of _____

($_____), at the payee's residence or at such other place as the holder here-of may direct in writing, with interest upon the unpaid principal balance at the rate of _____ percent (__%) per annum from the date of this instrument until maturity, and _____ percent (__%) per annum after maturity until paid, with attorneys' fees and costs of collection and without relief from valuation and appraisement laws, payment of the principal and interest to be made as follows:

On or before the _____ of each month, beginning _____maker shall make principal and interest payment of _____; the final installment shall be due and payable on or before _____.

In event of default in payment of any of said installments when due, the entire un-paid balance of principal and interest shall become due and payable immediately, without notice, at the election of the holder hereof.

No delay or omission on the part of the holder hereof in the exercise of any right or remedy shall operate as a waiver thereof, and no single or partial exercise by the hold-er hereof of any right or remedy shall preclude other or further exercise thereof or of any other right or remedy.

This note (may) (may not) [delete one] be assigned or negotiated without the written consent of the maker.

This note and all extensions or renewals hereof are not secured by any property.

Signed and delivered at _____, _____ this _____ day of _____, 20___.

_____ as President of ABC, Inc.

Estate Planning Information

Fill out this form before visiting your attorney for estate planning. Keep a copy and update it periodically, so that your heirs will know what property you own at your death.

Estate Planning Information Sheet

Name _____ Birth _____ SS# _____

Name of Spouse _____ Birth _____ SS# _____

Residence Address _____

Names of Children _____

Age _____ Marital Status _____ Number of Children _____

Assets

Real Estate (Residence and Other Land)

Description	Present Value	Purchase Price	Mortgage	How Owned

Business Interests (Sole Proprietor, Partnership, Corporation)

Form of Business	Value of Interest	Who Owns

Accounts (Bank, Brokerage, Certificates of Deposit)

Type of Account	Account Name	Value	Who Owns

Stocks and Bonds

Stocks/Bonds Company	Market Value	Cost	Who Owns

Motor Vehicles

Make	Model	Year	Value	Who Owns

Miscellaneous Personal Property
(Household Goods, Sporting Equipment, Jewelry, Art, etc.)

Type of Property	Value	Who Owns

Life Insurance

Insurance Company	Face Value	Cash Value	Insured	Owner	Beneficiary

Retirement Benefits
(401(k), Pension/Profit Sharing, IRA, Keogh, etc.)

Type of Plan	Owner	Beneficiary	Value to Date

Other Assets (Including Possible Inheritances)

Type of Asset	Owner	Value
_____	_____	_____
_____	_____	_____
_____	_____	_____
Total Assets $ _____		

Liabilities

Type of Liability	Amount	Who Owes
_____	_____	_____
_____	_____	_____
_____	_____	_____
Total Liabilities $_____		

Total Assets minus Total Liabilities equals Net Worth $_____

Last Will and Testament

This is a basic last will and testament for a married person with children who wants to leave his or her property to the spouse and then the children. The will may be modified to add to the "specific devises," such as "I devise 100 shares of XYZ stock to my daughter, Sarah Hiatt." Use the form as a tentative draft of your will, then submit it to your attorney for the final draft and signing.

Last Will and Testament

of

_____

I,_____, of _____, _____, being of sound and disposing mind and memory, do make, publish, and declare this to be my Last Will and Testament, and I hereby revoke all Wills and Codicils heretofore made by me.

I. Identification, Definitions, Comments

    A. I am married to _____. I have _____ children:

    _____.

    B. A beneficiary must survive me by thirty (30) days to be entitled to receive a devise.

C. "Issue" is to be construed as lawful lineal descendants, and include adopted persons. Issue shall receive any devise by representation, not per capita.

II. Debts, Expenses, Encumbrances, Taxes

A. I direct that my enforceable debts, expenses of my last illness, and funeral and administrative expenses of my estate shall be paid by my personal representative from my residuary estate. In his or her discretion, my personal representative may continue to pay any installment obligations incurred by me during my lifetime on an installment basis or may prepay any or all of such obligations in whole or in part, and my personal representative may, in his or her discretion, distribute any asset encumbered by such an obligation subject to the obligation.

B. I direct that all inheritance, estate, and succession taxes (including interest and penalties thereon) payable by reason of my death shall be paid out of and be charged generally against my residuary estate without reimbursement from any person.

III. Specific Devises

I devise all my personal effects and household goods, such as jewelry, clothing, furniture, furnishings, silver, books, pictures, motor and recreation vehicles to _____. If he (or she) does not survive me, I devise said property, in equal shares, to _____. If a child does not survive me, then his or her share devolves to the deceased child's issue, or if none survive me, then the share devolves, equally, to the surviving children.

IV. Residuary Estate

I devise my residuary estate to _____. If he (or she) does not survive me, I devise my residuary estate, in equal shares, to _____ _____. If a child does not survive me, then his or her share devolves to the deceased child's issue, or if none survive me, then the share devolves, equally, to the surviving children.

V. Personal Representative

I hereby appoint _____as personal representative. If he (or she) cannot serve, I appoint _____ as co-personal representatives. I authorize unsupervised administration of my estate. I request that the personal representative serve without bond, or if a bond is required, that a minimum bond be required. My personal representative shall have all powers enumerated and granted to personal representatives under the _____ Code, and any other power that may be granted by law, to be exercised without the necessity of Court approval, as my personal representative determines to be in the best interest of the estate.

VI. Guardian

I appoint _____ as guardian of the person and property of each of my minor children. If _____ cannot serve as guardian, I appoint _____ as alternate guardian. I request that no bond be required for the guardian; however, if such a bond is required, then I request that such bond be nominal in amount.

VI. Miscellaneous

If my spouse and I executed Wills at approximately the same time, this Last Will and Testament is not made pursuant to any contract or agreement with my spouse.

I have signed this Last Will and Testament in the presence of the undersigned witnesses on this _____ day of _____, 20___.

Signature _____

Printed Name _____

The foregoing instrument, consisting of two typewritten pages, this included, was at _____, _____, this _____ day of _____, 20__, signed, sealed, published, and declared by _____ to be her (or his) Last Will and Testament, in our presence, and we, at her (or his) request and in her (or his) presence and in the presence of each other, have hereunto subscribed our names as attesting witnesses.

_____ residing at _____

_____ residing at _____

Index

Symbols

401(k) plan, 158

A

AARP Web site, 324
acceptance, forming contracts, 191-192
accounting
 accountant services, 73-74
 cash basis versus accrual accounting methods, 53
 Operating Agreements and LLCs, 43
 partnership agreements, 20
acquisitions
 corporations, 36
 existing business purchases, 85-86
acts. *See also* statutes
 ADA, 134
  compliance with laws when renting, 124
  defining criteria, 172
  required accommodations, 172
 Age Discrimination in Employment Act, 134
 Equal Credit Opportunity Act, 241
 Equal Pay Act, 134
 ERISA, 136
 Fair Credit Billing Act, 242-243
 Fair Credit Reporting Act, 241
 Fair Debt Collection Practices Act, 243
 FLSA, 135
 FMLA, 136
 Freedom of Information Act, 277
 Government-in-Sunshine Act, 277
 Immigration Reform and Control Act, 135
 Magnuson-Moss Act, 198
 NLRA, 135
 OSHA, 136
 Pregnancy Discrimination Act, 151
 Regulatory Flexibility Act, 278
 Securities Act of 1933, 114
 Small Business Regulatory Enforcement Fairness Act, 278
 Truth in Lending Act, 242

ADA (Americans with Disabilities Act), 134
 compliance with laws when renting, 124
 defining criteria, 172
 required accommodations, 172
addition of members, Operating Agreements and LLCs, 44
ADEA waivers, 169
adjudications, violation of administrative regulations, 274-275
administrative laws
 adoption of rules and regulations, 271
  adoption of final rules, 271
  challenges, 272
  comment period, 271
  notice of proposed rules, 271
 small business rights, 277
  Freedom of Information Act, 277
  Government-in-Sunshine Act, 277
  Regulatory Flexibility Act, 278
 violation of regulations, 273
  adjudication, 274-275
  investigations, 273
 zoning boards, 275
  hearings, 277
  pre-hearings, 276
admission of facts, pretrial discoveries, 228
adoption of final rules, administrative agency regulations, 271
advertisements
 as a deductible expense (sole proprietorships), 54
 consumer protection laws, 235
  bait-and-switching, 238
  creating accurate advertisements, 237-238
  deceptive advertisements, 236-237
  endorsements, 239
  FTC actions, 237
  sale items, 238
 employee recruitments, 138
advisors, 7
 accountant services, 73-74
 bankers, 76
 computer experts, 78
 fellow business owners, 8
 financial planners, 78-79
 insurance agents, 75-76
 lawyers
  fees, 73
  roles, 7
  selection of, 72

real estate brokers, 76-77
 retired business owners, 79-80
Age Discrimination Act, 10
Age Discrimination in Employment Act, 134
agencies (administrative)
 adoption of rules and regulations, 271
  adoption of final rules, 271
  challenges, 272
  comment period, 271
  notice of proposed rules, 271
 authority from statutes, 269-271
 small business rights, 277
  Freedom of Information Act, 277
  Government-in-Sunshine Act, 277
  Regulatory Flexibility Act, 278
 violation of regulations, 273
  adjudication, 274-275
  investigations, 273
 zoning boards, 275
  hearings, 277
  pre-hearings, 276
agreements. *See also* contracts, documents
 Agreement to Sell Business forms, 351-352
 franchise agreements, 99-100
  disclosures, 100
  terms, 103
 limited partnerships, 25-26
 partnerships, 16
  accounting responsibilities, 20
  addition of new partners, 20
  appraisal of ownership interests, 21
  arbitrations, 22
  contract liabilities, 22-23
  dissolution requirements, 21-22
  expulsions, 21
  forms, 336-339
  fiduciary duties, 19
  management concerns, 19
  profit and loss shares, 18
  property designations, 24
  timeframes, 17
  withdrawing partners, 20
 pre-incorporation agreements, 30
 prenuptial agreements, 321-323
 purchase agreements, terms, 128-130
 rental agreements, 120
  assignments and subleases, 124

breaches, 125
cancellations, 125
compliance with ADA, 124
condition of premises, 122
improvements, 123
liability and insurance coverages, 124
rent payments, 121-122
rental periods, 120-121
signage, 125
space specifications, 122
usage restrictions, 123
security agreements, 250-251
shareholders
forms, 339-343
shareholders' stock purchase agreements, 31-32
alimony, 322-323
allocation of income among owners (operational tax tactic), 63
alternatives to lawsuits, 231
arbitration, 231
mediation, 231
Americans with Disabilities Act.
See ADA
anti-discrimination laws, compensation packages, 149
appeals, 230
Appeals Conferences (audits), 67
applications
employee recruitment, 139
insurance policies, 178
patents, 266
appraisals, 21
arbitrations, 22, 231
Articles of Incorporation, 30-31
Articles of Organization, 40
forms, 344-347
terms, 40-41
assaults, employer liabilities, 212
assets
bankruptcy protections
choice of entity, 295
insurance coverages, 297
personal loan guarantees, 296
pledging collateral, 297
pre-planning, 298
taxes, 297
determining for capital needs, 109
equity, 109
life insurance policies, 110
personal savings, 109
retirement plans, 110
estate planning, 307
business assets, 309-310
personal assets, 308
sale of corporate assets, 36
assignments, terms of rental agreements, 124
assumption of risks (negligence), 211
attitudes of employees, performance reviews, 165
attorneys. *See* lawyers
audits
Appeals Conference, 67

preparations, 65-66
process of, 67
automatic perfections, securing loans, 251-252

B

bait-and-switching advertisements, 238
bank loans, provisions
amounts, 111
collateral, 111
cosigners and guarantors, 112
defaults, 111
fees, 111
interest rates, 111
payment schedules, 111
prepayment penalties, 111
bankers, advisor duties, 76
bankruptcies, 253
Chapter eleven, 303-304
Chapter seven, 254, 302-303
Chapter thirteen, 256
decision process, 301
closing businesses, 301
dissolving entities, 302
selling businesses, 301
discharges, 256
distributions, 256
exempt properties, 255
protection of assets
choice of entity, 295
insurance coverages, 297
personal loan guarantees, 296
pledging collateral, 297
taxes, 297
pre-planning, 298
prevention
nonessential cutbacks, 299
warning signs, 298-299
working with creditors, 299
resource materials, 305
taxes, 304
voluntary personal bankruptcy petitions, 255
basis of property, 93
battery, employer liabilities, 213
benefit plans
child and dependent care, 155
compensation packages, 153
educational assistance, 155
employee discounts, 156
employee handbook guidelines, 162
fringe benefits, 148
group term life insurance, 154
health insurance, 154
listing of extras, 157
moving expenses, 156
operational tax tactics, 64
pay discrimination, 151-152
billing consumers, Fair Credit Billing Act, 242-243
board of directors, 33
breach of trusts, 34-35
roles, 33
bodily injury, liability insurance coverages, 182

borrowing
bank borrowing, 110-112
bank loans, 111
risks, 110
SBA-guaranteed loans, 112
breaches
contracts, 202
remedies
equity, 203-204
money damages, 203
purchase agreements, 130
rental agreements, 125
trusts, 34-35
brokers
advisor duties, 76-77
finding location for leases and purchases, 119-120
building inspections, 127
burglary insurance, 183
businesses
contracts, 11
elements of, 11
UCC versus common laws, 11-12
employment laws, 9
Age Discrimination Act, 10
Americans with Disabilities Act, 10
Civil Rights Act of 1964, 9
Fair Labor Standards Act, 10
OSHA, 10
State workers' Compensation Acts, 10
estate planning, 13
assets, 309-310
last will and testament, 13
life insurance, 13
successor plans, 14
interruption insurance, 182
intellectual property laws, 12
copyright protections, 12
patents, 12
plans, capital needs assessments, 107-108
raising capital for, 8-9
types and selection process, 4
advisor selections, 7-8
corporations, 4
limited liability companies, 4
partnerships, 4
personal liability concerns, 5
sole proprietors, 4
tax considerations, 5-7
buying
existing businesses
acquistion team, 85-86
closing process, 94
examining financial condition of company, 86-87
financing, 93
offers and negotiations, 90-93
potential legal problems, 87-89
selection process, 83-85
tax issues, 93
real estate, 126
building inspections, 127
function of attorneys, 128

location considerations, 119-120
mortgage financing, 127
terms of purchase agreements, 128-130
title insurance companies, 127
bylaws, 31

C

C corporations, 33, 60-61
cancellations
insurance policies, 179-180
terms of rental agreements, 125
capacities, contract requirements, 194-195
capital
bank borrowing, 110-112
contributions, operating agreements and LLCs, 42
determining assets, 109
equity, 109
life insurance policies, 110
personal savings, 109
retirement plans, 110
investors, 113
co-owners, 113
federal security laws, 114-116
outside investors, 113
state security laws, 116
needs assessment, 107-108
raising capital for businesses, 8-9
risks of borrowing, 110
SBA-guaranteed loans, 112
cash basis versus accrual method accounting, 53
cash payments from customers, 246
casualty losses as a deductible expense, 56
causation, negligence, 209-210
Chapter eleven bankruptcy, 303-304
Chapter seven bankruptcy, 254, 302-303
Chapter thirteen bankruptcy, 256
character of incomes (operational tax tactic), 63
charitable pledges, 194
check payments, 246
precautions, 246
prosecution of bad checks, 247
child and dependent care, benefit plans, 155
civil procedures (lawsuits)
claim of injury, 223
countersuits, 226
filing, 225-226
motions, 227
pleadings, 225
pretrial discoveries, 227-228
third parties and cross claims, 226
trials, 228-230
Civil Rights Act of 1866, 134
Civil Rights Act of 1964, 9
claim of injury, 223
closing arguments at trials, 229
closings
existing business acquisitions, 94

purchase agreements, terms, 128
sole proprietorships, 52-53
co-owner investors, 113
Code of Federal Regulations, 271
collateral
bank loans provisions, 111
bankruptcy protection, 297
securing loans, 248
automatic perfections, 251-252
mortgages, 249
security agreements, 250-251
security interests, 249-250
statutory liens, 248
collection of debts
collecting without suing, 252-253
agencies, 253
collection letters, 253
follow-up bills, 252
debtor bankruptcies, 253
Chapter seven, 254
Chapter thirteen, 256
discharges, 256
distributions, 256
exempt properties, 255
voluntary personal bankruptcy petitions, 255
Fair Debt Collection Practices Act, 243
comment period, proposed rules and regulations, 271
common and preferred stocks, federal security laws, 114
common laws
contract laws, 190
versus UCC, 11-12
communication skills, performance reviews, 165
community property laws, 309
companies, LLCs, 4. *See also* corporations
Articles of Organization, 40-41
maintenance of LLC status, 45-46
operating agreements, 41-44
resource materials, 47
tax considerations, 46
versus partnerships and corporations, 39-40
comparative negligence, 210
compensation
employment laws, 135
ERISA, 136
FLSA, 135
FMLA, 136
unemployment compensation, 136
minimum wage and overtime, 149-151
packages for employees, 147
anti-discrimination laws, 149
deferred compensation, 157
fringe benefits, 148, 153-157
medical insurance, 148
pension plans and ERISA provisions, 148, 157-158
salary and wages, 148, 152

pay discrimination, 151
fringe benefits, 151-152
wages, 151
computer experts, advisor duties, 78
condition of premises, rental agreement terms, 122
conduct of members, operating agreements and LLCs, 42
conferences, pretrial conferences, 228
confidentiality
employees' files, 167
employment contracts, 164
consents, forming contracts, 192
duress, 192
misrepresentations, 193
undue influences, 193
consultants. *See* advisors
Consumer Product Safety Commission. *See* CPSC
consumer protection laws
advertising, 235
bait-and-switching, 238
creating accurate advertisements, 237-238
deceptive advertisements, 236-237
endorsements, 239
FTC actions, 237
sale items, 238
telephone and mail orders, 239
credit laws, 241
Equal Credit Opportunity Act, 241
Fair Credit Billing Act, 242-243
Fair Credit Reporting Act, 241
Fair Debt Collection Practices Act, 243
Truth in Lending Act, 242
cyberlaws and privacy issues, 285
resource materials, 243
safety laws, 240
CPSC, 240
FDA protection, 240
Consumer Reports, 243
contents of employee handbooks, 161
benefits, 162
discipline and discharges, 163
grievance procedures, 163
introductions, 162
pay, 162
policies, 162
working hour requirements, 162
contracts, 11. *See also* agreements, documents
binding authority of agents, 204
breaches, remedies, 202-204
cyberlaws, 287
drafting checklists, 201-202
elements for legal existence, 190
acceptance, 191-192
capacities, 194-195
consents, 192-193

considerations, 193-194
offers, 191
employment, 163
confidential information, 164
covenant not to compete, 164
introductions, 163
pay, 164
period of employment, 163
terminations, 164
federal security laws, 114-115
forming, 189-190
insurance, 177-180
interference liabilities, 217-218
interpretations, 196
dictionary, 196
gap fillers, 197
performance, 197
trade usage, 197
laws
common law, 190
UCC, 190
liabilities and partnership agreements, 22-23
performance terms
excusing performance, 200-201
performance by parties, 199
subcontracting, 200
warranties, 198
Statute of Frauds, 12, 195-196
UCC versus common laws, 11-12
voidable, 195
contributions of property to entity, tax laws, 61
contributory negligence, 211
copyrights
printed or recorded works, 262-264
creating, 262-263
infringement and fair use, 264
protections, 263
protections, 12
corporations, 4, 35. *See also* companies
board of directors, 33
breach of trusts, 34-35
roles, 33
C Corporations, 60-61
dissolutions, 36
documents, 29
Articles of Incorporation, 30-31
bylaws, 31
pre-incorporation agreements, 30
resource materials, 38
mergers and acquisitions, 36
naming, 30-31
officers, roles, 35
S Corporations, 60-61
sale of corporate assets, 36
Shareholders' Stock Purchase Agreements, 31-32
sole proprietorships, 50

stock ownership and shareholders, 32
tax considerations, 36
C corporations, 37
S corporations, 37-38
versus LLCs, 39-40
cosigner, bank loans provisions, 112
countersuits, 226
court systems (filing lawsuits)
federal courts, 221-223
state courts, 223
covenants, 92-93
home-based business restrictions, 290
not to compete (employment contracts), 164
quiet enjoyment, 124
coverages
health insurance, 185
insurance policies, 179
liability insurance
bodily injury, 182
limits, 182
occurrences, 182
property damages, 182
pension plans, 158
property insurance, 180
amounts, 181
perils, 181
CPSC (Consumer Product Safety Commission), 240
credit card payments from customers, 246
credit laws, consumer protection, 241
Equal Credit Opportunity Act, 241
Fair Credit Billing Act, 242-243
Fair Credit Reporting Act, 241
Fair Debt Collection Practices Act, 243
Truth in Lending Act, 242
creditors
collection process, 252
collecting without suing, 252-253
debtor bankruptcies, 253-256
judgment and collections, 253
debt workout plans, 299
payment options, 245
cash, 246
checks, 246-247
credit card, 246
promissory notes, 248
securing loans with collateral, 248
automatic perfections, 251-252
mortgages, 249
security agreements, 250-251
security interests, 249-250
statutory liens, 248
cross claim lawsuits, 226
cutbacks (bankruptcy prevention)
business, 299
personal, 299
cyberpiracy, 282
cybersquatting, 282

D

damages, tort remedies, 218
debts
bankruptcy prevention
cutbacks, 299
warning signs, 299
working with creditors, 299
collection process, 252
collecting without suing, 252-253
debtor bankruptcies, 253-256
judgment and collection, 253
Fair Debt Collection Practices Act, 243
workout plans, 299
deceptive advertisements, consumer protection laws, 236-237
deductibles
insurance policies, 179
limitation on losses, 63-64
sole proprietorships, 54
advertising, 54
casualty losses, 56
depreciation, 55
employees' wages, 55-56
travel, 56
defamation, employer liabilities, 215-216
defaults (bank loans) 111
defenses for negligence, 210
assumption of risks, 211
comparative negligence, 210
contributory negligence, 211
deferred compensation, 157
defined benefit pension plans, 157
defined contribution pension plans, 157-158
dependability of employees, performance reviews, 165
dependent care, benefit plans, 155
depositons, pretrial discoveries, 228
deposits, security deposits, 122
depreciation as a deductible expense 55
design patents, 265
devisee, 317
dictionary interpretation of contracts, 196
directors and officers liability insurance policy, 184
disability insurance, 186
discharging bankruptcies, 256
discipline
employee handbook guidelines, 163
progressive discipline process, 167-168
disclosures
franchise agreements, 100
Truth in Lending Acts, 242-243
discounts for employees, benefit plans, 156
discrimination
employment laws, 134
ADA, 134
Age Discrimination in Employment Act, 134

Equal Pay Act, 134
Immigration Reform and
   Control Act, 135
NLRA, 135
Section 1981, Civil Rights Act
   of 1866, 134
state and local civil rights
   laws, 135
Title VII, 134
pay discrimination, 151
   fringe benefits, 151-152
   wages, 151
dissolutions
corporations, 36
operating agreements and LLCs,
   44
partnership agreements, 21-22
dissolving entities, bankruptcies,
   302
distributions
bankruptcies, 256
pension plans, 158
divorce (effects on businesses),
   320-321
alimony, 322-323
no-fault divorces, 322
doctrine of impossibility, 201
documents. *See also* agreements,
   documents
Articles of Organization, 40-41
bylaws, 31
corporations, 29
   Articles of Incorporation,
      30-31
   pre-incorporation agree-
      ments, 30
operating agreements, 41
   accounting, 43
   capital contributions, 42
   dissolutions, 44
   loss of members, 43
   maintenance of LLC status,
      45-46
   management concerns, 44
   members'conduct, 42
   naming company, 41
   profit and losses, 43
   purpose statements, 41
   terms, 41
domain names (World Wide Web),
   279
creation and registrations, 280
cyberpiracy, 282
cybersquatting, 282
tags, 282
trademark issues, 280-282
drafting agreements
checklists, 201-202
partnerships, 16
   accounting responsibilities,
      20
   addition of new partners, 20
   appraisal of ownership inter-
      ests, 21
   arbitrations, 22
   contract liabilities, 22-23
   dissolution requirements,
      21-22
   expulsion, 21
   fiduciary duties, 19

management concerns, 19
profit and loss shares, 18
property designations, 24
timeframes, 17
withdrawing partners, 20
drug test, testing of future employees, 142-143
duress, contracts, 192
duties, fiduciary duties, 19, 34-35
dying without a will, 316-317

E

e-commerce, 283
cyberlaws, 284
   contracts, 287
   jurisdictions, 288-289
   linking, 284-285
   privacy, 285-286
   publishing, 286-287
   spamming, 286
   taxes, 289
   torts, 287-288
development of Web sites, 283
operating sites, 283-284
resource materials, 291
earnest money, terms of purchase
   agreements, 128
ECOA (Equal Credit Opportunity
   Act), 241
educational assistance, benefit
   plans, 155
*EEOC's Uniform Guidelines on
   Employee Selection Procedures*, 137
effective dates of insurance policies,
   178
emotional harms, employer liabilities, 217
employees
compensation packages, 147
   anti-discrimination laws, 149
   deferred compensation, 157
   fringe benefits, 148, 153-157
   medical insurance, 148
   pension plans and ERISA pro-
      visions, 148, 157-158
   salary and wages, 148, 152
contracts, 163
   confidential information,
      164
   covenant not to compete,
      164
   introductions, 163
   pay, 164
   period of employment, 163
   terminations, 164
files
   confidentiality, 167
   contents, 166
handbooks, 161
   benefits, 162
   discipline and terminations,
      163
   grievance procedures, 163
   introductions, 162
   pay guidelines, 162
   policies, 162
   working hour requirements,
      162

hiring process, 140
interviews, 140
investigation of applicants,
   140-141
home-based businesses, 290
insurance coverages, 184
disability, 186
health, 185
life, 184
labor unions, 173-174
laws. *See* employment laws
minimum wage and overtime,
   149-151
pay discrimination, 151
   fringe benefits, 151-152
   wages, 151
performance reviews, 164-165
attitudes, 165
communication skills, 165
dependability, 165
organizational skills, 165
quality of work, 165
relating to others, 165
progressive discipline process,
   167-168
recruitment guidelines, 137
advertisements, 138
application requirements,
   139
job descriptions, 137-138
rights of ex-employees, 169
safety issues, 171
OSHA, 171
workers' compensation,
   171-172
sexual harassment
defining criteria, 169
policies, 170
terminations, 168-169
testing
medical and drug testing,
   142-143
skills tests, 142
torts and employer liabilites, 205
assaults, 212
battery, 213
defamation, 215-216
emotional harm, 217
employment requirements,
   206
false imprisonment, 213
invasion of privacy, 216
negligence, 207-211
nuisances, 215
products liability, 211-212
remedies, 218-219
resource materials, 219
scope of employment, 206
strict liabilities, 214-215
trespass and conversion,
   213-214
wrongful contract interferences, 217-218
versus hiring independent contractors, 143-144
employer liabilities, 205
assaults, 212
battery, 213
defamation, 215-216

emotional harm, 217
employment requirements, 206
false imprisonment, 213
invasion of privacy, 216
negligence, 207-211
nuisances, 215
products liability, 211-212
remedies, 218-219
resource materials, 219
scope of employment, 206
strict liabilities, 214-215
trespass and conversion, 213-214
wrongful contract interferences, 217-218
employment laws, 9, 133
ADA, 10, 134
defining criteria, 172
required accommodations, 172
Civil Rights Act of 1964, 9
compensation, 135
ERISA, 136
FLSA, 135
FMLA, 136
unemployment compensation, 136
Fair Labor Standards Act, 10
health and safety, 136
OSHA, 136
workers' compensation, 137
illegal discrimination, 134
Age Discrimination in Employment Act, 10, 134
Equal Pay Act, 134
Immigration Reform and Control Act, 135
NLRA, 135
Section 1981, Civil Rights Act of 1866, 134
state and local civil rights laws, 135
Title VII, 134
OSHA, 10
resource materials, 145
State workers' Compensation Acts, 10
employment practice insurance, 183
Employment Retirement Income Security Act. *See* ERISA
encryptions, 286
endorsements, deceptive sales practices, 239
environmental surveys, terms of purchase agreements, 129
Equal Credit Opportunity Act. *See* ECOA
Equal Pay Act, 134
equity
asset determination for capital needs, 109
line of credit, 109
refinancing, 109
second mortgages, 109
equity remedies (contract breaches), 203
reformations, 203

rescissions, 203
specific performance, 204
tort remedies, 218-219
ERISA (Employment Retirement Income Security Act), 136, 148
estate planning, 13
assets, 307
business, 309-310
personal, 308
information sheets, 353-356
last will and testament, 13, 316
devisee, 317
dying without wills, 316-317
guardians, 318
personal representatives, 317
life insurance, 13
living wills and power of attorney, 320
probate, 310
advantages of avoiding, 312
defining characteristics, 310-311
procedures, 311-312
resource materials, 324
successor plans, 14
taxes, 313-316
trusts, 316-317
essential contents, 319-320
living, 319
testamentary, 319
evidence presentation at trials, 229
excusing performances, contracts, 200-201
executive agencies, 270
exempt properties, bankruptcies, 255
existing business acquisitions, 85-86
closings, 94
examining financial condition of company, 86-87
financing, 93
offers and negotiations, 90-91
covenants, 92-93
purchase agreements, 91-92
potential legal problems, 87
contracts with suppliers and employees, 89
lawsuits, 89
leases, 88
service warranties and trademarks, 89
taxes, 89
titles and liens, 88
toxic waste, 88
zoning, 88
taxes, 93
selection process, 83-85
expulsion of partnership agreements, 21

F

Fair Credit Billing Act. *See* FCBA
Fair Credit Reporting Act. *See* FCRA
Fair Debt Collection Practices Act. *See* FDCPA
Fair Labor Standards Act. *See* FLSA
fair use (copyrights), 264

false imprisonment, employer liabilities, 213
Family and Medical Leave Act. *See* FMLA
family partnerships, taxes, 65
FCBA (Fair Credit Billing Act), 242-243
FCRA (Fair Credit Reporting Act), 241
FDA (Food and Drug Administration), 240-243
foods, 240
medications, 240
FDCPA (Fair Debt Collection Practices Act), 243
federal courts, filing lawsuits, 221-223
federal independent regulatory agencies, 270
Federal Register, 271
federal laws
security, 114
common and preferred stocks, 114
investment contracts, 114-115
SEC regulations, 115-116
stock warrants and options, 114
tax laws
C Corporations, 60-61
estate and gift taxes, 314-316
LLCs, 60
partnerships, 60
S Corporations, 60-61
sole proprietors, 59-60
fees
bank loans, 111
lawyers, 73
fiduciary duties, 19, 34-35
files (employees)
confidentiality, 167
contents, 166
filing
lawsuits
civil procedures, 223-230
federal courts, 221-223
state courts, 223
motions, 227
small claims court collections, 230
finances
examining finances of existing businesses, 86-87
existing business acquisitions, 93
financial plans, 108
mortgage financing, 127
sole proprietorships, 51-52
financial planners, advisor duties, 78-79
firing. *See* terminations
FLSA (Fair Labor Standards Act), 135
minimum wage, 149-151
overtime compensations, 149-151
FMLA (Family and Medical Leave Act), 136
food, FDA protection, 240
Food and Drug Administration. *See*

FDA
forms
  Agreement to Sell Business,
    351-352
  Articles of Organization, 344-347
  estate planning information
    sheets, 353-356
  installment promissory notes,
    352-353
  last will and testament, 356-358
  leases, 348-350
  partnership agreements, 336-339
  shareholder agreements, 339-343
franchises
  disclosures, 100
  overview of laws, 95-97
  problem solving, 106
  resource materials, 106
  selection process, 97-98
    expertise of franchise, 98
    investigation of franchise, 98
    reputation of, 99
    terms of franchise agreements,
      99-100
Freedom of Information Act, 277
fringe benefits
  child and dependent care, 155
  compensation packages, 148, 153
  educational assistance, 155
  employee discounts, 156
  group term life insurance, 154
  health insurance, 154
  listing of extras, 157
  moving expenses, 156
  operational tax tactics, 64
  pay discrimination, 151-152
FTC, evaluation of advertisements,
  237
fund raising (capital)
  bank borrowing, 110-112
  determining assets, 109
  investors and security laws,
    113-116
  life insurance policies, 110
  needs assessment, 107-108
  retirement plans, 110
  risks of borrowing, 110
  SBA-guaranteed loan, 112
FUTA tax, 148

G–H–I

gap fillers, interpretation of contracts, 197
garnishments, 253
gift taxes, 313-316
goodwill, 85
grievance procedures, 163
group term life insurance, fringe
  benefits, 154
guarantors, bank loans provisions,
  112
guardians, estates, 318

handbooks (employee handbooks),
  161
  benefits, 162
  discipline and discharge, 163

grievance procedures, 163
introductions, 162
pay, 162
policies, 162
working hour requirements, 162
health and safety employment laws,
  136
  OSHA, 136
  workers' compensation, 137
health insurance
  coverages, 185
  fringe benefits, 154
  providers, 185
hearings, zoning boards, 277
hiring employees, 140
  interviews, 140
  investigation of applicants,
    140-141
  versus independent contractors,
    143-144
home-based businesses, 289
  laws
    employment, 290
    licensing, 290
    restrictive covenants, 290
    zoning, 290
  resource materials, 291
  taxes, 291

illegal discrimination employment
  laws
  ADA, 134
  Age Discrimination in
    Employment Act, 134
  Equal Pay Act, 134
  Immigration Reform and
    Control Act, 135
  NLRA, 135
  Section 1981, Civil Rights Act of
    1866, 134
  state and local civil rights laws,
    135
  Title VII, 134
Immigration Reform and Control
  Act, 135
independent contractors versus hiring employees, 143-144
infringements (copyrights), 264
inspections
  building inspections, 127
  terms of purchase agreements,
    129
installment promissory note forms,
  352-353
insurance
  advisor duties of agents, 75-76
  bankruptcy protection, 297
  burglary and theft, 183
  contracts, 177-180
  directors and officers liability
    policy, 184
  disability insurance, 186
  employment practices, 183
  fringe benefits for employees
    group term life insurance,
      154
    health insurance, 154
    medical insurance, 148

health insurance
  coverages, 185
  providers, 185
interruption insurance, 182
liability insurance, 181
  bodily injury coverages, 182
  coverage limits, 182
  occurrence coverages, 182
  pollution liability, 183
  property damage coverages,
    182
  product liability, 183
life insurance, 184
  estate planning, 13
  term life, 184
  whole life, 184
policies
  application and effective
    dates, 178
  cancellations, 179-180
  coverages and deductibles,
    179
  duties and rights, 178
  misconduct by insured, 180
  riders, 180
property insurance, 180-181
rental coverages, 121, 124
resource materials, 187
saving premium costs, 187
tax issues, 186
title insurance, 127-129
intellectual property laws, 12
  copyright protections, 12
  patents, 12
interest rates, bank loan provisions,
  111
Internet. *See* World Wide Web
interpretations of contracts, 196
  dictionary, 196
  gap fillers, 197
  performance, 197
  trade usage, 197
interruption insurance, 182
interstate, 308
interview process, hiring employees,
  140
introductions
  employee handbooks, 162
  employment contracts, 163
invasion of privacy, employer liabilities, 216
investigations
  applicants for employment,
    140-141
  financial conditions of existing
    businesses, 86-87
  franchises, 98
  violation of administrative regu-
    lations, 273
investors, 113
  co-owners, 113
  federal security laws, 114
    common and preferred
      stocks, 114
    investment contracts,
      114-115
    SEC regulations, 115-116
    stock warrants and options,
      114

outside investors, 113
    private placement, 113
    stock market, 113
    strategic partners, 113
    venture capitalists, 113
state security laws, 116
irrevocable living trusts, 319

J–K–L

job descriptions for employee
  recruitment, 137-138
judgments, collection process, 253
jurisdictions, cyberlaws, 288-289
jury selections, 228
just cause, 102

labor unions, 173-174
landlords, avoiding problems with,
  126
last will and testament
    estate planning, 13, 316
        devisee, 317
        dying without wills, 316-317
        guardians, 318
        personal representatives, 317
    sample forms, 356-358
laws
    administrative
        adoption of rules and regula-
          tions, 271-272
        authority from statutes,
          269-271
        small business rights,
          277-278
        violation of regulations,
          273-275
        zoning boards, 275-277
    community property, 309
    consumer protection, 235
        creating accurate advertise-
          ments, 237-238
        credit laws, 241-243
        deceptive advertisements,
          236-237
        deceptive sales practices,
          238-239
        FTC actions, 237
        resource materials, 243
        safety laws, 240
    contract
        common law, 190
        UCC, 190
    copyrights
        creating, 262-263
        infringement and fair use,
          264
        protections, 263
    cyberlaws, 284
        contracts, 287
        jurisdictions, 288-289
        linking, 284-285
        privacy, 285-286
        publishing, 286-287
        spamming, 286
        taxes, 289
        torts, 287-288

employment laws, 9
    Age Discrimination Act, 10
    Americans with Disabilities
      Act, 10
    Civil Rights Act of 1964, 9
    compensation, 135-136
    Fair Labor Standards Act, 10
    health and safety, 136-137
    illegal discrimination,
      134-135
    OSHA, 10
    resource materials, 145
    State workers' Compensation
      Acts, 10
federal tax laws
    C Corporations, 60-61
    LLCs, 60
    partnerships, 60
    S Corporations, 60-61
    sole proprietors, 59-60
franchises, 95-97
home-based businesses, 290
    employment, 290
    licensing, 290
    restrictive covenants, 290
    taxes, 291
    zoning, 290
intellectual property laws, 12
    copyright protections, 12
    patents, 12
patents, 264
    creating, 265
    protection, 266
security laws
    federal, 114-116
    state, 116
lawsuits
    alternatives to, 231
        arbitration, 231
        mediation, 231
    civil procedures, 223
        claim of injury, 223
        countersuits, 226
        filing, 225-226
        motions, 227
        pleadings, 225
        pretrial discoveries, 227-228
        pretrial conferences, 228
        third parties and cross
          claims, 226
        trials, 228-230
    filing of, 221
        federal courts, 221-223
        state courts, 223
    legal problems of existing busi-
      nesses, 89
    resource materials, 232
lawyers
    fees, 73
    roles, 7
    selection of, 72
leases
    avoiding problems with land-
      lords, 126
    forms, 348-350
    legal problems of existing busi-
      nesses, 88
    location considerations, 119-120

rental agreements, 120
    assignments and subleases,
      124
    breaches, 125
    cancellations, 125
    compliance with ADA, 124
    condition of premises, 122
    improvements, 123
    liability and insurance cover-
      ages, 124
    rent payments, 121-122
    rental periods, 120-121
    signage, 125
    space specifications, 122
    usage restrictions, 123
legal problems, analysis of existing
  businesses, 87
    contracts with suppliers and
      employees, 89
    lawsuits, 89
    leases, 88
    service warranties and trade-
      marks, 89
    taxes, 89
    titles and liens, 88
    toxic waste, 88
    zoning, 88
letters
    collections, 253
    credit, 201
    Letter of Intent to Purchase, 90
    terminations, 168-169
liabilities
    employers, 205
        assaults, 212
        battery, 213
        defamation, 215-216
        emotional harm, 217
        employment requirements,
          206
        false imprisonment, 213
        invasion of privacy, 216
        negligence, 207-211
        nuisances, 215
        products liability, 211-212
        remedies, 218-219
        resource materials, 219
        scope of employment, 206
        strict liabilities, 214-215
        trespass and conversion,
          213-214
        wrongful contract interfer-
          ences, 217-218
    insurance, 181
        bodily injury coverages, 182
        coverage limits, 182
        occurrence coverages, 182
        pollution liability, 183
        property damage coverages,
          182
        product liability, 183
    partnership agreements, 22-23
    rentals, 124
licenses, home-based businesses,
  290
liens
    legal problems of existing busi-
      nesses, 88
    mechanics' lien, 128
    statutory liens, 248

life insurance, 184
  asset determination for capital needs, 110
  estate planning, 13
  term life, 184
  whole life, 184
limited liability company. *See* LLCs
limited liability partnerships. *See* LLP
limited partnerships, 4, 25-26
limits
  deductible tax losses, 63-64
  liability insurance coverages, 182
line of credit, 109
linking, cyberlaws, 284-285
liquidations, Chapter seven bankruptcy, 303
litigations
  alternatives to, 231
    arbitration, 231
    mediation, 231
  civil procedures, 223
    claim of injury, 223
    countersuits, 226
    filing, 225-226
    motions, 227
    pleadings, 225
    pretrial discoveries, 227-228
    pretrial conferences, 228
    third parties and cross claims, 226
    trials, 228-230
  filing lawsuits, 221
    federal courts, 221-223
    state courts, 223
  resource materials, 232
  small claims court
    filing claims, 230
    trials, 230-231
living trusts, 319
living wills, 320
LLCs (limited liability company)
  Articles of Organization, 40
    forms, 344-347
    terms, 40-41
  maintenance of LLC status, 45-46
  operating agreement terms
    accounting, 43
    addition of members, 44
    capital contributions, 42
    dissolutions, 44
    loss of members, 43
    management concerns, 44
    members'conduct, 42
    naming company, 41
    profit and losses, 43
    purpose statements, 41
  resource materials, 47
  sole proprietorships, 50
  taxes, 46, 60
  versus partnerships and corporations, 39-40
LLP (limited liability partnerships), registering, 24
loans
  bank loans, provisions 111-112
  SBA-guaranteed loans, 112

securing with collateral, 248
  automatic perfections, 251-252
  mortgages, 249
  security agreements, 250-251
  security interests, 249-250
  statutory liens, 248
local taxes
  property taxes, 69
  sole proprietorships, 56-57

M–N–O

Magnuson-Moss Act, 198
mail orders, deceptive sales practices, 239
management concerns
  operating agreements and LLCs, 44
  partnership agreements, 19
marks (trademarks), 260-261
  creating, 261
  protection, 261-262
marriage (effects on businesses), prenuptial agreements, 320-323
mechanics' lien, 128
mediation, 231
medical insurance, compensation packages, 148
medical tests, testing of future employees, 142-143
medications, FDA protection, 240
mergers (corporations), 36
minimum wages, FLSA coverages, 149-151
mitigations, 126
money damages, contract breaches, 203
mortgages, 88
  financing real estate purchases, 127
  securing loans, 249
motions
  filing of, 227
  post-trial motions, 230
moving expenses, benefit plans, 156
naming
  corporations, 30-31
  LLCs, 41
National Labor Relations Act. *See* NLRA
negligence, employer liability, 207-208
  causation, 209-210
  defenses, 210-211
  legal duties, 208-209
  personal injury and property damages, 210
  unreasonable conduct, 209
negotiation of existing business acquisitions, 90-91
  covenants, 92-93
  Purchase Agreements, 91-92
NLRA (National Labor Relations Act), 135
  labor unions, 173-174
no-fault divorces, 322

nondiscriminatory pension plans, 158
nuisances, employer liabilities, 215

Occupational Safety and Health Act. *See* OSHA
occurrence coverages (liability insurance), 182
offers
  existing business acquisitions, 90-91
    covenants, 92-93
    purchase agreements, 91-92
  forming contracts, 191
  terms of purchase agreements, 128
officers (corporate officers), roles, 35
opening statements at trials, 229
operating agreements (LLCs), 41
  maintenance of LLC status, 45-46
  terms, 41
    accounting, 43
    addition of members, 44
    capital contributions, 42
    dissolutions, 44
    loss of members, 43
    management concerns, 44
    members'conduct, 42
    naming company, 41
    profit and losses, 43
    purpose statements, 41
operational tactics (taxes), 62
  allocation of income among owners, 63
  character of income, 63
  fringe benefits, 64
  limitations on deductible losses, 63-64
  taxation of owners, 62
  timing, 63
organizational costs, tax laws, 62
OSHA (Occupational Safety and Health Act), 10, 136, 171
overtime employee compensations, FLSA coverages, 149-151
owners taxation (operational tactic), 62

P

partnerships, 4
  agreement terms, 16
    accounting responsibilities, 20
    addition of new partners, 20
    appraisal of ownership interests, 21
    arbitrations, 22
    contract liabilities, 22-23
    dissolution requirements, 21-22
    expulsions, 21
    fiduciary duties, 19
    forms, 336-339
    management concerns, 19
    profit and loss shares, 18
    property designations, 24

timeframes, 17
withdrawing partners, 20
family partnerships, 65
limited partnerships, 25-26
LLCs, 4
registered limited liability
partnerships, 4, 24
resource materials, 26-27
strategic partners, 113
taxes, 26, 60
versus LLCs, 39-40
patents, 12, 264
application process, 266
creating, 265
design patents, 265
protection, 266
utility patents, 265
pay
discrimination, 151
fringe benefits, 151-152
wages, 151
employee handbook guidelines,
162
employment contracts, 164
payments
options for paying creditors, 245
cash, 246
checks, 246-247
credit card, 246
promissory notes, 248
rental agreement terms, 121
advertising, 121
insurance, 121
real estate taxes, 121
repairs and maintenance, 121
security deposits, 122
utilities, 121
schedules, bank loan provisions,
111
penalties, prepayment, 111
pension plans, 157
compensation packages, 148
defined benefits, 157
defined contributions, 157-158
requirements, 158
coverages, 158
distributions, 158
nondiscriminatory, 158
vesting, 158
performance
contracts
excusing performance,
200-201
interpretation of, 197
performance by parties, 199
subcontracting, 200
warranties, 198
reviews, 164-165
attitudes, 165
communication skills, 165
dependability, 165
organizational skills, 165
quality of work, 165
relating to others, 165
perils, property insurance coverages,
181

personal loan guarantees, bankruptcy
protection, 296
personal assets, estate planning, 308
personal injury, empolyer liabilities,
210
personal representatives (estates),
317
planning (estate planning), 13
last will and testament, 13
life insurance, 13
successor plans, 14
policies
employee handbook guidelines,
162
insurance
application and effective
dates, 178
cancellations, 179-180
coverages and deductibles,
179
duties and rights, 178
misconduct by insured, 180
riders, 180
sexual harassment, 170
pollution liability insurance, 183
possession, terms of purchase agreements, 128
post-trial motions, 230
power of attorney (living wills), 320
pre-hearings, zoning, 276
pre-incorporation agreements, 30
preferred stocks, security laws, 115
Pregnancy Discrimination Act , 151
premium cost of insurance, savings
ideas, 187
prenuptial agreements, 321-323
prepayment penalties, 111
pretrial
conferences, 228
discoveries, 227
admission of facts, 228
depositions, 228
written interrogatories, 228
prevention of bankruptcies, 298
cutbacks, 299
warning signs, 298-299
working with creditors, 299
printed works, copyrights, 262-264
creating, 262-263
infringement and fair use, 264
protections, 263
privacy, cyberlaws
business information, 286
consumers, 285
private placement investors, 113
probate, 310
advantages to avoiding, 312
defining characteristics, 310-311
procedures, 311-312
product disparagement, 218
product liability
employer liabilities, 211-212
insurance, 183
profit and losses
operating agreements and LLCs,
43
partnership agreements, 18

progressive discipline process,
167-168
promissory estoppels, 194-195
promissory notes, 248, 352-353
properties
damages, employer liabilities,
210
designations, partnership agreements, 24
intellectual property laws, 12
copyright protections, 12
patents, 12
insurance and coverages, 180
amounts, 181
liability insurance, 182
perils, 181
lines, terms of purchase agreements, 129
taxes, local property taxes, 69
protections
bankruptcies
asset protection, 295-297
pre-planning, 298
copyrights, 263
patents, 266
trademarks, 261-262
provisions (bank loans), 111-112
proxies, 45
publishing, cyberlaws, 286-287
purchase agreements
creating, 91-92
terms, 128
breaches, 130
closing and possessions, 128
environmental surveys, 129
inspections, 129
offers, 128
property lines and zoning,
129
purchase price and earnest
money, 128
taxes and assessments, 128
title insurance, 129
purpose statements, operating
agreements, 41

Q–R–S

quality of work, performance
reviews, 165

real estate
brokers, advisor duties, 76-77
buying, 126
building inspections, 127
function of attorneys, 128
mortgage financing, 127
terms of purchase agree-
ments, 128-130
title insurance companies,
127
rental agreements, 120
assignments and subleases,
124
breaches, 125
cancellations, 125

compliance with ADA, 124
condition of premises, 122
improvements, 123
liability and insurance coverages, 124
rent payments, 121
rental periods, 120
signage, 125
space specifications, 122
usage restrictions, 123
taxes, 121
recorded works, copyrights, 262-264
creating, 262-263
infringement and fair use, 264
protections, 263
recruitment of employees, guidelines, 137
advertisements, 138
application requirements, 139
job descriptions, 137-138
refinancing, 109
reformations, contracts, 203
registered limited liability partnerships, 4, 24
registrations, domain names, 280
regulations. *See also* statutes
administrative agencies
adoption of regulations, 271-272
violations, 273-275
Regulatory Flexibility Act, 278
remedies
contract breaches, 202
equity, 203-204
money damages, 203
torts and employers liabilities, 218
damages, 218
equity, 218-219
rental agreements, terms
assignments and subleases, 124
breaches, 125
cancellations, 125
compliance with ADA, 124
condition of premises, 122
improvements, 123
liability and insurance coverages, 124
rent payments, 121-122
rental periods, 120-121
signage, 125
space specifications, 122
usage restrictions, 123
repairs and maintenance, rental payments, 121
reputation of franchises, 99
rescissions, 203
resource materials
bankruptcies, 305
consumer protection laws, 243
e-commerce, 291
employment laws, 145
estate planning, 324
franchises, 106
home-based businesses, 291
insurance coverages, 187
litigations and lawsuits, 232
LLCs, 47

sole proprietorships, 57
taxes, 69
torts and employer liabilities, 219
restriction on ownerships, tax laws, 61
restrictive covenants, home-based businesses, 290
retired business owners, advisor duties, 79-80
retirement plans
asset determination for capital needs, 110
successor planning, 323-324
revocable trusts, 320
riders, insurance policies, 180
rights
insurance policies, 178
ex-employee's, 169
risks of borrowing, 110
roles
board of directors, 33
corporate officers, 35
fellow business owners, 8
lawyers, 7
rules and regulations, administrative agencies
adoption of regulations, 271-272
violations, 273
Rules of Civil Procedure, 224

S corporations, 33, 37-38, 60-61
safety
consumer protection laws, 240
CPSC, 240
FDA protection, 240
workplace
OSHA, 171
workers' compensation, 171-172
salaries, compensation packages, 148, 152
sales
corporate assets, 36
deceptive sales, 238
bait-and-switching advertisements, 238
endorsements, 239
sale items, 238
telephone and mail orders, 239
tax, 68
SBA-guaranteed loans, 112
scope of employment, 206
SEC (Securities and Exchange Commission), 114-116
second mortgages, 109
Secretary of State, filing business documents, 6
secrets (trade secrets), 266-267
Section 1981, Civil Rights Act of 1866, 134
securing loans with collateral, 248
automatic perfections, 251-252
mortgages, 249
security agreements, 250-251
security interests, 249-250
statutory liens, 248

Securities Act of 1933, 114
Securities and Exchange Commission. *See* SEC
security deposits, rental payments, 122
security laws
federal laws, 114
common and preferred stocks, 114
contracts, 114
SEC regulations, 115-116
stock warrants and options, 114
state security laws, 116
selection process
existing business purchases, 83-85
franchises, 97-98
expertise of, 98
investigation of, 98
reputation of, 99
terms of agreements, 99-100
selling
businesses due to bankruptcies, 301
ownership interests, 65
service marks. *See* trademarks
service warranties, 89
sexual harassment
defining criteria, 169
policies, 170
shareholder
shareholders
agreements, forms, 339-343
stock ownerships, 32
Shareholders' Stock Purchase Agreements, 31-32
signage, terms of rental agreements, 125
skills tests, testing of future employees, 142
Small Business Regulatory Enforcement Fairness Act, 278
small businesses, federal statutes, 277
Freedom of Information Act, 277
Government-in-Sunshine Act, 277
Regulatory Flexibility Act, 278
small claims court
filing claims, 230
trials, 230-231
sole proprietorships, 4, 49
closing out, 52-53
corporations, 50
financing options, 51-52
LLCs, 50
resource materials, 57
set-up process, 50-51
taxes and deductible expenses, 53-54
advertising, 54
casualty losses, 56
depreciation, 55
employees' wages, 55-56
laws, 59-60
state and local taxes, 56-57
travel, 56
zoning regulations, 51

367

space specifications, rental agreement terms, 122
spamming, cyberlaws, 286
specific performance contracts, 204
state laws
    court systems, filing lawsuits, 223
    security laws, 116
    taxes, 68
        local property tax, 69
        sole proprietorships, 56-57
        state sales and use tax, 68
    state and local civil rights laws, 135
State workers' Compensation Acts, 10
statutes. *See also* acts, regulations
    Freedom of Information Act, 277
    Government-in-Sunshine Act, 277
    Regulatory Flexibility Act, 278
    Small Business Regulatory Enforcement Fairness Act, 278
    Statute of Frauds, 12, 195-196
statutory liens, 248
stocks
    market investors, 113
    ownership and shareholders, 32
    warrants and options, federal security laws, 114
strategic partners, 113
strict liabilities, employer liabilities, 214-215
subcontracting, performance contracts, 200
subleases, terms of rental agreements, 124
subpoena duces tecum, 273
successor planning, 323-324
successor plans
    estate planning, 14
    retirement, 323-324
surveys (environmental surveys), 129

federal. *See* federal tax laws
FUTA tax, 148
gift taxes, 313-316
home-based businesses, 291
    insurance coverages, 186
    operational tactics, 62
        allocation of income among owners, 63
        character of incomes, 63
        fringe benefits, 64
        limitations on deductible losses, 63-64
        taxation of owners, 62
        timing, 63
    organizational costs, 62
partnerships, 26, 60
purchase agreement terms, 128
real estate taxes, 121
resource materials, 69
restriction on ownership, 61
sale of ownership interests, 65
sole proprietorships, 53-54, 59-60
    advertising deductions, 54
    cash basis versus accrual accounting methods, 53
    casualty losses, 56
    depreciation, 55
    employees' wages, 55-56
    state and local taxes, 56-57
    travel, 56
state income taxes, 68
    local property tax, 69
    state sales and use tax, 68
    years, 61
team of advisors
    accountant services, 73-74
    bankers, 76
    computer experts, 78
    financial planners, 78-79
    insurance agents, 75-76
    real estate brokers, 76-77
    retired business owners, 79-80
telephone solicitations, deceptive sale practices, 239
term life insurance, 184
terminations
    employee handbook guidelines, 163
    employment contracts, 164
    letters of termination, 168-169
terms
    Articles of Organization, 40-41
    franchise agreements, 103
    insurance policies, 179
    operating agreements and LLCs, 41
        accounting, 43
        addition of members, 44
        capital contributions, 42
        dissolutions, 44
        loss of members, 43
        maintenance of LLC status, 45-46
        management concerns, 44
        members'conduct, 42
        naming company, 41

profit and losses, 43
    purpose statements, 41
partnerships, 16
    accounting responsibilities, 20
    addition of new partners, 20
    appraisal of ownership interests, 21
    arbitrations, 22
    contract liabilities, 22-23
    dissolution requirements, 21-22
    expulsions, 21
    fiduciary duties, 19
    limited partnerships, 25-26
    management concerns, 19
    profit and loss shares, 18
    property designations, 24
    timeframes, 17
    withdrawing partners, 20
purchase agreements, 128
    breaches, 130
    closing and possessions, 128
    environmental surveys, 129
    inspections, 129
    offers, 128
    property lines and zoning, 129
    purchase price and earnest money, 128
    taxes and assessments, 128
    title insurance, 129
rental agreements
    assignments and subleases, 124
    breaches, 125
    cancellations, 125
    compliance with ADA, 124
    condition of premises, 122
    improvements, 123
    liability and insurance coverages, 124
    payments, 121-122
    signage, 125
    space specifications, 122
    usage restrictions, 123
testamentary trusts, 319
testing future employees
    medical and drug testing, 142-143
    skills tests, 142
theft insurance, 183
third-party lawsuits, 226
timing taxations, 63
title insurance, 127-129
Title VII of the Civil Rights Act of 1964, 134
titles, legal problems of existing businesses, 88
torts
    cyberlaws, 287-288
    employers liabilities, 205
        assaults, 212
        battery, 213
        defamation, 215-216
        emotional harm, 217
        employment requirements, 206
        false imprisonment, 213

T–U–V

tags, domain names, 282
taxes
    analysis of business types, 5-7
    audits
        Appeals Conferences, 67
        preparations, 65-66
        process of, 67
    bankruptcies, 297, 304
    contribution of property to entity, 61
    corporations, 36
        C corporations, 37, 60-61
        LLCs, 46, 60
        S corporations, 37-38, 60-61
    cyberlaws, 289
    estate taxes, 313-316
    existing business acquisitions, 89, 93
    family partnerships, 65

invasion of privacy, 216
negligence, 207-211
nuisances, 215
product liability, 211-212
remedies, 218-219
resource materials, 219
scope of employment, 206
strict liabilities, 214-215
trespass and conversion, 213-214
wrongful contract interferences, 217-218
toxic waste, legal problems of existing businesses, 88
trade secrets, 266-267, 286
trade usage, interpretation of contracts, 197
trademarks, 260-261
creating, 261
domain names, 280-282
potential legal problems with existing business acquisitions, 89
protection, 261-262
travel as a deductible expense, 56
trespass and conversion, employer liabilities, 213-214
trials, 228
appeals, 230
closing arguments, 229
evidence presentations, 229
jury selections, 228
opening statements, 229
post-trial motions, 230
small claims court collections, 230-231
verdicts, 229
trusts, estate planning, 316-317
essential contents, 319-320
living, 319
testamentary, 319
Truth in Lending Act, 242

U–V

UCC (Uniform Commercial Code)
contract laws, 190
versus common laws, 11-12
unemployment compensation, 136
Uniform Commercial Code. *See* UCC
unions (labor unions), 173-174
unreasonable conduct, employer liability, 209
usage restrictions, rental agreement terms, 123
use taxes, 68
utility patents, 265

venture capitalists, 113
verdicts, 229
vesting, pension plans, 158

violation of administrative regulations, 273
adjudication, 274-275
investigations, 273
voidable contracts, 195
voir dire, 229
voluntary personal bankruptcy petitions, 255

W–X–Y–Z

wages
as a deductible expense, 55-56
compensation packages, 148
pay discrimination, 151
warning signs of financial trouble, 298-299
warranties, contract performance, 198
whole life insurance, 184
wills
estate planning, 13
last will and testament, 316
devisee, 317
dying without wills, 316-317
guardians, 318
personal representatives, 317
living wills, power of attorney, 320
withdrawing partners, 20
workers' compensation, 137, 171-172
workplaces
labor unions, 173-174
safety, 171
OSHA, 171
workers' compensation, 171-172
sexual harassment
defining criteria, 169
policies, 170
World Wide Web
cyberlaws, 284
contracts, 287
jurisdictions, 288-289
linking, 284-285
privacy, 285-286
publishing, 286-287
spamming, 286
taxes, 289
torts, 287-288
domain names, 279
creation and registrations, 280
cyberpiracy, 282
cybersquatting, 282
tags, 282
trademark issues, 280-282
e-commerce, 283
development of Web sites, 283
operating sites, 283-284
written interrogatories, pretrial discoveries, 228

zoning
boards, 275
hearings, 277
pre-hearings, 276
home-based businesses, 290
legal problems of existing businesses, 88
regulations, sole proprietorships, 51
terms of purchase agreements, 129